Each volume of this series of companions to major philosophers contains specially commissioned essays by an international team of scholars, together with a substantial bibliography, and will serve as a reference work for students and nonspecialists. One aim of the series is to dispel the intimidation such readers often feel when faced with the work of a difficult and challenging thinker.

William James (1842–1910) was both a philosopher and a psychologist. The essays in this companion deal with the full range of his thought, including technical philosophical issues, religious speculation, moral philosophy, and political controversies of his time. James's interactions with other philosophers of his time are also examined, as is his relationship to his brother Henry. By placing James in his intellectual landscape, the volume will be useful not only to philosophers but also to teachers and students in such areas as religious studies, history of ideas, and American studies.

New readers and nonspecialists will find this the most convenient and accessible guide to James currently available. Advanced students and specialists will find a conspectus of recent developments in the interpretation of James.

THE CAMBRIDGE CO...

WILLIAM JA...

The Cambridge Companion to

WILLIAM JAMES

Edited by Ruth Anna Putnam
Wellesley College

CAMBRIDGE
UNIVERSITY PRESS

PUBLISHED BY THE PRESS SYNDICATE OF THE UNIVERSITY OF CAMBRIDGE
The Pitt Building, Trumpington Street, Cambridge CB2 1RP, United
Kingdom

CAMBRIDGE UNIVERSITY PRESS
The Edinburgh Building, Cambridge CB2 2RU, United Kingdom
40 West 20th Street, New York, NY 10011-3211, USA
10 Stamford Road, Oakleigh, Melbourne 3166, Australia

First published 1997

Printed in the United States of America

Typeset in Trump Medieval

*A catalogue record for this book is available from
the British Library*

Library of Congress Cataloging-in-Publication Data

The Cambridge companion to William James / edited by Ruth Anna
Putnam.
    p.   cm.
    Includes bibliographical references.
    ISBN 0-521-45278-3 (hbk.). – ISBN 0-521-45906-0 (pbk.)
    1. James, William, 1842–1910. I. Putnam, Ruth Anna.
B945.J2C35   1997
191 – dc20   96-29099
                                                                 CIP

ISBN 0-521-45278-3 hardback
ISBN 0-521-45906-0 paperback

CONTENTS

v

CONTRIBUTORS

GRAHAM H. BIRD is the Sir Samuel Hall Professor of Philosophy at the University of Manchester, U.K., and has held posts at Oxford, Aberdeen, St. Andrews, and Stirling Universities. He is the author of *Kant's Theory of Knowledge* (1962), *Philosophical Tasks* (1972), and *William James* (1986).

THOMAS CARLSON farms just outside Vinton, Iowa. He has taught at Harvard, Howard, the University of Virginia, and Macalester. He is presently affiliated with the Project on Rhetoric of Inquiry at the University of Iowa.

JAMES CONANT is Assistant Professor of Philosophy at the University of Pittsburgh. He is the author of articles on Kant, Frege, Kierkegaard, Nietzsche, and Wittgenstein.

HARVEY J. CORMIER teaches philosophy at the University of Texas at Austin. He is currently completing a book on pragmatic theories of truth and their political implications.

JESSICA R. FELDMAN is Assistant Professor of English, University of Virginia. The author of *Gender on the Divide: The Dandy in Modernist Literature* (1993), she is currently completing a study of aestheticism in nineteenth-century England and America.

OWEN FLANAGAN is Professor of Philosophy, Experimental Psychology, and Neurobiology, and Adjunct Professor in the graduate program in Literature at Duke University. His interests are in philosophy of mind and ethics. He is the author of *Varieties of Moral Personality: Ethics and Psychological Realism* (1991), *Consciousness Reconsidered* (1992), and *Self-Expressions: Mind, Morals, and the Meaning of Life* (1996).

vii

RICHARD M. GALE is Professor of Philosophy at the University of Pittsburgh. He is the author of *The Language of Time* and *On the Nature and Existence of God.*

DAVID A. HOLLINGER is Professor of History at the University of California at Berkeley. He is the author of *Morris R. Cohen and the Scientific Ideal* (1975), *In the American Province* (1985), and *Postethnic America* (1995).

CHRISTOPHER HOOKWAY is Professor of Philosophy at the University of Sheffield. He is the author of *Peirce* (1985), *Quine: Language, Experience and Reality* (1988), and *Scepticism* (1990).

DAVID C. LAMBERTH is Assistant Professor of Religion at The Florida State University in Tallahassee. He is the author of *Metaphysics, Experience, and Religion in William James's Thought,* forthcoming in *Cambridge Studies in Religion and Critical Thought* from Cambridge University Press.

GERALD E. MYERS is Professor Emeritus at the City University of New York. He is the author of *William James: His Life and Thought* and numerous essays on James; he is co-editor of *Echoes from the Holocaust.* Currently he is philosopher-in-residence and director of humanities, American Dance Festival in North Carolina and New York City.

RICHARD R. NIEBUHR is Hollis Professor of Divinity at Harvard University. He holds degrees from Harvard, Union Theological Seminary, New York, and Yale University, has published on Friedrich Schleiermacher's theology and philosophy and other subjects, and has lectured at universities in England, Japan, and the United States.

ROSS POSNOCK is Andrew Hilen Professor of American Literature at the University of Washington and author, most recently, of *The Trial of Curiosity: Henry James, William James, and the Challenge of Modernity* (1991). Currently he is writing a book on black intellectuals and the politics of pragmatism.

HILARY PUTNAM is Cogan University Professor at Harvard University. His books include *Reason, Truth and History, Realism with a Human Face, Renewing Philosophy, Words and Life,* and *Pragmatism.*

RUTH ANNA PUTNAM is Professor of Philosophy at Wellesley College. She is the author of articles on William James, John Dewey, and in ethical theory. With Hilary Putnam she is currently working on a book on William James.

RICHARD RORTY is University Professor of the Humanities at the University of Virginia. His books include *Philosophy and the Mirror of Nature* and *Contingency, Irony and Solidarity*.

T. L. S. SPRIGGE was previously Professor of Logic and Metaphysics at the University of Edinburgh and now teaches there part time. His books include *Santayana: An Examination of His Philosophy* (1974), *The Vindication of Absolute Idealism* (1983), *The Rational Foundations of Ethics* (1987), and *James and Bradley: American Truth and British Reality* (1993). He is currently working on a book on the phenomenology of thinking.

BRUCE WILSHIRE is Professor of Philosophy at Rutgers University. He is the author of *William James and Phenomenology: A Study of "The Principles of Psychology," Role Playing and Identity: The Limits of Theater as Metaphor,* and *Wild Hunger: Nature's Excitements and Their Addictive Distortions.* He is the editor of *William James: The Essential Writings.*

METHOD OF CITATION

The complete works of William James have now been published in a scholarly edition by Harvard University Press. References to the volumes of this edition are given as follows:

ECR   *Essays, Comments and Reviews*
EPh   *Essays in Philosophy*
EPs   *Essays in Psychology*
EPR   *Essays in Psychical Research*
ERE   *Essays in Radical Empiricism*
ERM   *Essays in Religion and Morality*
MEN   *Manuscripts, Essays and Notes*
ML   *Manuscript Lectures*
MT   *The Meaning of Truth*
P   *Pragmatism*
PB   *Psychology: The Briefer Course*
PP   *Principles of Psychology* (followed by volume number)
PU   *A Pluralistic Universe*
SPP   *Some Problems of Philosophy*
TT   *Talks to Teachers on Psychology*
VRE   *Varieties of Religious Experience*
WB   *The Will to Believe*

Except for *ECR, EPh, EPs, ERM, EPR, MEN,* and *ML,* the original editions of these books were repeatedly reprinted keeping the same paginations. In the Harvard edition of the Works, the corresponding volumes provide a key correlating pagination. In this volume, references to the pagination of these original editions rather than that of the Harvard edition use the same abbreviations followed by *.

xi

References to the letters of William James are given as follows:

Coresp.	*The Correspondence of William James* (followed by volume number)
Letters	*Correspondence: The Letters of William James* (followed by volume number)
Sel.Letters	*Selected Letters of William James*

Additional letters may be found in Perry 1935 and the James Family Collection in Houghton Library, Harvard University, in this volume cited as Houghton.

THE CAMBRIDGE COMPANION TO

WILLIAM JAMES

Introduction

Jacques Barzun called his book about William James *A Stroll with William James* and explained that title as follows. Having said that he read widely and variously in philosophy, Barzun asked, "What then is the difference when I go back to William James?" and replied that

... his ideas, his words, his temperament speak to me with intimacy as well as force. ... "he does me good." ... He is for me the most inclusive mind I can listen to, the most concrete and the least hindered by trifles ... he helps me to understand what his contemporaries and mine were and are doing. I stroll with him again and again because he knows better than anyone else the material and spiritual country I am traveling through. (Barzun 1983, 4)

The contributors to this volume will, I trust, prove to be stimulating, informative, enlightening companions to readers who undertake their own stroll with James.

James was thirty-six years old when, in 1878, he published his first philosophical as well as his first psychological writings. Earlier in his life, he had studied painting, had joined Louis Aggassiz in a research expedition to Brazil, and had earned an M.D. from Harvard in 1869. In 1872, after recovering from ill health and depression, he began to teach at Harvard, where he would remain until his retirement in 1907. James began his academic career teaching physiology and anatomy; he taught his first psychology course in 1875 and his first philosophy course in 1879. During James's lifetime the disciplines of psychology and philosophy became independent of one another, and James contributed decisively to this separation. In one

I

remarkable paragraph of the preface to his monumental *Principles of Psychology* (1890), he wrote,

I have kept to the point of view of natural science throughout the book. Every natural science accepts certain data uncritically. . . . Psychology, the science of finite individual minds, assumes as its data (1) *thoughts and feelings,* and (2) *a physical world* in time and space with which they coexist and which (3) *they know.* Of course, these data are themselves discussible; but the discussion of them (as of other elements) is called metaphysics and falls outside the province of this book. This book, assuming that thoughts and feelings exist and are vehicles of knowledge, thereupon contends that psychology when she has ascertained the empirical correlation of the various sorts of thought or feeling with definite conditions of the brain, can go no farther – can go no farther that is, as a natural science. If she goes farther she becomes metaphysical. All attempts to *explain* our phenomenally given thoughts as products of deeper-lying entities . . . are metaphysical. This book consequently rejects both the associationist and the spiritualist theories; and in this strictly positivistic point of view consists the only feature of it for which I feel tempted to claim originality. (*PP,* 1:6)

Nevertheless, one finds philosophy throughout *Principles,* and that, as well as James's masterful style, accounts, I suspect, for its enduring appeal over and above its being, in Gerald Myers's phrase, "the classic – and most interesting – source for understanding nineteenth-century physiological psychology" (Myers 1986a, 54).

In this volume Myers (Chapter 1) examines sympathetically but critically the introspective method in psychology as it was used by James and his contemporary Titchner. Owen Flanagan (Chapter 2) rejects his own earlier "naturalistic" reading of James's theory of consciousness (Flanagan 1984, chapter 2). He examines with great care James's search, from 1884 to 1904, for an alternative to substance dualism. Finally, Richard Gale (Chapter 3) rejects forcefully John Dewey's "naturalizing" of James's ontology and thereby questions whether James could or did sustain the "monism" of his radical empiricism.

Psychologists assume, with common sense, the (distinct) existence of mental and physical events or states, and investigate, among other things, mind/body interactions or, as James had put it cautiously, empirical mind/brain correlation. But, he continued in the preface to *Principles,* "Men must keep thinking; and the data assumed by psychology, just like those assumed by physics and the other natural sciences, must some time be overhauled." It is fair to say, I think, that James devoted the rest of his life to the attempt to work out a satisfactory metaphysics and epistemology. For he rejected "associationist and spiritualist theories" not merely because they constituted unwarranted metaphysical intrusions into the science of psychology, but because as metaphysical doctrines, he found them profoundly unsatisfactory. Finally, especially after he had completed *The Principles of Psychology*, the interactionist dualism that psychology takes for granted seemed to him to be always on the verge of becoming a reductive materialism, and James found the idea of a universe that consisted ultimately of nothing but matter subject to deterministic laws deeply repellent. Always prone to depression, he had as a young man reached the very depth of despair when writings by the French philosopher Renouvier persuaded him that he was intellectually entitled to believe in free will. He decided – he described it as his first act of free will – to believe in free will.

Given James's profound mind and his intellectual integrity, this early decision, though never revoked, was simply another invitation to search for a comprehensive metaphysical position. But the nature of the "arguments" for metaphysical hypotheses forced James to inquire also into conditions of adequacy, or acceptability, of metaphysical positions. Early episodes in the latter inquiry can be found in the 1879 essay "The Sentiment of Rationality," seeking a criterion by which to determine the adequacy of a philosophy; in "The Dilemma of Determinism," presenting both metaphysical and moral considerations in favor of the belief in free will; and in the (in)famous and much misunderstood "The Will to Believe," defending one's right to believe ahead of the evidence in those cases, and only in those cases, where, (a) much is at stake, (b) the evidence at hand does not settle the case, and (c) one cannot wait for more evidence, either because no amount of evidence can settle the case, or because waiting itself is to decide not to believe. David Hollinger (Chapter 4) offers a careful reading not only of James's essay but of the essay by Clifford to which James responded. He places "The Will to Believe" in the wider context of James's lifelong endeavor to reconcile science and religion, an endeavor that succeeded, according to Hollinger, only in the lectures on *Pragmatism* delivered in the winter of 1906–7. Richard Rorty (Chapter 5) offers a radically different reading of "The Will to Believe" and a different perspective on the wider issue of religious belief in an age of science. James Conant (Chapter 10) applies the doctrine of "The Will to Believe" to pragmatism itself. There is more to be said about religious belief and about criteria of reasonableness for metaphysical doctrines. That more will be found in the essays by Richard Niebuhr (Chapter 11) and David Lamberth (Chapter 12).

For the moment, our stroll takes us into the most technical aspects of James's philosophy: his pragmatism and his radical empiricism. I shall begin with the latter, for as John J. McDermott pointed out in his introduction to the Harvard edition of *Essays in Radical Empiricism*, "James's writing on the 'will to believe,' *The Varieties of Religious Experience, Pragmatism, A Pluralistic Universe,* and 'psychical research' are rootless and subject to misunderstanding unless they are examined in the light of the considerations and claims of radical empiricism" (*ERE*, xii).

As early as 1897, in the preface to *The Will to Believe,* James referred to his own view as a radical empiricism, but did not yet present key elements of the view developed in a series of essays published during 1904 and 1905 and collected by Ralph Barton Perry in the posthumously published *Essays in Radical Empiricism*. In 1904, James stated one of these key elements, the basis of his rejection of associationism, as follows:

To be radical, an empiricism must neither admit in its constructions any element that is not directly experienced, nor exclude from them any element that is directly experienced. For such a philosophy, *the relations that connect experiences must themselves be experienced relations, and any kind of relation experienced must be accounted as 'real' as anything else in the system.* (*ERE*, 22; emphasis in the original)

McDermott has noted that the germs of this view were already present in 1884, and are found repeatedly in *Principles* (*ERE*, xviii ff.).

Another key element of James's radical empiricism is his rejection of mind/matter dualism as well as of its reduction to either materialism or idealism. In its place, he offers – it is the title of one of his essays – a world of pure experience. In that world consciousness *as an entity* does not exist. But neither is consciousness a function of matter, for matter *as an entity* also does not exist. Ultimately there are only pure experiences (and, perhaps, experienceables – this is a difficult interpretative question), experiences which only in retrospect are *taken* either as part of a stream of thought or as physical objects.

Although one is tempted to call this view a neutral monism, it is, in my opinion, more properly thought of as a neutral pluralism – neutral in not favoring either thought or matter, plural because "there is no *general* stuff of which experience at large is made. There are as many stuffs as there are 'natures' in the things experienced . . . and save for time and space (and, if you like, for 'being') there appears no universal element of which all things are made" (*ERE*, 14–15).

Radical empiricism is not only James's ontology, it is his theory of perception and his theory of intentionality. It explains how my percept of, say, a particular pen is indeed of that pen and not of the thousands of other virtually indistinguishable pens. It explains also how my percept and your percepts are of the same pen when, as we normally say, we are looking at the same pen. Finally, it explains how we succeed in thinking about an object, and how you and I can think of and converse about the same object. Radical empiricism, in other words, explains how it is that we live in a common world and can communicate about this common world. James's failure, in *Principles*, to explain how mental states are about their object drove him, as Bruce Wilshire (Chapter 6) explains, to develop the doctrine of radical empiricism. There was, to be sure, an alternative answer already to hand: that offered by the absolute idealism of James's Harvard colleague Josiah Royce. T. L. S. Sprigge (Chapter 7), in the context of James's reception in England, discusses not only the objections raised by Moore and Russell but Royce's challenge to James, James's response, and Bradley's critique of that response. James Conant (Chapter 10) explores the relation between Royce's philosophy and that of James in greater detail. Both Wilshire and Sprigge note the intimate connections between James's theory of intentionality and his theory of truth, a theory which results when the pragmatic method is applied to the concept of truth; Conant, in contrast, will argue that James does not and cannot have a *theory* of truth, that he offers rather a *conception*.

Although James claimed to have learned his theory (or conception) of truth from John Dewey and F. C. S. Schiller, he credited the pragmatic method and its maxim to Charles Sanders Peirce. Peirce's first statement of the maxim (in 1878) reads as follows, "Consider what effects, that might conceivably have practical bearings, we conceive the object of our conception to have. Then our conception of these effects is the whole of our conception of the object" (Peirce 1931–60, 5.402).

When James restated the maxim in *Pragmatism*, he wrote, "To develop a thought's meaning, we need only determine what conduct it is fitted to produce. That conduct is for us its sole significance." And, in the same paragraph, "To attain perfect clearness in our thoughts of an object, then, we need only consider what conceivable effects of a practical kind the object may involve – what sensations we are to expect from it, and what reactions we must prepare" (*P*, 29).

Christopher Hookway (Chapter 8) argues that the principle was a logical principle for Peirce but a philosophical principle for James. The maxim must not be confused with the positivist verifiability criterion of meaning; it is not used, by either Peirce or James, to condemn metaphysical statements as nonsense. It is used, particularly by James, to clarify metaphysical hypotheses; this may show them to be uninteresting – the doctrine of a substantial soul merely restates but does not explain one's sense of being a continuous self (*PP*, 1:326–8) – or morally repugnant – determinism, especially when coupled with the optimistic view that all is for the best, is seen by James as an invitation to moral sloth ("The Dilemma of Determinism" in *WB*).

However, some metaphysical hypotheses evidently survive this test. *Pragmatism*, a set of lectures James gave right after his retirement from Harvard, offers pragmatism as a philosophy that "preserves as cordial a relation with facts [as Spencer's]" and treats "religious constructions . . . cordially as well" (*P*, 26). Hollinger (Chapter 4) holds that James succeeded in *Pragmatism*, as he had not in "The Will to Believe," to develop a position that includes religion in the sphere of scientific inquiry. Concerning this little book, this set of eight lectures, James wrote to his brother Henry, "I have just finished the proofs of a little book called pragmatism which even you *may* enjoy reading. It is very 'sincere' . . . not particularly original at any one point, yet . . . with just that amount of squeak or shrillness in the voice that enable one book to *tell*, when others don't, to supersede its brethren, and be treated later as 'representative.' " He continues that he has no doubt that this way of thinking will triumph, "I believe it to be something quite like the protestant reformation" (*Corresp.*, 3:339).

James applied the pragmatic method not only to metaphysical hypotheses but at length, and notoriously, to the concept of truth. He devoted one and a half lectures to this subject alone, but the result proved disappointing. He was widely misunderstood – indeed, he is still widely misunderstood – and his attempt to clarify things by collecting various responses to these misunderstandings in *The Meaning of Truth* was less successful than he had hoped. Hilary Putnam (Chapter 9) not only offers a clear statement of James's views on truths (note the plural) but explains also the source of the misunderstandings. James Conant (Chapter 10) suggests that James's response to Royce's criticism – the criticism that the pragmatic theory of truth collapses into incoherence when we ask whether *it* is true – is to deny that pragmatism offers a *theory* of truth, that is, an assertion that is either true or false. Instead, Conant argues, James offers a *conception* of truth and suggests how to live with this notion.

Although James thought that one can be a pragmatist without being a radical empiricist, the two views are, at any rate in his writings, closely interwoven. While I do not want to say that all pragmatists must be "radical empiricists" in the narrow sense of James's doctrine, they must, I think, explain in some way, as radical empiricism does, how it is that you and I experience not separate private worlds but one common public world and how we succeed in communicating about this world. For it makes sense to seek shared knowledge and to be concerned about others' welfare because, and only because, we live in a common world. It is perhaps worth stressing, however, that radical empiricism does not provide a "foundation of knowledge"; a "pure experience" is not a knowing. For, on the one hand, "Only new-born babes, or men in semi-coma from sleep, drugs, illnesses, or blows, may be assumed to have an experience pure in the literal sense of a *that* which is not yet any definite *what*" (*ERE*, 46) and, on the other hand, any "definite what" (any concept) falsifies the continuity of actual experience, for "the essence of life is its continuously changing character; but our concepts are discontinuous and fixed, and the only mode of making them coincide with life is by arbitrarily supposing positions of rest therein" (*PU*, 113). This must not be understood as an irrationalism, however. James acknowledges the enormous practical importance of what he calls "the conceptual method."

This treatment supposes life to have already accomplished itself, for the concepts, being so many views taken after the fact, are retrospective and post mortem. Nevertheless we can draw conclusions from them and project them into the future. We cannot learn from them how life made itself go, or how it will make itself go; but, on the supposition that its ways of making itself go are unchanging, we can calculate what positions of imagined arrest it will exhibit hereafter under given conditions. (*PU*, 109)

This sort of knowledge, the kind of knowledge we acquire in everyday life and in science, is, of course, of the utmost practical importance. James's point here is not to denigrate it. His quarrel is not with scientists or engineers, not with farmers or plumbers, but only with philosophers who think that "the conceptual method" provides insight into reality, when it "touches only the outer surface of reality" (*PU*, 111).

A Pluralistic Universe was not only James's last attempt to develop a coherent and inclusive metaphysical position, it also supplied the philosophical discussion of religion that had only been sketched in the last of his Gifford Lectures, published as *The Varieties of Religious Experience*. In the latter book James shows himself to be indeed a radical empiricist, radical in carrying empirical methods into the study of religion. He not only provided a rich and detailed survey of religious experiences but raised questions concerning the spiritual value and moral consequences of religious experience. He asked, finally, whether religious experience provided evidence for the existence of a deity, and concluded that while no demonstration is possible, the common core found in the beliefs of both organized religions and the faith of individuals was objectively true. That core consists in the sense that one's conscious self is part of a wider self that is the source of one's moral ideals and one's religious experiences. Richard Niebuhr (Chapter 11) provides a wonderfully illuminating reading of *Varieties*. That book had been planned to be the first part of a larger work, the second part of which would have developed a philosophy of religion. Ill health prevented James from writing that book, but some part of that ambition was realized in *A Pluralistic Universe*. Not surprisingly, James returned in this book to the question raised in "The Sentiment of Rationality," the question of a criterion of reasonableness for metaphysical hypotheses. David Lamberth (Chapter 12) argues that intimacy is that criterion, and that the position James defends as meeting this criterion is a pluralistic panpsychism.

James's philosophizing was motivated by a deeply moral concern. He sought a world-view that would motivate a strenuous moral life. He held early and late that only a belief in free will, in a genuinely open future, in objective values, and in a deity who cooperates with us and needs our cooperation to bring about a better world could motivate such a life. James's most sustained attempt at ethical theory is "The Moral Philosopher and the Moral Life," an essay so rich and suggestive that Graham Bird (Chapter 13) found ample material for reflection in a few of its pages. James was aware of the complexity of our moral lives as few moral philosophers are. He rejected hedonism as falsely reductive, he attempted to do justice both to the existential moment of choice and to the authority, or objectivity, of moral values. Our most important judgments, our ideals, he held, were prospective rather than retrospective, though whether an ideal should have been realized can only be known in retrospect; in this sense, ethics, and this includes politics, is empirical. James was an ardent believer in tolerance, in respect for a multitude of ways of life. These commitments are most clearly expressed in "On a Certain Blindness in Human Beings," an essay of which he said that he wished he could have made it "more impressive" (*TT*, 4). I have examined this essay and its sister "What Makes a Life Significant" and tried to relate the views James defended there to some of his other activities as a public philosopher (Chapter 14). Jessica Feldman (Chapter 15), considering "On a Certain Blindness" in relation to the novels of Elizabeth Stoddard, draws a quite different lesson: she regards Jamesean pragmatism as "a product of turn-of-the-century decadence."

James's occasional lectures, those collected in *The Will to Believe*, those mentioned in the preceding paragraph, and some others now found in the volume *Comments, Essays and Reviews* of the standard edition, account perhaps more than his more technical philosophy for James's influence on his students and their students, although considerable credit must also be given to his personality. Ross Posnock (Chapter 16) exhibits James's influence on several of his most publicly visible students, in particular W. E. B. DuBois and Alain Locke. Posnock's essay may be taken to support Harvey Cormier's defense (Chapter 17) of James against criticisms from the left as formulated by Gramsci and Cornel West. Cormier returns us for this purpose to several chapters of *Pragmatism*. Our stroll with William James concludes with a long backward glance as Thomas Carlson (Chapter 18) argues for a Kantian reading of James.

This volume does not attempt to offer a single interpretation of

James's philosophy, nor even of any one aspect of his philosophy. On the contrary, I have sought, not always successfully, to find alternative readings. I believe that James would have wanted it this way. A man as passionately devoted to pluralism as he was would have wished to draw attention to plural understandings of his own work. As Barzun so clearly understood, one strolls with James, one does not follow a single track.

Finally, I wish to thank my husband, Hilary Putnam, for his unfailing encouragement and for his helpful criticisms of my own contributions to this volume.

1 Pragmatism and introspective psychology

The revival of interest in William James seems to result largely from a new fondness for American pragmatism. Given that, we should not be surprised that, for many philosophers presiding at the revival, Dewey and Peirce receive the lion's share of attention. Or that contemporary interest, when focused on James, renews efforts to get his pragmatism straight, since that is admittedly a thorny concept, especially if it is linked with such other Jamesean doctrines as the will-to-believe.

Today's returnees to James are apparently less stimulated by his having been one of the last major introspective psychologists prior to the behaviorist take-over. Why this is so may be elusive, but, for whatever reasons, introspective psychology at its demise seemingly took memories of itself to the grave as well. Those who do occasionally remember are mostly lonely cemetery-walkers talking to themselves for lack of conversational company.

This is regrettable on several counts. A full look at James's work forces one to stare hard and long at the notion of introspection, and, beyond interpreting James, at analyses that the notion deserves. Although the literature is liberally sprinkled with references to the concept, sustained treatments of it are uncommon. William Lyons's excellent contribution of a few years ago, so far as I know, is the only book-length study devoted to introspection.[1] An idea that is knocked about as introspection is ought to be laid out for patient diagnosis, a consequence that we might hope from a Jamesean revival.

There is the initial job of clarifying the concept. In addition, employing it should be recognized as being essential for interpreting the histories of philosophy and psychology. Without it, how can one comprehend Descartes, Locke, Hume, Bain, Spencer, Wundt, Titchener, and James? Or Dewey, Peirce, Watson, Ryle, Wittgenstein, Russell, Freud, Jung, and Skinner? And, turning to the present, how relevant is introspection to current philosophizing? Responding to this question, I believe, is more than a courtesy; it fulfills an intellectual and professional responsibility.

For James, a psychology that is pragmatic (rather than, say, rationalistic) uses introspection as an investigative tool just because it is practically valuable, and this cannot be ignored in fully deciphering his pragmatism. He expresses his conviction emphatically in the important 1884 essay "On Some Omissions of Introspective Psychology" that makes fragmented reappearances six years later in various chapters of *The Principles of Psychology*.[2] Today, when philosophers visit the topic of introspection, they are usually preoccupied with the question, Do we possess an *infallible* faculty of self-scrutiny? Their inquiry concentrates less on what introspection is than on whether, as is sometimes claimed, its disclosures are indubitable.

James's position here was characteristically middle-of-the-road. Unlike Brentano who seemed to be on the side of infallibility but also against Comte who appeared to condemn introspection as worthless, James insisted upon the fallible utility of introspection in experimental psychology. Indeed, his motive in the 1884 essay was to show how faulty introspecting by his predecessors had omitted important details of conscious experience that in fact, if carefully done, can be detected introspectively.

The grounds, then, for rejecting infallibility were empirical. But James appealed to another argument, one that has often been used before and since, and whether it is empirical or rather a priori, as we wonder in Comte's and James's cases, is up for interpretation. In any event, James held that "No subjective state, whilst present, is its own object; its object is always something else" (*EPs*, 142). Hence, if a subjective state such as anger is knowable introspectively, it can be present only to a *subsequent* subjective knowing state; that is, what we call introspection is really retrospection. And inasmuch as there is a temporal gap between the subjective state that is known and the state that knows it via sizing it up, reporting it, and so forth, the retrospective findings are inevitably risky and susceptible to error.

There is, I believe, a curious equivocation in James's use of "introspection" which can be seen by comparing the argument above with what, for example, he wrote in *Principles: "Introspective Ob-*

servation is what we have to rely on first and foremost and always. The word introspection need hardly be defined – it means, of course, the looking into our own minds and reporting what we there discover. *Everyone agrees that we there discover states of consciousness"* (*PP,* 1:185).[3]

Here, introspection is a kind of inner *observation* that we recognize because we so often do it; asked to introspect, we "look inside" and report what we "see." What we typically "see" are moods, feelings, impulses, thoughts, images, and so forth. But, in rejecting introspective infallibility, James moved the meaning of "introspection" away from being a relatively straightforward, not uncommon type of observation to a more complex (but also not uncommon) kind of inferential process called "retrospection." What is not clear is whether he always kept the two meanings distinct in his claims on behalf of an improved introspective psychology, claims that may require introspection as direct or simultaneous observation rather than subsequent retrospection.

Be that as it may, one can question the premise, that a subjective state can be known only by a later one, which is used for supporting the conclusion that what is commonly called introspection must be retrospection. The *feltness* of a state such as anger, James agreed, is self-intimating or self-revealing; it registers upon consciousness not later but while it occurs. Since no special theory of the unconscious was relevant to James's reasoning here, it would appear that, for his view, if a state is *felt* then it must in some sense be *noticed.* How can one's subjective state be determined to be felt without being noticed, being brought into one's attention in some degree? If so, then it must in some sense be *observed,* simply because noticing is a form of observation. Some subjective states, consequently, are observable simultaneously with their occurrences.

Whether introspection-as-*observation* exists, let us appreciate, is no minor nor merely fussy issue so far as either historical or contemporary philosophy is concerned. Ryle and Hebb, echoing Watson's earlier behavioristic polemics, denied its existence, although Skinner was closer to James and Titchener than to his own colleagues. Space does not permit a recapitulation here of the different arguments employed by these and other debaters about introspective observation, but a study of their writings will support, I submit, my point that what has been at stake is whether introspective observation (or whatever other name be given to it) is an available human capability.[4]

Our conclusion above, that observation and noticing can occur simultaneously with the subjective state that is noticed, that the noticing occurs embedded, as it were, in the noticed state – if adopted, that would help James's psychology. It would help because he clearly wanted to retain something of the traditional view of introspection-as-observation while apparently abandoning much of it in redefining it as retrospection, and because, in my judgment, retrospection cannot be made to do what only direct, simultaneous observation can accomplish. One can try to picture a retrospective state of awareness or cognition as being so closely juxtaposed in time to a prior state, say, of anxiety that the later awareness, though retrospective, may be said to "observe" the anxieties; being such a close temporal neighbor that it can eavesdrop on the (slightly earlier) anxiety.

But by hypothesis the alleged observation would be an illusion, opening the door to the kinds of errors that James emphasized always haunted retrospection. Admittedly, the risk of error is diminished if the retrospective judgment is virtually simultaneous with the "observed" state, but the diminished risk accompanies not observation but short-term memory; we generally recall more accurately the least remote of our experiences. To acknowledge this, however, does not force us to confuse short-term memory with observation.

Furthermore, if what some have called introspective observation turns out in fact to be retrospection, how is that fact determined? If by experience and not by some a priori argument, then by what kind of experience if not introspective observation? James apparently believed that (careful) introspection does show us that, when we suppose ourselves inwardly observing ongoing anxiety states, we are in fact retrospectively considering (immediately recalling) those states just past. But, to reiterate my point, it would seem that we require contemporaneous introspective observation precisely for making that determination, for bringing to introspective attention the difference between introspection-as-observation (contemporaneous with what is observed) and introspection-as-retrospection (short-term memory judgment).

An argument often brought against the claim that one can introspectively observe a contemporaneous subjective state is that the observing alters or interferes with the state that one attempts to perceive. The best evidence for this argument is that we do sometimes find this to be the case, but why should we conclude that it *must* always be so? Concluding this on a priori grounds is unwarranted, and surely the empirical clues indicate only the fallibility, not the inevitable failure, of introspective observation.[5]

James's prominent reason for identifying introspection with retrospection is that one's stream of consciousness happens so rapidly that by the time one can report it, it has already vanished. In some contexts, he also concurred that observation alters the observed state, but, curiously, that conflicts with a quite different conviction of his that he expresses thus: "To wrestle with a bad feeling only pins our attention on it, and keeps it still fastened in the mind: whereas, if we act as if from some better feeling, the old bad feeling soon folds its tent like an Arab, and silently steals away" (*TT,* 118).

James's statement here is significant for revealing how he, like countless others, worried about introspection's leading to morbidity, to self-preoccupation resulting in depression. And the connection that some discern between introspection and morbidity is evidently due to the belief that introspective observation does not alter or eliminate a subjective state but in fact *sustains* it. The problem with heeding your despair is not that you will change it but that you will prolong it and to your distress. Hence, denying introspective observation on the grounds just considered is certainly questionable.

We must concede to James, however, that even if observation can occur embedded, as it were, in a passing state of consciousness, what is often meant by "introspection" in philosophical and psychological literature is something different. The term was introduced to designate an alleged activity of attending to or studying another state of consciousness already existing; introspection, that is, has been typically construed as a heeding or "looking-at" that is superimposed upon a prior state, and the introspective intent is to locate details in that prior state that may elude casual or nonintrospective awareness. Construed as a kind of inward eye scanning an already laid-out consciousness, introspecting is an activity that is additional to the states that it is supposed to observe, that may require some time for doing its job, and that may find the job to be a tricky one. So conceived, introspection would have to be, as James insisted, fallible and needing supplementary testing and evidence; not only that, introspection as *studied* or searching observation would have to be retrospective, although, let us keep in mind because of what I have argued above, the retrospected data may need to include direct/contemporaneous introspective observations.

James defended a type of introspective psychology, but it was only a part of the experimental process. He wrote:

The English writers on psychology, and the school of Herbart in Germany, have in the main contented themselves with such results as the immediate introspection of single individuals gave, and shown what a body of doctrine they make. The works of Locke, Hume, Reid, Hartley, Stewart, Brown, the Mills, will always be classics in this line; and in Professor Bain's *Treatise* we have probably the last word of what this method taken mainly by itself can do – the last monument of the youth of our science, still untechnical and generally intelligible, like the Chemistry of Lavoisier, or Anatomy before the microscope was used. . . . But psychology is passing into a less simple phase. Within a few years what we may call a microscopic psychology has arisen in Germany, carried on by experimental methods, asking of course every moment for introspective data, but eliminating their uncertainty by operating on a large scale and taking statistical means. (*PP*, 1:191–2)

Previous or preexperimental introspective psychology, James said, suffered from its dependence on everyday language. Since our vocabulary is noun-dominated and refers primarily to external objects, we lack a subjective idiom for reporting all but the most obvious and recurrent subjective details. Empiricists, he argued, assumed that words mean by designating objects, and, accordingly, if there is no word for *x* then there is no *x*; lacking an adequate subjective vocabulary leads to the idea that there is not much subjectivity. "It is hard to focus our attention on the nameless, so there results a certain vacuousness in the descriptive parts of most psychologies" (*PP*, 1:192).

This fault consorts with another, of supposing, because we typically identify our awareness of an object through identifying the object, that our awareness must essentially resemble the object. For James, this has disastrous results, and he never tired of targeting it as what his introspective psychology sought to replace. The entire tradition of English psychology, derived from Locke and Hume, and the whole German movement begun by Herbart, in his opinion, treated consciousness as if, like the physical environment for which we have a common descriptive language, it is constituted by units ("ideas") that are discrete, independent, substantive, and even recurrent. The main objective of the famous chapter in *Principles*, "The Stream of Thought," is to refute this viewpoint and to replace it, largely on introspective grounds, with the picture of consciousness as a rapid continuous stream.

The special continuity that our successive subjective states display to (careful) introspection was overlooked, James held, by his predecessors (except for a few, including Herbert Spencer) whether English, German, or French. This was a glaring omission on the part of traditional introspective psychology that focused not on the "transitive" but the "substantive" parts of the conscious stream such as ideas, images, and sensations. The subjective glidings from one state to the next went unrecognized. The obsession with images and sensations, he said, led to "Hume's fantastical assertion that we can form no idea of a thing with either quality or quantity without representing its exact degrees of each. . . . Strange that so patent an inward fact as the existence of 'blended' images could be overlooked! Strange that the assertion could virtually be made that we cannot imagine a printed page without at the same time imagining every letter on it – and made too by a school that prided itself particularly on its powers of observation! However, of such blunders is the history of psychology composed" (*EPs*, 145).

Earlier introspective psychology had also failed our subjective life by never appreciating its subtleties, its exquisiteness of details, its range of modulations. Corresponding to every conjunction or preposition, to every adverbial phrase, syntactic form, or inflection of speech, James claimed (a claim that later evoked skeptical responses, for example, from Wittgenstein), there exists "some shading or other" in feeling or consciousness. There are, besides cognitions of objects, images, and sensations, feelings of relations. We can *feel* the glidings from one state to the next, so we "ought to say a feeling of *and*, a feeling of *if*, a feeling of *but*, and a feeling of *by*, quite as readily as we say a feeling of *blue* or a feeling of *cold*" (*EPs*, 146).

James charged the Lockean tradition with omitting other subjective details that he lumped under the heading "feelings of tendency." An example: the words "Wait!" "Hark!" and "Look!" when shouted at us, he contended, arouse three different types of tendencies or expectancies in us; we have no names for them but they can be introspectively recognized, and when we do so, we come to appreciate how richer our subjective life is than is indicated by previous psychologies.

Another example: if I'm trying to remember Spalding's name, my consciousness differs (in tendency or expectation) from what it is like when I'm trying to recall ("on the tip of my tongue") Bowles's name. This difference in subjectivity is evidently easy to overlook, providing another instance of how, because of careless or no introspection in league with an impoverished subjective vocabulary, we can end up with a barren conception of our inner lives.

That same tradition went astray, James held, in locating the basic unit of consciousness in something discrete like an image or sensation. The picture that resulted, of consciousness being compounded into "complex ideas," was especially mischievous. It not only fostered a wrongheaded kind of introspection, neglecting relations, feelings of continuity and changes in consciousness, and so forth, but it also promoted the notion that the basic units of consciousness resemble physical objects by being discrete, independent, substantive, and capable of being rearranged in successive complexes.

James had a lively time in attacking this conception. Its suggestion that subjective states like feelings, images, and sensations can endure and recur while remaining self-identical completely fudged, he urged, the all-important distinction between subjective experience and the physical world. But, he argued, it *is* refutable by combining careful introspection with further evidence from experimental and laboratory psychology. Carefully introspect and you will find nothing there that answers to the scheme of simple and complex ideas, pictured as mental atoms that retain their identity while entering and exiting successive molecular compounds. But you need not rely on introspection solely, because the laboratory shows that brain physiology is such that the brain never remains identical in successive moments. "For an identical feeling to recur, it would have to recur in an unmodified brain, which is an impossibility" (*EPs*, 152).

Supplementing introspective findings with those from physiology was but one example of how introspection would be checked out, James being of course not alone in trying to save introspection as an indispensable but fallible investigative method within a larger experimental setting. There was Wundt at Leipzig, Marbe and others at Würzburg, and Titchener at Cornell University. They were particularly interested in the experimental use of introspection for advancing "the psychology of thought." Titchener praised the "gradual and increasing recognition of the value of introspection, with its promise of a wide extension of the experimental method" (Titchener 1909, 4–5). A major obstacle, he emphasized, is the difficulty, due to their different mental constitutions, of obtaining the same results from different introspective psychologists. So, he asserted, "The creation of a scientific psychology of these differences is . . . one of the principal achievements of the experimental method" (6–7).[6]

The first step towards a scientific psychology, Titchener believed, was to place on the table, in full view, his own introspective tendencies. In what is perhaps the only psychology textbook that begins with an introspective confession, he offered a detailed self-study. An example: "When I am working for myself, reading or writing or thinking, I experience a complex interlacing of imagery which it is difficult to describe, or at any rate to describe with the just emphasis. My natural tendency is to employ internal speech; and there are occasions when my voice rings out clearly to the mental ear and my throat feels still as if with much talking. But in general the internal speech is reduced to a faint flicker of articulatory movement" (Titchener 1909, 9). So, Titchener argued, if different experimenters begin with a determination of their own introspective proclivities, it should be possible to bridge them scientifically, and his Cornell laboratory became the place in the twentieth century where the most extraordinary efforts were directed toward that end.

But Watson made the pronouncement that would generally prevail in psychology (and later in philosophy): "As a result of this major assumption that there is such a thing as consciousness and that we can analyze it by introspection, we find as many analyses as there are individual psychologists. There is no way of experimentally attacking and solving psychological problems and standardizing methods" (Watson 1924/1925, 6). Behaviorism would take over, and the introspective inquiries of Titchener, James, and others would, for the most part, be forgotten by the psychology profession.

It is not my purpose here to scour the historical kitchen for tasty tidbits that might sweeten the reputations of James and Titchener as experimental introspective psychologists. Today, of course, psychologists along with physicians and lab technicians continue to rely on first-person reports for diagnosing their subjects or patients; and, if this is called dependence on introspection, so be it. But routine noncontroversial first-person reports are hardly the probative introspection that James and Titchener sought. They sought via introspection "newsworthy" results that would seriously impact experimental psychology (and philosophy). The psychology profession, however, long ago rendered its verdict here, and I see no signs of its being reversed.

It will not be reversed because introspection is peculiar in being so hypostatic; in intent, technique, and effect it is preeminently *personal*. Borrowed for laboratory and contemporary purposes in the psychology profession, it is forced into impersonal posturing, becoming lifeless with a mainly unexciting yield. That James's most striking introspections in *Principles* are strikingly personal, often defying immediate comprehension, is therefore not surprising. Sympathetic to James's conception of our inner lives as rich but elusive lodes for introspective mining, I am almost always intrigued by his personal efforts, often themselves as elusive as they are suggestive, to decipher them. By the same token, I think (seeming to differ with James here) that some of his introspective claims are important, not because they emerge from difficult or ingenious introspectings, but because they are urged against theorists whose arguments simply bypass introspection. That is generally true of James's claims when they are of the "Anyone can introspect and see that . . . " kind; as, for example, of the claim that anyone can "look inside" and discover that experience is a "stream" and not a series of discrete items.

But many theorists are not content to downgrade the value of introspective searches solely within experimental and laboratory psychology, extending their reservations to the personal or idiosyncratic context as well. Yet, once fallibility and privileged access limitations are conceded, defending the role of introspection (both as direct observation and retrospection) in gaining self-knowledge becomes important and achievable. When I ask, "Why?" "What does it mean?" "Does it resemble anything in my previous experience?" Am I really sincere about it?" "Have I been denying (self-deceiving) all along?" "What conception fits this experience best?" and so forth – where what is at issue is a feeling, emotion, mood, attitude, impulse, impression, thought, altered consciousness, and so on – introspection both as observation and retrospection, I submit, is more often than not an essential part of the process of delivering responsible answers to such questions that we put to ourselves. Such questions occur in psychoanalytic and self-help contexts, but so do they in philosophical ones as well.[7]

James's pragmatism and his introspective psychology are reciprocative in two major respects. Convinced that experiences are richly textured and multiply veneered, perhaps superficially clear to the casual inner eye but increasingly murky to the searching eye, James recognized how introspective the task is of giving or finding the cash-value of terms such as "I," "will," "consciousness," "sense," "attention," "remember," "imagine," and so forth. Experiences are to be explored introspectively, partly for the experimental discoveries enjoyed, but also for revealing the pragmatic value of notions like, for instance, *oneself*. Failing to appreciate this, one will never survive a reading of *The Principles of Psychology*. It is a monumental attempt to connect, introspectively, key philosophical and psychological concepts with relevant experiences so that the experiential differences (cash-value) made by the distinctions contained in the concepts are disclosed. It was, of course, just this attempt that Wittgenstein, despite his admiration for James, criticizes at length and, in my opinion, with too much success. Elaborating our understanding of our more subjective vocabulary, *without* closely consulting the delicate details of ephemeral experiences, should look like what it is – an impossible assignment.[8]

The second intersection between James's pragmatism and his introspective psychology, while crucial, is strangely overlooked in Jamesean commentaries. Too often, his pragmatism is treated as being two theories, of meaning and truth, and they are evaluated, as it were, for their own sake. But, for James, pragmatically revising the concepts of truth ("workability") and meaning ("cash-value") represented no end in itself but rather pointed toward what he called "the pragmatic *method*." What kind of method? It is in fact a technique for decision making, for voluntarily assenting to *p* rather than *q*, especially when one is lost for compelling evidence for either *p* or *q*.

One of the more conspicuous formulations of the idea occurs in James's *Pragmatism*. " . . . I wish now to speak of the *pragmatic method*. The pragmatic method is primarily a method of settling metaphysical disputes that otherwise might be interminable. Is the world one or many? – fated or free? – material or spiritual? . . . disputes over such notions are unending. The pragmatic method in such cases is to try to interpret each notion by tracing its respective practical consequences. What difference would it practically make to anyone if this notion rather than that were true? If no practical difference . . . all dispute is idle" (*P*, 28). What is often overlooked is the utilitarian role played by James's pragmatic concepts of meaning and truth in serving the pragmatic method. Are we free or determined? We can debate this forever. How can we break free and adopt a belief one way or the other? After ascertaining the cash-value meanings of "free" and "determined," and discovering (perhaps by experiments in imagination) what it would mean to us "practically" if one side of the debate were true over the other, we could then *decide* what to believe. As is well known, James's own grounds for decision were highly personal or idiosyncratic. In such cases, he insisted, you have the right to choose the side whose consequences strike you as being practically "better" than the other's. I have in the past called this, accordingly, *subjective* pragmatism, a label that also serves to distinguish James's from Dewey's and Peirce's pragmatisms (Myers 1986a, 279–81).

Deciding which consequences of opposed propositions are practically "better" was for James a matter of deciding which are psychologically preferential, and, because determining this in the sorts of cases that he contemplated is markedly subjective, there is no evading the involvement of introspection in the process. Years before he officially espoused pragmatism, James displayed his adoption of it, signs of this occurring, for instance, throughout *Principles*. That the pragmatism emerged from his introspective psychology is indicated by this claim in *Principles: "That theory will be most generally believed which, besides offering us objects able to account satisfactorily for our sensible experience, also offers those which are most interesting, those which appeal most urgently to our aesthetic, emotional, and active needs"* (PP, 2:940).

Let James's thesis here be qualified somewhat, it can then be recommended as a regulative principle for contemporary philosophizing. It must add that introspection (both as observation and retrospection) is often required for deciphering what "really" appeals to one's aesthetic and emotional needs; recognizing one's needs or what appeals to them need not occur automatically or abruptly in a Eureka!-type moment. Noticing or logging one's feelings plus patient retrospection in the form of self-interrogation and diagnosis precede confident verdicts about one's own aesthetic, emotional, conceptual, and moral needs.

This suggests a further qualification for James's thesis, that one's beliefs are to be based only on what (presuming that considerations of truth and evidence have been satisfied as well as the circumstances permit) one believes *ought* to appeal to these needs that *ought* to be favored. So qualified, the importance of introspection as a process of self-dialogue that seeks to establish sincerity, understanding of purpose and motivation, and honesty in knowledge-claims is even more prominent.

The introspective process, of course, occurs not *in vacuo* but in a context where numerous factors, especially philosophical arguments, set the agenda. The philosopher's job, it is often said, is to find and follow the right argument wherever it leads, and that calls for intellectual acuity and probity, so forget introspective highjinks! But the problem here is the endemic inconclusiveness of philosophical arguments. It is not only the debates about metaphysical issues of the sort that occupied James throughout his career but all the current ones – about abortion, the death penalty, just wars, professional responsibilities, as well as about physicalism, essentialism, realism, and so on – that have no bottom lines. Nothing remains but for the *personal* element to intrude, to weigh the arguments but also the special (possibly compromising) relations that may obtain between them and oneself, if a responsible decision or choice of belief is to eventuate. In the spirit of James's subjective pragmatism, I have argued here that introspection, as previously delineated, is often a necessary condition for responsibly delivered conclusions.

The only kind of pragmatism that can connect hygienically with this so-called postmodern era, my ruminations tell me, is the Jamesean that is rooted in introspective psychology. We hear much about philosophy as conversation but not nearly enough about it as conversation with oneself. In an era when skepticism, relativism, antifoundationism, and the death of the author or self cloud the philosophical horizon, the finest irony is that a new sense of *oneself* is needed for finding one's way. Thinking and behaving nowadays requires an ego sufficiently intact to construct, for oneself anyway, a foundation or center of sorts from which and by which intellectual, moral, and aesthetic priorities get developed. Constructing an inner center of convictions that allows a hierarchy of beliefs and values, thereby escaping nihilism, will be, inevitably, an intensively introspective process.

NOTES

1 Edwin G. Boring's survey essay "A History of Introspection" is also useful and also deserves mention. Published originally in 1953 in the *Psychological Bulletin*, it is reprinted in Boring 1961.

2 "On Some Omission of Introspective Psychology," *Mind* 9 (1884), pp. 1–26. It reappears, in sections, in chapter 7 (Methods and Snares of Psychology), chapter 9 (Stream of Thought), chapter 10 (Consciousness of Self), and chapter 12 (Conception) of *The Principles of Psychology*. The 1884 essay is reprinted in *EPs*, 142–68.

3 The quoted passage continues immediately into an expression of doubt on James's part about the *metaphysical* status of "states of consciousness," a doubt that reappears throughout *Principles* and that, subsequent to *Principles*, leads to his concept of "pure experience." This idea, he believed, could be developed into a replacement of traditional Cartesian dualism.

   Since the issue of traditional metaphysical dualism is not my concern here, I omit James's references to it. But it is worth noting that the practical merits of introspection remain, whatever be the fate of dualism. James on this point could agree with such recent opinions as Churchland 1984, 32 ff., 73 ff., 158 ff. But compare, for a different contemporary viewpoint, Lyons 1986, 151 ff.

4 See Hebb 1949; Ryle 1949; Skinner 1976; Titchener 1909; and Watson 1919.

5 This remark applies also, I believe, to the celebrated critique of introspection by Nisbett and Wilson (1977, 231–59). Nisbett and Wilson are certainly persuasive in the evidence that they present for being skeptical about first-person subjective reports, but that is a far cry from dismissing introspection altogether as worthless.

6 For more on Titchener as well as Wundt and the Würzburg school, see Humphrey 1951.

7 For my defense of introspection in self-knowledge as well as for my fuller analysis of introspection-as-retrospection, see Myers 1986, 199–207.

8 For further arguments in this vein, see my introduction to *The Principles of Psychology, The Works of William James* (Cambridge: Harvard University Press, 1981), pp. xxvii ff.; and Myers 1986a, 346 ff.

2 Consciousness as a pragmatist views it

I INTRODUCTION

There is, of course, no one way a pragmatist must view the nature and function of human consciousness. I'll be concerned in this essay with the way William James understood consciousness. James's struggles with the problem of consciousness provide I believe a compelling example of the pragmatic method at work, the method of trying to keep all the things we need to believe in play at once. This is no easy task since the things we need to believe typically represent the needs of different aspects of human life, of different human practices. There will be the things we need to believe for purposes of doing psychology, for living morally, for making life significant, and so on. And there is no guarantee that the things we find ourselves needing to believe will not compete. Indeed, allowing, even relishing, competition among different beliefs, the constant shifting back and forth, revising, dispelling appearances of inconsistencies, refining, and drawing together various pieces of a view of the world that works, that makes sense, as much sense as can be made from here-and-now, is what makes James such a compelling figure. His modus operandi is as visible in his work on consciousness as anywhere else in his philosophy.

Pragmatism is a method for doing what matters most: finding a way of believing, thinking, and being that will make life meaningful, that will make life worth living in the widest possible sense. Pragmatism involves first and foremost the intellectual virtues of honesty and humility.

II PLURALISM AND POINTS OF VIEW

James questioned the philosophical aspiration to find a single way of seeing the world and insists throughout his corpus that experience resists reductive unifying analysis. In the preface to *The Will to Believe and Other Essays in Popular Philosophy*, James writes:

After all that reason can do has been done, there still remains the opacity of the finite facts as merely given, with most of their peculiarities mutually unmediated and unexplained. To the very last, there are various "points of view" which the philosopher must distinguish in discussing the world. . . . He who takes for his hypothesis the notion that [pluralism] is the permanent form of the world is what I call a radical empiricist. There is no possible point of view from which the world can appear an absolutely single fact. Real possibilities, real indeterminations, real beginnings, real ends, real evil, real crises, catastrophes, and escapes, a real God, and a real moral life, just as commonsense conceives these things, may remain in empiricism as conceptions which that philosophy gives up the attempt either to "overcome" or to reinterpret in monistic form.[1] (*WB*, viii–ix)

The commitment to pluralism involved for James a commitment to the existence of different points of view that serve different purposes. It follows that we will not be able to understand James's views on consciousness without paying close attention to the point of view from which he is speaking.

III NONNATURALISM

In the past, I have thought this emphasis on point of view permitted me to provide a reading of James's theory of consciousness, based solely on the *Principles of Psychology* and *Psychology: The Briefer Course*, both written from the point of view of the empirical psychologist, as involving a consistent and farseeing naturalism. I have come to see that this cannot be done. There are parts of James's overall philosophy that require him to resist naturalism, and even the texts written from the point of view of "psychology as a natural science" cannot, without a good deal of interpretive sleight of hand, be given a consistent naturalistic reading.[2] What can be established, however, is that James was always searching for a way around substance dualism, a dualism he ambivalently adopted for methodological purposes in the *Principles*, but eventually saw his way out of in the *Essays in Radical Empiricism*. But even in the "Stream of Thought" chapter, written in 1884 – and thus one of the earliest pieces of the monumental project that became the *Principles* – we see ample evidence that James was struggling against substance dualism before completing the book in which he provisionally assumed this very form of dualism.

To prove my point, I discuss what seem to me to be several *prima facie* inconsistent texts devoted to the discussion of consciousness. The texts are the paired *Principles of Psychology* and its short and somewhat different version, *Psychology: The Briefer Course*, published in 1890 and 1892, respectively; the essays written between the early 1880s and the mid 1890s and collected in *The Will to Believe and Other Essays in Popular Philosophy*, which was published in 1897; the 1898 Lecture on "Human Immortality"; and the essays "Does Consciousness Exist?" and "A World of Pure Experience," written in 1904 and collected posthumously in the *Essays in Radical Empiricism*. Some of the *prima facie* inconsistent passages occur, as I have just suggested, within *Principles* themselves, so the interpretive problem does not occur simply among different texts, but also within them.

IV TEXTUAL INCOHERENCE?

The *prima facie* inconsistency among the texts is easy to see. In *Principles*, James writes that psychology is the science of "finite human minds" (*PP*, 1:v), and that *"Introspective Observation is what we have to rely on first and foremost and always. The word introspec*tion need hardly be defined – it means of course, the looking into our own minds and reporting what we discover. *Everyone agrees that we there discover states of consciousness"* (*PP*, 1:185).

In the essays collected in *The Will to Believe and Other Essays in Popular Philosophy*, the dominant theme is that belief in freedom of the will – consciously orchestrated freedom of the will – is required to make life meaningful, whereas in the *Principles* we learn that psychology must assume determinism.

In the lecture on "Human Immortality," published in 1898, James suggests that we assume that *"Thought is a function of the brain"* (*ERM*, 81). He then goes on to argue that this assumption creates no obstacle to the doctrine that our conscious self "may still continue when the brain itself is dead" (*ERM*, 82). In effect, a science of finite human minds, which assumes that consciousness is functionally linked to the brain, is compatible with the thesis that after the functional link between brain and consciousness ceases to exist due to bodily death, consciousness may continue to exist for all eternity.

Finally, in the paper "Does Consciousness Exist?" published fourteen years after *Principles* and eight years after the lecture on "Human Immortality," James writes "[Consciousness] is the name of a non-entity, and has no right place among first principles. Those who still cling to it are clinging to a mere echo, the faint rumor left behind by the disappearing 'soul,' upon the air of philosophy" (*MEN*, 169).

V CHANGING HIS MIND?

Taking these passages at face value suggests that the wisest tactic might be to simply assert that James changed his mind about consciousness or that he was inconsistent. Consciousness is the primary datum in *Principles*, but it goes the way of phlogiston in the *Essays on Radical Empiricism*. Psychology assumes determinism, but moral philosophy requires free will – an assertion made not only in most of the essays in *The Will to Believe*, but also in *Psychology: The Briefer Course* of 1892.

Consciousness is a property of finite minds with brains in *Principles* but can exist without the brain according to the view enunciated in "Human Immortality." Finally, personal immortality which involves my continued existence as a disembodied conscious self appears to require an assumption, the assumption that consciousness exists, which in the later work is seen to depend upon the silly adherence to an unwarranted posit – *Consciousness* – "a mere echo, the faint rumor left behind by the disappearing 'soul,' upon the air of philosophy."

Such are a few of the interpretive problems. I'll resist the tactic of arguing either that James changed his mind in any fundamental way about the nature and function of consciousness or that he was simply inconsistent. Whether I can succeed in giving a coherent non-naturalist reading remains for the reader to judge.

VI THE PSYCHOLOGY

James writes in the "Preface" to the *Principles* that "I have kept close to the point of view of natural science throughout the book. . . . This book, assuming that thoughts and feelings exist and are vehicles of knowledge, thereupon contends that psychology when she has ascertained the empirical correlation of the various sorts of thought and feeling with definite conditions of the brain, can go no farther – can go no farther, that is, as a natural science. If she goes farther she becomes metaphysical" (*PP*, 1:v–vi).

The first point to notice is that the point of view of natural science in the case of psychology is not one in which consciousness *is* a brain process. Consciousness is correlated with certain brain processes. The second point I want to insist on is this: For James, as for contemporary philosophers such as John Searle and Galen Strawson, the mind/body problem *is* the consciousness/brain problem. This is because the meaning of "mental" involves essentially the idea of experience. When we describe unconscious visual processes or the processes which get us from thinking to performing speech acts that express our thoughts as "mental processes," it is a sort of linguistic courtesy, akin to calling a boy a "young man." Unconscious visual processing is "mental" only in the sense that it takes place in or supervenes on brain processes and has some interesting relation to conscious visual experience. Getting the vocal apparatus to produce speech undoubtedly involves a complex set of neural processes, and typically saying what one intends involves consciousness of the beginning and the end of the process. But we are clueless about how saying what we mean happens.

Furthermore, there is nothing like a Freudian Unconscious in *Principles* – indeed, the possibility, insofar as it is entertained, is rejected. And although dissociative, disunified minds are discussed, as are cases of hysterical blindness, where, for example, the patient insists that she does not see anything, while evidence shows that she is seeing some things in her visual field, these are all explained in terms of what James called "secondary consciousness" – a variation on the theme, not something unconscious.

This much is secure – when James is concerned with the mind/body problem in the *Principles*, he is concerned with the problem of consciousness – its nature, function, and relation to the brain and the rest of the body.

There are several deflationary views that James rejects on the mind/brain relation. What he calls the "automaton-theory" comes in two versions: an epiphenomenalist version and a parallelist version.

Epiphenomenalism is the theory that conscious mental life is a causally inconsequential byproduct, or side effect, of physical processes in our brains. James quotes Huxley's startling version of epiphenomenalism:

The consciousness of brutes would appear to be related to the mechanism of their body simply as a collateral product of its working, and to be completely without any power of modifying that working, as the steam-whistle which accompanies the work of a locomotive engine is without influence upon its machinery. Their volition, if they have any, is an emotion *indicative* of physical changes, not a *cause* of such changes. . . . The soul stands to the body as the bell of a clock to the works, and consciousness answers to the sound which the bell gives out when it is struck . . . to the best of my judgment, the argumentation which applies to brutes holds equally good of men. . . . We are conscious automata. (*PP*, 1:131)

James aptly refers to the epiphenomenalist position as the "inert spectator" view of the mind.

The epiphenomenalist's position is implausible, if not incoherent. First, assuming that epiphenomenalism is meant as a response to the interaction problem facing classical Cartesian dualism, it undermines its own rationale, which is to keep distinct metaphysical kinds from interacting, by allowing causal interaction between body and mind in one direction. On the epiphenomenalistic view, conscious mental states are the causal outcome of certain physical processes – the terminal side effects of biological processes. The epiphenomenalist, however, provides no intelligible reason as to why causality in the body/mind direction is any less problematic or worrisome than in the mind/body direction.

Alternatively, if we really take the locomotive engine-steam whistle analogy seriously we have no reason to think of conscious mental states in immaterial terms in the first place. A steam whistle's "toot" is, after all, an utterly physical process. But if we are under no pressure to think of conscious mental states in nonphysical terms, then we have no metaphysical interaction problem to worry about, and epiphenomenalism loses its appeal as a solution to *that* problem.

Furthermore, as soon as we take note of this fact that the epiphenomenalist position is compatible with consciousness being a physical process involving what we would nowadays call some sort of supervenience relation, it loses its status as a distinctive solution to the mind–body problem and becomes instead simply a particular theoretical position on the relative *causal efficacy* of the different physical components and processes that make up a person. On this interpretation, epiphenomenalism is the thesis that conscious mental life has the same incidental relation to the whole person as the steam whistle has to the locomotive engine.

To James such a view seems highly implausible on, as he puts it, "common-sensical" grounds. All the evidence points to conscious mental life as more analogous to the steam engine, which powers the locomotive and produces the steam, than to the quaint but terminal toot. James insists that epiphenomenalism is an *"unwarrantable impertinence in the present state of psychology"* (*PP*, 1:138).

Against the epiphenomenalist, James musters the commonsensical evidence that we often seem to bring about what we in fact mentally intend. He then joins this evidence to evolutionary theory, arguing that it is "inconceivable that consciousness should have *nothing to do* with a business which it so faithfully attends." And the question, "What has it to do?" is one which psychology has no right to "surmount," for it is her plain duty to consider it (*PP*, 1:136). James, however, immediately adds that "the whole question of interaction and influence between things is a metaphysical question about which we are entirely without knowledge."

The second type of "automaton-theory" is parallelism-with-an-eliminativist-agenda. James describes the position this way:

If we knew thoroughly the nervous system of Shakespeare, and as thoroughly all his environing conditions, we should be able to show why at a certain period of his life his hand came to trace on certain sheets of paper those crabbed little marks which we for shortness' sake call the manuscript of *Hamlet*. We should understand . . . all this without in the slightest degree acknowledging the existence of thoughts in Shakespeare's mind. [B]ut, on the other hand, nothing in all this could prevent us from giving an equally complete account of . . . Shakespeare's spiritual history, an account in which gleam of thought and emotion should find its place. The mind history would run alongside the body-history of each man, and each point in the one would correspond to, but not react upon, a point in the other. (*PP*, 1:136–7)

This sort of parallelism is logically identical to the sort of parallelism familiar from the writings of Leibniz and Malebranche. But Leibniz and Malebranche proposed their somewhat different forms of the doctrine in an attempt to solve the problem of interaction between the two distinct metaphysical kinds that Cartesianism requires, while at the same time maintaining the metaphysical and explanatory primacy of mentalistic explanation.

The sort of parallelism James takes as his target sees the possibility of parallel, but distinct, mental and physical stories as warranting the elimination of the mental story from science.

Why would one favor the elimination of the mentalistic story? Mental phenomena are metaphysically spooky, ontologically orthogonal to the materialistic perspective dominating the rest of the natural sciences, and thus worth eliminating. Furthermore, parsimony favors eliminating one of two stories supposing both have equal explanatory power, especially when one is metaphysically weird.

As with all positions on the mind/body problem, James acknowledges that parallelism cannot be straightforwardly proved or disproved. But parallelism has several worrisome features. First, there is the unyielding puzzle as to why there are these two utterly independent but parallel chains of events – itself a metaphysically odd state of affairs. No less odd, after all, than if the two metaphysically distinct kinds interacted. Second, there is the puzzle as to how the two chains keep their perfect symmetry. The only decent answer to this question ever proposed in the philosophical literature has been theological: God flawlessly orchestrates the parallel symmetry – either by setting the mental and physical streams in harmony at the point of creation or birth (Leibniz) or by maintaining the harmony on each and every occasion (Malebranche). The first kind of parallelism might be dubbed "deistic parallelism," the second "pantheistic parallelism."

Perhaps parallelism finesses the interaction problem. Still, even as God is invoked, it looks as if parallelism must be a deterministic doctrine. God does all the work of keeping mental events and bodily events in harmony, and both the mental and the bodily paths look *prima facie* to be deterministic. It is not as if I ever truly *choose* any sequence of acts along the mental path, nor that I ever *choose* to perform any bodily movements.

Determinism to one side, even on the supposition that there might be two utterly distinct stories about Shakespeare's writing of *Hamlet*, one the story of the mental sequence, the other of the coordinated sequence of bodily movements, this fact hardly favors elimination of the mental story. The reason is simple. The two stories do not explain the same phenomena. Eliminating the mental account of Shakespeare's composition of Hamlet eliminates something fundamental that is in need of explanation, namely, the intentional character of Shakespeare's production of *Hamlet* and our intentional appropriation of the written play as about what it is about. Surely from a physical point of view this play called *Hamlet* is just a series of ink marks on paper, but to Shakespeare and to us it is a story, a meaningful intentional object. Any analysis of a significant human act framed totally in the languages of the natural sciences, neuroscience included, will fail to capture certain facts related to the meaning and significance of that act. A science of mind may well require different levels of description, some intentional, some not, in order to answer different explanatory questions. But even on parallelist assumptions, the purely physical chain of events hardly explains the same thing as the mental chain does.

For James, the fundamental flaw of parallelism runs even deeper. It is the same as the epiphenomenalist's, namely, the evidence for interaction is overwhelming. It is simply too implausible to assume that Shakespeare's decision to write a play was not causally related to his taking pen in hand, but rather that the two events, the decision to write a play and the movements of his hand over paper, just happened to coincide!

Dewey ("The Vanishing Subject," 1940) claimed that James himself was a parallelist. But James's parallelism and his commitment to what he called the "pre-established harmony" between Object and Subject is, as best I can discern, epistemic, not metaphysical, or possibly a confused admixture of the two. The "thoroughgoing dualism" James insists is the psychologist's starting point involves, in the first instance, a distinction between the cognizing organism and the things-it-knows. After James quotes a long passage from Borden Parker Browne in which sense data are introduced as an intermediary between the cognizing subject and the things in the world, he makes the odd and textually singular assertion about the need to assume a "dualism of Object and Subject and their pre-established harmony" (*PP*, 1:218–21). These words invoke the specter of parallelism. But in context, I claim the best interpretation is that James was thinking here of "pre-established harmony" as involving the generally well coordinated links between knower and known, the fact that the world somehow has evolved to put the metaphysically distinct relata of mind, brain, and external world into such relations that "willing" and "knowing" can occur.

James often makes the point that we must assume that for every mental event there exists a brain correlate. But this doctrine does not require advocacy of any traditional form of parallelism. To be sure, the correlations are brute and provide no warrant for identifying the mental with the neural – as for example some sort of identity theory or double aspect theory might do. Nonetheless, mental events and neural events interact in both directions. My seeing you will be correlated with neural event n, both at time t; but if when I see you, I then decide to tell you a juicy piece of gossip, that decision at t_1, which will also have its own neural correlate at t_1, will temporally precede my speech act which it will cause at t_2.

In the *Principles*, James also considers a *Master Homunculus Theory*, a sort of Consciousness as CEO model. This model comes in two varieties: a materialist version and a spiritualist version. The materialist proposes that there exists "among the cells one central or pontifical one to which our consciousness is attached" (*PP*, 1:179).

James objects to this brazen materialistic tactic of claiming the existence of a physical location for our mental masterworks on the grounds that there is absolutely no physical evidence that there is any one such place in the brain. "There is no cell or group of cells in the brain of such anatomical or functional preeminence as to appear to be the keystone or centre of gravity of the whole system" (*PP*, 1:180).[3]

Waiting in the wings, of course, is our old friend the Cartesian, who holds what James calls the "spiritual monad theory." He holds that every remotely plausible theory of the mind requires the existence of a Master Homunculus who comprehends and orchestrates the goings-on of the cognitive system. The Cartesian insists that because there is no evidence that this Master Homunculus is located in the two and one-half pounds of gray matter between our ears, we are logically compelled to assume that it exists nonphysically – as an immaterial *soul* or *thinking substance.*

James is very much attracted to the spiritual monad view although he sees ways the psychologist can avoid committing himself to it. First, the Cartesian can produce no direct empirical evidence for his immaterialist hypothesis. Therefore, his theory must have either strong intuitive, introspective, and phenomenological warrant, or it must have logic and parsimony on its side. But James insists it does not have the former since we do not ever introspect a Cartesian *soul* – even less so a *pure immutable ego.* Rather we introspect our ordinary everyday self thinking. So, Cartesianism fails the introspective test one would expect to be its primary warrant.

What about its warrant on grounds of logic and parsimony? Not surprisingly, given what I've said so far, James brushes away standard worries about interaction between two metaphysically different kinds of substances on the grounds, *pace* Hume, that all causality is completely mysterious (*PP*, 1:181).

James writes, "the only trouble that remains to haunt us is the metaphysical one of understanding how one sort of world or existent thing can affect or influence another at all. This trouble, however, since it also exists inside of both worlds, and involves neither physical improbability nor logical contradiction, is relatively small. [I] confess, therefore, that to posit a soul influenced in some mysterious way by the brain-states and responding to them by conscious affections of its own, seems to me the line of least logical resistance, so far as we have yet attained" (*PP*, 1:181). But once again James reminds us that in fact we do not experience a "soul," but only states of consciousness. Believing in a soul that orchestrates mental and bodily life is an option, but psychology may, for its purposes, be able to do with less.

This suggestion is developed in the "Stream of Thought" chapter which was written in 1884, although not published in the *Principles* until 1890. James says here, and in the next chapter, "The Consciousness of Self," that the thoughts themselves are the thinkers. I am a cognitive creature or, if this is too materialistic a way of putting things, I am a unified thinking thing. This is enough to explain why I have my own experiences, and not yours. Thinking or experiencing are powerfully appropriative. So my thinking now carries its past to itself, a past that gives my thinking, texture, richness, and meaning. Furthermore, I have been led to construct concepts of "me," "myself" and "I." These are useful ways of conceiving of me or of what-is-happening-here or of different ways of the stream of consciousness appropriating itself from different vantage points. But what these pronouns pick out is not a substantial Cartesian mind nor a Kantian transcendental ego, but this metaphysically complex organism, this subject of experience, appropriated in different reflexive ways. These themes about the constructive quality of pronouns, of different ways of conceiving of the self (in bodily, psychological, or social terms), of the idea that consciousness is an entity, and of the distinctions between mental states and physical ones are key to the later writings on neutral monism.

We have experiences which we then categorize and parse. On what basis do we categorize and parse? On the basis of human interactions – some with world-historical force behind them – revealed in the languages we are taught, prior common sense, and philosophizing – and some that are called for by our time-and-place, our unique situation in the world.

VII EVOLUTION

It might be thought that reading James as a nonnaturalist, as a dualist of some sort, is in tension with (indeed, incompatible with) his Darwinism. It seems right to think that James's commitment to Darwin's theory of evolution required him to provide a theory of the nature and function of conscious mental life that explained how it could be the adaptive, causally efficacious trait he thought it was. But it might seem that James's view in *Principles* that consciousness is immaterial is incompatible with Darwinism. There may be ways around this problem, even as Darwinism has developed in our time. Let me explain. Nature selects what it can see. What she sees is reproductive success. Reproductively successful organisms get to pass on their traits, which results in increased frequency of the traits that lead to success. Now if Homo sapiens happen to have developed the quirky, hard-to-understand capacity to "load the dice," to select courses of action by conscious will, to broadcast information of important events to self and other, then they will do well in the struggle to survive. But here one might think the following problem will prove insuperable: we need to understand the process of the transmission and maintenance of consciousness within the species. Nature does not see consciousness. She cannot. She only sees the effects that consciousness reliably produces and that are implicated in reproductive success. So long as consciousness is linked to the production of the relevant effects, there is no problem in there being selection pressures for consciousness. Unless, that is, consciousness is immaterial. Nowadays, we would say that if there are genes that select for consciousness and if creatures with consciousness behave in reproductively successful ways, then the genes that select for consciousness will increase in frequency, or maintain themselves as characteristic of the species. The problem is this: How does selection of phenotypic traits such as the behaviors or traits that are thought to be caused by consciousness, that is, by selective attention, capacities to do what one intends, to "load the dice," and the like, also select for what produces these behaviors and traits, unless what produces the behaviors and traits is linked to what we now call "genes"? Selection pressures operate on sperm and ova and what we have come to think they carry – genetic material.

Although I personally do not find this response appealing, James could maintain the immateriality of mind and the idea that there were powerful selective pressures pulling for it. First, there is his ever-ready argument about our fundamental ignorance about causality. We do not know – may never know – how causality works. But if we are dualists who believe in the interaction of the mental and physical in the domain of mind/brain relations, there is no internal incoherence in believing that evolution also operates over the mental and the physical. We happen to understand only the mechanisms governing the physical transmission. But either our ignorance or God can be left to do some work.

Alternatively, one could opt for the standard, purely physicalist, theory of selection and maintain that certain genes, once on-line, have as emergent properties the production of a mysteriously causally efficacious immaterial mind. James's acceptance of the Humean doctrine that all causality is mysterious gives him lots of room to operate.

I will conclude this section with this claim: In *Principles* James was a dualist. His dualism involved a commitment to interaction between the mental and the physical. It follows that all the statements about psycho-physical correlations need to be taken, not as support for any kind of parallelism, but as involving the belief that for each token mental event, there will be a corresponding brain event (probably not the other way around). Finally, the sort of dualistic interactionism that James accepts in *Principles* is ambivalently Cartesian, an ambivalent form of substance dualism. The ambivalence shows up in many places, especially in the passages in the "Stream of Thought" and "Consciousness of Self" chapters where the view that will be adopted later that "consciousness is not a thing" begins to reveal itself.

VIII VOLUNTARISM

One reason James is not – indeed, cannot be – a naturalist has to do with his commitment to voluntarism. James either did not understand compatibilism or else he did not respect it as a solution to the free will/determinism problem – possibly both. For him, two live options existed: a libertarian conception of free will and hard determinism. The meaning of life was at stake, not just the prospects for a scientific psychology. Meanwhile, James insisted that scientific psychology must assume determinism.

When James says the psychology must assume determinism what exactly does he mean? One thing he most certainly thinks is that each token mental event has a brain correlate, possibly one to which it appears to have a necessary connection (such connections, once again, however, bespeak "constant connection," and apparent necessary causality, but are, at root, mysterious). But in the second place, since consciousness can load the dice and influence the direction of bodily action, he must mean that we should assume that whatever laws describe this interaction will be deterministic.

Why think this? One possibility is that assuming determinism might make discovery of whatever sort of lawlike generalizations psychology might eventually yield more probable, even if these generalizations turn out to be nondeterministic – even if determinism is false. The idea is similar to the idea that if I assume I will one day become rich, I may be more careful than I would otherwise have been with my investments and in this way become wealthier than I would have been had I not made this assumption, even if I never do become rich by any measure.

Still one might wonder about the plausibility of making even the regulative assumption that the laws of psychology, if there are such laws, will be deterministic, when already in James's philosophy is the assumption that we have free will. To stick with the example of my financial future, it seems like assuming that I could become rich even in a situation where I had independent reason to believe that no one can ever become rich. Am I not doing something odd, if I look for what I know, on other grounds, cannot be found? James gives no answer to these questions.

One possibility is that he thought that psychology cannot get behind consciously initiated action; but that if it allows its generalizations to start with consciously generated actions, it might end up with deterministic laws linking conscious will with action: "If a person P consciously decides to do x, and there are no obstacles to her doing x, she will do x." To the further question: "Why did P decide to do x?" two answers suggest themselves: "P just decided, it was a matter of free will"; or, if this seems like stonewalling, we might advert to the realm of reasons that are distinct from causes to rationalize P's choice, but not causally explain it.

Another possibility is that James found the state-of-the-art reassuring. The sort of law mentioned above will, in fact, be nondeterministic, wearing various *ceteris paribus* clauses on its sleeve. So long as psychology had not discovered any laws, the deterministic assumption is truly regulative, not constitutive – in a way, I think it could not be conceived if physics were the science under discussion. In the epilogue to his *Psychology: The Briefer Course*, published two years after *Principles*, James writes:

When we talk of "psychology as a natural science," we must not assume that that means a sort of psychology that stands at last on solid ground. It means just the reverse; it means a psychology particularly fragile, and into which the waters of metaphysical criticism leak at every joint, a psychology all of whose elementary assumptions and data must be reconsidered in wider connections . . . it is strange to hear people talk of "the New Psychology" . . . when into the real elements and forces which the word covers not the first glimpse of clear insight exists. A string of raw facts; a little gossip and wrangle about opinions; a little classification and generalization on the mere descriptive level . . . but not a single law in the sense in which physics shows us laws, not a single proposition from which any consequence can causally be deduced. . . . This is no science, it is only the hope of a science.

James then repeats in the last sentence of the book the caveat that "the natural science assumptions with which we started are provisional and revisable things" (*PB*, 334–5). Restricting natural science assumptions to the discovery of psycho-physical correlations, not one of which has yet yielded a genuinely predictive law, explains in part why James felt perfectly comfortable saying only a few paragraphs earlier:

Let psychology frankly admit that *for her scientific purposes* determinism may be *claimed*, and no one can find fault. . . . Now ethics makes a counterclaim; and the present writer, for one, has no hesitation in regarding her claim as the stronger, and in assuming that our wills are "free" . . . the deterministic assumption of psychology is merely provisional and methodological (*PB*, 328).

This passage is emblematic of a certain sort of move characteristic of James's philosophy. First, there is the idea that points of view can be in competition. Inconsistency is, however, avoided by noting the provisionality or methodological nature of certain points of view.

James often speaks as if all points of view are equally partial, provisional, interest relative, fallible, and so on. But sometimes there is a moment when he stands by metaphysics or morals and gives them final authority, the last say – a point at which he allows them to assert a view that is not merely provisional or methodological, but true. Second, free will and consciousness are deeply connected in James's thought since "consciousness" is causally efficacious in willing – it "loads the dice." Third, we know from the corpus and every biography of James that he was obsessed with the problem of freedom of the will. The discussion of free will in *Principles* (*PP*, 2:572) – "the question of free will is insoluble on strictly psychologic grounds" – resonates with, indeed almost duplicates, the line of argument in the famous papers from the mid-1880s collected in *The Will to Believe* where James argues from the premises that philosophical arguments for or against God and free will are inconclusive, and that belief in God and free will contribute to a meaningful life while atheism and determinism undermine meaning, to the conclusion that believing in God and free will are warranted, all things considered. In the work on immortality, James is clear that even if a brain/body are necessary for consciousness to appear as it does for *embodied beings*, it does not follow that consciousness, identity, and their suite require a brain or a body. Belief in personal immortality, like the belief in free will and God, are options for philosophically honest persons trying to find the beliefs that will support a meaningful life.

It is not clear that the position James takes on points of view is stable. So long as psychology contains not one predictive law, the provisional deterministic assumption can hardly claim to be the point of view that best captures the nature of all things. What is less clear is how one could resist giving this provisional assumption more than provisional weight if it worked to yield an explanatory and predictive science of the mind. If one starts to give two competing views more than provisional or methodological weight, it is hard to see how one will keep from courting inconsistency. One will surely court some sort of cognitive dissonance.

IX MY IMMORTAL SOUL

As I have just indicated, in the lecture on "Human Immortality," James complicates matters further. He writes, "For the purposes of my argument, now, I wish to adopt this general doctrine as if it were established absolutely, with no possibility of restriction. During this hour I wish you also to accept it as a postulate, whether you think it incontrovertibly established or not; so I beg you to agree with me to-day in subscribing to the great psycho-physiological formula: *Thought is a function of the brain*" (ERM, 81).

He then asks whether this doctrine logically compels us to reject the idea of personal immortality and answers, "no." James's reasoning requires distinguishing three different kinds of function, and thus three different ways we might understand the thesis that "*Thought is a function of the brain.*" There are, first, productive functions, as operate when a hot kettle produces steam. Second, there are releasing or permissive functions. "The trigger of a crossbow has a releasing function: it removes the obstacle that holds the string, and lets the bow fly back to its natural shape" (ERM, 85). Third, there are transmissive functions. Light hits a prism and surprising colors are transmitted; an organ transmits sounds.

Once the distinctions are in place, James says: "My thesis now is this: that, when we think the law that thought is a function of the brain, we are not required to think of productive function only; *we*

are entitled also to consider permissive or transmissive function"
(*ERM*, 86).

I don't claim to completely understand the distinctions, but it is clear in the lecture that James intends something like the following proposal. If all functions are "productive" then to say that thought is a function of the brain is tantamount to asserting that thought cannot exist without the brain. Brains produce thoughts. They are the only things that produce thoughts; and when the brain dies, so dies thought.

On the other hand, if thought is a function of the brain in the sense that for embodied beings the brain permits and/or transmits thought, if it is a conduit more than a producer, then there is no incoherence in the idea that thought, including the stream of thought, can be (1) of a different metaphysical kind than the brain, which (2) interacts with the brain while we are alive, and that (3) absorbs and retains the identity, personality, and memories constitutive in this interaction, and finally (4) can continue to go on without the brain.

To take the metaphor literally requires thinking something like this: whereas only boiling water produces steam, prismatic arrays and music, despite requiring prisms and musical instruments in the actual world, can possibly exist without that which typically permits or transmits them.

James writes, "when finally a brain stops acting altogether, or decays, that special stream of consciousness which it subserved will vanish entirely from this natural world. But the sphere of being that supplied the consciousness would still be intact; and in that more real world with which, even whilst here, it was continuous, the consciousness might, in ways unknown to us, continue still" (*ERM*, 87).

X POSSIBILITY

I will only add this much: James is right. All this is possible. Someone, possibly most modernists or postmodernists or whatever it is we now allegedly are, will think it old-fashioned and improbable. What James shows (to his great credit, I think) is that when one takes as the data all that experience has thus far offered and will offer down the road, the concept of old-fashioned might find its place, but what is more or less probable is an utterly obscure notion. Peirce's concept of what we will be warranted to assert at the end of inquiry is just one way of alerting us to the fact that assertions of what is probable now can at most take account of a small portion of actual and possible experience. How partial, like how probable, is something we cannot say. But humility is in order.

XI CONSCIOUSNESS: EPISTEMOLOGICAL NOT METAPHYSICAL

The last texts I will consider in this essay are from the *Essays in Radical Empiricism*. These, more than any other essays in the corpus, are thought to express a change in James's position about the nature of consciousness. My view, as I said at the start, is that they express the culmination of two decades worth of thinking that there was something wrong with substance dualism, and possibly with dualism, generally. In "Does 'Consciousness' Exist?" James admits that for over twenty years, and therefore before the writing of *Principles*, he had "mistrusted 'consciousness' as an entity" (*ERE*, 4). What could this mean? James answers, "I mean only to deny that the word stands for an entity, but to insist more emphatically that it stands for a function" (*ERE*, 4). Part of the general motivation is to provide a route away from substance dualism, and indeed from a host of other closely related posits. The postulation of mental and physical substance is a construct, as is the metaphysical distinction between object and subject, especially the objective and subjective worlds. There are powerful historical pressures that incline us to adopt these distinctions in their standard forms, but the pragmatic value of these dualisms and distinctions, once reexamined, suggest that their cash-value is overrated.

James has two arguments for his view. One I like, the other I do not. First, the one I do not like. It consists in the articulation of what Russell called "neutral monism." James writes: " 'Pure experience' is the name [for] . . . the immediate flux of life which furnishes the material to our later reflection with its conceptual categories. Only new-born babes, or men in semi-coma from sleep, drugs, illnesses, or blows, may be assumed to have an experience pure in the literal sense of a *that* which is not yet a definitive *what*" (*ERE*, 46).

This statement is from a 1905 essay. But in both *Principles* of 1890 and *Psychology: The Briefer Course* of 1892, James speaks of the mental life of infants and makes a similar point. Infants do not take metaphysical positions, they do not divide the world into mental and material substance, possibly not even into me and not-me, and perhaps they lack concepts altogether. Something like this is true even for noninfants – us grown-ups, although our conceptual apparatus is so near at hand that we lose sight of the fact that we first have experiences, and then and only then put them into compartments, into worlds – mental-physical, real-unreal, and so on.

Such an experience as *blue*, as it is immediately given, can only be called by some such neutral name as that *phenomenon*. It does not come to us *immediately* as a relation between two realities, one mental and one physical. It is only when still thinking of it as the *same* blue . . . that it doubles itself, so to speak, and develops in two directions; and, taken in connection with some associates, figures as a physical quality, whilst with others it figures as a feeling of mind. (PB, 332)

Experiences occur, and then practical needs and existing social and linguistic practices guide us to construct the concepts of inner and outer, mind and matter, consciousness and content. James insisted on this point from 1890 on. What is different about the post-1904 work is that he seems – or has been so interpreted – to want to take this phenomenological fact as having metaphysical significance, that is, as showing something about what is ontologically basic. If we are radical empiricists then we will insist that both mind and matter are constructs. Pure experience, which is neutral between the two, is primordial.

I'm not convinced that neutral monism should be read as an ontological as opposed to an epistemic or psychological doctrine. But assuming it is intended ontologically, then I think there is a mistake, a form of the genetic fallacy, mistaking what comes first or early in the order of experience as having ontological bearing. Pragmatism, I would have thought, is a wait-and-see approach.

The metaphysical reading is one way to read the argument for neutral monism. And if this way of reading James is right, then he makes the mistake of thinking, something he insists we should not think, that the way things *seem* has obvious or significant metaphysical import. The argument, interpreted as moving from the atheoretical experience of the uninitiated to a metaphysical conclusion, requires something like the assumption that *ontology recapitu-*

lates ontogeny. This does not seem to me to be a good premise to implicitly import – no matter where one is coming from.

James might be completely correct that what he calls "pure experience" is what phenomenology reveals as primordial, both in the infant's case and in the noninfant's case when as adults we can bracket out our weighty conceptual baggage. But being right about that has no consequences whatsoever for what is metaphysically basic. Neutral monism makes sense as phenomenology – quite possibly the primacy of "pure experience," if true, has some epistemological significance. But as far as I can tell such phenomenological primacy carries no ontological weight. James writes in "La Notion de Conscience," one of the essays collected in the *Essays in Radical Empiricism*, that:

Les attributions sujet et objet, représenté et représentatif, chose et penseé, signifient donc une distinction practique qui est de la dernière importance, mais qui est d'ordre FONCTIONNEL seulement, et nullement ontologique comme le dualisme classique représente. (*ERE*, 117)

Even if all these distinctions are functional, not ontological, it does not follow that what presents itself as functionally undivided is ontologically basic. Assuming this is the doctrine, then this is what I do not like about the papers in which neutral monism is defended. Hopefully, I have put my finger on the logical mistake being made – so that this is not simply an issue about taste.

What I like about the papers is something altogether different; and I think what I like is something that has no important conceptual connection to neutral monism. What is it?

It is the doctrine that consciousness is not a thing, a substance, or an entity. Consciousness does not belong on our list of first principles as a substance – either as immaterial substance or as a *faculty* of the brain. Once James announces his rejection of the idea that consciousness is a thing, he immediately adds, so as to correct the impression that he now thinks of consciousness as akin to phlogiston or the ether, that "thoughts undeniably exist . . . there is a function in experience which thoughts perform. . . . That function is *knowing* . . . 'Consciousness' is supposed necessary to explain the fact that things not only are, but get reported, are known. Whoever blots out the notion of consciousness from his list of first principles must still provide in some way for that function's being carried out" (*ERE*, 4).

I will have to explain what I think James means here in a nutshell since exegesis of these late metaphysical writings is a topic in itself. First, nothing in *Essays in Radical Empiricism* suggests that James is an eliminativist about conscious experience. Experience, as I said at the beginning, is for James what we would now just call "conscious experience" – although it is not clear now, just as it was not clear then, that there is a contrastive category of "unconscious experiences" to call attention to. Second, James's belief that things get reported and are known does not require the posit of a faculty of consciousness, immaterial or material. Experiences will do. What will happen, and this is the third point, is that our experiences will relate in ways that typically lead to the constructions of certain distinctions, for example, between what is mental and nonmental. But this distinction can be made without commitment to some essential underlying ontological difference. It can be like the distinction between up and down, in and out, and the like. Fourth, this pragmatically motivated distinction will lead to a distinction among experiences, events, things – I do not care what you call them – with different causal properties. We will learn that "mental water" does not put out "fire" whereas "water" does. We will learn that attention and concentration help to solve arithmetic problems on paper. When distinction making ensues – and it is guaranteed to be supported, but not always most wisely, by the community which participates in the project of interpreting our "pure experiences" – we are then engaged in the lifelong project of knowing, conceiving, and thinking of the world in ways that seem, indeed that might truly be, useful. But opportunities for mistakes abound. One mistake we might make is the one James made in thinking that substance dualism had to be assumed for the sake of doing scientific psychology, namely, giving too much weight to previous philosophizing and to common sense. Whitehead called this sort of mistake "the fallacy of misplaced concreteness." One makes into a thing or an entity something that reveals itself vividly and powerfully. Why do we do this? Perhaps, in the case of thinking of consciousness as an entity or a thing, there is the combined weight of the philosophical tradition which has pretty much cleared only this path, as well as certain tendencies of thought that Homo sapiens are prone to. This is not a line James took, but Quine has suggested, and I agree, that we go for physical hunks over time slices and undetached parts when individuating things. It would not be particularly surprising if either natural tendencies or some sort of metaphorical extension from the normal physical case led to reification when doing mental individuation.

XII C'EST FINI

One must stop somewhere and sometime. I choose now. William James is my favorite philosopher. There is almost no view he holds that I agree with. But this is not because I think his arguments are generally bad. I would prefer that James believed in compatibilism, that he saw the possibility that some "mental" events might be conscious, and that those that are might have causal powers, distinct from those that do not possess the relevant property. I wish he did not, if he did, hold neutral monism as a metaphysical thesis and several other things, too. Why do I love him? Let me count the ways? Not enough space or time. Simply put, the attraction of James the philosopher is that he is to me the best example I know of *a person doing philosophy;* there is no hiding the person behind the work, no way of discussing the work without the person, no way to make believe that there is a way to do philosophy that is not personal. Furthermore, the problems that absorbed, possibly obsessed, James are good problems to worry about. What are experiences? What capacities does a creature for whom *there is something it is like to be* that creature have that an automaton lacks? How do such concepts as agency, self, free action, and the like fit with the effort to develop a scientific psychology, and, most importantly of all, what makes life worth living? James never let these questions drop off the agenda in an effort to focus his efforts on giving a picture of only a piece of the world. He wanted and worked at a picture of the whole thing.

Most child psychologists now think that James was wrong in thinking that the world of the infant is a "blooming, buzzing confusion." I have come to think that for William James, the philosopher and the man, experience almost certainly seemed this way. His greatness as a philosopher and as a person comes from allowing this "blooming, buzzing confusion" to continually present itself to himself. No experience is to be disallowed; everything is to be attended to, even if not accounted for; and all the interests and projects we have as conscious beings are to be taken seriously. For James, the philosopher and the man, this attitude brought with it no small amount of intellectual and personal trouble. But it makes him at the same time a model for philosophers even today, a worthy model, indeed.

NOTES

1 One might think that it is a characteristic feature of pragmatism that it will resist any totalizing view – naturalistic or nonnaturalistic, that it must be pluralistic in the sense James describes in this passage above. But I do not think this is right, since Dewey and Quine are pragmatists who are also thoroughgoing naturalists, whereas Goodman and Hilary Putnam are pragmatists who are pluralists.

2 I am grateful to W. E. Cooper (1990) for an excellent and decisive critique of my attempt to provide a consistent naturalistic reading even of the purely psychological works. Cooper's essay abounds with insights about the difficulty of interpreting James's theory of mind. Not only does my own naturalistic reading require correction, but so too do neutral monist, panpsychist, and protophenomenological readings, according to Cooper. I am extremely grateful to him for his extremely patient, thoughtful, and scholarly essay.

3 In case anyone is wondering, this is still true. No respectable neuroscientist is looking for some "Holy Seat" in brain tissue (which, by the way, is different from looking for characteristic neural patterns that might subserve conscious experiences – this is very much the game as I write).

3   John Dewey's naturalization of William James

William James was John Dewey's philosophical hero, because his "biological psychology" of the 1890 *The Principles of Psychology* led Dewey out of bondage in the land of Hegel and into the wonderful land of naturalism. Dewey attempted to repay his debt by passionately expounding and defending James's philosophy over a period of fifty-one years, stretching from 1897 to 1948. While not calling into question the philosophical brilliance of these essays, it will be shown that they gave a blatantly distorted, self-serving account of James's philosophy, the basic aims of which were to despookify and depersonalize it so that it would agree with Dewey's naturalism and socialization of all things distinctively human. The intent of my "exposé" of this act of hero worship-turned-philosophical usurpation, however, is to bring into bold relief the salient features of their philosophies by highlighting their deep-seated differences. Because of the limitations of space, only Dewey's attempted naturalization of James will be considered.

"Naturalism" has meant very different things to different philosophers. Since my claim is that Dewey attempted to make James into "a good naturalist like himself," it is Dewey's sense that is relevant. His naturalism comprises two components. First, there is no ontological dualism between the mental and the physical, be it in the form of an irreducible mental/physical substance or a mental/physical event dualism, psychological states and processes being reducible to certain distinctive ways in which an organism interacts with its natural environment. This is called "biological behaviorism" by Dewey and is invidiously contrasted with a "physiological behaviorism" that understands mental phenomena exclusively in terms of physical processes and states *within* the organism. Second,

49

the sciences alone give us knowledge of reality, and they accomplish this through an objective common pattern of inquiry. Thus, every kind of individual is a "natural kind" in the sense that its nature is to be determined through scientific inquiry. Though Dewey would abhor this terminology, this in fact is what his scientism is committed to, minus, of course, any kind of fixity of species or nonfallibilist claims to certainty. Each of these two components will now be discussed in turn.

I ONTOLOGICAL NATURALISM

Dewey's attempt to transform James into an ontological naturalist occurs primarily in his 1940 "The Vanishing Subject in the Psychology of James."[1] Because this essay shifts back and forth between an italicized and unitalicized use of "Psychology," its thesis is ambiguous between the self and consciousness in general, disappearing from the book, *Psychology* (which was Dewey's abbreviation for *The Principles of Psychology*), and its disappearing from the psychology developed therein. (Notice the unitalicized "Psychology" in the essay's title but the italicized use of "Psychology" on *LW*, 14:156, 166.) This distinction is important because there are numerous metaphysical and epistemological excursions interspersed with psychology throughout the book, in spite of James's repeated resolutions to the contrary. That Dewey argues for the stronger disappearance-within-the-book thesis, and thus for the self's disappearance from James's philosophy in general, becomes apparent when Dewey appeals for support to James's 1904–5 doctrine of pure experience, which is the centerpiece of James's metaphysics and epistemology. *Pace* Dewey, it will be argued that the self disappears neither from James's psychology nor from his book *The Principles of Psychology*, nor from his philosophy in general.

Throughout *The Principles of Psychology*, James strictly adheres to the commonsense dualism between conscious experiences and the physical objects and events that are perceived and referred to by these experiences. Dewey claims that James's acceptance of this dualism is merely verbal, a concession that he made for tactical purposes to his opponents – the associationists, rationalists, and automatists – all of whom accepted this dualism. This is not unreasonable, since James's major purpose in *Principles* was to draw together all of the recent work in psychology for the purpose of helping it to attain the status of a legitimate science. To challenge the almost universally accepted mental/physical dualism would have alienated his audience and thus been a self-defeating distraction.

Dewey advances a number of considerations in support of this thesis. First, there is James's subsequent claim in his 1904 "Does 'Consciousness' Exist?" that "For twenty years past I have mistrusted 'consciousness' as an entity" (*ERE*, 4). James is referring back to his 1884 "The Function of Cognition" in which the "epistemological gulf" is eliminated "so that the whole truth-relation falls inside of the continuities of concrete experience, and is constituted of particular processes, varying with every object and subject, and susceptible of being described in detail."[2] While there is no explicit denial of the ontological dualism between the mental and the physical, there is a hint at one place of his later doctrine of pure experience when he says that " . . . we believe that we all know and think about and talk about the same world, because *we believe our PERCEPTS are possessed by us in common*" (*MT*, 29–30). Herein there is no duplication in consciousness of the outer objects perceived, otherwise two minds could not share one and the same percept. Dewey speculates that if James were to have rewritten *Principles* after 1904, he would have completely dispensed with consciousness as a special sort of entity, be it of a substantial or eventful sort, and replaced it with a full-blown biological behaviorism.

If Dewey's disappearance thesis were based only on this speculation as to how James would have rewritten *Principles*, it does not show that within the book or the psychology developed within it there is any such disappearance, nor even doubts about the mental/physical dualism. According to Dewey, the doubts about consciousness are expressed not just subsequent to *Principles* but in *Principles* itself. James had whittled the self down to the passing thought – a momentary total stage of consciousness – and, supposedly, he then went on "to express a doubt about the existence of even a separate 'thought' or mental state of any kind as the knower, saying that it might be held that 'the existence of this thinker would be given to us rather as logical postulate than as that direct inner preception of spiritual activity which we naturally believe ourselves to have' " (*LW*, 14:157). Immediately upon expressing this "doubt," James refers to an "important article" by Souriau in which the existence of

consciousness as some sort of aboriginal stuff is denied, which anticipates James's doctrine of pure experience.

Pace Dewey's account, James does not express any doubts of *his own* in *Principles* about the existence of consciousness, but merely alludes to a theory that is eliminative of consciousness. Immediately upon his brief exposition of this theory he adds that "Specula-
tions like this traverse common-sense" and he "will therefore treat the last few pages as a parenthetical digression, and from now to the end of the volume revert to the path of common-sense again" (*PP*, 1:291). This hardly is an expression of doubt on James's part. Far from expressing any doubts about consciousness in *Principles*, James, as will be seen, availed himself of every opportunity to take the spooky route.

Fortunately, Dewey has stronger things to say in favor of his disap-
pearance thesis than the false claim that James expressed doubts about consciousness in *Principles* and counterfactual speculations about how James would have rewritten his psychology subsequent to 1904. Of more weight is Dewey's appeal to the overall orientation and tenor of *Principles*, along with the biological-behavioristic approach to certain topics, most notably the self.

As for general orientation, there is a concerted attempt, no doubt due to James's medical background, to give a biological grounding to psychology which "if it had been consistently developed it would have resulted in a biological behavioristic account of psychological phenomena" (*LW*, 14:158). Dewey also enlists in support of his be-
havioral interpretation James's claim that "pursuance of future ends and choice of means for their attainment are the mark and criterion of mentality in a phenomenon" (*PP*, 1:21). But, as Dewey correctly points out, since this is said to be only "the mark and criterion by which to circumscribe the subject-matter of this work *as far as action enters in*," it allows for psychic phenomena that do not admit of a behavioral analysis (*LW*, 14:158–9).

The strongest support for the disappearance thesis comes from the way James handles specific topics. An important case in point is James's account of habits in terms of neural pathways in the brain established by past experiences that allow for subsequent reflex arc-
type behavior. Discrimination, in turn, is based on habit, a point which James did not sufficiently emphasize. And what is true of discrimination will also hold for attention (as well as the will and

belief, since each, for James, is a way of attending). Dewey also cites James's account of interest – the linchpin of his psychology and the basis of his later pragmatism. "Officially he assumes interest to be mentalistic. What he actually says about it is most readily understood in terms of the selection by motor factors in behavior" (*LW*, 14:160).

James did not treat sensations or impressions as physiological processes, but he should have, since he allowed for them to occur unnoticed (*LW*, 14:159). (Herein Dewey overlooks James's introduction of secondary selves to whom these sensations are consciously present.) An indication of just how desperate Dewey is to show that sensations really are physiological for James is that he offers on page 160 two allegedly corroborating quotations from *Principles* that do no such thing.

Dewey also appeals to James's example of "Baby's first sensation" in which there is no distinction between the mental and the physical, it being the entire world to the baby, as containing the germ of James's later theory of neutral entities.

The direct empirical meaning of *neutral* in this connection would seem to be that of indifference to the distinction between subjective and objective, this distinction arising when the proper guidance of behavior requires that we be able to tell whether a given sound or color is a sign of an environing object or of some process within the organism. Unfortunately his later writings seem at times to give the impression that these entities are a kind of stuff out of which both the subjective and objective are made – instead of the distinction being a question of the kind of an object to which a quality is referred. (*LW*, 14:164)

Herein Dewey is amplifying on his 1907 "The Postulate of Immediate Empiricism," in which he gave his variant of James's 1904–5 doctrine of pure experience. It is interesting to note that Dewey's denial therein that immediate experience is "any aboriginal stuff out of which things are evolved" (*MW*, 3:166) is almost a direct quotation from James's claim in "Does Consciousness Exist?" that "I have now to say that there is no *general* stuff of which experience at large is made" (*ERE*, 14). James's denial seemingly contradicts his claims within the very same essay that "My thesis is that if we start with the supposition that there is only one primal stuff or material in the world, a stuff of which everything is composed, and if we call that stuff 'pure experience,' then knowing can easily be explained as a particular sort of relation towards one another into which portions of pure experience may enter" (*ERE*, 4) and "But thoughts in the concrete are made of the same stuff as things are" (*ERE*, 19), as well as his identification of pure experience with "*materia prima*" in "The Place of Affectional Facts in a World of Pure Experience" (*ERE*, 69; see also 13 and 46). This characterization of pure experience as a kind of prime matter, no doubt, is what Dewey had in mind when he mockingly said in a letter to Bentley that "at times he [James] seems to mix his neutrals with a kind of jelly-like cosmic world-stuff of pure experience . . . " (Ratner and Altman 1964, 115).

I believe that the way to neutralize this surface inconsistency, which James himself saw but did not attempt to resolve, is to distinguish between metaphysical and empirical (or scientific) constituents. His prime matter is meant to be a metaphysical constituent of everything, which is consistent with his denial that there are any empirical or scientific entities, such as atoms, of which everything is composed.

Running throughout *Principles* is a kind of phenomenological materialism that reduces many psychic phenomena to physical sensations within the body. There is James's famed theory of emotions as physiological sensations and, most noteworthy for Dewey, his phenomenological reduction of the spiritual self, that inner active self from whom fiats and efforts seem to originate, to a collection of intracephalic sensations, and "what is further said about personal identity is consistent with this behavioral interpretation. The appropriations of the passing thought are 'less to itself than to the most intimately felt part of its present Object, the body, and the central adjustments, which accompany the act of thinking, in the head' " (*LW*, 14:165–6). But, as T. L. S. Sprigge has perceptively pointed out, "James's phenomenological materialism does not imply that the consciousness of these physical processes is itself a physical process in any ordinary sense. It claims rather that our mode of "being in the world" is through and through a physical one" (Sprigge 1993, 76).

It now will be shown that Dewey's attempted ontological naturalizing of James fails to address the overall spookiness of *Principles*, as well as the extreme spookiness of *The Varieties of Religious Experience* and *A Pluralistic Universe*, in regard both to its metaphysics and treatment of important psychological topics, such as the self and paranormal phenomena. The major causes of this failure are due to a total overlooking of the spooky parts of James's metaphysics and psychology, and a failure to appreciate the restrictions James placed upon his materialistic claims. Dewey's ignoring of this spookiness resembles a parent making a point not to notice a child's unruly behavior, hoping thereby to help make it go away. There is some excuse for such omissions in essays that deal with some limited aspect of James's philosophy, such as the 1908 "What Pragmatism Means by Practical" (*MW*, vol. 4) and the 1925 "The Development of American Pragmatism," both of which zero in primarily on his pragmatic theory of meaning and truth, but none for the many articles that attempt a broad overview of his philosophy, most notably the two death notices in 1910, the 1920 China lecture on James (*MW*, vol. 12), and the two James's centennial essays of 1942, "William James and the World Today" and "William James as Empiricist" (*LW*, vol. 15). More specifically, the following will be shown: (i) Far from adopting dualism in name only in *Principles*, he *argues* for its most virulent form, interactionism. (ii) A will-to-believe type justification is given for believing in contracausal spiritual acts of effort or attention. (iii) Paranormal phenomena, wherein he thought the future of psychology lay, *pace* Dewey's speculations about how James would have subsequently rewritten his psychology, are given a spiritualistic explanation that lay the foundation for the subsequent enveloping world soul(s) ontology of *Varieties* and *A Pluralistic Universe*.

(i) For starters, James presents a proto-version of a conceptually based property objection argument for the nonidentity of consciousness with any physical goings-on. "Everyone admits the entire incommensurability of feeling as such with material motion as such. 'A motion became a feeling!' – no phrase that our lips can frame is so devoid of apprehensible meaning" (*PP*, 1:149). It looks like he is arguing for the nonidentity of the mental and physical on the basis of their necessarily not having all their properties in common, assuming, as would James, the indiscernibility of identicals.

Chapter 5, attacking "The Automaton-Theory," is an extended metaphysical defense of an interactionist sort of dualism. The following is an argument for the causal efficaciousness of consciousness based on evolutionary success.

... the study *a posteriori* of the *distribution* of consciousness shows it to be exactly such as we might expect in an organ added for the sake of steering a nervous system grown too complex to regulate itself. The conclusion that it is useful is, after all this, quite justifiable. But, if it is useful, it must be so through its causal efficaciousness, and the automaton-theory must succumb to the theory of common-sense. (*PP*, 1:147)

(ii) Throughout his adult life, James ardently believed in the Libertarian doctrine of free will, replete with its contracausal spiritual efforts. It was this belief that sustained him through his emotional crises by enabling him to lead the morally strenuous life. Dewey completely ignores James's passionate defenses of this doctrine in the chapters on "Attention" and "Will." Instead, he zeroes in exclusively on James's phenomenological reduction of the active self to a collection of intracephalic sensations.[3] The cornerstone of his despookification of James is James's claim that

the *"Self of selves," when carefully examined, is found to consist mainly of the collection of these peculiar motions in the head or between the head and throat . . . it would follow that our entire feeling of spiritual activity, or what commonly passes by that name, is really a feeling of bodily activities whose exact nature is by most men overlooked.* (*PP*, 1:288)

What Dewey fails to realize is that James's identification of the active self with these physical sensations is restricted to phenomenological appearances. At the beginning of his analysis James makes this restriction manifest when he says "*Now*, let us try to settle for ourselves as definitely as we can, just how this central nucleus of the Self may feel, no matter whether it be a spiritual substance or only a delusive word." There are several other places in *Principles* where James makes tough-minded claims but restricts them to a certain interest or perspective (see *PP*, 1:33 and 2:1179). In the chapter on "The Perception of Reality" James develops a radically relativized account of reality according to which something is real only in relation to or *qua* someone's interest in a certain "world," such as the world of commonsense objects, the theoretical entities of science, fictional realms, Platonic abstracta, and so on. He is a veritable Poobah, the character in the *Mikado* who held all the offices of state and always spoke *qua* this or that official, only for James it is *qua* this interest or that. It is "*qua*"-clauses all the way on down until

James gets to the content of mystical experiences, for which unrestricted reality claims are made.

Dewey deliberately overlooked certain passages in *Principles*, primarily in the interconnected chapters on "Attention" and "Will." Basically, volition is nothing but attention to an idea. Belief, in turn, is a state in which an idea fills consciousness without competitors, with the consequence that, in certain cases, we can believe at will or voluntarily, as is required by his will-to-believe doctrine, with its *option* to believe a proposition. For James, all actions initially are involuntary. In some cases a sensory idea of the motion or its immediate effects is formed. This creates a neural pathway from the brain to the concerned motor organ so that now mere consciousness of this idea causes the action. In the simplest cases, that of the "ideomotor" will, there is no fiat or effort. But human beings quickly become more complex so that for many ideas they might entertain there is a competing idea which blocks its motor discharge. Such a case of conflict sets the stage for an occurrence of an effort to attend to one of these competing ideas so that it alone will fill consciousness for a sufficient time with sufficient intensity and thereby lead to its motor discharge. This effort to attend is the voluntary will. *"The essential achievement of the will . . . when it is most 'voluntary,' is to ATTEND to a difficult object and hold it fast before the mind.* The so-doing is the *fiat;* and it is a mere physiological incident that when the object is thus attended to, immediate motor consequences should ensue" (*PP*, 2:1166).

James assumes that it is causally determined both which ideas enter consciousness and whether an effort is made to attend to one of them to the exclusion of its competitors. The question of all questions for James is whether the *amount* of this effort to attend also is causally determined, our answer determining "the very hinge on which our picture of the world shall swing from materialism, fatalism, monism, towards spiritualism, freedom, pluralism, – or else the other way" (*PP*, 1:424). The reason is that the amount of this effort, especially in cases in which we try to resist acting in the course of least resistance, can be the decisive factor in determining which idea emerges victorious and thus what action ensues, which, in turn, can have momentous consequences. It is only "the *effort to attend,* not to the mere attending, that we are seriously tempted to ascribe spontaneous power. We think we can make more of it *if we will;* and the amount which we make does not seem a fixed function of the ideas themselves, as it would necessarily have to be if our effort were an effect and not a spiritual force" (426–7).

James characterizes this spiritual force as an "original force" and the "star performer" (*PP,* 1:428). To be an original force, for James, it must be an irreducibly conscious event that is not causally determined. After giving a very fair and forceful exposition of the "effect theory" of the amount of the effort to attend, according to which it is only a causally determined effect of physiological events, he expresses his personal preference for the "cause-theory." "The reader will please observe that I am saying all that can *possibly* be said in favor of the effect-theory, since, inclining as I do myself to the cause-theory, I do not want to undervalue the enemy" (424–5). The basis of his preference is "ethical," since "the whole feeling of reality, the whole sting and excitement of our voluntary life, depends on our sense that in it things are *really being decided* from one moment to another, and that it is not the dull rattling off of a chain that was forged innumerable ages ago" (429).

James's version of libertarianism is far superior to that of others, from Aristotle down through Sartre and Chisholm, for he alone gives a detailed, close-up picture of just how free will works. What is distinctive about his version is that the immediate effect of a free volition, the amount of the effort to attend, is the sustaining and intensifying of an idea in consciousness rather than a bodily movement, as in Aristotle's example of the stick moves the stone, the hand moves the stick, and the man moves his hand. There is reason to think that this approach might have these two further advantages over its competitors, which, surprisingly, have not been mentioned by either James or his expositors. First, it avoids troublesome questions about backward causation, for when Aristotle's man freely moves his hand, he brings about *earlier* events along the efferent nerves linking his brain with his hand. (By clenching my fist I ripple my forearm muscles.) Second, it gives some hope of escaping a violation of the conservation of angular momentum, since its immediate effect, being the strengthening of an idea in consciousness, does not involve an acceleration, as happens when the man moves his hand.

James sets up a will-to-believe option, as already developed in his 1878 "Some Reflections on the Subjective Method," to justify belief in the reality of such contracausal spiritual acts of attention. One has such a right or permission to believe when the proposition in question cannot be determined on intellectual or epistemic grounds and by believing it one helps to bring about some morally or even prudentially desirable state of affairs.[4]

That the amount of these efforts to attend against the course of least resistance, such as in a case of moral temptation, are causally undetermined cannot be epistemically determined, since we cannot make sufficiently fine-grained measurements of brain events so as to discover whether the effect-theory is true. "The feeling of effort certainly *may* be an inert accompaniment and not the active element which it seems. No measurements are as yet performed (it is safe to say none ever will be performed) which can show that it contributes energy to the result" (*PP*, 1:428).

Thus, "The last word of psychology here is ignorance, for the 'forces' engaged are certainly too delicate and numerous to be followed in detail" (*PP*, 1:429).

When it comes to what good is realized by someone of a similar psychological constitution as himself believing in the cause-theory of the will, he comes across like an itinerant New England preacher intent on saving our souls, which is what he essentially was. Our very sense of our own self-worth as persons and ability to function as moral agents depends on this belief, since "the effort seems to belong to an altogether different realm, as if it were the substantive thing which we *are*, and those ['our strength and our intelligence, our wealth and even our good luck'] were but externals which we *carry*" (*PP*, 2:1181). James extolls the stoical hero who, regardless of external deterrents, can still find life meaningful "by pure inward willingness to take the world with those deterrent objects there" (1181). "The world thus finds in the heroic man its worthy match and mate; and the effort which he is able to put forth to hold himself erect and keep his heart unshaken is the direct measure of his worth and function in the game of human life" (1181). This sets the stage for the eloquent concluding paragraph of the section on free will.

Thus not only our morality but our religion, so far as the latter is deliberate, depend on the effort which we can make. *"Will you or won't you have it so?"* is the most probing question we are ever asked; we are asked it every hour of the day, and about the largest as well as the smallest, the most theoretical as well as the most practical, things. We answer by *consents or non-consents* and not by words. What wonder that these dumb responses should seem our deepest organ of communication with the nature of things! What wonder if the effort demanded by them be the measure of our worth as men! What wonder if the amount which we accord of it be the one strictly underived and original contribution which we make to the world! (*PP*, 2:1182)

Here is the passionate, existential James, and it is a source of amazement how Dewey could have completely overlooked it in all his many expositions of James's philosophy, and in particular when he claimed that *Principles* was dualistic only in terminology.[5] Whereas the active, inner self, *qua* phenomenological object, is nothing but cephalic sensations, as Dewey was right to point out, *qua* metaphysical entity required for being a morally responsible agent, it is a "spiritual force" that is the "substantive thing which we *are*" (*PP*, 2:1181). And which perspective we adopt is to be decided in terms of the moral benefits that accrue.

(iii) Paranormal phenomena consisting of insane delusions, alternating selves, and mediumship are given prominence in *Principles*. In his later works James developed a panpsychical metaphysical theory to explain these phenomena, along with mystical and conversion experiences. It really is a unifying inference to the best explanation that postulates a mother-sea of consciousness, of which there might be more than one, that is revealed in these exceptional experiences. In the 1898 lecture on "Human Immortality" it is said that in veridical mediumship contact is made with conscious states in a

transcendental world, and all that is needed is an abnormal lowering of the brain-threshold to let them through. In cases of conversion, in providential leadings, sudden mental healings, etc., it seems to the subjects themselves of the experience as if a power from without, quite different from the ordinary action of senses or of the sense-led mind, came into their life, as if the latter suddenly opened into that greater life in which it has its source. . . . All such experiences, quite paradoxical and meaningless on the production-theory [according to which consciousness is causally dependent upon brain events], fall very naturally into place on the other theory [that the brain merely is a filter through which consciousness passes and gets focused]. We need only suppose the continuity of our consciousness with a mother-sea, to allow for exceptional waves occasionally pouring over the dam. (*ERM*, 93–4)

This mother-sea of consciousness theory becomes dominant in his most mature work, wherein it is given a panpsychical twist. In the "Conclusions" to *A Pluralistic Universe* he writes:

... the drift of all the evidence we have seems to me to sweep us very strongly towards the belief in some form of superhuman life with which we may, unknown to ourselves, be co-conscious. ... The analogies with ordinary psychology, with certain facts of pathology, with those of psychical research ... and with those of religious experience establish, when taken together, a decidedly *formidable* probability in favor of a general view of the world almost identical with Fechner's. (140)

The same Fechnerian mother-sea(s) theory informs the 1909 "Confidences of a Psychical Researcher."

... we with our lives are like islands in the sea ... there is a continuum of cosmic consciousness, against which our individuality builds but accidental fences, and into which our several minds plunge as into a mother-sea or reservoir. Our 'normal' consciousness is circumscribed for adaptation to our external earthly environment, but the fence is weak in spots, and fitful influences from beyond leak in, showing the otherwise unverifiable common connexion. Not only psychic research, but metaphysical philosophy and speculative biology are led in their own ways to look with favor on some such 'panpsychic' view of the universe as this. (*EPR*, 374)

The 1902 *Varieties* also appeals to this theory to explain what is revealed by mystical and conversion experiences. James develops a perceptual model of mystical experience according to which, when veridical, they are direct apprehensions of this surrounding sea of consciousness. They are "windows through which the mind looks out upon a more extensive and inclusive world" (339). In conversion experiences this subliminal or transmarginal consciousness is a medium through which the divine consciousness in this more extensive and inclusive world salvifically flows into the subject. In general, the religious life shows "That the visible world is part of a more spiritual universe from which it draws its chief significance" (382). It supports

Fechner's theory of successively larger enveloping spheres of conscious life ... the tenderer parts of his personal life are continuous with a *more* of the same quality which is operative in the universe outside of him and which he can keep in working touch with, and in a fashion get on board of and save himself ... we inhabit an invisible spiritual environment from which help comes, our soul being mysteriously one with a larger soul whose instruments we are. (*PU*, 139)

It is very difficult to the point of being impossible to treat the mother-sea of consciousness and our variegated experiences of it as neutral experiences – as neither physical nor mental simpliciter, counting as one or the other only when placed in a series of surrounding experiences, a mental series, unlike a physical one, being one in which the content of the successive experiences are not nomically connectible. It is for this reason that Dewey's beloved neutrals of James's 1904–5 essays have become the spiritual denizens of a panpsychical pluralistic universe. Even in these essays there are hints of panpsychism, as for example when he deals with the problem posed by unperceived events future. His way out of the difficulty seems to go the panpsychic route because he says of them that "If not a future experience of our own or a present one of our neighbor, it must be . . . an experience *for* itself . . . ," thereby imputing an inner consciousness to every physical event (*ERE*, 43). Viewed in its historical setting, the phenomenological neutrals of 1904–5, although apparently materialism friendly, really are a trojan horse gift, for, unbeknownst to Dewey and his cohorts, it is only veridical *sense* perceptions that qualify as ontologically neutral, and not the motley crew of religious and paranormal experiences that James, in his extreme radical empiricism, also counted as cognitive.

Not only does Dewey overlook all of the spookiness of the post-*Principles* writings, he even overlooks their presence in *Principles* itself. Everything within the James corpus makes an appearance in *Principles*, even the theories of the mother-sea of consciousness and the brain as a filter through which this flows. James asks in *Principles* what "more" the soul is than just a succession of Thoughts. His reply: "For my own part I confess that the moment I become metaphysical and try to define the more, I find the notion of some sort of an *anima mundi* thinking in all of us to be a more promising hypothesis, in spite of all its difficulties, than that of a lot of absolutely individual souls" (328). This "anima mundi," which becomes Fechner's mother-sea of consciousness in his later writings, is implicitly appealed to when he says that "the perfect object of belief would be a God or 'Soul of the World,' represented both optimistically and moralistically . . . and withal so definitely conceived as to show why our phenomenal experiences should be sent to us by Him in just the very way in which they come" (944–5). The filtration-theory is hinted at by his remark that the brain is an instrument of possibilities, but of no certainties. But the consciousness, with its own ends present to it, and knowing also well which possibilities lead thereto and which away, will, if endowed with causal efficacy, reinforce the favorable possibilities and repress the unfavorable or indifferent ones. The nerve-currents, coursing through the cells and fibres, must in this case be supposed strengthened by the fact of their awakening one consciousness and dampened by awakening another. (144–5)

II METHODOLOGICAL NATURALISM

Throughout *Principles*, James employs a dual method for investigating a psychic phenomenon, one based on an introspective "analysis" of what it is like to experience it, the other, the "historical" method, a third-person based description of its publicly observable causes. "There are, as we know, two ways of studying every psychic state. First, the way of analysis. What does it consist in? What is its inner nature? Of what sort of mind-stuff is it composed? Second, the way of history. What are its conditions of production, and its connection with other facts?" (2:913).

While Dewey praises James's introspective analyses as an advancement beyond those given by the rationalists and empiricists because it alone recognizes relations as given, he downplays its centrality and wishes that James would completely jettison it in favor of the "outer" causal approach, as is required by Dewey's methodological naturalism.

An example of Dewey's downplaying the importance of introspection to James is the remark in his 1920 China lecture on Bergson that whereas Bergson assigned a major role to introspection James did not (*MW*, 12:21). Another example is Dewey's claim that "The work of James replaces a dialectic analysis of experience with one based upon scientific knowledge . . . ," which omits mention of James's reliance on introspection. One of the tricks Dewey used to downplay James's reliance on introspection is to convert his introspective analyses into something else, a good example of which is Dewey's construal of James's analysis of connections in the 1942 "William James and the World Today." When Dewey wrote this he was preoccupied with the challenge to democracy posed by totalitarianism to show how a society can be both unified and yet contain genuine individuals. Dewey finds a solution in James's "each-form" analysis in *A Pluralistic Universe* – that immediately conjoined neighbors, be it in space or time, interpenetrate and melt into each other but without losing their own identity, as is seen by the fact that this melting or fusing relation is not transitive. (If you don't understand this, then you understand it, since it is a mystical doctrine.) These "confluence" relations can unify a society, because even if two persons are not directly connected by such a relation they are indirectly connected by a chain of such relations (*LW*, 15:5–6). Dewey's deployment of James's each-form analysis, though brilliant in its own right, fails to note that James's analysis, in spite of his use of the metaphor of a "federal republic" for his pluralistic world (*PU*, 145), was not a political but a phenomenological one. It is an attempt to improve on *Principles*'s specious present phenomenological description of our experience of change, according to which each pulse of sensory experience has a temporally extended content of *distinct* successive events, with a Bergsonian analysis that fuses them into a cotton-candyish glop.

Because Dewey held that philosophical theories ultimately were sociopolitical in origin and intent, he might have believed that he was well within his rights to politicize James's phenomenological description of the flow of experience. In his 1904 graduation address at the University of Vermont he said:

It is today generally recognized that systems of philosophy however abstract in conception and technical exposition lie, after all, much nearer the heart of social, and of national, life than superficially appears . . . philosophy is a language in which the deepest social problems and aspirations of a given time and a given people are expressed in intellectual and impersonal symbols. (*MW*, 3:73)

Dewey's metaphilosophical thesis faces a counterexample in James's Bergsonian account of change. Dewey, after correctly pointing out that Bergson's "intuition" of the "duree" is a form of mysticism, accounts for this mystical strain in terms of Bergson being a Jew from Alexandria, a crossroads for mystical cultures (*MW*, 12:227). But James's description of change is, according to James himself, identical with Bergson's, and thus every bit as mystical. Are we to infer that James was Jewish and reared in an area that is a fleshpot of mysticism! James's rival sentiment-of-rationality metaphilosophical thesis, that one's philosophy is an expression of psychological predilections, seems far more in agreement with the empirical facts. The mystical mindset knows no sociopolitical boundaries.

Rather than being a fifth wheel, introspection is accorded pride of place in James's existentially oriented philosophy. Even before James came out explicitly for panpsychism in his final years, there is a desperate effort, such as is found in many of the essays in the 1897 *The Will to Believe* and especially in "On a Certain Blindness in Human Beings," to penetrate to the inner life of everything. Whereas Dewey viewed the other person primarily as a co-worker in a cooperative venture to realize some shared goal, James wanted to "I-Thou" this person, in fact the universe at large. In *A Pluralistic Universe* he even speaks of penetrating by an act of "intuitive sympathy" (117) to "the inner life of the flux" (110), to "the inner nature of reality" – "what really *makes it go*" (112). *A Pluralistic Universe* is a plea for a philosophy of "intimacy" according to which "The inner life of things must be substantially akin anyhow to the tenderer parts of man's nature" (19).

How does this quest to penetrate to the inners of things pertain to James's attachment to introspection? The use of it does not *per se* commit one to a mental/physical dualism, no less panpsychism; recall James's phenomenological materialism about the active self and the emotions in this regard. However, if one already believed that everything had an inner conscious life that gave value and meaning to its existence, as did James, then pride of place would be given to the introspective method. For through its use we can discover in our own case what it is like to enjoy or be some quality or thing, which then can be projected on to others via an act of "intuitive sympathy," sometimes buttressed, as it was for James, by a Cartesian type of analogical argument.[6] The great attraction of introspective analysis for James is that it afforded him a way of preventing the bifurcation of man and nature, which is his ultimate enemy because it strips the world of any human meaning or value (*PP*, 2:940–1).

These existential themes clearly emerge in James's treatment of the identity of the self over time, another part of James that Dewey totally ignores. His analysis is exclusively introspective, thereby assuring that our concept of what we are will have the required intimacy, given that what we are, our nature, is tied to our identity conditions. It is given exclusively in terms of first-person criteria –

states of consciousness that are introspectively available to the subject. This approach fits his antibifurcationist demand because it is based on what is important to us as emotional and active beings. It is just such considerations of importance that form the underlying leitmotif of James's analysis of the self.

This "inner" approach to understanding the identity of persons contrasts with the "outer" objective approach that treats persons as what could be called in a somewhat extended sense of the term a "natural kind," meaning a type of object whose nature is to be determined through natural science. It was suggested that Dewey's scientism places him squarely within the natural kind camp. These contrasting approaches are at the foundation of the split in twentieth-century philosophy between so-called continental and analytic philosophy. They also form the basis of James's contrast between the tough- and tender-minded given in *Pragmatism* (13). The traits listed under "The Tender-Minded," for the most part, are those that assure an unbifurcated world and are vouchsafed through the inner approach, as contrasted with those listed under "The Tough-Minded," which represent the natural scientist's temper of mind, with its scientistic natural kinds approach to understanding the nature of persons and their world.

James's analysis is patterned after Locke's and holds that successive thoughts are co-personal just in case the later one "appropriates," that is, judges, the former to be its own on the basis of its having a special sort of warmth and intimacy.[7] While James alludes at a couple of places to third-person criteria that could challenge or defeat a judgment of self-identity over time based on these sort of apparent memories, the only defeater he seems to recognize is the existence of a better or equally good claimant, someone else whose apparent memories are more or just as rich and coherent and also match some real life person's past. James's version of a memory-theory of personal endurance treats persons as nonnatural kinds, since it includes no causal requirement for memory. "The same brain may subserve many conscious selves, either alternate or coexisting . . . " (379), thus permitting persons to switch bodies *à la* Locke's prince and cobbler. This is the single most important feature of his analysis and sharply distinguishes it from natural kind memory theories that treat memory as a causal process that is ultimately to be understood by natural science.

James's chapter on "Memory" is placed six chapters later than the one in which he gives an introspective analysis of personal endurance. He follows his usual pattern of first giving an introspective analysis, followed by an historical or causal one. After repeating his introspective analysis from the earlier chapter, he presents a straightforward neurophysiological analysis of the causes of memory. "Whatever accidental cue may turn this tendency [to recall] into an actuality, the permanent *ground* of the tendency itself lies in the organized neural paths by which the cue calls up the experience ... the condition which makes it possible at all ... is ... the brain-paths which *associate* the experience with the occasion and cue of recall" (*PP*, 2:616).

You would think that this physicalist, natural kind account of memory would supply third-person criteria for defeating introspectively based memory claims and the claims of personal endurance that they carry. Such claims could be defeated by showing that the right sort of physical process does not connect the apparent memory with the past event. But James never places any causal requirement on memory. The turkey is on the table and all carved. All he has to do is sit down and eat. But he doesn't, thus following the nonnatural kind approach to the nature of the Self.

It is reported that in 1905 James and Dewey sat over a Ouija board together (Dearborn 1988, 95). If the general thesis of this paper is correct – that Dewey's philosophy is naturalistic all the way on down and James's spooky all the way on up – Dewey must have had a big smirk on his face while the sweat of earnest conviction was pouring off James's.

NOTES

1 Reprinted in *John Dewey, The Later Works*, vol. 14 (Carbondale: Southern Illinois University Press, 1988). All references will be to the pagination in this volume and will appear in the body of the paper. All references to Dewey will be to this press's editions and will use the following system of abbreviations: *EW, MW*, and *LW* standing respectively for *Early, Middle*, and *Later Works*, to be followed by the volume and page number.

2 This essay later appears as chapter 1 of *The Meaning of Truth*. Reference is to page 32 of that volume.

3 This oversight in his 1940 essay is especially surprising since in his 1897

"The Psychology of Effort," Dewey recognized that James's account of the will is "spiritual" with respect to moral effort; but, even then, he tries to finesse James into the naturalist camp by pointing out that this ought not to be his considered position since it is inconsistent with James's claim that his sensationalizing of emotions did not detract from their spiritual significance (*EW*, 5:149).

4 For a full account see Gale 1991, chapter 9.

5 Strange to say, even James himself overlooks it at times, as for example when he made this disclaimer in his 1904 "The Experience of Activity": "I have found myself more than once accused in print of being the assertor of a metaphysical principle of activity. Since literary misunderstandings retard the settlement of problems, I should like to say that such an interpretation of the pages I have published on effort and on will is absolutely foreign to what I meant to express. . . . Single clauses in my writing, or sentences read out of their connexion, may possibly have been compatible with a transphenomenal principle of energy; but I defy anyone to show a single sentence which, taken with its context, should be naturally held to advocate such a view" (*ERE*, 93). The sentences that have just been quoted from *Principles* on effort as an "original spiritual force" more than meet James's challenge. It might be conjectured that the reason for James going back on his "metaphysical" account of the will in *Principles* is that he wanted to impress the "brethren" in the American Psychological Association, to whom his 1904 address was given, that he was as tough-minded as they.

6 See *ERE*, 38 for James's presentation of the analogical argument for other minds; and for his commitment to a private language, a presupposition of this argument, see *PP*, 1:40 and *SPP*, 57.

7 Because of space limitations, my account necessarily is very sketchy. For all the details see Gale 1994.

4   James, Clifford, and the scientific conscience

However diverse our opinions of William James today, we generally agree that the great pragmatist was right about one thing: the pretensions of the Victorian "positivists." James exposed the epistemological naivete of these cultural imperialists. He celebrated openness of mind over the arrogant, dogmatic closures we associate with the nineteenth-century scientific intelligentsia. These contemporaries of Darwin ascribed to the sciences a God's-eye view, and to the world a set of hard features discoverable by men and women bold enough to replace fantasy and superstition with facts. These Huxleys and Tyndalls and Cliffords thought themselves a new priesthood, and, while telling everyone what to believe, functioned as the thought-police of their age. So deep were the roots sunk in the western mind by this vine of conceits that we seem never to be able to get it out of our system. We attack it and attack it and attack it, and quote modern thinkers as diverse as Quine and Kuhn and Wittgenstein and Foucault against it. And we quote James. We honor him for being one of the first to take up the cause, for being among the great prophets of epistemic humility, a founder of truly "modernist" or even "postmodernist"[1] thought.

Especially in "The Will to Believe" did James vindicate the right of the average man and woman to resist the directives of the self-appointed spokespersons for science. James understood that scientific inquiry took place in a socially and historically specific matrix, and that every inquirer was both enabled and confined by cultural and psychological predilections. James's world was plural and contingent, and what features it afforded to our disciplined gaze remained, to a large extent, ontological enigmas. If the quality of James's argumentation in this legendary essay was sometimes sloppy – as has

69

been so often lamented by sympathetic commentators[2] – the lapse has been largely forgiven in the context of the essay's prophetic role in "the revolt against positivism."[3] But we seem unwilling to forgive the chief target of James's righteous wrath in "The Will to Believe," the English mathematician W. K. Clifford. James's dispatching of Clifford was so effective that commentators on "The Will to Believe" rarely even read the arguments of the thinker James was most concerned to answer. Clifford's historical significance is, thanks to James, akin to that of some of Socrates's more obliging stooges. He was foolish enough to voice opinions that a wiser intellect could refute with wholesome and lasting effects.

But scrutiny of what Clifford wrote reveals that he was not quite as foolish as James has led us to conclude, and that James's representation of Clifford's arguments was less than fair. Some philosophers who now claim to write in James's "spirit" might feel closer to Clifford than to James, were they to assess the two side-by-side.[4] Walking to the library to read Clifford's "The Ethics of Belief" may seem an extraordinarily simple act, but the existing scholarship on "The Will to Believe" – by far the most widely renown of all James's essays – displays little awareness of what Clifford actually said.[5]

To call attention, as I will be doing here, to James's misrepresentations of Clifford is not simply to invite a scolding of James, nor to indulge an antiquarian's interest in Jamesiana. These misrepresentations served to conceal important intellectual ground that James actually shared with Clifford. The points genuinely at issue between James and Clifford can be distinguished from the red herrings James fed to a readership eager for any excuse to keep agnostics at bay. A more accurate understanding of James's relation to Clifford can enable us to clarify the terms on which James contested Clifford over the structure of plausibility that would obtain in the culture of educated inhabitants of the North Atlantic West. Both understood that the character of this structure of plausibility was at issue in their time. "The Will to Believe" was a distinctive moment in James's search for a scientifically respectable framework in which the essential religious sensibility of the liberal protestantism of his milieu could be affirmed. When read against Clifford, and against *Pragmatism*, which James wrote ten years after "The Will to Believe," the latter emerges as a brilliant spasm, but a spasm nevertheless. James was lashing out against a scientific conscience that held enormous power over him. In *Pragmatism*, James made a tense, but steadier and more genuine peace with this scientific conscience than he had been able to do in the jumpy, and sometimes disingenuous "The Will to Believe."

Clifford did assert that "it is wrong in all cases to believe on insufficient evidence."[6] This is the adamant, rather precious claim invariably linked with Clifford's name. The rigid, absolutist tone of the remark was made to sound silly by the practical, flexible, down-to-earth James. Our pragmatist knew that real people have to make choices between alternatives that are not always subject to clear and convincing proofs. "Clifford's exhortation" was "thoroughly fantastic" to James. It meant keeping our minds "in suspense forever." Not by such withdrawal could knowledge be expanded, and appropriate action be performed. Clifford's injunction was "like a general informing his soldiers that it is better to keep out of battle forever than to risk a single wound" (*WB*, 24–5). Thus did James drive a cross through Clifford's infidel heart.

The victory was made more easy by the fact that Clifford lay eighteen years in the grave. James published "The Will to Believe" in 1897; Clifford died in 1879. Had "that delicious *enfant terrible*" – as James called (*WB*, 17) the brilliant mathematician killed by tuberculosis while still short of his thirty-fourth birthday[7] – been around to dispute the point, Clifford could have quoted with telling effect the very essay James ridiculed. "We have no reason to fear lest a habit of conscientious inquiry should paralyze the actions of our daily life," Clifford had explained, as though answering James directly. We encounter "many cases in which it is our duty to act on probabilities, although the evidence is not such as to justify present belief." Clifford had taken pains, then, to avoid exactly the misreading that James carried out, a misreading in which Clifford was alleged to have been oblivious to the need to live on the basis of incomplete and imperfect information. It was "precisely by" doing this, by taking chances on the basis of the best available information and observing the results, "that evidence is got whereby to justify future belief" (Clifford 1877, 296).

Far from advocating the passivity James ascribed to him, Clifford extolled action based on the most critically defensible belief available at any given time. What Clifford argued against vehemently was the holding of beliefs uncritically, the shielding of such beliefs from the "habit of conscientious inquiry." "Sufficiency" of evidence was a relative ideal, but James, by quoting Clifford selectively, made it sound absolute and unattainable. James thus dealt with Clifford through the classic device of appropriation and effacement: he appropriated for himself the more sensible qualifications that Clifford had built into his own argument to begin with, and then effaced these commonsense caveats from his summary of Clifford.

James was almost as cavalier on the matter of the uniformity of nature. Against the narrow construction of this principle by Clifford and his scientific compatriots James warned sagely that nature might not be so absolutely uniform, after all. Scientists refuse to look for "evidence of telepathy" because it would threaten their dogmas. To illustrate the bad faith of the scientists, James cited "a leading biologist" who told him that even if telepathy were true "scientists ought to band together to keep it suppressed and concealed." But James admitted that this unnamed scoundrel was, like Clifford, "now dead" (WB, 19).

What had Clifford said about the uniformity of nature? Nothing so outrageous as the sentiments of the biologist conveniently unavailable for confirming interrogation. Clifford argued that our reasoning about new experiences should begin with an assumption that these experiences can be explained by the same forces that have explained previous experiences. We assume a continuity between "what we do not know" and "what we do know." This simple assumption helps us to allocate our energies in our experiments, and to guide our actions in daily life. If what we see of the sun in our spectroscope "behaves as hydrogen under similar circumstances would behave on earth," we have good reason to think there is hydrogen in the sun. And Clifford again took pains to prevent being charged as an absolutist: he answered with a resounding "no" the question he, himself, raised: should we believe "that nature is absolutely and universally uniform?" Clifford used this preposterously extreme uniformitarianism as an example of an idea in which "we have no right to believe" (Clifford 1877, 306, 308).

For Clifford, the principle of the uniformity of nature was a guide to action, and a foundation for the asking of new questions about our world. But to believe in it as an absolute truth was an example of believing on "insufficient evidence," the very vice against which

Clifford's essay was directed. James, of course, turned this around entirely, so that generations of James's readers have assumed that Clifford was one of those trusting monks of the positivist faith who believed the "evidence" was "sufficient" to believe absolutely in the uniformity of nature.

Not every impression James left about Clifford was misleading. Clifford was truly less respectful than James of the religious beliefs of the masses of humankind, beyond as well as within the Christian tradition. James was correct to identify Clifford as the voice for a sensibility different from his own. If James was inclined, as his friend Justice Holmes once complained, "to turn down the lights so as to give miracle a chance,"[8] Clifford was unattractively eager to carry the torch of the Enlightenment into the prayer room in the hope of embarrassing some pious, if misguided soul.

In several other respects, too, James left a fair impression. Clifford had more confidence than James did in the body of existing knowledge, was more inclined to stress its durability, and was less cognizant than James was of the power of a cultural inheritance to shape the course of inquiry. James was more concerned than Clifford with the psychological realities of the process of inquiry, and less piously moralistic about what the two agreed were the imperatives guiding this process. Clifford still praised a studied detachment in science that James skewered eloquently: "If you want an absolute duffer in an investigation . . . take the man who has no interest whatsoever in its results." The best investigator, James insisted in a voice appreciated by most twentieth-century thinkers, "is always he whose eager interest in one side of the question is balanced by an equally keen nervousness lest he become deceived" (WB, 26).

James's relation to Clifford was dominated by James's determination to protect "religious" belief from the critical spirit James himself appreciated, even as presented in Clifford's "The Ethics of Belief." James was a man of science, and deeply proud of it. Not only his earlier Principles, but his later The Varieties of Religious Experience were among the most formidable applications of Wissenschaft to any aspect of human life produced by his generation of American intellectuals. James was haunted, throughout his career-long effort to vindicate religion, by a scientific conscience.[9] This conscience he associated with Clifford more than with any other single individual. At the end of Varieties, for example, James invoked the long-dead Clifford once again, and in his capacity as the conscience of science. Clifford had identified "that inward monitor" which whispers "Bosh!" in one's mind when one is tempted to go beyond an "objective" assessment of experience (VRE, 408). In this particular instance the "conscience" served, as so often when invoked by James, to ironically prevent one from accepting as "scientific" the agnosticism preached by Clifford. The gravamen of James's disagreement with Clifford was the extent to which beliefs Anglophone intellectuals of the late-Victorian era called "religious" could be held without a guilty conscience.

The core of these beliefs was an exceedingly general theism. "The essence of the religious principles for James," Edward H. Madden has cogently summarized, "was a god strong enough to ensure that moral values are not a fleeting aspect of man's short existence but have a permanent residence at the heart of things."[10] In "The Will to Believe" no less than throughout his entire career James shied away from defending more specific religious doctrines, despite the fact that his books and essays were filled with sympathetic portrayals of believers in this or that specific faith.[11]

This disposition was fully in keeping with the "essentialism" of the liberal Protestant culture of James's milieu.[12] The "essentials" of Christianity were to be affirmed, while its anachronistic overlays – the products of well-meaning if unsophisticated disciples who had projected their own cultures onto the eternal gospel – were to be cast aside. The generality of "the religious hypothesis," as James often phrased his unelaborated theism, did not go very far as theology. But as a common denominator around which the embattled Protestants of James's time and place could rally, James's formulation of the core of religion was a spectacular success. James's readers could connect to this hypothesis whatever specific beliefs they thought implied by it. In the minds of the most highly educated segment of the population, the basic theism defended by James was the bedrock of a Christian faith that had been liberalized in response to the fear of Schleiermacher and a host of other Protestant leaders that the world's cognitive future lay with the secular, scientific intellect. Even those good Congregationalists and Episcopalians who had welcomed the emphasis on "feelings" and "conduct" following upon the scaling down of Christianity's cognitive claims remained committed, of course, to the concept of God. Hence, agnostics posed a real challenge: they undermined the remaining cognitive foundation of the Christian edifice that housed religious emotions and the social gospel.

Clifford had not attacked theism directly, nor was he forthright in his approach to Christianity. "The Ethics of Belief" was a passionate vindication of critical inquiry, and a vociferous attack on the habit of accepting, unexamined, the truth-claims that come to us from political or religious authority, social custom, or undisciplined feeling. Clifford's essay bears more comparison than it has received to a great American apotheosis of scientific method that appeared in the same year, Charles Peirce's "The Fixation of Belief" (1877). Peirce brought science to bear on the entirety of belief, explicitly including religious belief, and he did so with a spirit of moral rectitude. To "avoid looking into the support of any belief from a fear that it may turn out to be rotten," Peirce intoned with a righteous indignation worthy of Clifford, "is quite as immoral as it is disadvantageous."[13] But the beliefs of Christians figured in Clifford's text only marginally. Clifford quoted Milton and Coleridge to the effect that one should love "truth" itself above Christianity and the words of its preachers, but the religion of Clifford's readers was hidden, for the most part, behind carefully constructed stand-ins such as the "medicine-man in Central Africa" whose absurd ideas Clifford invoked coolly. Clifford's most extended example of unfounded religious belief was that of "a Mohammedan." Clifford had this imaginary apostle of a specific religion anathema to most of his readers voice the general arguments for faith common among educated Christians (the virtues of the great prophet, the miraculous events that testify to God's greatness and power, etc.). Clifford faulted these arguments as insufficiently grounded in conscientious inquiry (Clifford 1877, 297–300, 302). This was not quite Galileo inserting the Pope's arguments in the mouth of a character called "Simplicio," but Clifford's casting the Infidel Turk in the role of spokesman for "religion" had some of the same flavor.

The beliefs that get called "religious" were, for Clifford, merely cases of belief in general. Part of the power of Clifford's presentation derived from his locating of religious belief next to a variety of other kinds of belief, including scientific belief and the beliefs that inform the conduct of everyday life in the home, the workplace, and the tavern. "Every rustic who delivers in the village alehouse his slow, infrequent sentences," Clifford allowed with a patrician's sensitivity to the strivings of the respectable poor, "may help to kill or keep alive the fatal superstitions which clog his race" (Clifford 1877, 293).

Clifford's cardinal example, however, was that of a shipowner who stifled his doubts about the seaworthiness of his vessel and, putting "his trust in Providence," allowed the ship to carry its load of immigrants to their death at sea. The shipowner "did sincerely believe in the soundness of his ship," but he had *"no right to believe on such evidence as was before him"* because he had not earned it in "patient investigation" (Clifford 1877, 289–90; emphasis in original). This extended example opened the essay and provided Clifford with his major theme: that beliefs have social consequences and must, on that account, be held responsibly, which is to say, "ethically," on the basis of the best evidence to be obtained through conscientious investigation.

James's lack of attention to this theme is one of the most instructive features of "The Will to Believe," and it is a feature that becomes all the more striking if one is aware of the extraordinary emphasis Clifford had placed on the consequences of belief for social action. It is the pragmatist James, after all, who is properly remembered in the history of thought for insisting on the transcendent importance of the practical consequences of belief. And nowhere does he affirm this classically Jamesean sentiment more fiercely than in "The Will to Believe" itself:

The whole defence of religious faith hinges upon action. If the action required or inspired by the religious hypothesis is in no way different from that dictated by the naturalistic hypothesis, then religious faith is a pure superfluity, better pruned away, and controversy about its legitimacy is a piece of idle trifling, unworthy of serious minds. (WB, 32)[14]

Yet nowhere in "The Will to Believe" did James indicate what actions follow from religious belief of even the most generic sort, to say nothing of any specific belief. Do men and women who believe in God comport themselves more compassionately toward their fellow humans? Do they make and sustain better families? Are religious believers more reliable citizens than are the agnostics? Are they more selfless? Are religious people more diligent in their callings than are free-thinkers? James may have believed some of the assertions implied by these questions, but he neither defended nor even formulated them as claims. James managed to avoid altogether Clifford's pointed challenge about social action.

For James, the consequences of religious belief, such as they were, were worked out either within the individual psyche – James used to say that religious belief kept him sane (*VRE*, 408) – or in a celestial city: perhaps religious believing did make more likely the believer's eternal oneness with God? Action in this world was not on James's agenda in "The Will to Believe."[15] Yet James sought to leave the opposite impression, especially in his melodramatic closing calling upon his readers to envision a decision to believe in God as comparable to worldly action in a life-or-death situation under horrendous, physically real conditions. "We stand on a mountain pass in the midst of whirling snow and blinding mist," James quoted from Fitzjames Stephen, "through which we get glimpses now and then of paths which may be deceptive." We are obliged to make a "leap in the dark." We cannot stand still, for if we do,

we shall be frozen to death. If we take the wrong road, we shall be dashed to pieces. We do not certainly know whether there is any right one. What must we do? "Be strong and of good courage." Act for the best, hope for the best, and take what comes . . . If death ends all, we cannot meet death better. (*WB*, 33)[16]

This philosophically obscurantist ending is another sign of the spasmic character of "The Will to Believe." Action is mystified, and its stakes are represented as truly momentous. A "leap in the dark" is celebrated as the best possible mode of death. And such florid stuff is offered by someone who, only a few pages before, had mocked Clifford for a certain "robustious pathos in the voice" (*WB*, 18).

Clifford called attention to the injuries done to individuals and groups as a result of the exercise of power sanctioned by beliefs held on "insufficient evidence." For Clifford, society as a whole paid for lax standards for belief. What of the shipowner's uncritical habits of belief? What of a population victimized by the mystifications of priests? Did the average citizen not need to scrutinize public questions with a more critical eye? "The credulous man is father to the liar and the cheat," warned Clifford; social solidarity and wholesome, collective action were promoted by "our powers . . . of judicially and fairly weighing evidence" (Clifford 1877, 294).

The ostensibly authoritarian Clifford displayed more concern about the manipulation of the public by charlatans and frauds than did the homespun American champion of "everyman," who betrayed an almost aristocratic aloofness from the social matrix in which cognitive choices are made. "The Will to Believe" defended the sensibilities of individual souls altogether removed from the fields of social power, while "The Ethics of Belief" defended social actors from death, injustice, crime, and exploitation that can be visited upon them by unjustified (although Clifford did not use this Foucaultian term) "regimes of truth." Foucault would find in Clifford a soul more kindred than the James of "The Will to Believe."

Clifford had good reason to comprehend alternate structures of plausibility as vehicles for power. British intellectuals of his generation had to contend with an established church which, in 1877 even more than when James wrote twenty years later, continued to exert enormous authority over education and public culture. It was not silly of Clifford to view the Enlightenment as an embattled cause, struggling against entrenched and resourceful enemies. But James flourished amid the enormous expansion of American universities, and in a society that treated religion as a more private matter than it was assumed to be in Britain. James thought the Enlightenment was doing so well among the educated classes that its excesses could be criticized without fear of undermining it. Clifford called attention to the "professional training" of the chemist that gave others a sound basis for listening to his testimony about chemicals (Clifford 1877, 301), while James, witnessing the most rapid and successful rise of academic professionals in history, was instead worried that professionals would intimidate the layman into undue deference.

The socially complacent American worried about the damage a strict scientific conscience could do to the peace of mind of individuals, while the politically engaged Englishman of a generation before had worried about the damage religious authority could exact on a credulous population learning only gradually the liberating potential of a critical mind. Clifford feared falsity in a social order he thought could only be improved by the truth; James defended freedom against what he saw as the cognitive tyranny of science. "Our errors are surely not such awfully solemn things," said James. Clifford spoke as though the creation and maintenance of culture was a zero-sum game and the stakes were high for all, while James spoke as though culture could expand indefinitely, making room for everyone's favorite faith without hurting anyone. "Live and let live," James urged; "tolerance" should be our ideal "in speculative as well as in practical things" (WB, 25, 33).

When James thus extolled laissez-faire as an adequate principle for the life of the mind he was thinking about questions on one side of a portentous divide. James distinguished between questions that could be decided "on intellectual grounds" and those that "by nature" could not (WB, 20). Clifford was right about the need for a scientific conscience, according to James, but mistaken about the cognitive terrain in which it was to operate. The function of James's boundary between spheres was of course to protect religious belief from critical challenge: it was all-or-nothing, either there was compelling intellectual evidence, or there was not, and in the second instance the passions were at liberty to choose our beliefs for us. James also made other distinctions discussed at length by his commentators – between options that were living or dead, forced or avoidable, and momentous or trivial – but the most salient distinction was that between intellectually resolvable and intellectually irresolvable questions. James drew the line between scientifically warranted beliefs and the rest of our opinions more sharply than the positivist Clifford did, and he pushed that line back selectively until it no longer threatened the varieties of supernaturalism favored by the most sophisticated of Protestant believers.

The absolute character of James's distinction between spheres of belief in "The Will to Believe" is worth dwelling upon because it contrasts so sharply to the more thoroughly secular approach to true belief James was just beginning to develop under the inspiration, in part, of Peirce. Although *The Will to Believe* was dedicated to Peirce, who was quick to acknowledge his appreciation for this book's title essay even while lamenting James's preoccupation with religious belief,[17] Peirce's influence on James was much more pronounced a decade later in *Pragmatism*. In that much less impetuous work, to which we will attend more extensively in a moment, James presented belief as a monolith, embracing both religious and scientific ideas, just as Peirce had done in "The Fixation of Belief." The self has an undifferentiated "mass of opinions" that is tested by the course of experience and critically revised as a result (P, 35). But in "The Will to Believe" James was still held in thrall by an older, highly nonpragmatic strategy for defending religious belief: the assertion of the reality of separate spheres for religious and for scientific cognition.

A host of James's interpreters have been troubled by James's refusal, in "The Will to Believe," to recognize degrees of confirmation. Even so sympathetic a reader as Gerald E. Myers, for example, has voiced "the suspicion that James has fabricated an artificial situation in which the will or right to believe applies." Intellectual evidence comes in many kinds, Myers adds, and fewer people than James supposed "assume that we hold or reject religious beliefs in a complete vacuum of evidence." It was the character and location of the line James etched between intellectual evidence and everything else that inspired Holmes's complaint that James "turned down the lights" to shield the warrants of religious faith from close scrutiny. "If we reduce knowledge, inflate ignorance, and summon feelings to center stage," as Myers puts it, "everything is set for faith's appearance" (1986a, 454).

During the decade between "The Will to Believe" and *Pragmatism* James came to accept more fully an idea he had long suspected was true but had often resisted: that scientific discourse was the field on which the culture of the future would be determined. James had recognized from the start that his dispute with Clifford had to do with what structure of plausibility would prevail in the world's most advanced societies. But until around the turn of the century James episodically indulged the hope – displayed the most openly in "The Will to Believe" – that a doctrine of separate spheres would preserve a place in which traditional religious emotions could continue to flourish unintimidated.

As I have shown elsewhere,[18] *Pragmatism* was the point in James's career at which he consolidated his defense of religious belief so that it could more easily operate within, rather than outside of, scientific inquiry. He downplayed the distinction that had been central to "The Will to Believe." In *Pragmatism*, religious beliefs were to be put at risk in conscientious investigation, the better to maximize the chances of their being proven true. James feared that the agnostics would create the culture of the future if the religious believers abdicated their responsibility and left the design and execution of research programs to the likes of Clifford. There would be no one, then, to actually test "the religious hypothesis," because all of the investigators would have concluded that it was dead from the start. James was "advanced" enough to understand that the results of inquiry were deeply affected by the premises that informed it, and he was determined, in *Pragmatism*, to inspire persons with religious faith to put their beliefs at risk in the scientific arena. Religion might then have a chance to be vindicated through the *wissenschaftliche* study of the world.

"What are needed to bring the evidence in," James insisted on the last page of *Pragmatism*, was the "various over-beliefs of men, their several faith ventures" (*P*, 144). James's project of defending religious belief had now come within the Cliffordian framework he had still been resisting in "The Will to Believe": "evidence" was what decided the merits of religion in the long run, and it was up to people who believed in religion to go out and get that evidence, thereby putting their cherished ideas at empirical risk. Religious faith was now integrated into the culture of inquiry. In *Pragmatism*, James was able to make the case for religion within, rather than as an exception to, the historicist and pragmatist outlook for which he is rightly celebrated as a giant of "the revolt against positivism."

A reading of "The Will to Believe" against James's chief foil, Clifford, and against James's own later work can thus remind us of the depth and intensity of the religious road James traveled to reach the formulations for which he is most honored today by persons who no longer share James's religious preoccupations. Such a reading may tempt one to resuscitate Clifford, whose critical spirit might seem attractive to today's intellectuals, troubled, perhaps, by cable television's endless string of advertisements for the services of "psychics," and by other signs that belief without sufficient evidence remains a problem in our society. But Clifford's preachy histrionics and his insufficiently historicist understanding of the scientific enterprise render him even more thoroughly Victorian than James. Both can continue to inspire our own struggles with decisions about belief, but neither can help us much without a generous portion of correction from the other.

NOTES

1 For representative examples of the invoking of James as a precursor of postmodernism, see Best and Kellner 1991, 28; and Livingston 1994, 273–9.

2 Two recent examples are Myers 1986a, esp. 451–2; and Levinson 1981, esp. 55.

3 For the classic narrative of this revolt and a typical account of James's role in it, see Hughes 1958. For a more recent account, distinguished by an excellent treatment of James, see Kloppenberg 1986.

4 See, for example, Gale 1980, 1–14. Gale characterizes (14) his own analysis of the problem of the ethics of belief as capturing "some of the spirit and thrust" of James's "The Will to Believe." But Gale could more justly be described as salvaging James by critically expanding James's argument in Clifford's direction. This is not to find fault with Gale's discussion of the ethics of belief, which is one of the most rigorous and illuminating in the literature. It is a sign of the effectiveness of James's destruction of Clifford that later philosophers arguing more in Clifford's tradition than James's can ignore Clifford and claim James as their inspiration. Another of the leading studies of "The Will to Believe" enters decidedly Cliffordian caveats against James without apparently realizing it. The thoughtful article by Kauber and Hare (1974) defends James by drawing out "implications" of James's argument that (1) rule out any "technique" that leads a believing subject away from seeking more evidence (339), and (2) support an actual "duty" to induce belief under certain conditions (342).

5 One of the very few philosophers to show signs of studying Clifford's essay has ended up offering a mildly sympathetic reading of it: See Harvey 1979. Another philosopher who has actually studied Clifford's text is Wernham, whose James's Will-to-Believe Doctrine: A Heretical View (1987) came to my attention only after this article was completed. A refreshing feature of Wernham's discussion is its sensitivity to the extent to which James misrepresented Clifford; see esp. 69–74.

6 Clifford 1877, 309.

7 For a convenient, brief account of Clifford's life and career, see Macfarlane 1916, 78–91. Clifford is a major character in the history of agnosticism, as recounted splendidly by Lightman 1987. Lightman points to the exceptional esteem the young Clifford enjoyed within the Victorian intellectual elite of his time. T. H. Huxley thought him "the finest scientific mind born in England in fifty years." While Clifford was dying he was attended regularly by no less a personage than Leslie Stephen himself, who then assumed the task of editing Clifford's papers and the mission of keeping Clifford's flame. See Lightman 1987, 95.

8 Holmes to Frederick Pollock, 1 September 1910 (Howe 1941, 1:67). I have dealt with Holmes's relation to James's pragmatism and his religious views in Hollinger 1992, 216–28, 307–13, esp. 217–18 and 221–2.

9 For the argument that the bulk of James's career as a philosopher should

be seen in terms of James's concern with the fate of religion in an age of science, see Hollinger 1985, 3–22. The present study of James and Clifford is an elaboration and extension of the basic interpretation of James developed in this earlier study.

10 Edward H. Madden, "Introduction," *WB*, xxvi.

11 Never was Ralph Barton Perry more accurate about James than when he proposed that James was "deeply concerned" with the right to believe, "but made no considerable use of that right" (1935, 2:211).

12 For a helpful overview, see Hutchinson 1977.

13 Peirce's "The Fixation of Belief" was originally published in *Popular Science Monthly* 12 (November 1877), 1–15. For the passage cited, see the essay as reprinted in Hollinger and Capper 1993, 23–4.

14 Clifford, too, held forth (1877, 298) rather "pragmatically" about belief and action: " . . . no belief is real unless it guide our actions, and those very actions supply a test of its truth."

15 Even George Cotkin, perhaps the most assiduous of the scholars who have portrayed James as an "activist," is unable to find in "The Will to Believe" a hint of an analysis of what actions are required by theistic belief. See Cotkin 1990, 80–1.

16 James was here quoting Fitzjames Stephen (1874, 353).

17 "Religion *per se* seems to me a barbaric superstition," Peirce complained to James, but went on to praise the social gospel at its most social: "The clergymen who do any good don't pay much attention to religion. They teach people the conduct of life, and on the whole in a high and noble way." This letter of Peirce's to James, dated 13 March 1897, is quoted in Myers 1986a, 605.

18 This paragraph summarizes an argument developed in Hollinger 1985.

5 Religious faith, intellectual responsibility, and romance

In thinking about William James, it helps to remember that James not only dedicated *Pragmatism* to John Stuart Mill, but reiterated some of Mill's most controversial claims. In "The Moral Philosopher and the Moral Life," James says that "The only possible reason there can be why any phenomenon ought to exist is that such a phenomenon actually is desired" (*WB*, 149). This echo of the most ridiculed sentence in Mill's *Utilitarianism* is, I suspect, deliberate. One of James's most heartfelt convictions was that to know whether a claim should be met, we need *only* ask which other claims – "claims actually made by some concrete person" – it runs athwart. We need not also ask whether it is a "valid" claim. He deplored the fact that philosophers still followed Kant rather than Mill, still thought of validity as raining down upon a claim "from some sublime dimension of being, which the moral law inhabits, much as upon the steel of the compass-needle the influence of the Pole rains down from out of the starry heavens" (*WB*, 148).

The view that there is no source of obligation save the claims of individual sentient beings entails that we have no responsibility to anything other than such beings. Most of the relevant sentient individuals are our fellow humans. So talk about our responsibility to truth, or to reason, must be replaced by talk about our responsibility to our fellow human beings. James's account of truth and knowledge is a utilitarian ethics of belief designed to facilitate such replacement.[1] Its point of departure is Peirce's treatment of a belief as a habit of action, rather than as a representation. A utilitarian philosophy of religion must treat being religious as a habit of action. So its principal concern must be the extent to which the actions of religious believers frustrate the needs of other human beings, rather than the extent to which religion gets something right.

Our responsibility to truth is not, for James, a responsibility to get things right. Rather, it is a responsibility to ourselves to make our beliefs cohere with one another, and to our fellow humans to make them cohere with theirs. As in Habermas's account of "communicative rationality," our obligation to be rational is exhausted by our obligation to take account of other people's doubts and objections to our beliefs.[2] This view of rationality makes it natural to say, as James does, that the true is "what would be better for us to believe" (P, 42).

But of course what is good for one person or group to believe will not be good for another person or group. James never was sure how to avoid the counterintuitive consequence that what is true for one person or group may not be true for another. He fluctuated between Peirce's identification of truth with what will be believed under ideal conditions, and Dewey's strategy of avoiding the topic of truth and talking instead about justification. But for my present purpose – evaluating James's argument in "The Will to Believe" – it is not necessary to decide between these strategies.[3] For that purpose, I can duck questions about what pragmatists should say about truth. I need consider only the question of whether the religious believer has a right to her faith – whether this faith conflicts with her intellectual responsibilities.

It is a consequence of James's utilitarian view of the nature of obligation that *the obligation to justify one's beliefs arises only when one's habits of action interfere with the fulfillment of others' needs.* Insofar as one is engaged in a private project, that obligation lapses. The underlying strategy of James's utilitarian/pragmatist philosophy of religion is to *privatize* religion. This privatization allows him to construe the supposed tension between science and religion as the illusion of opposition between cooperative endeavours and private projects.[4]

On a pragmatist account, scientific inquiry is best viewed as the attempt to find a single, unified, coherent description of the world – the description which makes it easiest to predict the consequences of events and actions, and thus easiest to gratify certain human desires. When pragmatists say that "creationist science" is *bad* science their point is that it subordinates these desires to other, less widespread desires. But since religion has aims other than gratification of our need to predict and control, it is not clear that there need be a quarrel between religion and orthodox, atoms-and-void science, any more than between literature and science. Further, if a private relation to God is not accompanied with the claim to knowledge of the divine will, there may be no conflict between religion and utilitarian ethics. A suitably privatized form of religious belief might dictate neither one's scientific beliefs nor anybody's moral choices save one's own. That form of belief would be able to gratify a need without threatening to thwart any needs of any others and would thus meet the utilitarian test.

W. K. Clifford, James's chosen opponent in "The Will to Believe," thinks that we have a duty to seek the truth, distinct from our duty to seek happiness. His way of describing this duty is not as a duty to get reality right but rather as a duty not to believe without evidence. James quotes him as saying "if a belief has been accepted on insufficient evidence, the pleasure is a stolen one. . . . It is sinful, because it is stolen in defiance of our duty to mankind. . . . It is wrong always, everywhere, and for anyone to believe anything upon insufficient evidence" (WB, 18).

Clifford asks us to be responsive to "evidence," as well as to human needs. So the question between James and Clifford comes down to this: is evidence something which floats free of human projects or is the demand for evidence simply a demand from other human beings for cooperation on such projects?

The view that evidential relations have a kind of existence independent of human projects takes various forms, of which the most prominent are realism and foundationalism. Realist philosophers say that the only true source of evidence is the world as it is in itself.[5] The pragmatist objections to realism start from the claim that "it is impossible to strip the human element from even our most abstract theorizing. All our mental categories without exception have been evolved because of their fruitfulness for life, and owe their being to historic circumstances, just as much as do the nouns and verbs and adjectives in which our languages clothe them" (ECR, 552).[6] If pragmatists are right about this, the only question at issue between them and realists is whether the notion of "the world as it is in itself" can be made fruitful for life. James's criticisms of correspondence theories of truth boil down to the argument that a belief's purported "fit" with the intrinsic nature of reality adds nothing which makes any practical difference to the fact that it is universally agreed to lead to successful action.

Foundationalism is an epistemological view which can be adopted by those who suspend judgment on the realist's claim that reality has an intrinsic nature. A foundationalist need only claim that every belief occupies a place in a natural, transcultural, transhistorical order of reasons – an order which eventually leads the inquirer back to one or another "ultimate source of evidence."[7] Different foundationalists offer different candidates for such sources: for example, Scripture, tradition, clear and distinct ideas, sense-experience, and common sense. Pragmatists object to foundationalism for the same reasons they object to realism. They think that the question of whether my inquiries trace a natural order of reasons or merely respond to the demands for justification prevalent in my culture is, like the question whether the physical world is found or made, one to which the answer can make no practical difference.

Clifford's demand for evidence can, however, be put in a minimalist form – one which avoids both realism and foundationalism, and which concedes to James that intellectual responsibility is no more and no less than responsibility to people with whom one is joined in shared endeavor. In its minimalist form, this demand presupposes only that the meaning of a statement consists in the inferential relations which it bears to other statements. To use the language in which the sentence is phrased commits one, on this view, to believing that a statement S is true if and only if one also believes that certain other statements which permit an inference to S, and still others which can be inferred from S, are true. The wrongness of believing without evidence is, therefore, the wrongness of pretending to participate in a common project while refusing to play by the rules.

This view of language was encapsulated in the positivist slogan that the meaning of a statement is its method of verification. The positivists argued that the sentences used to express religious belief are typically not hooked-up to the rest of the language in the right inferential way and hence can express only pseudo-beliefs. The positivists, being empiricist foundationalists, equated "the right inferential way" with eventual appeal to sense experience. But a nonfoundationalist neopositivist might still put forward the following dilemma: If there are inferential connections, then there is a duty to argue; if there are not, then we are not dealing with a belief at all.

Even if we drop the foundationalist notion of "evidence," Clifford's point can still be restated in terms of the responsibility to *argue*. A minimal Clifford-like view can be summed up in the claim that, although your emotions are your own business, your beliefs are everybody's business. There is no way in which the religious person can claim a right to believe as part of an overall right to privacy. For believing is inherently a public project: all we language users are in it together. We all have a responsibility to each other not to believe anything which cannot be justified to the rest of us. To be rational is to submit one's beliefs – all one's beliefs – to the judgment of one's peers.

James resists this view. In "The Will to Believe" he gave an argument for doing so. Most readers of that essay have thought it a failure, and that in it James offers an unconvincing excuse for intellectual irresponsibility. James argues that there are live, momentous, and forced options which cannot be decided by evidence – cannot, as James put it, "be decided on intellectual grounds." But people who side with Clifford typically rejoin that, where evidence and argument are unavailable, intellectual responsibility requires that options *cease* to be either live or forced. The responsible inquirer, they say, does not *let* herself be confronted by options of the sort James describes. When evidence and argument are unavailable, so, they think, is belief, or at least *responsible* belief. Desire, hope, and other noncognitive states can legitimately be had without evidence – can legitimately be turned over to what James calls "our passional nature" – but *belief* cannot. In the realm of belief, which options are live and forced is not a private matter. The same options face us all; the same truth-candidates are proposed to everyone. It is intellectually irresponsible either to disregard these options or decide between these truth-candidates except by argument from the sort of evidence which the very meanings of our words tell us is required for their support.

This nice sharp distinction between the cognitive and the noncognitive, between belief and desire, is, however, just the sort of dualism which James needs to blur. On the traditional account, desire should play no role in the fixation of belief. On a pragmatist account, the only point of having beliefs in the first place is to gratify desires.

James's claim that thinking is "only there for behavior's sake" (*WB*, 92) is his version of Hume's claim that "reason is, and ought to be, the slave of the passions."

If one accepts either claim, one will have reason to be as dubious as James was of the purportedly necessary antagonism between science and religion. For, as I said earlier, these two areas of culture seem to fulfill two different sets of desires. Science enables us to predict and control, whereas religion offers us a larger hope, and thereby something to live for. To ask "which of their two accounts of the universe is true?" may be as pointless as asking "is the carpenter's or the particle physicist's account of tables the true one?" For neither question needs to be answered if we can figure out a strategy for keeping the two accounts from getting in each other's way.[8]

Consider James's characterization of the "religious hypothesis" as (1) that "the best things are the more eternal things . . ." and (2) "that we are better off even now if we believe [1]" (*WB*, 29–30).[9] Many people have said, when they reached this point in "The Will to Believe," that if that hypothesis exhausts what James means by "religion," then he is not talking about what they, or Clifford, are interested in. I shall return to this objection shortly. For now I merely remark that if you had asked James to specify the difference between accepting this hypothesis (a "cognitive" state) and simply trusting the larger hope (a "noncognitive" state) – or the difference between believing that the best things are the eternal things and relishing the thought that they are – he might well have replied that such differences do not make much difference.[10] What does it matter, one can imagine him asking, whether you call it a belief, a desire, a hope, a mood, or some complex of these, so long as it has the same cash-value in directing action? We know what religious faith is, we know what it does for people. People have a right to have such faith, just as they have a right to fall in love, marry in haste, and persist in love despite endless sorrow and disappointment. In all such cases, "our passional nature" asserts its rights.

I suggested earlier that a utilitarian ethics of belief will reinterpret James's intellect/passion distinction so as to make it coincide with a distinction between what needs justification to other human beings and what does not. A business proposal, for example, needs such justification, but a marriage proposal (in our romantic and democratic culture) does not. Such an ethics will defend religious belief by saying, with Mill, that our right to happiness is limited only by others' rights not to have their own pursuits of happiness interfered with. This right to happiness includes the rights to faith, hope, and love – intentional states which can rarely be justified, and typically should not have to be justified, to our peers. Our intellectual responsibilities are responsibilities to cooperate with others on common projects designed to promote the general welfare (projects such as constructing a unified science or a uniform commercial code) and not to interfere with their private projects. For the latter projects – such as getting married or getting religion – the question of intellectual responsibility does not arise.

James's critics will hear this riposte as an admission that religion is not a cognitive matter, and that his "right to believe" is a misnomer for "the right to yearn" or "the right to hope" or "the right to take comfort in the thought that. . . ." But James is not making, and should not make, such an admission. He is, rather, insisting that the impulse to draw a sharp line between the cognitive and the noncognitive, and between beliefs and desires, even when this explanation is relevant neither to the explanation nor the justification of behavior, is a residue of the false (because useless) belief that we should engage in two distinct quests – one for truth and the other for happiness. Only that belief could persuade us to say *amici socii, sed magis amica veritas*.

The philosophy of religion I have just sketched is one which is shadowed forth in much of James's work and is the one he *should* have invoked when replying to Clifford. Unfortunately, in "The Will to Believe" he attempts a different strategy and gets off on the wrong foot. Rather than fuzzing up the distinction between the cognitive and the noncognitive, as he should have, James here takes it for granted and thus yields the crucial terrain to his opponent. The italicized thesis of "The Will to Believe" reads: "Our passional nature not only lawfully may, but must, decide an option between propositions, whenever it is a genuine option that cannot by its nature be decided on intellectual grounds" (*WB*, 20). Here, as in his highly unpragmatic claim that "in our dealings with objective nature we obviously are recorders, not makers of the truth" (*WB*, 26),[11] James accepts exactly what he should reject: the idea that the mind is divided neatly down the middle into intellect and passion, and that possible topics of discussion are divided neatly into the cognitive and the noncognitive ones.

When philosophy goes antifoundationalist, the notion of "source of evidence" gets replaced by that of "consensus about what would count as evidence." So objectivity as intersubjectivity replaces objectivity as fidelity to something nonhuman. The question "Is there any evidence for p?" gets replaced by the question "Is there any way of getting a consensus on what would count in favor of p?" The distinction between settling the question of p on intellectual grounds and turning it over to one's passional nature thus turns into the question: "Am I going to be able to justify p to other people?" So James should have rephrased the issue between Clifford and himself as "What sort of belief, if any, can I have in good conscience, even after I realize that I cannot justify this belief to others?" The stark Cliffordian position says: no beliefs, only hopes, desires, yearnings, and the like. The quasi-Jamesean position I want to defend says: do not worry too much about whether what you have is a belief, a desire, or a mood. Just insofar as such states as hope, love, and faith promote only such private projects, you need not worry about whether you have a right to have them.

Still, to suggest that the tension between science and religion can be resolved merely by saying that the two serve different purposes may sound absurd. But it is no more nor less absurd than the attempt of liberal (mostly Protestant) theologians to demythologize Christianity, and more generally to immunize religious belief from criticism based on accounts of the universe which trace the origin of human beings, and of their intellectual faculties, to the unplanned movements of elementary particles.[12]

For some people, such as Alasdair MacIntyre, the effect of this latter attempt is to drain all the interest out of religion. Theologies which require no *sacrificium intellectus* are, these people think, hardly worth discussing. MacIntyre disdainfully remarks of Tillich that his "definition of God in terms of ultimate human concern in effect makes of God no more than an interest of human nature" (MacIntyre and Ricoeur 1969, 53). A pragmatist however, can reply that Tillich did nothing worse to God than pragmatist philosophy of science had already done to the elementary particles. Pragmatists think that those particles are not the very joints at which things as they are in themselves divide but are objects which we should not have come across unless we had devoted ourselves to one of the many interests of human nature – the interest in predicting and controlling our environment.

Pragmatists are not instrumentalists, in the sense of people who believe that quarks are "mere heuristic fictions." They think that quarks are as real as tables, but that quark-talk and table-talk need not get in each other's way, since they need not compete for the role of What Is There Anyway, apart from human needs and interests. Similarly, pragmatist theists are not anthropocentrists, in the sense of believing that God is a "mere posit." They believe that God is as real as sense-impressions, tables, quarks, and human rights. But, they add, stories about our relations to God do not necessarily run athwart stories about our relations to these other things.

Pragmatist theists, however, do have to get along without personal immortality, providential intervention, the efficacy of sacraments, the virgin birth, the risen Christ, the covenant with Abraham, the authority of the Koran, and a lot of other things which many theists are loath to do without. Or, if they want them, they will have to interpret them "symbolically" in a way which MacIntyre will regard as disingenuous, for they must prevent them from providing premises for practical reasoning. But demythologizing is, pragmatist theists think, a small price to pay for insulating these doctrines from "scientific" criticism. Demythologizing amounts to saying that, whatever theism is good for, it is not a device for predicting or controlling our environment.

From a utilitarian point of view, both MacIntyre and "scientific realists" (philosophers who insist that, in Sellars's words, "science is the measure of the things that are, that they are") are unfairly privileging some human interests, and therefore some areas of culture, over others.[13] To insist on the "literal reality" of the Resurrection is of a piece with insisting, in the manner of David Lewis, that the only non-"gerrymandered" objects in the universe – the only objects that have not been shaped by human interests – are those of which particle physics speaks (Lewis 1984, 226–8). Pragmatists think that we shall only see religion and science as in conflict if we are unwilling to admit that each is just one more attempt to gratify human needs and admit also that there is no way to gratify both sets of needs simultaneously.

Scientific realism and religious fundamentalism are products of the same urge. The attempt to convince people that they have a duty to develop what Bernard Williams calls an "absolute conception of reality" is, from a Tillichian or Jamesean point of view, of a piece with the attempt to live "for God only," and to insist that others do so also. Both scientific realism and religious fundamentalism are private projects which have gotten out of hand. They are attempts to make one's own private way of giving meaning to one's life – a way which romanticizes one's relation to something starkly and magnificently nonhuman, something ultimately true and real – obligatory for the general public.

I said earlier that many readers of "The Will to Believe" feel let down when they discover that the only sort of religion James has been discussing is something as wimpy as the belief that "perfection is eternal." They have a point. For when Clifford raged against the intellectual irresponsibility of the theists, what he really had in mind was the moral irresponsibility of fundamentalists – the people who burnt people at the stake, forbade divorce and dancing, and found various other ways of making their neighbors miserable for the greater glory of God (Clifford 1879, 2:244–52). Once "the religious hypothesis" is disengaged from the opportunity to inflict humiliation and pain on people who do not profess the correct creed, it loses interest for many people. It loses interest for many more once it is disengaged from the promise that we shall see our loved ones after death. Similarly, once science is disengaged from the claim to know reality as it is in itself, it loses its appeal for the sort of person who sees pragmatism as a frivolous, or treasonous, dereliction of our duty to truth.

A pragmatist philosophy of religion must follow Tillich and others in distinguishing quite sharply between faith and belief. Liberal Protestants to whom Tillich sounds plausible are quite willing to talk about their faith in God but demur at spelling out just what beliefs that faith includes. Fundamentalist Catholics to whom Tillich sounds blasphemous are happy to enumerate their beliefs by reciting the Creed and identify their faith with those beliefs. The reason the Tillichians think they can get along either without creeds, or with a blessedly vague symbolic interpretation of credal statements, is that they think the point of religion is not to produce any *specific* habit of action but rather to make the sort of difference to a human life which is made by the presence or absence of love.

The best way to make Tillich and fuzziness look good, and to make creeds look bad, is to emphasize the similarity between having faith in God and being in love with another human being. People often say that they would not be able to go on if it were not for their love for their spouse or their children. This love is often not capable of being spelled out in beliefs about the character, or the actions, of these beloved people. Furthermore, this love often seems inexplicable to people acquainted with those spouses and children – just as inexplicable as faith in God seems to those who contemplate the extent of seemingly unnecessary human misery. But we do not mock a mother who believes in her sociopathic child's essential goodness, even when that goodness is visible to no one else. James urges us not to mock those who accept what he calls "the religious hypothesis" – the hypothesis that says "the best things are the more eternal things" (WB, 29) – merely because we see no evidence for this hypothesis, and a lot of evidence against it.

The loving mother is not attempting to predict and control the behavior of her child, and James's assent to the religious hypothesis is not part of an attempt to predict and control anything at all. Concentration on the latter attempt, the attempt to which most of common sense and science is devoted, gives rise to the idea that all intentional states are either beliefs or desires, for the actions we take on the basis of prediction and in the hope of control are the results of practical syllogisms, and such syllogisms must include both a desire that a given state of affairs obtain and the belief that a certain action will help it do so. The same concentration gives rise to the idea that anything that counts as a belief – as a cognitive state – must be capable of being cashed out in terms of specific practical consequences, and to the related idea that we must be able to spell out the inferential relations between any belief and other beliefs in considerable, and quite specific, detail.

These two ideas have often led commentators to see a tension between James's pragmatism and his trust in his own religious experiences, and between the Dewey of *Reconstruction in Philosophy* and the Dewey of *A Common Faith*. The question of whether the tension seen in James and Dewey's work is real or apparent boils down to the question: can we disengage religious belief from inferential links with other beliefs by making them too vague to be caught in a creed – by fuzzing them up in Tillichian ways – and still be faithful to the familiar pragmatist doctrine that beliefs have content only by virtue of inferential relations to other beliefs?[14]

To give up this latter claim would be to abandon the heart of both classical and contemporary pragmatism, for it would be to abandon the holistic view of intentional content which permits pragmatists to substitute objectivity as intersubjectivity for objectivity as correspondence to the intrinsic nature of reality. But what becomes of intersubjectivity once we admit that there is no communal practice of justification – no shared language-game – which gives religious statements their content? The question of whether James and Dewey are inconsistent now becomes the question: Is there some practice other than justification of beliefs by beliefs which can give content to utterances?

Yes, there is. Contemporary externalists in the philosophy of mind insist, and James and Dewey could heartily agree, that the only reason we attribute intentional states to human beings at all is that doing so enables us to explain what they are doing and helps us figure out what they might do next. When we encounter paradigmatic cases of unjustifiable beliefs – Kierkegaard's belief in the Incarnation, the mother's belief in the essential goodness of her sociopathic child – we can still use the attribution of such beliefs to explain what is going on: why Kierkegaard, or the mother, is doing what he is doing. We can give content to an utterance like "I love him" or "I have faith in Him" by correlating such utterances with patterns of behavior, even when we cannot do so by fixing the place of such utterances in a network of inferential relations.

The fact that Kierkegaard is not about to explain how Christ can be both mortal and immortal, nor the mother to say how a good person could have done what her child has done, is irrelevant to the utility of ascribing those beliefs to them. Just as we can often answer the question "Why did she do that?" by attributing a practical syllogism to the agent, so we can often answer it simply by saying "She loves him" or "She hopes against hope that he . . ." or "She has faith in him." The "him" here may be either her son, her lover, or her God. We thereby give an explanation of action which is not capable of being broken down into beliefs and desires – into individual sentential attitudes connected with other such attitudes by familiar inferential links – but which is nonetheless genuinely explanatory.

So far I have been content to accept James's own description of the religious hypothesis. But it is, I think, an unfortunate one. Just as I think James took the wrong tack, and partially betrayed his own pragmatism, in his reply to Clifford, so I think that he betrayed his own better instincts when he chose this definition of religion.[15] For that definition associates religion with the conviction that a power not ourselves will do unimaginably vast good rather than with the hope that we ourselves will do such good. Such a definition of religion stays at the second of Dewey's three stages of the development of the religious consciousness – the one Dewey called "the point now reached by religious theologians" – by retaining the notion of something nonhuman which is nevertheless on the side of human beings.[16]

The kind of religious faith which seems to me to lie behind the attractions of both utilitarianism and pragmatism is, instead, a faith in the future possibilities of mortal humans, a faith which is hard to distinguish from love for, and hope for, the human community. I shall call this fuzzy overlap of faith, hope, and love "romance." Romance, in this sense, may crystallize around a labor union as easily as around a congregation, around a novel as easily as around a sacrament, around a God as easily as around a child.

There is a passage in the work of the contemporary novelist Dorothy Allison which may help explain what I have in mind. Toward the beginning of a remarkable essay called "Believing in Literature," Allison says that "literature, and my own dream of writing, has shaped my own system of belief – a kind of atheist's religion . . . the backbone of my convictions has been a belief in the progress of human society as demonstrated in its fiction" (Allison 1994, 166). She ends the essay as follows:

There is a place where we are always alone with our own mortality, where we must simply have something greater than ourselves to hold onto – God or history or politics or literature or a belief in the healing power of love, or even righteous anger. Sometimes I think they are all the same. A reason to believe, a way to take the world by the throat and insist that there is more to this life than we have ever imagined. (181)

What I like best about this passage is Allison's suggestion that all these may be the same, that it does not greatly matter whether we state our reason to believe – our insistence that some or all finite, mortal humans can be far more than they have yet become – in religious, political, philosophical, literary, sexual, or familial terms. What matters is the insistence itself – the romance, the ability to experience overpowering hope or faith or love (or, sometimes, rage).

What is distinctive about this state is that it carries us beyond argument, because beyond presently used language. It thereby carries us beyond the imagination of the present age of the world. I take this state to be the one described (in italics) by James as "a positive content of experience which is literally and objectively true as far as it goes [namely] the fact that the conscious person is continuous with a wider self through which saving experiences come" (VRE, 405). The images and tropes which connect one with this wider self may be, as Allison suggests, political or familial, literary or credal. I think James would have liked Allison's pluralism, and would have thought that what she says in the above passage harmonizes with his own praise of polytheism in the final pages of Varieties and with his insistence that "The divine can mean no single quality, it must mean a group of qualities, by being champions of which in alternation, different men may all find worthy missions" (VRE, 384).

In past ages of the world, things were so bad that "a reason to believe, a way to take the world by the throat" was hard to get except by looking to a power not ourselves. In those days, there was little choice but to sacrifice the intellect in order to grasp hold of the premises of practical syllogisms – premises concerning the after-death consequences of baptism, pilgrimage, or participation in holy wars. To be imaginative and to be religious, in those dark times, came to almost the same thing – for this world was too wretched to lift up the heart. But things are different now, because of human beings' gradual success in making their lives, and their world, less wretched. Nonreligious forms of romance have flourished – if only in those lucky parts of the world where wealth, leisure, literacy, and democracy have worked together to prolong our lives and fill our libraries.[17] Now the things of this world are, for some lucky people, so welcome that they do not have to look beyond nature to the supernatural and beyond life to an afterlife, but only beyond the human past to the human future.

James fluctuated between two states of mind, two ways of dealing with the panic which both he and his father had experienced, and the return of which he always dreaded.[18] In one of these the Whitmanesque dream of plural, democratic vistas stretching far away into the future was enough.[19] Then he would respond to the possibility of panic by saying, as in the quotation from Fitzjames Stephen which ends "The Will to Believe": "Act for the best, hope for the best, and take what comes. . . . If death ends all, we cannot meet death better" (WB, 33). In those moods, James could find this bravura as appropriate for the death of the species as for that of an individual.

But in other moods James was unable to shrug off panic in the name of healthy-mindedness, unable to rid himself of a panic-inducing picture of mankind as

in a position similar to that of a set of people living on a frozen lake, surrounded by cliffs over which there is no escape, yet knowing that little by little the ice is melting, and the inevitable day drawing near when the last film of it will disappear, and to be drowned ignominiously will be the human creature's portion. (VRE, 120)

In such moods he is driven to adopt the "religious hypothesis" that somewhere, somehow, perfection is eternal and to identify "the notion of God" with the "guarantee" of "an ideal order that shall be permanently preserved" (P, 55). In such moods he demanded, at a minimum, what Whitehead called objective immortality – the memory of human achievements in the mind of a "fellow-sufferer who understands" (Whitehead 1929, 532–3). At the maximum, he hoped that in his own best moments he had made contact with that mind.

All of us, I think, fluctuate between such moods. We fluctuate between God as a perhaps obsolete name for a possible human future and God as an external guarantor of some such future. Those who, like Dewey, would like to link their days each to each by transmuting their early religious belief into a belief in the human future, come to think of God as Friend rather than as Judge and Savior. Those who, like me, were raised atheist and now find it merely confusing to talk about God, nevertheless fluctuate between moods in which we are content with utility and moods in which we hanker after validity as well. So we waver between what I have called "romance" and needy, chastened humility. Sometimes it suffices to trust the human community, thought of as part of what Dewey called "the community of causes and consequences in which we, together with those not born, are enmeshed . . . the widest and deepest symbol of the mysterious totality of being the imagination calls the universe" (Dewey 1934, 85). Sometimes it does not.

James was not always content to identify the "wider self through which saving experiences come" with Dewey's "widest and deepest symbol" of the universe. In Whitmanesque moods he could identify this wider self with an Americanized humanity at the farthest reach of the democratic vistas. Then he could (to paraphrase the title of his father's book) think of Democracy as the Redeemed Form of God. But in Wordsworthian moods he held what he called an "over-belief" in something far more deeply interfused with nature than the transitory glory of democratic fellowship. Then he thought of the self from which saving experiences come as standing to even a utopian human community as the latter stands to the consciousness of our dogs and cats (VRE, 518–19).

We can, I think, learn two lessons from recapitulating what Henry Levinson calls "the religious investigations of William James." The first is that we latest heirs of time are lucky enough to have considerable discretion about which options will be live for us and which will not. Unlike our less fortunate ancestors, we are in a position to put aside the unromantic, foundationalist view that all the truth-candidates, and thus all the momentous options, have always already been available, live, and forced – because they are built into a language always and inevitably spoken by common sense. We can, with James, relish the thought that our descendants may face live and forced options which we shall never imagine. The second lesson is that letting his liveliest option be the choice between Whitman and Wordsworth – between two romantic poets rather than between an atheistic creed and a theistic one – was enough to satisfy William James's own religious needs.

James combined, to an extent of which most of us are incapable, honesty about his own needs with concern for those of others. So the upshot of his investigations is worth bearing in mind.

NOTES

1 Ruth Anna Putnam has suggested that I might wish to use "consequentialist" in place of "utilitarian" in this description of James. On reflec-

tion, I have retained the latter term. This is because I think that, for James, J. S. Mill was the paradigm utilitarian, and that Mill was as aware as James and Dewey that there can be no Benthamite measuring of context-free quantities of need-satisfaction, and that consequently there will always be agonizing moral dilemmas. I find "consequentialist" a rather flexible and pallid term, whereas "utilitarian" has a sharp-edged polemical force, thanks to its associations with the tough-minded Huxleyite suggestion that human beings be thought of as complex, needy animals. There seem to me to be Huxleyite overtones throughout James's work, and my use of "utilitarian" is intended to bring these out.

2 But Habermas, unlike James and Dewey, still believes in a "transcendent moment of universal validity." I have argued against Habermas's retention of this Kantian doctrine in Rorty 1994a.

3 In fact I prefer a third strategy, that of Davidson, who cuts truth off from justification by making it a nonepistemic notion. I defend the counterintuitive implications of this strategy in Rorty 1995.

4 Many people would agree with Stephen Carter's claim that this reduces religion to a "hobby," and would accept his invidious contrast between a mere "individual metaphysic" and a "tradition of group worship." (See Carter 1993, esp. chapter 2.) I argue against Carter's views in Rorty 1994.

5 See, for example, John McDowell's claim that without "direct confrontation by a worldly state of affairs itself" thought's "bearing on the world" will remain inexplicable (1994, 142–3).

6 Cf. Nietzsche, *The Will to Power*, § 514.

7 See Williams 1993, 116: ". . . we can characterize foundationalism as the view that our beliefs, simply in virtue of certain elements in their contents, stand in *natural epistemological relations* and thus fall into *natural epistemological kinds.*"

8 Although I have no proof text to cite, I am convinced that James's theory of truth as "the good in the way of belief" originated in the need to reconcile his admiration for his father with his admiration for such scientistic friends as Peirce and Chauncey Wright.

9 Note that for a pragmatist (2) is superfluous. "P" and "we are better off even now if we believe p" come pretty close, for pragmatists, to saying the same thing.

10 Pragmatists can, of course, make a distinction between hope and knowledge in cases where knowledge of causal mechanisms is available. The quack hopes, but the medical scientist knows, that the pills will cure. But in other cases, such as marriage, the distinction often cannot usefully be drawn. Does the groom know, or merely hope, that he is marrying the right person? Either description will explain his actions equally well.

11 Here James buys in on a dualism between objective nature (The Way the World Is) and something else – a dualism which critics of the correspondence theory of truth, such as the future author of *Pragmatism*, must eventually abjure.

12 Paul Tillich claimed that his existentialist, symbolic theology was an expression of "the Protestant Principle" – the impulse that led Luther to despise scholastic proofs of God's existence and to label Reason "a whore." James said that "as, to papal minds, protestantism has often seemed a mere mess of anarchy and confusion, such, no doubt will pragmatism often seem to ultra-rationalist minds in philosophy" (*P*, 62; see also *VRE*, 396).

13 My fellow-pragmatist Barry Allen remarks that Hume saw no need to proclaim himself an atheist (Allen 1994). Holbach and Diderot, by contrast, did see a need, for, unlike Hume, they substituted a duty to truth for a duty to God, a duty explained in terms of what Allen elsewhere (1993) has called an "onto-logical," specifically antipragmatic account of truth. Holbach would, today, proclaim himself a scientific realist and *therefore* an atheist. Hume would proclaim himself neither.

14 Davidson and other externalists have emphasized that this claim is compatible with saying that we can attribute content to intentional states only if we are able to correlate utterances with their extramental causes. They have, I think, thereby shown us how to be radically holistic and coherentist without running the danger of "losing touch" with the world. Realist philosophers such as McDowell, however, have doubted whether Davidson's view allows "cognitive" as opposed to merely "causal" connections with the world. I attempt to reply to these doubts in Rorty forthcoming.

15 Acceptance of the claim that "perfection is eternal" was not, of course, James's only definition of religion. He had as many conflicting quasi-definatory things to say about religions as he did about truth.

16 See Dewey 1934, 73. Dewey's own conception of "the human abode" is not of something nonhuman but friendly, but rather of a Wordsworthian community with nonhuman nature, with Spinoza's "face of the whole universe."

17 James said that there is reason to think that "the coarser religions, revivalistic, orgiastic, with blood and miracles and supernatural operations, may possibly never be displaced. Some constitutions need them too much" (*VRE*, 136). He could have added that people placed in some circumstances (no wealth, no literacy, no luck) also need them too much.

18 "Not the conception or intellectual perception of evil, but the grisly blood-freezing heart-palsying sensation of it close upon one. . . . How

irrelevantly remote seem all our usual refined optimisms and intellectual and moral consolations in presence of a need of help like this! Here is the real core of the religious problem: Help! help!" (*VRE*, 135).

19 See James's "pluralistic way of interpreting" Whitman's "To You" (*P*, 133), and his account of "the great religious difference," the one "between the men who insist that the world *must and shall be,* and those who are contented with believing that the world *may be,* saved" (*P*, 135).

6 The breathtaking intimacy of the material world: William James's last thoughts

When William James began to write in the nineteenth century, technological, industrial, and political revolutions had destroyed ways of life evolved over centuries of adaptation to nature. James belongs with those who tried to reweave a coherent world in thought and experience. At the end of his life, he evolved what he called a "comminuted" – pulverized – "*Identitätsphilosophie.*" Without grasping this world-view, there is no way to know what James was up to, for example, his pragmatic theory of truth.

I

The view that spirit (or mind) and nature (or matter) are identical was advanced most famously by Schelling very early in the nineteenth century, with key concepts refined, disciplined, and constricted by Hegel a little later. Early on, James has little or nothing to say about Shelling, as if even acknowledging his existence were to give him too much credit. With regard to Hegel, he bristles with contempt. We will see how he inched over the decades toward the views he ridiculed. He tried to retain a vision of the individual's intimate inclusion in a whole, but a whole construed pluralistically. His method was a phenomenology divested of rationalistic presuppositions.

In his 1882 essay "On Some Hegelisms" (*WB*, 196–221), James scathingly attacks Hegel's way of connecting things: in being other from each other they are all Other. They are bonded with each other in the very act of differentiating themselves from each other. What Hegel calls the activity of Absolute Spirit, James derides as a mere playing on the ambiguity of the term "other." This alchemical mixing of apparent opposites ecstatically James also finds in nitrous oxide intoxication (see his "Note on the Anaesthetic Revelation" appended to "On Some Hegelisms"). They have their place in that sort of experience, James thinks in 1882 – not in serious philosophy. While the experience is at its height, the flowing interfusions of opposites seem to make perfect sense. But when during the sober hours James reads his jottings made during the experience, they seem nothing but nonsense. He thinks he has located the root of Hegel's dialectical logic in a deep and desperate craving for harmony and inclusion, for belonging and sharing. Concluding his "Note" he writes,

the identification of contradictories, so far from being the self-developing process which Hegel supposes, is really a self-consuming process, passing from the less to the more abstract, and terminating either in a laugh at the ultimate nothingness, or in a mood of vertiginous amazement at a meaningless infinity. (WB, 21)

But in the nearly three decades before his death James moved toward some Hegelian views. He will not accept Hegel's notion of an Absolute Mind, an all-binding reality, but he offers a "pulverized identity-philosophy": things and events are what they are because, within a certain sector of the universe, they flow into each other, into what intellectualistic logic maintains they are *not*. Once we elucidate James's key discoveries and turns, his development toward a strange and explosive pluralism seems inevitable.

Charles Peirce was quicker to see the living resources of idealism and *Identitätsphilosophie*. His willingness to divide "intellectual purport" from meaning in other senses, and to give priority to it, his absorption in mathematics, logic, and mathematical physics – all this rendered him more patient with the earlier idealists' relative neglect of the organism caught up in the surround immediately. James cannot tolerate that neglect.

Peirce saw that idealists had attained a point of leverage from which the Cartesian stranglehold on philosophy could begin to be broken. In "Some Consequences of Four Incapacities" (1868), Peirce attacks Descartes with a ferocity and concision never seen before (nor since, perhaps). The whole idea of a consciousness individuated through its native powers of self-reflection or introspection, and constituting the sure foundation of all further knowledge, seems absurd to Peirce, unscientific in every sense. A demon may deceive me in everything, writes Descartes. But if I doubt that I exist, I the solitary thinker at least must exist to doubt it. I think, therefore I am.

But what are the conditions, Peirce asks, for Descartes to begin his "solitary" questionings? Where does he stand when he reflects his consciousness within itself? Why suppose that consciousness is a self-standing domain sealed off within itself? Consciousness fades off on every side through fuzzy fringes, say both Peirce and James, and it cannot inventory introspectively all its "contents." It blurs into the not-yet-reflected, or the never-to-be-reflected. In other words, it blurs into the whole pre-reflective life in which it is engaged in the public *world*. And this is the position, unacknowledged by Descartes, necessary for him to begin introspecting and doubting and affirming his "solitary" existence.

Schelling and Hegel saw that if the self is to be affirmed the world must be likewise. In mathematics it is acceptable to suspend the question of where thinkers stand when they begin to think. An axiom concerns formal entities only and can float: $1 = 1$. So the mathematically inclined philosopher is tempted to say I = I, Ego = Ego. But Schelling and Hegel think the philosopher should be concerned with *Wirklichkeit* (actuality, existence). Peirce early picks up on this. To think about thinking we must think about world. (In his preferred language, all thinking is in signs and signs are *of* a world.) This is the primal level of thinking: phenomenological description of where we always already are. In one form or another, idealists and pragmatists are all phenomenologists.

Peirce abjures any dualism of psychical and physical substances. If, *per impossible*, the two existed, there could be no intercourse between them, cognitive *or* causal. Any hypotheses about their action or interaction would be hypotheses about the unknowable. But since hypotheses are attempts to *explain*, such formulations would be absurd. So mind and matter must merely be two aspects of a single, continuous, self-organizing and self-generalizing reality he calls (somewhat inadequately) "feeling." This is the basic level of *phaneron* (phenomenon) as best he can describe it. In "Man's Glassy Essence" (1892) he writes,

But all mind is directly or indirectly connected with all matter, and acts in a more or less regular way; so that all mind more or less partakes of the nature of matter. Hence, it would be a mistake to conceive of the psychical and the physical aspects of matter as two aspects absolutely distinct. Viewing a thing from the outside, considering its relations of action and reaction with other things, it appears as matter. Viewing it from the inside, looking at its immediate character as feeling, it appears as consciousness. (Peirce 1931–60, 6.268)

In a letter of 28 January 1894 Peirce writes to James,

My views were probably influenced by Schelling – by all stages of Schelling, but especially the *Philosophie der Natur.* I consider Schelling as enormous; and one thing I admire about him is his freedom from the trammels of system, and his holding himself uncommitted to any previous utterance. In that, he is like a scientific man. If you were to call my philosophy Schellingism transformed in the light of modern physics, I should not take it hard. (as quoted in Esposito 1977, 203)

II

The gist of Schelling's identity-philosophy finally influences James's thought, more than will Hegel's, although that will too. Schelling's growing doubts about an Absolute Mind – its pure dialectical reason supposed to be the accessible ground of being – his awareness that art opens up and reveals ourselves-in-the-world at a more fundamental level than discursive intellect, all this will show up in modified form in James's thought. Schelling very acutely sees that the idea of two realms, a self-standing psychical and a self-standing physical, is an abstraction from what we immediately live, an abstraction that fails to grasp itself and its alienating effect. Shape construed by mechanistic physics as a "primary quality" is an abstraction useful for physics. But the reality from which it abstracts is revealed through the artist's shaping of materials. Schelling writes,

According to the oldest account, plastic art is silent poetry. The originator of this definition doubtless meant that the former is to express spiritual thoughts just like the latter; except not by speech, but by shape, by form, by corporeal, independent works – like silent nature. . . . Therefore it is evident that plastic art stands as a uniting link between the soul and nature, and can only be grasped in the living center of both. (Schelling 1807, 128–30)

In contrast to Hegel, Schelling's rendering of art reveals a phenomenology less wedded to ideas of iron-clad dialectical progressions dictated by Pure Reason, Logic, and Absolute Consciousness.

To reclaim our reality now, so says this mercurial philosopher of identity, we must feel our way back down into art and myth, into the time before the split between subject and object. Behind Schelling's "new" dialectical thought are discernible very ancient notions of cyclical, ever-regenerating life, the dark depths of Earth, interdependence of light and darkness, clarity and vagueness, birth-death-rebirth. All this lives underground in James's thought and finally emerges in stark new forms. Though slower than Peirce, he was more patient, more self-consolidating, better able perhaps to develop the living resources of idealism.

III

James's massive *The Principles of Psychology* (1890) was twelve years in the writing, and stands as the first peak in a range of remarkable and surprising mature work in the next two decades. His only degree was M.D., his first job was teacher of physiology, and he was much influenced by Darwin. In *Principles* he says his approach to psychology will be natural-scientific and nonphilosophical. He will simply try to discover causal laws of functional covariation between mental states and brain states. He realizes that there are philosophical problems of how mind and brain could interact, and also of how mind could know the world, but he believes that for his purposes he can avoid them.

Of the many valuable insights and results of *Principles*, the most valuable is that James does not succeed in his grand design of avoiding philosophy. He cannot begin to correlate mental states and brain states until he specifies mental states, and he cannot specify mental states until he specifies how they are about their objects in the world. Not only can he not avoid philosophical problems, he sees that the problems are intermeshed and that the "cognitive relation" of mental states to the world is the most basic. (The question of how objects "get known into" mental states he had most wanted to avoid.)

In other words, James sees that he cannot avoid asking where he can stand intellectually if he would begin his natural scientific investigation. He cannot avoid a reflective excavation of the presuppositions of inquiry, cannot avoid turning around, so to speak, from his "main" natural-scientific project. Although he is reluctant to admit it, he is caught up in a transcendental investigation of the conditions of the experienceability and knowability of the world. His excavation of presupposition is an implicit but extensive and rich phenomenological description of where we always already are in the experienceable world. To go forward scientifically he must also go backward. *Principles* offers the spectacle of a man unable to run backward fast enough to keep up with himself.[1]

For the sake of his avowed natural scientific program, James sets up an analytic framework, dividing the "irreducible data of psychology" into four "water-tight" compartments (*PP*,* 1:184): "(1) The Psychologist; (2) The Thought Studied; (3) The Thought's Object; (4) The Psychologist's Reality (the real world)." To his increasing but more or less suppressed chagrin, he finds that while he wants to study (2), the thought or mental state, so that he can correlate it causally to the brain state (4), he cannot specify the mental state until he specifies what it is *of*, that is, (3) The Thought's Object. And this "Object" cannot be a particular object, like a particular brain state – or a particular anything else. He means "all that thought thinks just as thought thinks it." An example he gives is hearing thunder. We do not perceive thunder pure and simple, but "thunder-breaking-in-on-silence-and-contrasting-to-it." To specify the mental state we must specify it in terms of this Object. The *particular* object it is of is only the "topic" of the total "Object" (in Husserlian terms, the particular is only the "noematic kernel or nucleus" of the "total noematic object"). The particular may just as well be a particular brain state or event as a particular clap of thunder.

It takes no genius to see what is happening: Thought's Object (3), described phenomenologically, engorges both (2) the mental state and (4) the brain state. It is the full sweep of the experienceable world.

But does the natural scientific investigator, (1) The Psychologist, not stand off from all this, a kind of self-constituting, self-reflecting, and inventorying consciousness somehow inside an organism? No. James is no more able to believe this than could Peirce. James launches an intriguing description of identity of self as "the passing thought." "The passing thought is the thinker." But we have seen that "the passing thought" (2) can be specified only in terms of (3), the total Object. The Psychologist (1) is also absorbed into (3); The Psychologist cannot stand outside the phenomena to be described.

The Object becomes all-engulfing: thinkers or experiencers ab-

sorbed in the experiencing-experienced-experienceable world. What
started as natural science becomes a world-view, with all the philosophical problems and opportunities attendant upon that. The way
opens inexorably for James's later metaphysics, "A World of Pure
Experience," and for his phenomenology as the basis of this radically
empiricist thought – and this is the matrix essential for grasping
what he wants to say about truth.

James could begin to admit this frankly only after fourteen years of
gestation and struggle, in the *Abridgment* of *the Principles* (1892).
With stunning candor he writes in its last pages that "the waters of
metaphysical criticism leak into every joint" of his four-part analytic framework for a natural scientific psychology. And he clearly
prefigures his metaphysics of "pure or neutral" experience in a
memorable phenomenological description of looking into the blue
sky. As immediately seen and lived, the blue is pure or natural: it is
not confined in either a subjective (mental) or an objective (physical)
"compartment." The *very same blue* that figures in his "inner"
ongoing experiencing of it figures as well in the total context of the
experienced world's history at large (e.g., "The sky is blue whether I
am experiencing it or not"). Only in retrospection, however rapid, is
the pure or neutral experience of blue sorted into the different contexts. In breathtaking immediacy and intimacy, experiencers belong
in the experienced world, and that world belongs to them.

IV

Clearly, James has been profoundly influenced by absolute idealism
and *Identitätsphilosophie*. There can be no sensible talk of particulars pure and simple, brute particulars, either mental or physical.
What things are, is not dissociable from the ideas and standards
implicit in their experienceability. And we are those beings who can
experience the rest of the experienceable world in certain ways.
Human mind is human minding (let us not hypostatize the noun
"mind"), and this is just one aspect of one sort of processual context
within the single world of pure or neutral experience – the world,
the context of contexts. Atomism, either in its Cartesian or British
empiricist forms, is jettisoned in favor of his metaphysics of radical
empiricism.

But equally clearly, James cannot accept the earlier idealist-phenomenologists insofar as their reading of presuppositions is, he believes, insensitive to the many facets of an organism's evolving experience: organism as experiencer experiencing an experienced and experienceable world. The idealists accept more of the sensationist, atomistic tradition of mental "contents" than they have any right to. Then they have to import a transempirical Absolute Mind armed with its native battery of universals to organize everything. This is an all-inclusive atomism on a world scale – a World Atom – and it is not evident experientially or phenomenologically, James believes.

He puts tremendous pressure on his concept of experience. It must serve many roles, be multivocal. Yes, thinking beings are experiencing organisms that get constituted within an experienceable world – the constitution consisting largely of how they can experience others experiencing *them* as experienced and experienceable. Yes, experienceability requires universal concepts, but concepts are "teleological instruments," sorting devices, employed by experiencing organisms to achieve satisfaction of needs and interests in the wide world. James seems committed, along with Peirce, to some kind of objective idealism. But it is not an absolute idealism in which experience must disclose itself and be ordered in one definite "self-validating" dialectical progression. That approach smacks both of apriorism and transcendent monism – the world as Atom.

V

But how *does* James make a *world* of pure experience? As it took him twelve years to gestate his *Principles,* so it takes him another twelve to prepare for a systematic account of his radical empiricist metaphysics. As usual, he fights shy of anything resembling an architectonic system limned in advance by pure reason. He trusts his halting intuitive grasp of his own experiencing as he lives through its immediate vivacity, simultaneity, concreteness, and compulsion (not by accident he once intended to be an artist).

Before the first technical *Essays in Radical Empiricism* appear in 1904, he publishes a strange exploratory book, *The Varieties of Religious Experience* (1902). If experience is to be radical – "to the roots" – he must dig in the dark soil of his own primal experiencing.

Like Schelling, he must recontact mythic roots. His father – a powerful, strange, and imposing figure – had been a Swedenborgian mystic, and though James could never bring himself to believe in any formulable religion, he believed in belief, as it were. That is, belief is foundational, the direct "feeling" or "sense of reality," and if one does not understand this, one does not understand experience and how it can form a world experienceable as real (*PP*,* 2:283ff.).

James immersed himself in his intimations of how one world whole could take shape in experience. He focuses on religious experiences in which experiencers feel so powerfully and abruptly at one with the world that a radical reconfiguring of self may occur, a conversion. James writes:

Religion, whatever it is, is a man's total reaction upon life. . . . Total reactions are different from casual reactions, and total attitudes are different from usual or professional attitudes. To get at them, you must go behind the foreground of existence and reach down to that curious sense of the whole residual cosmos as an everlasting presence, intimate or alien, terrible or amusing, lovable or odious, which in some degree every one possesses. This sense of the world's presence . . . is the completest of all our answers to the question, "What is the character of this universe in which we dwell?" (*VRE*, 36–7)

For there to be *a real* world we must be "over our heads" in experience – in belief, in the *feeling* of reality. Yet we must also be able to make some sense of it. Differently put, the sheer *that* of things must be evident in our bones and viscera and fabricating hands, but we must also be able to learn *something* about *what* some of these realities are. This amplifies what he had said in *Principles* about the meaning of *real* things – their voluminousness, their overflowingness: they exceed any final knowledge of *what* they are. And it is the whole experienceable world that must be shown to overflow, to be real: the great *That* that perpetually exceeds our ability to grasp all of what it is.

James's version of identity-philosophy is "pulverized." His critique of the detached natural scientific psychologist looking on at a phenomenal world "out there" is also an implied critique of the absolute idealists' identity-philosophy. While they are deeply sensitive to the need to ground all inquiry metaphysically, they incorporate far too many traditional rationalistic assumptions to suit James.

Their initial steps are immense abstractions and de facto leaps of faith: to wit, reality is determinate, an all-inclusive organization of thats that are also whats.[2] So reality and truth are convertible. And since we are speaking of all of reality it must be One. And since the One is real there must be truth about the Oneness. And how could there be truth without a knowing of that truth within the Oneness itself?

Indeed, the knowing of the truth constitutes the ultimate structure of reality, according to absolute idealists: the drawing together of every objective manifold into the unity of an ultimate subjectivity, the identity of subject and object (which incorporates also the ancient idea of identity – the identity of particulars through the universals that join them).[3]

James cannot follow these leaps of abstraction. They dissociate him from concrete phenomena, from what real things are known as; in fact, from what truth itself is known as. He does offer a very schematic diagram of what he means by pure or neutral experience, of how a numerically identical "piece" of experience can figure simultaneously in both a minding being's personal history and in the history of the world at large. It is comparable to a point that can figure on two lines at once if placed at their intersection (ERE,* 12). But this schema must be fleshed out to conform to James's love of "concreteness and adequacy" (as A. N. Whitehead put it). A pure experience of blueness never stands alone but is embedded in the total Object of thought. It is the blue of the *sky*. Moreover, it catches us up in itself, we bodily beings beneath the sky. Very often we do not deliberately look up into it, but live involuntarily in its presence. As I might try to put it: skyified-my-head-is-turned-upwards-into-the-blue. We are possessed to some degree by the sky. A different example: We are irradiated and transfixed by the presence of a wild animal.

James's phenomenology places him much more intimately within phenomena than do the phenomenologies of the absolute idealists. His world will be messier, more pluralistic, pulverized, and "irrational" than they (particularly Hegel) could possibly abide. It *will* be a world, but a "concatenated" one "hanging together from next to next," with no single strand of identity, no absolute mind pulling everything together through their necessarily connected essences which that mind itself constitutes in its knowing (PU,* 321 ff.).

"And" names a "genuine reality," says James. Some things are merely "along with" other things, and no necessity whatsoever connects them. Every real thing has some "external environment," and unless some real threshold is passed there is no influence of one event upon another. For example, a horse sneezes in Tartary and a grain of cosmic dust falls on a planet's moon in another galaxy. These events have no causal connection and are merely "along with" each other in the universe. There is a world, but the Absolute is absent.

Belief is the feeling of the real world in which we organisms are caught up. Belief is a function of its "circumpressure." Belief is not only some assent we confer on a proposition when evidence justifies this. Nor is it only a willingness to believe that helps create in certain situations the very evidence that confirms the belief (like believing one can jump a chasm, which nerves and energizes us to do it), something James was immensely interested in. It also happens when we are caught up in the surround, and led and moved in certain ways. Pure experiences are variously "thick," moving, momentous, mood-and-activity-imbued. The idea that traditional pure reason's typical oppositions – mind/matter, self/other, human/animal, present/past, one/many – can contain the overflowing thatness of the world is presumptuous, preposterous.

To be sure, James grants that concepts are necessary if we are to have an experienceable *world*. They form a "coordinate realm of reality" – they can substitute for perceptions – as if a third line were drawn through that single point which is the pure experience. But, again, the danger is hypostatization, floating abstraction, which must be counteracted with the question, What are concepts "known as" within the living and lived total Object? Answer: they are our teleological instruments. James writes in his last, unfinished *Some Problems of Philosophy: A Beginning of An Introduction to Philosophy:*

Use concepts when they help, and drop them when they hinder understanding; and take reality bodily and integrally up into philosophy in exactly the perceptual shape in which it comes. The aboriginal flow of feeling sins only by a quantitative defect. There is always much-at-once of it, but there is never enough, and we desiderate the rest. The only way to get the rest without wading through all future time in the person of numberless perceivers, is to substitute our various conceptual systems which, monstrous abridgments though they be, are nevertheless each an equivalent, for some partial aspect of the full perceptual reality which we can never grasp. . . . [C]oncepts . . . must never be treated after the rationalistic fashion, as if they gave a deeper quality of truth. The deeper features of reality are found only in perceptual experience. Here alone do we acquaint ourselves with continuity, or the immersion of one thing in another, here alone with self, with substance, with qualities, with activity in its various modes, with novelty, with tendency, and with freedom. (*SPP,** 96–7)

The categorial concepts and oppositions of discursive reason must never presume to exhaust the great That, the world. The lessons of *Varieties of Religious Experience* must be retained:

. . . our normal waking consciousness, rational consciousness as we call it, is but one special type . . . whilst all about it, parted by the filmiest of screens, there lie potential forms of consciousness entirely different . . . definite types of mentality which probably somewhere have their field of application and adaptation. . . . The keynote is invariably reconciliation . . . something like what the hegelian philosophy means, if we could only lay hold of it more clearly. (*VRE*, 307–8)

It is presumptuous to think that all reality is determinate, that is, determinable by the categories of our reason. Why not suppose chronically borderline tendencies, systems, systematically overlooked? The world is the supreme *that* that cannot be broken down exhaustively into any set of *whats*, no matter how large. Discursive reason cannot penetrate a domain that, by hypothesis, is beyond it. James resorts to music for clues:

. . . music gives us ontological messages which non-musical criticism is unable to contradict, though it may laugh at our foolishness in minding them. There is a verge of the mind which these things haunt; and whispers therefrom mingle with the operations of our understanding. (*VRE*, 334)

Which exhibits affinities to Schelling's use of artistic process to analogize world-process insofar as they are suprarational. In great art a subconscious current combines with a conscious, as if emanating from a center common to both the mental and the physical.

The supreme *that*, the world, is dumbly presupposed by all thought, feeling, and action – the basis of common sense. The world presents itself as having been before we knew anything about it and did anything in it, and which will, in all probability, be after all our knowing and doing has passed away. "Julius Caesar was real, or we can never listen to history again. Trilobites were once alive, or all our thought about the strata is at sea" (*MT,* 54). If all is "at sea" there is no world, and we cannot think that.

VI

Only when we understand that the experienceable world is the ultimate presupposition of all inquiry can we grasp James's pragmatic theory of truth. Correspondence theorists presume that statements or judgments stand on their own and, when corresponding to the "outer or objective world," possess the property of truth whether we know it or not. This, James believes, is addictive verbalism that conceals the ground of meaning-making in the world.

There are no statements or judgments that stand on their own because there is no truth without meaning, and meaning is made about something when the organism anticipates that something's consequences for the organism's experience in the world. If those consequences actually occur, truth *occurs* (but see note 5). Specifically, truth happens when the past "builds itself out fruitfully" into the present and future.

Critics have maintained for decades that James has confused truth and the confirmation of truth. Take the statement, "The dog is in the garage." We confirm that it is true. The critic asks, "But wasn't it true that the dog was there before the meaning or belief about him was confirmed? So wasn't the statement " 'The dog is in the garage' true all along whether we know it or not?"

This is an appeal to common sense. But it is perverse because, in the end, it undermines the very common sense upon which it trades: We *define* declarative statements or propositions such as "The dog is in the garage" as either true or false, as either "corresponding" to reality or not. If we then confirm that one does, then *of course* we must think that it did so before it was confirmed. We *must* think that it already had the "property" truth. Even if we say at 8:16 PM "The dog is in the garage now," and we go and check at 8:17 PM and don't find him, we *must* believe that he might have been there a minute earlier, and that, if he was, the statement with its time qualifier has the "property" of truth. We *must* believe whatever is necessary to have a *real* world in our experience, to *mean* it. So we are not crazy enough to think that when we confirm something's existence we *create* that thing, or when we disconfirm something about it we *annihilate* it!

But what makes possible this "obvious" thought about truth? It is all too easy to isolate the statement "The dog is in the garage now" and to think that it stands alone with its "property" of truth. Yet without a living situation that prompts the statement, or poses a problem or question to which that statement is a response, there would be no sense in making it. It has the meaning or sense it has because of the situations in the world in which it makes sense to make it. The sense of these situations is the inherited matrix of common sense. Because the statement, with its "property" of truth, presumes independence of this matrix, it undermines common sense.

James believes that the correspondence-theory of truth, seemingly obvious, prompts us to ignore the evolving contexts in the world, mood-and-action-imbued, in which our lives have meaning – our probing, our bodily responses to our probing, our needs, suspecting, anticipatings, valuings, believings. Obvious and prosaic "objective truth" – truth about "what's out there" – bought at a price of an anorexic constriction of existence and meaning is bought too dear. Addictive, no quantity of it can ever satisfy.[4] Hence James believes that truth in the fullest sense does not preexist its discovery.[5]

Truth must be an actual co-creation of our inquiring selves and the rest of the world. So, about any *determinable* matter, James wants to say that *once a question is asked* (his italics) there is the possibility of only one true answer (*MT*, 56). Lacking evidence, we do not know which answer this is. All we can responsibly mean by truth is the answer that would come to our question were we to get the evidence.

VII

James seems to believe that most philosophers have not really pressed the question of the concrete *meaning* of truth. What could it mean aside from "leadings" in experience that lead where we expect them to whether we are happy with the results or not? (But perhaps he does not advance a single view of the meaning of truth. See Hilary Putnam's article in this volume.) We attribute certain characteristics to an experienced or experienceable thing and the thing accepts them. It's as if we were botanists grafting a branch from one tree onto another and the graft "takes." Our career as minding organisms intertwines and blends fruitfully with the career of what is minded. No need to search dreamily for a reality outside "subjective" experience to which our thinking might "correspond." James says that what advances and consummates or blocks and disappoints our thinking is found *within* experience. We are fated never to leave the experienceable world.

For any questioning or inquiring to begin effectively, most other questions must, for some stretch of time, be regarded as settled. This is dialectical ballast within the evolving body of human experience. Spontaneous, creative, perhaps daring engagement in the instant requires a relatively stable context in which the past can be taken for granted. There is no extraexperiential support. It is pragmatically and phenomenologically necessary to believe whatever is required to form a *world* in our experience. It makes no sense to say that this is "merely helpful" or "subjectively necessary," for there is no meaningful alternative; all there is are words about a world "out there" that float without experiential content. Hence we must believe where is no good reason to doubt – belief is the sense of reality. James writes,

Somewhere being must immediately breast non-entity. Why may not the advancing front of experience, carrying its immanent satisfactions and dissatisfactions, cut against the black inane as the luminous orb of the moon cuts the caerulean abyss? (*MT*,* 92)

Without our belief in an ongoing world that exists and has existed, that discloses itself here and now, and that grows and enhances its coherence through our very knowing of it, "truth" loses meaning.

James is generating a unique phenomenology of pre-reflective experience, the immediate engagement of body-self, body-thinker, and the rest of the world – our "living forward" in "the instant," as Kierkegaard had it. Always polemical with respect to Kant, James writes at the end of *Does Consciousness Exist?* "The 'I think' which Kant said must be able to accompany all my objects, is the 'I breathe' which actually does accompany them." (Though, not to be forgotten, he acknowledges that thinking does go on.)

This phenomenology comes closest to consummation in his last writings, particularly *A Pluralistic Universe*. He attacks "vicious intellectualism" and verbalism: the belief that what a name or definition fails explicitly to include it actively excludes (*PU,* 218). According to this "vicious" habit of thought, if a pure experience is of a specific nature, a *what*, it cannot be a *that*, but only an essence; if something is *present* it cannot be *past* or *future*; if something is a *part* it cannot be a *whole*; if the *self* it cannot be the *other*.

His last forays in the dialectics of experience complement his metaphysics of radical empiricism. For it is not sufficient to call blue, say, "a specific nature" that can figure in several contexts. Even colors, real colors in nature, are located on a continuum and fade into other colors. Essential to the supremacy of the *that*, the world, things finally overflow our pigeonholes and categories, and "bleed" through their boundaries into the evolving surround.

If experienced or experienceable things bleed through their boundaries, every pulse of experienc*ing* does this exceedingly. Every pulse is "its own other." It "buds out of" what it is and spreads into what it is not (not, according to intellectualist logic). Every pulse contains a spread or stretch that includes in immediate experience past, present, and future indissoluably fused and evolving. Experiencing forever rushing out through its fringes toward an ideal-expected (ideal relative to our needs and interests), something experienceable that may turn out to be exhibited in one of those experienced things we call actual existing things.

In fact, the instant's shock of experience may well be a *that* that is not yet a *what* – and, of course, not yet contextualized retrospectively into either our personal history or the history of the world at large. We are so vulnerable, so much a piece of the intimate otherness of the world, that the indeterminateness of the experience may reduce *us* to intolerable indeterminateness. We may faint. (Edmund Husserl's homey example: we drink milk absent-mindedly, expecting it to be water, and in that instant it is "mere sensuous matter"; no wonder we may spit it out in disgust.) In fact, in the instant the *other* can so possess *ourselves* that we are possessed, angelically or demonically.

This is the delayed unfolding of belief as "the feeling of reality" and "the excitement of reality." This is the phenomenological-pragmatic linchpin of all his radical empiricism and theory of truth.

Not only the absolute is its own other, but the simplest bits of immediate experience are their own other, if that hegelian phrase be once for all allowed. . . . In the pulse of inner life immediately present now in each of us is a little past, a little future, a little awareness of our own body, of each other's persons, of these sublimities we are trying to talk about, of the earth's geography and the direction of history, of truth and error, of good and bad, and of who knows how much more? Feeling, however dimly and subconsciously, all these things, your pulse of inner life is continuous with them, belongs to them and they to it. . . . The real units of our immediately felt life are unlike the units that intellectualist logic holds to and makes its calculations with. They are not separate from their own others, and you have to take them at widely separated dates to find any two of them that seem unblent . . . my present field of consciousness is a centre surrounded by a fringe that shades insensibly into a subconscious more. . . . Which part of it properly is in my consciousness, which out? If I name what is out, it already has come in. The centre works in one way while the margins work in another, and presently overpower the centre and are central themselves. What we conceptually identify ourselves with and say we are thinking of at any time is the centre; but our full self is the whole field, with all those indefinitely radiating subconscious possibilities of increase. (*PU*,* 282ff.)

VIII

What is still pregnant in his last complete book, *The Pluralistic Universe*, can be traced along a number of dimensions. In fact, the book is itself a *that* that opens horizons beyond our ability to survey just *what* is involved.

We just do not doubt that you and I meet in one place – really compenetrate to some degree – when I hold you by the arm. This is the excitement of reality. And since we share the same "at" experien*ced*, why should not our experien*cing* of this be shared or shareable somehow? Let us pick up a passage from an *Essay in Radical Empiricism* and then try to follow into a speculative horizon opened abruptly in *A Pluralistic Universe*.

. . . whatever differing contents our minds may eventually fill a place with, the place itself is a numerically identical content of the two minds. . . . The receptacle of certain of our experiences being thus common, the experiences themselves might some day become common also. (*ERE*,* 85–6)

Has James finally arrived at the Absolute Mind in disguise? No, it's something far more primally human than the massive abstractions of absolute idealists: their beliefs in the convertibility of reality and truth, and in the necessary play of essences – the logistic intellect's imaginings. It's a version of shamanism returning to startle us at the dawning of the twentieth century. The theoretical possibility of this was already present in the direct realism of radical empiricism and neutral experience. When encountering a wild animal, say, this creature *itself*, this *numerically identical* creature, figures in our personal history. If we do not close off in panic, but dilate to it, its presence animates and refreshes our lives. If a bear, say, we may experience again in this hybernating and reawakening creature what our gatherer-hunter ancestors did: a living embodiment of the regenerative and healing powers of nature.

Our experiencing is not completely private. To a great extent it is experienceable by others, and their experiencing infiltrates (sometimes floods) ours. As an auditory or visual sensation can keep its identity even when "summed" in a larger whole of consciousness, might not we keep our identity if summed or conjoined in a larger conscious whole? Of course, this will be an individual identity very different from Descartes's daydream of identity, or the clearness, distinctness, privacy (and invulnerability?) that so many philosophers seem to want.

Consciousness is not parcelled out into hermetically sealed atoms. It is something that organisms, interfusing with others in the excitement of reality, *do*. Might there be more direct communications of "private" experiencing than we now even imagine? There are indisputable experiences of mimetic engulfment, ecstatic absorption in corporate bodies, as humans – human organisms – celebrate their placement in the regenerative rhythms of Earth.

James flirts seriously with Gustav Fechner's idea of an Earth-Soul. He speculates: Might not plants and animals and even Earth have their own sort of consciousness? Might not there even be the "knower of all" and we be "one with the knower of all and its constituent knowers" (*PU*,* 155)? Such a knower would not be a dialectical logician. Broaching involvement with plant and animal beings, plant and animal consciousness, James is retrieving, at least implicitly, primal religious experience, Paleolithic, shamanic. Here repudiation of Cartesian point-instant mechanics generates startling consequences: the presence of the mythic past, the primal other, in the present pulse of experience. What will it amount to today shorn of its traditional cultural and natural matrix. James cannot or will not tell us.

James is trying to kill a number of rare birds with one stone. He tries to do justice to the vastness of the universe, and in terms of its experienceability. We see now how this may be experienceability for a more nearly inclusive, a larger or higher, consciousness – "unperceived relations accrue from the collective form" (*PU,* 173).

But, he later writes, to be real, the possible super-human consciousness must have an external environment, must be finite (*PU,* 310–11). So how can everything real be experienceable by it? Despite his metaphysics's startling reach, it might seem to be incomplete. But perhaps we are able to imagine that there may be realities, *thats*, that may never become *whats* – or be in any way contactable – by *any* minding being? We would be stretching experienceability to mean: experienceable *as* not actually experienceable. Such an experienceable, if entertained – such an intentional object – would be a some-*what* in some sense: *the mysterious.*[6]

IX

I want to extrapolate briefly on a promising horizon of James's thought, his suggestions of archaic mythic involvements touched on just above. To do this we must bring the body into play.[7] As I said, he writes little about the body at the end. But he suggests how the "I breathe" as stand-in for the "I think" could begin to be fleshed out.

To affirm something's existence is not just to perform a "mental act inside a consciousness" or "inside language" (a "propositional attitude"?). It is to accept the thing, to allow it to be at a place that I and others might share, to allow it to compenetrate and interfuse the body. One can take its presence into one's body through the inhaling, inspiring breath ("And the Lord God formed man of the dust of the ground, and breathed into his nostrils the breath of life; and man became a living thing.") To deny is the reverse. Feel the dissonance as you try to simultaneously deny something's existence and inhale.

Notice how James's thought can supply an interpretive context for a contemporary's experience. Conger Beaseley recounts accompanying an official of the Alaska Department of Fish and Game in an expedition on the Bering Sea. The goal was to shoot four seals so that biologists could analyze blood and tissue samples for toxins, trace minerals, and parasites.

Revolted, Beaseley gropes nevertheless for some redeeming qualities in the experience. After a seal is shot, its blood boils up around it in the icy water. The redeeming feature is there: for the first time Beaseley realizes viscerally his consanguinity with seals. He is bonded to a fellow mammal. As they open up the seal's abdomen and extirpate its vital organs, Beaseley notes,

I developed an identification with the animal that carried far beyond mere scientific inquiry . . . the abdomen of an adult harbor seal is approximately the size of an adult human male's. Each time I reached into the tangled viscera, I felt as if I were reaching for something deep inside myself. As I picked through the sticky folds of the seal's heart collecting worms, I felt my own heart sputter and knock. (Beaseley 1990, 16–23)

As they extirpate the seal's vital organs, Beaseley realizes – viscerally – that "the physical body contains functional properties, the proper acknowledgment of which transforms them into a fresh order of sacraments" (23). Coiled intestines intertwine with coiled intestines of all animate things. In the recoiling intake of air, in the gasp of awe induced involuntarily in our bodies, we pay tribute to the wilderness *mana* energies we share with all animals. In the intake of breath we let them into our being. The sacrament is the involuntary acknowledgment of our kinship and our common preciousness – an acknowledgment that resonates, nevertheless, through our voluntary consciousness and career. It is sacrifice in the sense of sacrifice of ego: the acknowledgment of all that we do not know and cannot control, and upon which we depend. It names the sacred.

James leaves us to explore this regenerative gasping on our own. At sixty-seven he was too close to death to do much more battle with the academic establishment, full of those who exhibited an inability to understand his theory of truth "that was almost pathetic." And he thought his speculations along Fechnerian (and shamanic) lines were "too spook haunted to interest an academic audience" – speculations, "wild beasts of the philosophic desert" (*PU,* 299, 330).

The return to life can't come by talk. It is an *act.* (*PU,* 290)[8]

NOTES

1 For a fuller account, see Wilshire 1979.
2 Kant's Idea of Pure Reason – reality as a totality of determinate states of affairs – is no longer merely heuristic, but constitutive.
3 A point well made by Paul Tillich (1974).
4 Concerning the addictive quality of truth construed exclusively on the "correspondence" model, see Wilshire forthcoming (a), chapter 10.
5 He does allow, however, that it was "virtually true" that something happened, say, when all that was lacking was the recognition of that. See "Humanism and Truth," the last pages, in *MT.* This is his way of conceding, I think, that propositions can have the "property" of truth even when unconfirmed. (Similarly, Dewey asserts that "truth" *can* be "confirmed to designating a logical property of propositions," but then it lacks its full character of "existential reference" – Dewey 1958, 161.) And it seems that James would have to allow that some propositions might be true even if unconfirmable, for example, "There are no extra-terrestrial intelligent beings" (though probably false) may be true, and, manifestly, there would be no way to confirm its truth if it were true. James's idea of intentionality is relevant to the truth and confirmation debate. "Truth" is ambiguous. It *occurs* in our experienc*ing*. But what is experienc*ed* or experience*able* can be stated in "the eternal present." In the case of the above proposition, perhaps all James's radical empiricism requires is that the *meaning* of its words be in terms of possible experience, that is, experienceability. Perhaps he could grant that the proposition (apparently unconfirmable) might be *true,* though this truth is neither experienced nor experienceable. I do not know.
6 This reasoning is amplified in Quentin Smith 1986. See "The Veil," and "The World-Whole Can Be Apparent to Me as Not Being Apparent to Me," and "The Happening of the Nonapparent World-Whole Can Appear to Me," 268 ff.
7 Phenomenologists trace essential connections between mental life and postures and attitudes of the body. See Merleau-Ponty 1968 and Todes 1987. James's "Pure Experience" should be connected with Merleau-Ponty's "Flesh of the World" that folds back on itself – for "reversibility is the ultimate truth." That is, the perceiver is a perceiving-perceptible. In James's terms, an experience contextualized as my experiencing is no

more intimately a part of my being than that same experience construed as being-experienced-by-another: the context of the other's experiencing intersecting and interfusing mine. Shame, for example, is profoundly mine because it is equiprimordially being-shamed-by-another.

8 See also an interview with Hilary Putnam, *U.S. News and World Report*, 25 April 1988, 56: Philosophy cannot be concerned only with "logical puzzles," but must also deal with "regenerative possibilities of experience."

7 James, aboutness, and his British critics

Then for the first time did I realize the enormous capacity of the philosophic mind for misconstruing James. (Schiller 1934, 97)

I G. E. MOORE'S CRITIQUE OF PRAGMATISM

Shortly after the publication of his lecture series, *Pragmatism*, in 1907, James's pragmatism, and in particular his pragmatic conception of truth, was subjected to some harsh examination in articles by two leading British philosophers, G. E. Moore and Bertrand Russell. These must surely have contributed significantly to the tendency, at least in Britain, to think of James as a rather second-rate thinker. For, upon the face of it, their rather commonsense objections seem quite devastating. It is only more recently, as certain philosophical trends, of a kind often described as pragmatic, have hit the philosophical headlines, that objections like those pressed by Moore and Russell have come to seem less forceful. However, I am doubtful whether even now most commentators make it quite clear what it is that is largely wrong in these criticisms.

In his address on "Professor James' 'Pragmatism' " to the Aristotelian Society in 1908 (reprinted in Moore 1922) Moore begins by painfully assembling evidence to the effect that James intends to affirm both the following two propositions.

(1) All, and only, true ideas are verifiable.
(2) All, and only, true ideas are useful.

He then shows that there must be many a true idea which is not verifiable. For example, if after a game of whist the players disagree as to whether one of them did or did not have the seven of diamonds,

125

it may be impossible to verify the matter (Moore 1992, 101–2). Yet one of these opinions must be true and hence an example of an unverifiable but true idea.

As for the converse claim that all verifiable ideas are true, Moore accepts this, but only as the trivial claim that if something has genuinely been shown to be true, and not merely supposed to have been shown to be so, then it is true (Moore 1922, 107).

So Moore regards James's first claim as simply hopeless. But perhaps, so he suggests, James is really more concerned to establish the second statement, that all, and only, true ideas are useful.

In discussing the first limb of this, namely that all true ideas are useful, Moore tries first to remove an ambiguity. Does James mean that every true idea is useful whenever it occurs to anyone, or only that a true idea is one which can on occasion be useful. Deciding that only that latter is a remotely plausible interpretation, he attacks it by pointing out that there may be some trivial ideas which may only occur once to anyone, and which may be harmful rather than helpful on their one occurrence. For they may distract attention from something more important which is what we should have been currently getting on with (Moore 1922, 111–12). For instance, slightly to alter Moore's actual example, if, instead of getting on with preparing a lecture, I fall to idly counting the number of dots on a wall pattern, I may form a true idea of the number which is at best useless for me.

Moore turns next to the claim that all useful ideas are true. He takes this to mean that any idea which is at any time useful is a true idea and he tells some stories in which an idea is supposed to be useful but not true (Moore 1922, 112–14). For example, a man, because his watch was slow, might believe that it was one time when really it was another and, as a result, might miss a train. Suppose now that the train crashes. Then his idea was very useful to him but it was scarcely therefore true. Again, it is a perfectly coherent view that a belief in rewards and punishments after death is useful but not true.

Thus it is "intensely silly" to suppose that all true ideas are sometimes useful or all ever useful ideas are true (Moore 1922, 115). And James could hardly think this if he reflected on the matter. Yet it also seems clearly to be what he is saying.

So far, says Moore, he has been taking James's claim as an empirical one. But actually, he continues, it would seem that James regards it as somehow a necessary truth. (Moore puts this by saying that James appears to hold that an idea which is useful would be true, and vice versa, whatever other properties the idea might have or fail to have [Moore 1922, 126–7].) But this, says Moore, implies that if such an idea on his part as that "Professor James exists, and has certain thoughts, *were* useful, this idea would be true *even if* no such person as Professor James ever did exist" (Moore 1922, 127). This is the kind of jibe against James which looks most telling and is most calculated to produce that sense of him as a rather lightweight philosopher which has, upon the whole, been the dominant view of him in Britain.[1]

Moore finally considers James's claim that "to an unascertainable extent our truths are man-made products" (Moore 1922, 139–43). (The passage is actually from James's account of the "humanism" of F. C. S. Schiller, James's one vigorous British ally, but James endorses it; see *P*,* 242.) After thrashing around with various interpretations of what James might mean by this he concludes that it must imply that somehow "to an unascertainable extent" my own activity plays a part in constituting the truth of all my true beliefs (not just about my own behavior and its consequences). From which it would follow, says Moore, that

I must have had a hand in causing the French Revolution, in causing my father's birth, in making Professor James write this book. Certainly he implies that some man or other must have helped in causing almost every event, in which any man ever truly believed. That it was we who made the planets revolve round the sun, who made the Alps rise, and the floor of the Pacific sink – all these things, and others like them, seem to be involved. And it is these consequences which seem to me to justify a doubt whether in fact "our truths are to an unascertainable extent man-made." (Moore 1922, 142–3)

Anyone who learnt of James's views only from this address must have concluded that James was not much of a thinker. The coup de grace is, of course, the ironic suggestion that, on these principles, it might be true that Professor James existed even though he did not.

II RUSSELL'S CRITIQUE OF JAMES'S PRAGMATISM

Bertrand Russell had a respect for James which Moore evidently quite lacked (and indeed engaged himself seriously with James's

neutral monism and what he saw as his essentially behaviorist account of belief; see Russell 1986, 193–5, 240–1, and passim). But in
his two articles on pragmatism of this period, his treatment of
James's account of truth is not so dissimilar to Moore's.

In "Pragmatism," which appears as chapter 4 of Russell's 1910
Philosophical Essays (Russell 1966, 79–111) and was first published
in 1909 in the *Edinburgh Review*, Russell dwells particularly on the
extent to which the pragmatic conception of truth, of both James
and F. C. S. Schiller,[2] is a psychologist's theory, tending to substitute
for the question what it is for a belief to be true, the psychologist's
question what tends to make us hold it true. Its usefulness in a wide
variety of ways is a good answer to the second question, but unless
"useful" means question-beggingly "useful for finding the truth," a
bad answer to the first. Russell also traces what he sees as the development of the pragmatic conception of truth from the doctrine of
the "The Will to Believe," which he thinks confuses adopting a
belief as a working hypothesis with believing it to be true. Finally,
Russell contends that pragmatism presupposes a metaphysics which
F. C. S. Schiller had developed most fully, that of humanism (101–2).
And he objects to the pettiness of the vision to which this metaphysics would restrict us, for it "appeals to the temper of mind which
finds on the surface of this planet the whole of its imaginative material" (110). Basically he is charging it with what Santayana called
"cosmic impiety."

In the more important, for my purposes, "William James's Conception of Truth," chapter 5 of his 1910 *Philosophical Essays* (Russell
1966, 112–30) and originally called "Transatlantic Truth" when it
appeared in the *Albany Review* in 1908, Russell develops, in effect,
eight main objections to the pragmatic conception of truth.

(1) The claim that a belief is useful seems itself to be something
true or false, so that the identification of truth with utility leads to
an infinite regress.

(2) Pragmatists confuse suggesting a criterion of truth with elucidating the meaning of truth (Russell 1966, 120–3). (Note how "criterion" has changed its meaning as a result of Wittgenstein.) Even if
theirs were a good criterion, it would not give the meaning, since
there is an obvious passage of thought from seeing that a belief is
useful to thinking it true.

(3) But it is not a good criterion as it is often more difficult to know whether it is satisfied than whether the belief is true (118–19).

(4) Pragmatism's confusion between criterion and meaning stems partly from its concentration on scientific hypotheses. We are, indeed, often more concerned with whether these work than with whether they are true. The pragmatist interprets this as showing that their truth just is their working. But (a) this is a special case where we are not primarily interested in truth; (b) "working" in this context means "leading to truth at an observational level" (126–9).

(5) The view that a belief can be true because it is emotionally satisfying implies that it can be true that something exists even though it does not exist.

(6) If we use "true" in the pragmatist's sense we need another predicate to express the difference between a belief in what actually exists and one in what does not actually exist (119–20).

(7) So if we are shown that a belief is true in the pragmatist's sense, namely, that it pays, we will not be thereby brought to have the belief, since that requires that our belief answers to that other predicate. Thus the pragmatist may convince us that "God exists" is true because it pays to believe it, but he cannot thereby raise in us the belief that God exists (124).

(8) Pragmatism's account of truth is an ill-conceived "generalization from the procedure of the inductive sciences" (126). Scientific hypotheses, in Russell's opinion, are accepted because they work in organizing our spontaneous beliefs or predicting what beliefs will present themselves as similarly obviously true in the future (129). But in accepting them because they work in this sense we are (a) not accepting them as true, (b) nor accepting them as working in an emotional way, but as leading to what we incline to think true in a nonpragmatic sense. So the authority of science cannot be invoked on behalf of pragmatism.

III MOORE'S AND RUSSELL'S FAILURE TO GRASP WHAT JAMES WAS REALLY UP TO

I would not deny that Moore and, to a greater extent, Russell make some good points against James. Moreover, James's 1909 reply to the second Russell article in "Two English Critics" (i.e., Russell and R. G. Hartry; *MT*, 146–53) seems to make him even more vulnerable to them.

One striking point which he makes is that Russell runs together the belief that P with the belief that P is true. James insists that, if I believe that God exists, I am not thereby believing that my belief that he does so is true. *Someone else* considering my belief will regard it as true if and only if he thinks that it works for me, but *I* am believing simply that God actually exists.

In short, what makes my idea true is not the same as what I believe (*MT*, 146–7). True, he goes on to insist that, of course, if the belief that *X* exists is true, then *X* does exist; but the context suggest that, while if I call my own belief in its existence true, then *X* does indeed exist from my point of view, equally, it may not exist from another person's point of view (who does not have a true, i.e., useful belief to that effect). Russell's claim that James confuses the psychology of the matter with the logic seems to have some justice here. But perhaps the point that James is really making, in a rather confusing way, is that, in deciding whether to call an idea true or false, one must do so either from one's own particular view as to what really exists, judging ideas as true or false according as they stand to this, or internally from the point of view of the person whose ideas they are, in which case they will have to count as true or false according to how far they work well for him (cf. *MT*, 104–7, 131–2; *MT* and related works passim).

As for Moore, James clearly felt as little respect for Moore as Moore did for him. In the preface to *Meaning of Truth* he is included among a list of critics some of whom "seem to me to labor under an inability almost pathetic, to understand the thesis which they seek to refute" (*MT*, 10).

IV PRAGMATISM AND ABOUTNESS

It must be admitted that James often expresses himself on the subject of truth in a manner confusing and perhaps confused. This is, as it seems to me, because his pragmatism, and in particular its account of truth, operated for him as a summary of some quite various – I do not say necessarily incompatible – themes in his thought over the years (for a virtual admission of this see *MT*, 100).

Chief among these are:

(1) The doctrine of the will to believe (that our reasons for belief may legitimately be chosen to suit our emotional needs where cognitive considerations cannot settle an important issue).

(2) The more logically positivist aspect of pragmatism (that there must be observable tests as to whether a concept has application and that the point of thought about empirical matters is to anticipate, or control, one's future experience, rather than to correspond with something extra-experiential; see especially *P*, lectures 2 and 3).

(3) That truth is a feature of mental states or acts, not mere "propositions" (*MT*, 154–9; a point with which Moore and Russell, incidentally, agreed).

(4) That our awareness of the world articulates reality into particular units and patterns which reflect our specifically human interests rather than some independent articulation of reality. (Note how completely unaware Moore shows himself of the challenge of this reflection, when he mocks James for suggesting that it is our true beliefs about it now which caused the French revolution. Surely it is only too obvious that our opinions about this are bound to organize that chaotic time into *gestalten* which suit our particular interests and ideologies.)

(5) That if truth consisted in representations which were mere copies of things in the world it would be pointless, unless this copying served some purpose, which might perhaps have been served by a quite different style of representation (*P*, lecture 5).

(6) A view about the relation between thought and its object which we shall be discussing.

As a result pragmatism is presented rather differently according as to which theme was presently dominant in James's mind. How far they can be the joint basis of a single coherent doctrine is a difficult question which I shall not consider here. I must also bypass the interesting question of how the pragmatic conception of truth stands to pragmatism as a whole. James's claim that it is simply one among many applications of the pragmatic way of analyzing concepts is quite unsatisfactory (*P*,* 198–201). In fact, I shall examine only the bearing of the sixth theme on the interpretation of pragmatism, thus doubtless presenting a somewhat unbalanced account. However, we have James's own word for it that one of the chief sources of the pragmatic conception of truth was his reflection on the problem of how thought relates to the object it is about (see *MT*, 32).

We have seen how, in his formal reply to Russell, James seems almost ready to grant him that the belief that something exists may be true even though it does not (which surely would be sufficient to refute pragmatism). Elsewhere, however, he clearly rejects any such idea. "Truth is essentially a relation between two things, an idea, on the one hand, and a reality outside of the idea, on the other" (see also *MT*, chapters 9 and 10). And, as we shall see, so far as pragmatism is conceived in relation to this sixth theme, he had good reason for doing so.

This theme is of peculiar interest in the context of current discussions of "mental content," of what it is, when someone has a thought to a certain effect, that constitutes its being to that effect. Two types of view are usually contrasted on this matter, though there are various intermediate positions. The first, the internalist view, holds that what makes a thought (or belief) on someone's part a thought (or belief) to a certain effect is a matter entirely of the character of what is literally or metaphysically going on inside him; the externalist holds that the internal state which somehow constitutes his thought (though it must doubtless have a certain structure to be a thought of the relevant kind) is only a thought to a certain definite effect in virtue of the way in which it is related to states of affairs lying outside him.[3]

These discussions are most often conducted by philosophers of a materialist persuasion, so that for them the question is whether someone is having thoughts to a certain effect in virtue of some holistic character of his current (perhaps taken together with some past) brain states, or whether his brain states are only thoughts to any particular effects in virtue of how they (or their constituents) have been caused by or cause states of affairs in the world beyond his head. James would surely have rejected this materialist slant on the matter. However, if one overlooks the materialist guise in which the internalist/externalist debate usually presents itself today, one can take it as a dispute as to how far what is strictly occurring in a thinker's stream of consciousness settles what it is that he is thinking, and how far it is a matter of how what is going on there relates to something outside his subjective state. If we pose the issue in this way we can see that James, in his struggles with the aboutness of thought, had a strong tendency to move in an externalist direction.

To appreciate how this came about, it is important to realize the enormous impact upon James's view of the relation between thought and its object of an argument for absolute idealism put forward by his colleague Josiah Royce (Royce 1885, chapters 9 and 11).

V ROYCE'S PROOF OF THE ABSOLUTE

Royce starts from the undeniable existence of such a thing as error (something we cannot be wrong about, for if we think there is, then there is, either because we are right or because we are wrong). But error requires that an idea in our mind be applied to something which is not in our mind, and which does not really answer to that idea. That shows, he contends, that the object of an idea is not determined by how the idea characterizes the object, for, if so, our ideas would either not apply to anything or would apply only to that which they correctly characterize. Put otherwise, if the immediate content of a mental act is the sole determinant of its object, then it cannot have an object discordant with that content.

Royce then points out that the matter would be different if the idea and its object were both components of the same total state of consciousness. For then the targeting of the object by the idea could be an actually lived-through experience. Thus I can center my attention on some sense impression, note its quality, and play with the idea of its having another incompatible quality. Such targeting is then something we can understand by a direct experience of it.

It follows that the mystery of how an idea of ours can refer to an object which it mischaracterizes is solved (as Royce claims it cannot be otherwise) if we suppose that both the idea and its object, though not present together in our experience, are co-present in a more inclusive consciousness which deliberately directs the one at the other. Evidently that more inclusive consciousness would be well aware whether the idea did or did not correctly characterize its object. But if it were articulated into lesser consciousnesses, each of which only included some of its contents, then some of these could be ideas of things which they characterize wrongly, because, though the ideas fall within its compass, the targeting of them upon their objects does not. Such, argues Royce, is our situation when we are in error.

A less farfetched explanation, it may be suggested, is that we can identify something by a characterization which applies to it alone, but leaves much open to be mischaracterized by concomitant thoughts about it (essentially along the lines of Russell's theory of descriptions). Royce, understandably, is not very alive to such an objection; but it is clear enough that his reply would be that this would not explain how our ideas can be targeted on any reality beyond our own consciousness at all rather than just upon its present contents.[4] And perhaps this reply should command more sympathy than it did when Russell's theory of descriptions, or something very similar, was widely accepted as an adequate account of how we can have thoughts about particular things outside our subjective states. For there is a widespread belief that the content of my thought is not just a matter of what is going on "in my head," but is determined also by what lies beyond. This relation is usually interpreted in an "externalist" manner, as a causal or behavioral one, but many of us feel that somehow the distinctively mental character of thought's aboutness is lost on such accounts. Royce's account scores better here, since for it the relation of thought to its object is a distinctively mental type of directedness on the Absolute's part.

So far it has only been shown, in our exposition of Royce, that the fact that I am sometimes in error can only be explained by postulating a larger consciousness of which mine is a fragment, not that that larger consciousness is a universal consciousness fit to be called God or the Absolute. However, such a conclusion follows when we realize that it is possible for me to think erroneously about the cosmos as a whole, for that shows that my consciousness must be part of an "infinite" consciousness which includes the whole cosmos.

It may be objected that Royce's account misses any genuine aboutness of my thought quite as much as do those of a merely causal or behavioral type since what goes on outside my consciousness, even if it is a genuinely mental affair on the Absolute's part, can hardly affect what I personally am seeking to characterize by my idea. For Royce, however, in the depths of my mind I am somehow at one with the Absolute; so it is, in a sense, I myself who target the object which my idea misrepresents.

But why should the Absolute play this strange game of creating such beliefs within the finite minds which it includes when it knows them to be erroneous? For Royce this is one with the problem of why the Absolute produces all sorts of evils within itself. It cannot be because the Absolute is evil, for evil is the product of a will which battles vainly with other wills, a battle for which that which includes and creates all willing within itself can have no cause. The answer can only be that the greatest goods which there are, are the gradual overcoming of error and evil in that total history of the cosmos which the Absolute experiences in one, as it were, eternal specious present.

VI JAMES'S STRUGGLE WITH ROYCE

Whatever the reader may think of Royce's argument, James was certainly deeply impressed by it and for many years was inclined to think, very much against his will, that Royce had proved the existence of his Absolute. However, he eventually thought that he had escaped by offering an alternative, more naturalistic account of how thought relates to its object, or, as he put it, of how a thought can know or intend a certain real object. James's alternative was, in its essentials, put forward in 1885 in an article called "The Function of Cognition" as a reasonable account from a "practical and psychological point of view," even if it did not reach to the bottom of matters from a more philosophical or "transcendental" perspective (*MT*, 23n).

The article's essential contention is that if one knows about something by way of pictorial imagery, what makes one's image knowledge of *that thing in particular* is not just that it resembles it (for it may resemble all sorts of things which it has nothing to do with) but also that it somehow thereby enables one to operate upon that object. It is a similar relation that links a percept to what it is a percept of, while knowledge which takes the form of verbal thought is about such objects as it is liable to lead us to percepts of.

In the reprint of this article in *Meaning of Truth* (1909), James rightly says that it contains the essential seeds of the pragmatic account of truth and the aboutness of thought (*MT*, 32). It does, indeed, he notes, suffer from certain deficiencies. There is, for example, perhaps an excessive emphasis on resemblance, while there is insufficient attention to the fact that if the idea is to be true of its object the operations upon it which it promotes must be in some way satisfactory.

However, properly revised, we virtually have the pragmatic conception of truth. Moreover, while originally he had thought it simply a useful empirical, but philosophically inadequate, account of the knowing relation, he had come to realize, eventually, that it reached to the heart of the matter (thus rescuing him from absolute idealism).

It must be said that neither in this early treatment nor in his full-blown pragmatism is James very clear about the relation between intending (that is, a thought's being about something) and truth, nor how exactly falsehood fits in with either. (It is, indeed, mildly odd that in his response to an argument which, on Royce's part, took the existence of *error* as its starting point, James almost always discusses the relation of *true* thought to its object, largely leaving it to us to reflect on how this bears on error.) However, the upshot of his position is evidently this: knowledge, or true thought, does indeed require an object external to itself with which it is in agreement (even if, for James as radical empiricist, this can consist only in actual or possible future experience for oneself or others). But this agreement for him consisted, not in some form of copying, nor some other ill-explained form of correspondence, but in the fact that the thought is a mental event with a tendency to put one into behavioral relations with that something, if it exists and has a certain character, of a useful or satisfactory kind. In contrast, an idea will be false if there is no such object as it is fitted to put us into satisfactory relations with, either because there is no such object to be engaged with in a manner prompted by the idea, or because such object as there is lacks essential features required if that engagement with it is to be successful (see, e.g., *MT,* 51, 80, 91, 104–7, 112, 117–20, 129–31; *ERE,** 197–8). Thus an idea ascribes to its object that character which it must have if the behavior toward it which the idea prompts is to be successful.

When we realize how basic this idea was to James's pragmatism we see why he was so little impressed by the objection that, on his account, truth did not require any kind of agreement or correspondence with a real object. What he denied was that this either consisted simply in its "copying" it or was too mysterious for empirical explication. Thus his account of truth, as an idea's power to lead us into satisfactory relations with its object, is advanced as an account of agreement or correspondence rather than its denial (P,* 198–202, 211). (James's seemingly odd opinion that unverified, but verifiable, ideas are only true in a secondary sense turns on the conception of agreement with a reality as a relation mediated by activity, rather than one of passive mirroring, so that possible leading underpins possible rather than actual truth; see, e.g., *MT*, 67–8.)

There is, indeed, a problem here as to what constitutes satisfactoriness or success and why, on which James does not say enough, using such phrases as "expedient in almost any fashion" and "in the long run" (P,* 222). Assisting survival (*ERE*,* 96) and procreation are obvious candidates from a Darwinist point of view, but James certainly also has in mind experiences which contribute enduringly to all sorts of ways of feeling good (see Sprigge 1994, 58–9). And, even apart from this particular problem, converting James's suggestive ideas into a full account of what it is for an idea to have a certain propositional content would require exactitude on various matters which James leaves vague; indeed, I have been elaborating on his position somewhat already.[5] But the general lines of such an account are laid down.

VII BRADLEY'S CRITIQUE OF JAMES'S PRAGMATISM AND RADICAL EMPIRICISM

If James's views on aboutness were his response to the greatest American absolute idealist, Josiah Royce, they received perhaps their most effective criticism from the greatest of British absolute idealists, F. H. Bradley. Bradley had, indeed, criticized the pragmatism of James, Dewey, and Schiller, in a manner sometimes not so dissimilar from, though from a very different perspective than, Moore and Russell (Bradley 1914, chapters 4 and 5). My present concern is, however, with his critique of James's claim that what I am thinking, or thinking about, can be explicated in terms of that to which the thought leads, or might have led. (See appendixes 2 and 3 to chapter 5.)

Bradley has some persuasive criticisms of this. Thus he describes various cases where thought either leads to an object without being in any proper sense about it or is about something to which it could not possibly lead, as when the object is in the past, and concludes that leading and aboutness cannot therefore possibly be identified. Indeed, where any kind of leading of any relevance does occur, it is because the leading is guided by a thought of the object it is steering us toward, so that aboutness guides, rather than is, the process of leading.

However, Bradley remarks, there is an ambiguity in James's view. Much of the time James treats the leading relation as explicable in terms not drawn from the language of thought, terms such as "sensible continuity" or "causal connection." And this does imply the view to which Bradley is taking objection, that there is nothing in a thought, taken at the moment of its actual occurrence, in virtue of which it is really *about* anything, this being solely a matter of its subsequent effects.

Yet James also speaks of a feeling of fulfillment which occurs as the experience which mediates between thought and its object unrolls. That suggests that there is something about the thought from the start which fits it to be fulfilled by just such an object. This, however, tacitly acknowledges that mysterious "transcendence" on the part of thought, that power to leap beyond itself, which it was advertised as the great achievement of the theory to dispel (Bradley 1914, 154; cf. Pratt 1909, lecture 4).

Bradley is right in detecting, if not exactly an ambiguity, then a tension, between two different emphases. On the one hand, James is anxious to emphasize how a thought, considered strictly when it occurs, is just a "flat" piece of experience, with nothing about it in virtue of which it inherently points toward, or is about, anything other than itself. For what makes it a thought about some particular thing (and perhaps a thought to a certain effect about it) is not its own inherent character but certain "*extrinsic* phenomena" (*MT*, 62), namely, that it leads us (or at least would have counterfactually done so under certain conditions) to an encounter with what it is therefore about (*ERE*,* 57–8, 67–76):

Whenever certain intermediaries are given, such that, as they develop towards their terminus, there is experience from point to point of one direction followed, and finally of one process fulfilled, the result is that *their starting point thereby becomes a knower and their terminus an object meant or known.* That is all that knowing (in the simple case considered) can be known-as, that is the whole of its nature, put into experiential terms. Whenever such is the sequence of our experiences we may freely say that we had the terminal object "in mind" from the outset, even although *at* the outset nothing was there in us but a flat piece of substantive experience like any other, with no self-transcendency about it, and no mystery save the mystery of coming into existence and of being gradually followed by other places of substantive experience, with conjunctively transitional experiences between. That is what we *mean* here by the object's being "in mind." Of any deeper more real way of being in mind we have no positive notion, and we have no right to discredit our actual experience by talking of such a way at all. (*ERE,** 57–8)

Thus "there is no self-transcendency in our mental images [of what we are thinking about] *taking by themselves* . . . and [their] pointing [to what they are of is] an operation as external and adventitious as any that nature yields" (*MT,* 34).

On the other hand, although these descriptions have a thoroughly "externalist" ring about them, they tend to go together with expressions, such as feelings of "fulfilled intention" (*ERE,** 56) or of a "fringe" feeling of more or less definite tendency (*ERE,** 71; *PU,** 283, echoing *PP,** 1:258–9) suggesting the more "internalist" idea that, after all, *a thought* and *the object which it is about* in virtue of its power to lead us to it have a certain intrinsic fit, which explains why the one is experienced, when directly given in perception, as the fulfillment of the other. This probably influenced Husserl's talk of intuitive fulfillment (Husserl 1970, Investigation 6 §1).

The two contrasting emphases come neatly together in the following note:

A stone in one field may "fit," we say, a hole in another field. But the relation of "fitting," so long as no one carries the stone to the hole and drops it in, is only one name for the fact that such an act *may* happen. Similarly with the knowing of the tigers [in India which I may think of when at Harvard] here and now. It is only an anticipatory name for a further associative and terminative process that *may* occur. (*MT,* 34n2)

This may remind us of the description in *Principles* (*PP,** 1:251) of the difference between the mental gap in our consciousness when we forget one name and when we forget another; in each case there is a differently "shaped" gap which can only be filled by the name we are currently trying to remember. However, there it was a matter of the intrinsic fit between something *forgotten* and our current mental state, whereas here the fit (the importance of which James anyway plays down) is between our present mental state and what we currently *know!*

Perhaps his most stable view is this: When an idea triggers a series of experientially lived activities (or would have done, had it been given its head) culminating in an experience of its object, each subsequent moment of the series has a character which allows it to be felt as that which was prefigured by, if one by their "fringes," the earlier ones (and in paradigm cases also, and especially, by the triggering idea), though slightly different ones would have allowed this equally. However, so far as the idea's inherent character goes, each of various other such series, each with a different object at the end, could have been that which the idea initiated (or would have initiated if we had followed its promptings), in which case it would have been an idea of that object instead.

VIII JAMES AND OUR CONTEMPORARY EXTERNALISM ABOUT MENTAL CONTENT

It is evident that much of what James says about the aboutness of thought is quite similar to modern externalist conceptions of mental content. He is, indeed, similarly seeking a more naturalistic substitute for what Hilary Putnam calls "magical theories of reference" and, in effect, *sense* too. In short, he seems to have anticipated their view that a phenomenological investigation of thought, meaning, and reference is misguided, and that thought must be related to its objects by our concrete physical and behavioral relations to them (Putnam 1981, 3–5, 17–21).

There certainly is this affinity. On the other hand, there are also striking differences between James's account and that of most of our contemporary externalists who subscribe to this position.

First, James is certainly not a materialist. It is the physical world which has to be conceived through concepts whose most obvious application is to what is usually called "subjective experience," not the latter which has to be explained in terms more obviously applicable to the former. James is up to a point a reductionist about intentionally (*MT*, 34–5) but not about "lived experience."

Second, as we have seen, he also strives to lessen the sheer externality of the relation between thought and its object by holding that, in paradigm cases, the subject of the experience actually experiences the process by which the original thought leads to its object. This process is often described in terms of behavior, but it is evident that the behavior is what phenomenologists call "lived behavior" rather than mere physical teleologically explicable movement. James insists that aboutness is intra-experiential though not "saltatory" (*MT,* 79–80).[6]

I think there are difficulties in this, because if one holds, as one may have learnt to do from James himself, that all one ever actually experiences is what falls within one specious present, then it seems that one does not genuinely experience this leading, even if it consists in a series of one's own experiences.

Third, the tendency of modern externalists is to explain the reference and content of a thought by way of the *causation* of the inner process which is its occurrent being. James, in contrast, conceives the relation as being from the thought to *resultant* (experienced) behavior bringing us in perceptual contact with its object. (This poses a difficulty for him where the object of my thought lies wholly in the past. His too vague answer is that a thought can be about something by being able to lead us not to it but to its effects or associates; see, for example, *P,** 214–15; *MT,* 75, 121).

Fourth, modern externalists tend to regard the externalist account of things as applying not just to "thought" or "belief" but to perception also (see Davies 1991/92). That is, the inner occurrence which is my perception of an object is so because it is caused by the object rather than because of its inherent character. The opaqueness of the world to thought, which externalism suggests, holds just as much of perception as its proponents usually understand it. For James, however, there is a great difference between thought's and perception's relation to its object. The former has its sense and reference in virtue of its power to lead to perceptual awareness of the object (this covering all sorts of experiences of direct encounter with it). The latter, in contrast, is a kind of merging of one's stream of consciousness with the stream of being of the object perceived, so that its very self is somehow an immediate presence as objects merely thought of cannot be (*MT,* 87). (I must pass over the fact that James sometimes also abandons externalism about thought with the suggestion that its object is similarly contained within it. See *ERE,** 17–22.)

On all these points it seems to me that James has the advantage. Philosophers like Hilary Putnam say that the intentionality of our thoughts is not an introspectible characteristic. But it would seem that the way our thoughts link up with objects, through our behav-

ioral transactions with them, would be equally opaque to our awareness if our experience of them consisted only in mental or brain
events whose *of-ness* of them was merely a particular way of being
caused by them.

IX MOVING BEYOND PRAGMATISM WITH JAMES

It is an oddity of James, as a pragmatist opposed to a "copy" theory of
truth, that if there was ever a philosopher who wanted reality revealed to him in a more intimate way than that of mere effective
interaction with it, it was James himself. The following reflections
may cast some light on this.

(1) It is worth insisting again that the pragmatic account of reference and truth is concerned only with how *thinking* relates to its
object and is not supposed to explain how perceptual experience
does so. For in the light of his radical empiricism (according to
which reality consists in nothing but experience) James had attempted to work out a view according to which, in perception, and
in any experience of directly handling things, we do not merely have
true thoughts about an object which remains outside our minds but
rather, so to speak, so absorb the object that it becomes a component
of our own mental state (*MT*, 35–6, 73–4; *ERE*,* 10–15, 197).

Sometimes this idea seems intended in a basically phenomenalist
way. On this account the object is a system of possible experiences,
and when we perceive it these possibilities are actualized strictly
within our experience. At other times it is suggested, rather, that the
sense datum which occurs in my stream of experience, when I perceive something, is a temporary visitor there from a wider world in
which streams of sense data, or sensibilia (as Russell called them
when promoting a similar view) develop and interact with each
other according to the laws of physical nature, while when they
enter into our personal streams of experience they get caught up also
in processes governed rather by special psychological laws.

(2) James, however, was never quite satisfied with views of this
sort, unless perhaps as an account of how things ordinarily seem to
be (*MT*, 35–6, 73), and he pushed on to a metaphysically more radical
position of a panpsychist character (see, e.g., *SPP*,* 218–19). On this
view physical objects, as they exist independently of us, do indeed
consist in streams of experience, but these are rather their own way

of experiencing themselves than series of sense data such as we experience when perceiving them.

The trouble is that this panpsychist view seems incompatible with the idea, of which James was so enamored, that in perception the object itself is an ingredient in our stream of consciousness. For our personal perceptual perspective on an object can hardly be part of that stream of experience which is the object's own inner being.

(3) To meet this James has two main proposals: First, we may at least be on the brink of merging with the object in perception, so that even if it does not actually enter into our experience it is within an inch of doing so (*MT*, 87–8; *ERE*,* 73, 199–202). Second, we may sense imaginatively something of its inner nature by extrapolation from our own experience.

This leads, I think, to what is in effect a strong qualification of the pragmatic conception of truth, as consisting of ideas which work. For James seems to hold, in the end, that there are two different sorts of true idea. The truth of ideas of a discursive conceptual kind is that of "splendidly useful" tools for coping with a reality which remains opaque. However, some ideas are true in a more profound way, by directing us to reality in its true character as we live through it or can empathically imagine it. The first is truth of the ordinary everyday kind, the second is a deeper kind of truth which should be the basis of an ultimate metaphysics.

This view comes close, it seems to me, to an abandonment of the pragmatic account of truth in the case of metaphysics, treating it only as a theory of everyday and scientific truth.[7] But it is hard to say how far James would have accepted this way of putting it. Pragmatism is always presented as a form of empiricism, and it is empiricism, too, which leads him to the view that concepts being static and sharply bounded cannot do justice to the mobile fluidity of the pure experience in which reality consists (*PU*,* 290–3; *SPP*,* 78–96, 147; 189–219; *EPh*, 152–5).

Bergson (so close to James on such matters) perhaps put it best in his introduction to the French translation of *Pragmatism*. He says there:

The definition that James gives of truth is of one flesh with his conception of reality. If reality is not that economical and systematic universe that our logic likes to represent, if it is not sustained within an intellectual framework, truth of an intellectual order is a human invention the function of which is to utilise reality rather than to introduce us to it. And if the reality does not form an ensemble, if it is multiple and mobile, composed of criss-crossing currents, the truth which is born from a direct participation in one of these currents – truth felt before being conceived – is more capable than the truth, which is simply thought, of seizing and storing up reality itself. (Bergson 1959, 1449).

NOTES

1   For a similar but more justified charge against F. C. S. Schiller's pragma-tism or humanism see Stout 1907, 587.

2   As presented in James's *Pragmatism* and Schiller 1907.

3   Relevant discussions include Burge 1979; Burge 1986; Davies 1991/92; Evans 1982; Fodor 1992; Pettit and McDowell 1986; Millikan 1984; Putnam 1975, 1981; Rey 1992.

4   And Royce thinks, in effect, that all thought must have this *de re* feature (see Royce 1965, 395–6 and passim).

5   Actually, as Russell says, James has a tendency to reism, in Brentano's sense, for instance to treat presumed objects rather than presumed states of affairs as the objects of belief, though I think this less significant than it may seem to the logically pedantic. (See Russell 1986, 194.) And what would James say about Frege's sense/reference distinction? However, there is no point in torturing James's position into alien formulas.

6   "Now the most general way of contrasting my view of knowledge with the popular view . . . is to call my view ambulatory, and the other view saltatory . . . I say that we know an object by means of an idea, whenever we ambulate towards the object under the impulse which the idea com-municates" (*MT,* 79–80). James rather forgets that sometimes the bene-fit gained by knowledge of an object is to warn us to avoid any contact with it!

7   This would be akin to Santayana's distinction between symbolic and literal knowledge, the first a tool, the second a revelation. Though Santa-yana criticized James in terms often similar to Moore's and Russell's, he realized, as they did not, at least in 1908/09, the extent to which pragma-tism was above all a theory of reference (Santayana 1920, 158–60), one indeed echoed in his own account of intending (Santayana 1923, 172–7).

8 Logical principles and philosophical attitudes: Peirce's response to James's pragmatism

I INTRODUCTION: TWO PRAGMATISTS

William James was generous in acknowledging his debts to fellow pragmatist Charles Sanders Peirce. As well as dedicating *The Will to Believe* to his "old friend . . . to whose philosophical comradeship in old times and to whose writings in more recent years I owe more incitement and help than I can express or repay," he emphasized Peirce's role in the birth of pragmatism in lecture 2 of *Pragmatism: A New Name for some Old Ways of Thinking.* Remarking that the word "pragmatism" derives from the Greek word for action from which our words "practice" and "practical" come, he noted that it was "first introduced into philosophy by Mr. Charles Sanders Peirce in 1878" (*P*, 28).[1] In one respect, memory failed him: Peirce did not use the word in print in the papers James referred to – he did not use it in print (or, indeed, in his manuscripts) until after James had done so. But the views expressed in Peirce's writings of 1878 had been presented and discussed in a "Metaphysical Club" whose regular meetings both attended. Peirce later recalled:

1871, in a Metaphysical Club in Cambridge, Massachusetts, I used to preach this principle as a sort of logical gospel, representing the unformulated method followed by Berkeley, and in conversation about it I called it "Pragmatism." In December [November] 1877 and January 1878 I set forth the doctrine in the *Popular Science Monthly.*[2] (*CP*, 6.482)[3]

Although these meetings witnessed the birth of the pragmatist "tradition," the work of the two philosophical comrades steered it in rather different directions: Peirce famously remarked that James pushed their shared doctrine "to such extremes as must tend to give us pause" (*CP*, 5.2). Some hold that James corrupted the pure

"Peircean" pragmatism (later called "pragmaticism" to distinguish it from other versions of the doctrine) thereby blocking philosophical progress; others, like Richard Rorty, find in his work a decisive pragmatist break with the traditional philosophical concerns which continued to dominate Peirce's thought.[4]

A careful comparison of these two "pragmatisms" will contribute to the understanding of both thinkers, and to an appreciation of the philosophical importance of "pragmatism." Many attempts to formulate the difference – by saying, for example, that James transformed Peirce's theory of *meaning* into a theory of *truth* – are less helpful than they at first appear. My strategy in this essay will be to begin by looking at some of Peirce's comments about James's use of pragmatism in an attempt to identify just where and why James amended his friend's doctrine.

Although Peirce is usually reported as being dismissive of James's pragmatism, his attitude was actually somewhat ambivalent. James provided a statement of his doctrine for Peirce's entry on pragmatism in Baldwin's *Dictionary of Philosophy and Psychology*. It defined pragmatism as a philosophy which claims that "the whole meaning of a concept expresses itself either in the shape of conduct to be recommended or of experience to be expected." Peirce noted that "between this definition and mine there certainly appears to be no slight theoretical divergence, which, for the most part, becomes evanescent in practice" (CP, 5.466). And, in another passage critical of James's claims about the content of his pragmatism, Peirce again concludes that "practically, his view and mine must, I think, coincide, except where he allows considerations not at all pragmatic to have weight" (CP, 5.494). So Peirce seems to have believed both that James's version of pragmatism was technically and theoretically flawed, but that "in practice" the two versions were likely to be very close. A suggestive comment is found in the following passage: "I am inclined to think that the discrepancies reside in other than the pragmatistic ingredients of our thought. If pragmatism had never been heard of, I believe the opinions of James on one side, of me on the other would have developed substantially as they have; not withstanding our respective connecting them at present with our conception of that method" (CP, 5.466).

Let me note one further point of convergence (which may illustrate the claim made in this comment). On at least two occasions,

Peirce acknowledged that his pragmatism was closely tied to James's "radical empiricism." In 1903, he called himself a "pragmatist or radical empiricist" (*CP*, 7.617); and two years later he attributed James's endorsement of pragmatism to a recognition that "his radical empiricism substantially answered to the writer's definition of pragmatism, albeit with a certain difference in the point of view" (*CP*, 5.414). If Peirce was sympathetic to radical empiricism and saw it as extremely closely tied to pragmatism, we should set against this James's insistence (in the introduction to *Pragmatism*) that "there is no logical connexion between pragmatism, as I understand it, and a doctrine which I have recently set forth as 'radical empiricism.' The latter stands on its own feet. One may entirely reject it and still be a pragmatist" (*P*, 6). In the closing sections of this paper, I shall offer some comments on this matter.

II FORMULATIONS: LOGICAL PRINCIPLE VS. PHILOSOPHICAL ATTITUDE

Peirce presented his pragmatism as a rule or method for clarifying ideas and concepts. He introduced the doctrine, without using its name, in "How to make our ideas clear" (1878). It received this classic formulation: "Consider what effects, which might conceivably have practical bearings, we conceive the object of our conception to have. Then, our conception of these effects is the whole of our conception of the object" (*CP*, 5.402). Illustrating his doctrine. Peirce clarifies what we mean by calling a thing *hard*. "Evidently that it will not be scratched by many other substances, the whole conception of this quality, as of every other, lies in its conceived effects" (*CP*, 5.403).[5] In general, we clarify a proposition by listing the experiential consequences we expect our actions to have if the proposition is true. As he later noted, it reflects an experimentalist's view of truth and inquiry (*CP*, 4.411). Applying the rule to concepts and propositions of a priori metaphysics, he concludes that these are empty; they have no cognitive "intellectual" meaning at all. Alluding to this formulation, James ascribed to Peirce the view that "to develop a thought's meaning, we need only determine what conduct it is fitted to produce: that conduct is for us its whole significance" (*P*, 29). He continued:

And the tangible fact at the root of all our thought-distinctions, however subtle, is that there is no one of them so fine as to consist in anything but a possible difference of practice. To attain perfect clearness in our thoughts of an object, then, we need only consider what conceivable effects of a practical kind the object may involve – what sensations we are to expect from it, and what reactions we must prepare. (P, 29)

Echoing Peirce, James concluded: "Our conception of those effects, whether immediate or remote, is then for us the whole of our conception of the object, so far as the conception has positive significance at all." So far, the differences seem small: each offers a rule for clarifying our thoughts; and each seeks clarification by looking at how accepting the thought would modify our practical plans and expectations.

We see that more substantial differences lie beneath the surface when James praises "pragmatism" for its "anti-intellectualism," emphasizing its links with nominalism (in its stress upon particulars) and with utilitarianism (in its emphasis upon practical factors) and identifies it with a distinctive philosophical attitude:

The attitude of looking away from first things, principles, 'categories,' supposed necessities; and of looking forward to last things, fruits, consequences, facts. (P, 32; emphasis in original)

Peirce, who repudiated "nominalism" as the source of all philosophical error, who saw a system of categories as fundamental to his philosophy, and who thought that science should be grounded through a system of philosophical architectonics, would presumably have been appalled by this philosophical outlook. Peirce saw his pragmatism as part of a philosophical system which was realist in its orientation and grounded philosophy in a system of categories; James embraced his pragmatism as a means of overcoming this conception of philosophy.

Evidence that this was Peirce's reaction is easily found. He described his pragmatism as a "logical doctrine" and a "theory of logical analysis" (CP, 6.490), claiming that he regarded it in the 1870s as "a sort of logical gospel" (CP, 6.482). "How to make our ideas clear," the essay in which it was published, belonged to a series of "Illustrations of the logic of Science": pragmatism was presented as a methodological rule, enabling us to clarify hard words and abstract concepts in order that we may inquire into the truth of theories incorporating them in a responsible and reflective manner. Commenting on later developments in pragmatism, he noted that "very few people care for logic," and remarked that the doctrine received little attention until James "remodelled the matter, and transmogrified it into a doctrine of philosophy, some parts of which I highly approved, while other and more prominent parts I regarded, and still regard, as opposed to sound logic" (CP, 6.482).

When comparing his views with those of other "pragmatists," Peirce rarely tired of pointing out that he was alone in regarding pragmatism as a part of logic. The work of other pragmatists "seems to me to be characterized by an angry hatred of strict logic, and even some disposition to regard any exact thought which interferes with their doctrines as all humbug" (CP, 6.385). Celebrating James's philosophical merits in 1911, he commented upon "his almost unexampled incapacity for mathematical thought, combined with an intense hatred for logic – probably for its pedantry, its insistence on minute exactitude" (CP, 6.182). And he attributed James's lack of ease at expressing his ideas to the fact that "rhetoric was his antipathy and logic an inconvenience to him" (CP, 6.184). If we see an acceptance of "intellectualism" and a taste for first principles as linked to an interest in logic, we can see that James saw "virtues" in pragmatism which had no place in Peirce's scheme of things. But we shall only understand these differences fully when we grasp the crucial but rather unclear difference between a logical principle and a "doctrine of philosophy."

When Peirce speaks of the "theoretical divergence" between himself and James, he generally draws attention to differences of opinion concerning which effects or consequences are relevant to the pragmatic clarification of a concept or hypothesis. This may suggest that they differ only over how the principle is to be applied in practice: a shared principle is applied with different results because of disputes about which consequences of the truth of a proposition contribute to its meaning or significance. That way of presenting things can be misleading, however, and we shall do best to begin by examining some more abstract considerations about their different philosophical aims and the role of a principle for clarifying ideas in achieving their differing philosophical aspirations.

What is involved in turning a doctrine of logic into a doctrine of philosophy? Pragmatists agree that they are recommending a technique or method for clarifying words, concepts, thoughts, ideas, hypotheses, and so forth. Techniques and methods are, presumably, adopted as means to ends: they are answerable to our purposes, evaluated in terms of how well they enable us to achieve them. Superficially similar techniques or methods may differ because they are designed as means to different ends. If James and Peirce have different aims in view in seeking a method for clarifying concepts and propositions, then it may be unsurprising if they light upon different features of their meanings or significance. When Peirce contrasts his doctrine of logic with James's doctrine of philosophy, he may intend to highlight the fact that they are adapting the shared belief that the meaning of a conception lies in its consequences to different philosophical purposes. And, since the defense of the principle must consist in showing that it serves the intended goal, there are likely to be corresponding differences in the ways in which the different versions of pragmatism are defended as well as in the ways in which they are formulated.

Methods can only be evaluated by reference to a goal or purpose: the method is judged by how well it meets its intended purpose. In that case, we would expect someone who advocates a "method for clarifying ideas" to specify the goal or end which they have in view. As we shall see, Peirce's pragmatism meets this requirement that a goal be specified. The "transmogrification" into a philosophical doctrine, which receives expression in an "attitude," may involve adopting a different cognitive goal. Peirce presents his pragmatist principle as a means to achieving a very definite goal which is closely linked to the aims of logical investigation: logic is primarily concerned with showing how we can carry out the evaluations required if we are to pursue this goal in a rational manner. James might differ in adopting a different overarching goal by reference to which pragmatism is to be judged. Alternatively – and this might fit the interpretation that finds in his work a decisive break with the philosophical tradition – he might have no very definite goal in mind. Either way, I suggest that we shall best understand these different strands in pragmatism by examining the views of Peirce and James about the goals to be met by adopting the pragmatist principle. Before doing that, however, we should try to become clear about exactly where the differences in their versions of pragmatism appear to lie.

IV "UTILITARIANISM": MEANING AND CONSEQUENCES

In a manuscript we have discussed before, Peirce noted that "[t]he most prominent of all our school and the most respected, William James, defines pragmatism as the doctrine that the whole 'meaning' of a concept expresses itself either in the shape of conduct to be recommended or of experience to be expected" (*CP*, 5.466). He immediately pointed out that "[b]etween this definition and mine there certainly appears to be no slight theoretical divergence." A major difference is expressed already in this brief definition. What could it be? All we can find in the passage is the appeal to two kinds of "effect":

    (i) Experiences to be expected.
    (ii) Conduct to be recommended.

A similar claim is found in *Pragmatism:* we are to take account of "what conceivable effects of a practical kind the object may involve – what sensations we are to expect from it, and what reactions we must prepare" (*P*, 29).

Elsewhere Peirce notes that James's definition of pragmatism "differs from mine only in that he does not restrict the 'meaning,' . . . , as I do, to a habit, but allows percepts, that is, complex feelings endowed with compulsiveness, to be such." He worries, mysteriously, that "if he is willing to do this, I do not quite see how he need give any room at all to habit" (*CP*, 5.494).

Some more passages offer illumination. Consider the following from the entry on "Pragmatism" in Baldwin's *Dictionary of Philosophy and Psychology:*

The doctrine appears to assume that the end of man is action – a stoical axiom which, to the present writer at the age of sixty, does not recommend itself so forcibly as it did at thirty. If it be admitted, on the contrary, that action wants an end, and that that end must be something of a general description, then the spirit of the maxim itself, which is that we must look to the upshot of our concepts in order rightly to apprehend them, would direct us towards something different from practical facts, namely to general ideas as the true interpreters of our thought.[6]

He concludes that the meaning of a concept does not lie in "individual reactions" but in the way in which such reactions contribute to the growth of what he calls "concrete reasonableness" (CP, 5.3). Avoiding the distraction of trying to make sense of "concrete reasonableness," we can take it that the crucial difference between the two pragmatisms is that where James simply looks for the experiences that would result if the proposition were true or the conduct one should carry out in those circumstances, Peirce looks for patterns in experience and lawlike interrelations of action and experience: our understanding of a proposition is manifested in some (possibly quite complex and almost certainly conditional) habits of expectation. Using his version of the pragmatist principle we clarify a concept or proposition by identifying the habits of expectation which are associated with it. Peirce's "consequences" are general; James allows that they may also be particular actions and perceptions – or, at least, he does not decree that they must take the form of laws and patterns ("habits").

We can bring out what this difference appears to involve by recalling James's claim that, pragmatism "agrees . . . with utilitarianism in emphasizing practical aspects" (P, 32). The clearest similarity between pragmatism and utilitarianism lies in their shared orientation toward the future. Thus, Peirce referred to "the consciousness of the future (whether veridical or not is aside from the question) in expectation, which enters into all general ideas according to my variety of pragmatism" (CP, 8.291 – from a letter to James). Pragmatism clarifies an hypothesis by listing the consequences we expect our actions to have if it is true. And the definition which James contributed to Baldwin's *Dictionary of Philosophy and Psychology* is explicitly consequentialist:

The doctrine that the whole "meaning" of a conception expresses itself in practical consequences, consequences either in the shape of conduct to be recommended, or in that of experiences to be expected, if the conception is true; which consequences would be different if it were untrue, and must be different from the consequences by which the meaning of other conceptions is in turn expressed. (See CP, 5.2)

Propositions are distinguished by the "consequences" of their being true. We clarify a proposition by investigating its "consequences"; we reject a philosophical distinction by finding no difference in the consequences of the distinguished items; and we undermine metaphysical theses by showing that they have no experiential consequences.

We can distinguish two sorts of consequentialism. The simplest holds that an action or utterance is to be evaluated according to its *actual* consequences: if an utterance is not (as a matter of fact) falsified by a surprising experience, it is true; if an action (as a matter of fact) leads to an increase in human happiness, it is good. A more sophisticated form of consequentialism appeals to possible consequences too, and insists that evaluating propositions and actions requires us to investigate counterfactual possibilities. An utterance would then be true if it *would* not be falsified in a range of possible worlds which includes, as well as the actual world, others in which inquiries are carried out more efficiently, more time is available, better instruments are to hand, and so on. And an action would be good if it would promote happiness in a range of possible situations which includes the actual one but also a number of other possibilities: a bad action can have good consequences "by accident." Peirce's remarks suggest that he regards *his* pragmatism as embodying a form of consequentialism of this second more sophisticated kind, while he finds it difficult to see how James's position differs from the kind which is content to judge actions or propositions in accord with their actual consequences.

What is at issue in Peirce's insistence upon the role of "habit"? Compare the following questions:

    I. What will I experience if *C* is true?
    II. What should I do if *C* is true?
    III. If *C* is true, what would I experience if I were to carry out action *A*?

James's formulations of his pragmatist principle suggest that we should clarify our conception *C* by asking I and II: what experiences are to be expected, what actions are to be performed? It is clear that for Peirce, III is the crucial question. III is in the subjunctive mood: our answer to it will reflect a general habit of expectation which traces systematic connections between action and experience if the conception or proposition we are trying to clarify is true. It assumes that there are facts about the consequences which possible actions (which were never carried out) *would* have had. Although appeal to such habits of expectation may have an invaluable heuristic role in forming a response to I or II, there is no *requirement* that we should approach these questions in this way. III asks for systematic connections which could easily be relevant to making predictions; I and II ask for predictions. I and II concern the actual future; an answer to III gives information about possible, nonactual futures as well as the actual future. For Peirce, the content and truth value of a proposition is a function of possible consequences as well as actual consequences. James's reference to nominalism and to utilitarianism suggests that he would disagree. This may, of course, simply reflect unclarity in presentation. But it may indicate a deeper disagreement. Does turning pragmatism into a philosophical doctrine somehow account for the different orientation we have just described? We shall discuss this below.

If this is correct, we may be able to understand Peirce's ambivalence about James's pragmatism. In practice, prediction depends upon law or generality. Our judgments of what will happen are likely to rest on habits of expectation, upon grasp of law, upon our answers to III. Even if James's pragmatism focuses on I and II rather than III and is hence, by Peirce's lights, confused, his application of his pragmatism in practice may be indistinguishable from Peirce's use of his version of the doctrine: answers to III are heuristically valuable (and often indispensible) when we try to answer I and II. It will only be in very special cases that differences will show up, cases where this heuristic approach is not the best one to employ. If this is correct, then we shall understand the roots of James's distinctive kind of pragmatism only by investigating why he does not follow Peirce in insisting that the consequences we refer to when we clarify meanings must involve general patterns. The first sentence of the quotation from Baldwin's *Dictionary* cited above suggests Peirce's view of the source of this difference: James assumed that the fundamental human end was "action" and used his principle to clarify hypotheses in the interests of efficient and successful action; Peirce's principle served a rather different end. I shall argue that, if this is his view, Peirce has misunderstood James's pragmatism. If so, it is very revealing misreading.

First, why does Peirce place so much stress upon habits and possibilities in applying his pragmatist principle? A helpful passage is:

According to . . . Pragmatism, the true meaning of any product of the intellect lies in whatever unitary determination it would impart to practical conduct under any and every conceivable circumstance, supposing such conduct to be guided by reflexion carried to an ultimate limit. (*CP*, 6.490)

According to Peirce, logic investigates the norms and methods which enable us to subject our activities to reflective self-control. His pragmatism offers a clarification of hypotheses and conceptions which will make this possible. Planning and monitoring our activities requires information about what would occur if we were to act in various ways. The subjective formulation ("it would impart") meets this need. It is characteristic of philosophy and science to embody reflective, systematic thought. The ideal "reflexion carried to an ultimate limit," the extreme of rational self-monitoring and self-control sets the tone for much of his later writings. This can be seen in three areas of his work.

Theory and practice

Shortly after the publication of James's *The Will to Believe* and his endorsement of pragmatism in "Philosophical Conceptions and Practical Results," Peirce delivered some lectures in Cambridge, Massachusetts, recently published as *Reasoning and the Logic of Things* (1992). In the first of these, he launched an attack on the idea that philosophy and logical reflection had much to offer with respect to "vital questions" and to matters of practical ethics and the like. Drawing a sharp distinction between scientific questions and practical matters, he urged that theory, logic, and "reflexion" had little or nothing to contribute to the latter. His "conservatism" called upon us to rely upon sentiment or common sense in seeking answers to such problems, denouncing it as a treason against reason to use reflective self-control in trying to answer vital questions.

If pragmatism is a technique of reflective self-control, and if instinct is more important than reflection in responding to vital matters, pragmatism will not have much of a role in dealing with practical matters. The distinctive character of Peirce's pragmatism depends upon a view about the scope of reflective thought: it offers a clarification which is to be valuable where reflection has a fundamental role and is not intended for use in other areas of life.[7] The only "consequences" of a concept or proposition which are "pragmatically relevant" will then be those which are pertinent to "reflective inquiry"; aspects of meaning which are of importance in attempting to answer "vital" questions need not be taken into account.

Reflection and the method of science

For Peirce, the scientific method of inquiry rests upon a distinctive assumption. This is the view that there are "real things," which are entirely independent of our opinions about them but which affect our senses in regular law-governed ways (*CP*, 5.384). If we carry out our inquiries correctly, then we shall eventually discover their properties. Scientific inquiry employs rules and methods which can be defended by reference to this underlying assumption. Specific logical procedures (for example, rules of statistical inference) are justified by showing how they contribute to the discovery of laws and other truths about realities. The method of science can be self-consciously adopted only by someone who identifies himself, or herself, with the wider scientific community. An individual's research is of value only for the contribution it makes to the progress toward the truth of the wider scientific community. This identification with the wider community is, for Peirce, one way of achieving a rational and fulfilling life; it is the only kind of life which is compatible with logical reflection taken to the utmost.[8]

If we have this "realist" conception of the concerns of science and our aim is to formulate and test hypotheses, hoping to reach the truth about the laws governing the universe, then, when we clarify such an hypothesis, we are looking for guidance with topics like experimental design and for help with decisions about how best to organize our inquiries. We need to consider different possible courses of action and to know what experiences we should expect from each: we need to know what would happen in a variety of different possible circumstances. We are interested in the habits of expectation that go with the truth of the hypothesis. Peirce's version of pragmatism accords with his view that it is an aid to scientific testing, that scientific reasoning is the only sort which is compatible with full rational reflection and a view of science which might be described as "realist."

The concern of science is with seeking the explanations of regularities and patterns in our experience. Although we may not now possess the truth on all matters, science possesses a method which will enable us to free ourselves of error and to contribute to progress and an increase in understanding. A proposition is true if anyone who inquires into its truth-value long enough and well enough is fated eventually to recognize that it is true (of course, this does not apply strictly to the vague propositions which are pervasive in the sciences, but Peirce's logic of vagueness is supposed to provide the necessary qualifications.⁹ Logic provides the materials required to contribute to science efficiently and reflectively. Clarifying hypotheses using the pragmatist principle provides all of the information about their meanings that we need to achieve ultimate reflectiveness. And this must include information about the experiences that would be expected if different courses of action or different experiments were undertaken. Science requires reflective self-control; Peircean logic serves such self-controlled inquiry; and the pragmatist principle reveals the aspects of meaning which are relevant to this task.

Ethics

Peirce's work in ethics is motivated by a desire to explain the possibility of adopting the life of science as he understands it. According to Peirce, the ethical good is to possess an ultimate aim, an overarching goal for conduct which gives meaning to one's activities. Such goals are tested by investigating whether they can be sustained come what may, that is, that they can provide a principle of integration for the self in any circumstance that can arise. The reflective self is thus required to examine what it would be like to live by his envisaged goal in a variety of counterfactual circumstances: "reflexion carried to an ultimate limit" calls for thought about a variety of possible futures. According to Peirce, responsible reflective adoption of an ultimate ideal requires a clear grasp of what it would commit us to, and what it would be like to try to live by it, in any possible circumstance. It is not enough that it *will* give us a satisfying life. We need to reassure ourselves that it would do so in other possible circumstances (*CP*, 5.130–2). Once again, we see that reflection and self-control require information about laws and general patterns, information about what we would experience and how we would react in counterfactual possibilities. And we see how Peirce's work is driven by a metaphysical picture, by the aspiration to a kind of ultimate reflective self-control which renders our lives, in a sense, risk free.

VI JAMES'S PRAGMATISM

As we have just explained, Peirce's pragmatism is a technique defended because it helps us to inquire responsibly and well into the truths of nature: it serves a specified role, and, indeed, not a strictly philosophical one. Logic, a branch of philosophy, tells us that scientists would do well to use the principle when planning their inquiries; and metaphysicians should rely upon it if they wish to apply the method of science in their metaphysics. If James's pragmatism is to have a distinctively "philosophical" cast, it must occupy a different role, meeting intellectual needs which are internal to philosophy. His texts support this view: he presents pragmatism as a device for identifying the worth of philosophical proposals and eliminating merely verbal debates.

In that case, we might suppose, James should identify the "aim" of philosophy and then defend the principle by showing that it provides the best means to achieving that aim. Peirce, as we have seen, suggested that pragmatism as James envisaged it was intended to enable us to act successfully – and, presumably, thought that James expected philosophy to satisfy that aim too. This would account for the "transmogrification" into a doctrine of philosophy. If this is what is going on, however, it is a little surprising that James refers to his pragmatism as an "attitude." Moreover, when he presents the doctrine in *Pragmatism*, the discussion is not accompanied by a general statement of what the goal of philosophy is. Pragmatism is not defended by showing that it meets some independently identifiable goals. It is defended, rather, by showing how it enables us to resolve a variety of otherwise interminable disputes. It is plausible that James does not have a clearly formulated statement of the goal of philosophy. Indeed, it would conflict with many aspects of his outlook to think that we could have one. At best, he has a second-order view, a view about the sorts of aims that responsible philosophical inquiries can have. We may put it thus: a philosophical position is respectable only if it makes a detectable contribution to the realization of purposes and aspirations whose achievement could be apparent from experience. As he would later say in defining his radical empiricism: "the only things that shall be debatable among philosophers shall be things definable in terms drawn from experience" (MT, 6). For James, pragmatism is a proposal which is vindicated in a range of areas of application by its varied fruits. For Peirce, on the other hand, it is a technique which is to be defended by showing that it helps us to achieve a definite purpose: making scientific progress.

An example will help us to sharpen the difference between Peirce and James. We shall present some of James's "pragmatist" remarks on the concept of freedom and consider how Peirce would react to them. For James, the question of freedom does not revolve around the possibility of self-control, of taking responsibility for our actions. Nor is it primarily a question of accountability: our instinctive and customary practices of praise and blame would not be touched by a victory for either side in the dispute – not least because it is hard to see how we can be blamed for our actions which are not (in some way) determined. The appeal of the doctrine of free will lies in its allowing for *"novelties in the world"*: it is a "melioristic doctrine," a doctrine of "relief" or "promise." It holds up improvement as at least possible; whereas determinism assures us that our whole notion of possibility is born of human ignorance, and that necessity and impossibility between them rule the destinies of the world (P, 59–61). James's suggestion seems to be that "intellectually" ("cognitively"?) free will is an empty doctrine, but the believer in free will is thereby enabled to sustain a kind of optimism: all is well with the world and things can get better:

Pragmatism alone can read a positive meaning into [Free Will and other "theological" notions], and for that she turns her back upon the intellectualist point of view altogether. "God's in his heaven and all's right with the world!' – *That's* the real heart of your theology, and for that you need no rationalist definitions. (P, 62)

James's pragmatism displays the role in our lives of belief in free will, it shows what this means to us and explains why we should not regard it as a quasi-scientific or cognitive claim. The believer will act differently and form different vague expectations: the "proposition" makes a difference. That it is a noncognitive "difference" should not lead us to condemn those who defend freedom of the will. Rather, recognizing this makes possible a positive appreciation of what such belief provides. Once we have this clear grasp of its role, we will lose the temptation to criticize it for failing to be what it blatantly is not. Pragmatism enables us to appreciate the force of something whose role is not narrowly "cognitive."

For Peirce, by contrast, pragmatism can help us to see whether the hypothesis has a scientific meaning. If so, it can be tested within one of the special sciences or within a system of metaphysics which employs the scientific method. If not, then the concept has no place within a scientific philosophy, which means that it has no place within philosophy at all.[10] He does hold that we are required to *hope* that we possess free will, because, without it, self-control and reflection carried to the ultimate will be an illusion. But this calls for a metaphysical or cosmological account of the possibility of freedom, of the possibility of responsible, ultimate, rational self-control.

Thus we can see that James and Peirce employed their differing versions of pragmatism for rather different purposes. And this will have important implications both for what the principle requires of them when they try to use their principles to clarify problematic concepts and for the styles of argument which become appropriate when they defend their views. It also means that their doctrines stand in rather different relations to the concept of truth. Each will use his pragmatism to arrive at a clear perspicuous representation of what truth involves. But while Peirce's pragmatism is answerable to the needs of a project (scientific inquiry) which already uses a substantive conception of truth, James's doctrine is not so answerable. His pragmatism has application at a stage of inquiry where the nature of truth and the role of the concept in our activities is still problematic.

VII NOMINALISM AND RADICAL EMPIRICISM

In the first section, we noted Peirce's avowal of "radical empiricism" and his suggestion that "radical empiricism" and "pragmatism" were equivalent. This seemed surprising in light of James's insistence, in the preface to *Pragmatism*, that "there is no logical connexion between pragmatism, as I understand it, and a doctrine which I have recently set forth as 'radical empiricism'." I lack the space to adjudicate the matter and we should note that Peirce is not alone in seeing close connections between these doctrines.[11] My aim in this section is to show that the account of the differences between the pragmatisms of Peirce and James which has been offered in this paper enables us to make sense of their different attitudes to this issue. Had he not accepted something close to radical empiricism, Peirce would have had to give up his pragmatism. James is not in the same position.[12]

The clearest formulation of "radical empiricism" is in the preface to *The Meaning of Truth*. It involves a postulate or recommendation that "the only things that shall be debatable among philosophers shall be things definable in terms drawn from experience." In addition it embraces the "fact" that "the relations between things, conjunctive as well as disjunctive, are just as much matters of direct particular experience, neither more or nor less so, than the things themselves." And the conclusion to be drawn from this is that "the parts of experience hold together from next to next by relations that are themselves parts of experience." The elements of experience are not connected by us. Experience itself possesses "a concatenated or continuous structure" (*MT*, 6–7). The important point is that experience itself is richer than earlier atomistic forms of empiricism had allowed.

When James asserted that pragmatism was independent of his radical empiricism, he can hardly have intended to deny that a pragmatist is committed to the "postulate" that the only issues for debate among philosophers concerned items definable in terms of experience. A pragmatist who rejected radical empiricism would, presumably, deny that relations among experienced items were experienced: pragmatic clarification would then display a more austere world than James presents to our view. The argument for pragmatism rests upon the hope that interminable debates be avoided; it does not rest upon any claims about the structure of experience, although acceptance of the position may make us more sensitive to its complexities.

As we have noticed, and as he often insisted, Peirce described himself as a realist. We have knowledge of a world of realities which exists independently of us. And there are objective modal facts about what experience we *would* have enjoyed had we been differently placed or acted differently. This requires there to be real connections between actual and possible objects of experience which can be known by us. When I discuss what is "possible," I do not necessarily intend to make a point about my epistemic position: to say that something is possible is not just to say that it is the case for all I know. When I claim that had I overslept this morning I would have missed the bus to work, I make an objective claim about "would-be's," about other possible worlds. The laws that ground assertions about what could occur and what would have occurred do not simply describe regularities between distinct events. Instead, they describe fundamental truths about the connections between events: the laws explain or mediate the sequences of events which we experience. When Peirce insisted that his pragmatism would never have entered the mind of anyone who did not accept "realism" rather than nominalism, this was the point at issue. He risked refutation through a demonstration that his pragmatist principle *used* concepts – those linked to the objectivity of "would be's" – which would be dismissed as metaphysical if we tried to clarify them by using the pragmatist principle.

When Peirce tried to meet these challenges by insisting that mediation, law, and external things are directly present in experience, he agreed with James in insisting that experience is richer than earlier empiricists had supposed. And when he argued that law and mediation were present in experience through our experience of real *continuity*, the connections with radical empiricism are very strong indeed. Moreover, he thought that unless experience was continuous, so that we were directly aware of temporal ordering within it, we could have no concept of time or any answer to Zeno's paradox. Thus unless we experience real continua, Peirce thought, his realism was indefensible and his pragmaticism was fatally flawed. And if science used concepts which could not be clarified using the pragmatist principle, it was pragmatism that would have to be abandoned.

VIII JAMES, SCIENCE, AND REALISM

James and Peirce have rather different views of science and of modal notions such as possibility and necessity. Unlike the mature Peirce,

James often espoused a subjective or epistemic account of possibility: this term is applied to things of the conditions of whose coming to be we are (to some degree at least) ignorant (*SPP*, 113). Dismissing our unreflective tendency to view possibility as a distinctive ontological status ("a sort of third estate of being, less real than existence, more real than non-existence" [*P*, 136]), he treats something being possible as consisting in a "lack of anything extant capable of preventing" it and in the existence of conditions of its production. A possible chicken involves an absence of small boys and other enemies and the existence of an egg (*P*, 136). This is not Peirce's mature opinion.

James might have been describing Peirce when he spoke of those who are "so carried away by the clearness, beauty and simplification that resulted that they believed themselves to have deciphered authentically the eternal thoughts of the almighty" (*P*, 33). In contrast, James insists that theories are only "a man-made language, a conceptual shorthand . . . in which we write our reports of nature: their great use is to summarize old facts and to lead to new ones." Theory choice involves "human arbitrariness" which appears to undermine any realist understanding of law and theoretical truth: James happily embraces the claim that theories, when true, are true "instrumentally." They bring us into a satisfactory relation with experience.

If all of this is correct, we can appreciate the force of Peirce's claim that the fundamental differences between the "pragmatisms" of Peirce and James reflect differences elsewhere in their thought. It is wrong to interpret James as misreading or misunderstanding Peirce's pragmatic maxim. Rather, he seized its fundamental insight about meaning, consequences, and the future, and employed it in the service of a different set of philosophical aims and a contrasting conception of science and its aims.

NOTES

1 In 1905, Peirce actually distinguished his pragmaticism from "practicalism." His point is to reject the Kantian doctrine that the ideas of practical reason have a regulative role in scientific or theoretical discourse. The only concepts used in science, he insisted, were those occurring in what Kant called "pragmatic beliefs," those concerned with anticipating the future run of experience (*CP*, 5.412). This rejection of "practicalism" need not conflict with this Jamesean claim.

2 Although Peirce here seems confident of his role in the origin of pragmatism, his 1900 letter to James requesting help with his entry for Baldwin's dictionary asks "Who originated the word *pragmatism*, I or you? Where did it first appear in print?" James's reply acknowledged that it was Peirce's term (*CP*, 8.253).

3 References to *The Collected Papers of Charles Sanders Peirce* are all given in this standard form. *CP*, 6.482 refers to numbered section 482 of volume 6.

4 See his suggestion that Peirce contributed no more than a name to pragmatism in Rorty 1982, 161.

5 A more detailed discussion of Peirce's pragmatism with further examples is in Hookway 1985, chapter 8.

6 Note how the first sentence of this quotation illustrates how Peirce viewed his methodological principle in means-ends terms. Permitting particular perceptions or actions to count as the "effects" which are elaborated when the pragmatist principle is applied can be understood only if application of the principle is understood as a means to achieving clarity about how we should *act*.

7 One passage which may conflict with this is found in the first lecture on *Pragmatism*, delivered at Harvard in 1903. Having noted that pragmatism is valuable in all the sciences as well as in philosophy, Peirce noted that "My want of skill in practical affairs does not prevent me from perceiving the advantage of being well imbued with pragmatism in the conduct of life" (*CP*, 5.14).

8 How Peirce argues for the set of views and what is involved in adopting the method of science are large questions which go beyond the scope of this paper. For further discussion, see Hookway 1993.

9 This qualification is important since it brings out the idealization involved in Peirce's claims about truth: unforced consensus among conscientious inquirers is assured only for propositions which have a definite content; but Peirce acknowledges that all the propositions actually used in science are vague. Meanings are developed and refined as inquiry proceeds and there is no guarantee (or requirement) that all inquirers do this in the same way. See Hookway 1990.

10 We can illustrate the difference between the two friends – albeit with an element of exaggeration – by considering the attitudes each would take to the themes of "The will to believe." Peirce and James would agree that where "intellectual methods" (reflection and the method of science) cannot settle a live or vital question, then we should rely upon sentiment (or the passions). But where we can read this as consonant with James's pragmatism, the answer being justified by the effect it has on conduct, Peirce argues that such issues are outside the scope of the

sort of rational logical self control within which his pragmatism finds a home.

11 The chapter on James in Flower and Murphey 1977 finds a closer connection between pragmatism and radical empiricism than James does.

12 There is a question about how far Peirce understood James's doctrine of radical empiricism. I shall not explore that here.

9   James's theory of truth

The pronouncements on the nature of truth in *Pragmatism* evoked howls of indignation (e.g., Russell 1945) as well as exaggerated praise. The howls (and some of the praise) came from readers who thought that James identified truth as whatever it gives us "satisfaction" to believe: the critics believed that this amounted to irrationalism, while the enthusiasts thought that the idea that truth is jibing with reality *deserves* to be abandoned (Rorty 1982), and the Italian pragmatist Giovanni Papini thought that irrationalism is a good thing (Perry 1935, 2:570–9).

The howlers and the enthusiasts were careless readers, however. They virtually ignored what James wrote about truth elsewhere. But it is not easy to say in a few words what James *did* think about truth, for, as I shall argue, James's view developed in complicated ways as he worked out his metaphysical system. In the present essay, I isolate the elements in James's theory of truth and show how they were linked by James's metaphysics of radical empiricism.

Here is a rough outline: I shall first describe two strains in James's thought: (1) A Peircean strain (as we shall see, this strain is quite strong, but James's critics ignore it). (2) The *un*-Peircean idea that truth is partly shaped by our interests. After that, I examine two more strains which reflect the metaphysics of radical empiricism, even though in *Pragmatism* James (unsuccessfully) attempted to avoid presupposing it. These are (3) a realist strain, summed up in the claim that truth involves agreement with reality, although that agreement is not one single relation, and (4) an empiricist strain, summed up in the claim that "truth *happens* to an idea." I also describe the way in which these strains reappear in the *Meaning of Truth*. My purpose here is almost entirely exegetical; nevertheless, I shall close with a brief comment on James's theory.

I THE PEIRCEAN STRAIN

Peirce famously defined truth as "the opinion which is fated to be ultimately agreed to by all who investigate" (5.407).[1] In spite of the many undeniable differences between James's metaphysical system and Peirce's, variants of this definition abound in James's writing.

They appear long before *Pragmatism*. In the concluding paragraph of the relatively early (1878) "Remarks on Spencer's Definition of Mind as Correspondence," we find the characteristically Jamesean idea that human beings "help to create" truth combined with the Peircean idea that the true judgments are the ones that we are fated to believe, not at any given instant, but in the long run, on the basis of "the total upshot of experience." Let us look at this passage closely. Here is how the paragraph opens:

> I, for my part, cannot escape the consideration forced upon me at every turn, that the knower is not simply a mirror floating with no foot-hold anywhere, and passively reflecting an order that he comes upon and finds simply existing. The knower is an actor, and coefficient of the truth on one side, whilst on the other he registers the truth which he helps to create. Mental interests, hypotheses, postulates, insofar as they are bases for human action – action which to a great extent transforms the world – help to *make* the truth which they declare. (*EPh*, 21)

Here the idea that we help to make the truth is spelled out in an innocuous way: our actions partially determine what will happen, and hence what will be true of the world. (In his later writings James will propose a more controversial sense in which we help to make truth.) But James is not primarily thinking of historical truth even here. For he immediately raises the question whether "judgments of the *should-be*" can correspond to reality and responds by declaring that this possibility should not be ruled out:

We know so little about the ultimate nature of things, or of ourselves, that it would be sheer folly dogmatically to say that an ideal rational order may not be real. The only objective criterion of reality is coerciveness, in the long run, over thought. . . . By its very essence, the reality of a thought is proportionate to the way it grasps us. Its intensity, its seriousness – its interest, in a word – taking these qualities, not at any given instant, but as shown by the total upshot of experience. If judgments of the *should-be* are fated to grasp us in this way they are what "correspond." The ancients placed the conception of Fate at the bottom of things – deeper than the gods themselves. "The fate of thought," utterly barren and indeterminate as such a formula is, is the only unimpeachable regulative Law of Mind. (*EPh*, 21–2)

Although "the reality of a thought" is an unfortunate expression, James is not here confusing how a thought "grabs" us with the reality of things external to us ("the objective criterion of reality" in the sense of the criterion for something's *being real*). What he means is that the criterion for something's being real is precisely that we are fated in the long run to believe that it is – that the belief that it is real – where the "it" may be something as large as "an ideal moral order" – exhibits "coerciveness over thought."

Nor did Peirce himself fail to appreciate the measure of both agreement and disagreement. Hence the curiously grudging tone of the following:

In the first place, there is the definition of James, whose definition differs from mine only in that he does not restrict the "meaning," that is the ultimate logical interpretant, as I do, to a habit, but allows percepts, that is, complex feelings endowed with compulsiveness, to be such. If he is willing to do this, I do not quite see how he need give any room at all to habit. But practically, his view and mine must, I think, coincide, except where he allows considerations not at all pragmatic to have weight. (5.494)

Peirce refers to James's interpretation of the pragmatic maxim (which James states in *P*, 28–9)[2] and the reservation is occasioned by the fact that James allows "[an idea's] intensity, its seriousness – its interest, in a word" to have weight.

It is true that on Peirce's view interests also have a role in determining the truth. For Peirce himself writes that the ultimate aim of inquiry is a finished knowledge, which we are to approach in the limit but never actually achieve and which will have an "aesthetic quality" that will be a "free development of the agent's own aesthetic quality" and will, at the same time, match the "aesthetic quality" of "the ultimate action of experience upon him" (5.136). However, Peirce supposes that all rational inquirers will share this "ultimate aim," while James believes that more practical and more immediate aims and sentiments must also play a role in determining what the "ultimate consensus" will be.

Moreover, the sense in which Peirce and James think of our "interests" or our "ultimate aim" as *determining* truth is complex. For both James and Peirce truth is a property of beliefs or judgments, and without thinkers there are no beliefs to be true or false. In that sense, both Peirce and James can agree that being interested in having true beliefs determines whether there will be truth. Moreover, our various interests determine what inquiries we shall pursue, what concepts we will find useful, and so on; that is, they determine *which* truths there will be. But James is willing to draw radical consequences from this last idea, consequences Peirce is not willing to draw because of his scholastic realism, his belief that ultimately only those concepts survive that correspond to real Thirds. The element in James's thought that Peirce objected to is clearly expressed in "The Sentiment of Rationality." There James writes:

> ... of two conceptions equally fit to satisfy the logical demand, that one which awakens the active impulses, or satisfies other aesthetic demands better than the other, will be accounted the more rational conception, and will deservedly prevail. ...
>
> ... a thorough-going interpretation of the world in terms of mechanical sequence is compatible with its being interpreted teleologically, for the mechanism itself may be designed.
>
> If, then, there were several systems excogitated, equally satisfying to our purely logical needs, they would still have to be passed in review, and approved or rejected by our aesthetic and practical nature. (*WB*, 66)

But the disagreement – and it is very important – over just this claim of James's should not obscure the fact that James, like Peirce, declares his allegiance to a notion of truth *defined in terms of ultimate consensus*.

But, one might object, the reason that the community of inquirers will agree on a certain opinion in the long run is that the opinion is *true*. "Consensus theory of truth" suggests the reverse, that the opinion to which the community of inquirers will agree in the long run is true because they agree on it. Surely neither Peirce nor James would say that! The answer is that it is virtually a conceptual truth for both Peirce and James that the long-run opinion of those who inquire, the opinion that they are "fated" to hold, is the true one. This is their *constitutive* account of truth. But neither James nor

Peirce thinks that the community of inquirers can simply *decide* what the long-run opinion is to be; both stress how tightly we are coerced by both reality and the body of previous belief.

Any comparison of James with Peirce must face two difficult exegetical questions, however. (1) Although Peirce in places does speak of "the opinion which is fated to be ultimately agreed to by all who investigate," he later glosses this as the opinion which we *would* converge to *if* inquiry were indefinitely continued (5.494). Would James accept a similar modification? And (2) Peirce insists that the convergence to the final opinion which is formulated by a true belief be determined by an "external permanency" (he also writes "by nothing human"). Would James agree?

With respect to the first question, I shall argue that James is talking about an ultimate convergence to be actually, not just counterfactually, brought about. But I shall postpone this discussion until we have examined what James says about truth in *Pragmatism*.

The second question is somewhat easier. Contrary to some misreaders, James *does* insist that a truth must put us in ("fruitful") contact with a reality (*MT*, 104–7). This strain in James's thought is termed (by him) his "epistemological realism," and Perry admits that his famous work "largely ignores" it (Perry 1935, 2:591). Early and late James speaks of "agreement" with reality and even (as in the passage quoted above) of "correspondence" (although he also insists that correspondence is a notion that must be *explained*, not one that can simply function as the *explanation* of the notion of truth (*P*, 96). However, James also thinks that what kinds of contact with realities will count as "fruitful" depends on our "aesthetic and practical nature." Thus James rejects both the view that agreement with reality is not required for truth and the Peircean view that our convergence to certain beliefs will be forced on us "by nothing human."

While these differences from Peirce are certainly momentous, the points of agreement should not be missed. They share the idea of truth as a final opinion to be converged to and determined (although not, in James's case, exclusively determined) by reality.

The 1878 formulation of what I shall call "James's ultimate consensus theory of truth" that I quoted earlier and the discussion of the objectivity of moral value in "The Sentiment of Rationality" (1879) were written long *before* James arrived at his metaphysics of radical empiricism, which was first published in a series of eleven articles that appeared in 1903–4. (These essays, plus one other, were posthumously published as *Essays in Radical Empiricism*. In "The Will to Believe" (1896) truth is also defined as "the total drift of thinking" (WB, 24). By 1906, however, the metaphysics of radical empiricism was worked out to his satisfaction, as was his answer to Royce's claim that pragmatism cannot account for reference to objects outside the mind (Royce 1969, 321–53; this should be read in the light of 1969, 681–709), and the complex architecture of *Pragmatism* reflects the fact that James was now working from within a rich framework of metaphysical ideas. Particularly relevant is the fact that James now distinguishes between "half truths" – the statements we accept at a given time as our best posits – and "absolute truths." The passage in which the distinction is drawn is difficult to interpret – I shall examine it closely in the course of this essay – but as James later explains it in *The Meaning of Truth*, the claim is that we *do* attain absolute truth, although we can never guarantee that we do; and James posits that pragmatism itself is absolutely true. In *The Meaning of Truth*, absolute truth is characterized by James as membership in an "ideal set" of "formulations" on which there will be "ultimate consensus" (MT, 143–4) – yet another Peircean formulation.[3]

II JAMES ON "AGREEMENT WITH REALITY"

Pragmatism is deliberately popular in style, so much so that both Royce (who disagreed with James) and Bergson (who largely agreed) hinted that it might be misunderstood (Royce 1971, 511) and Barzun 1983, 107). The lectures which it contains describe pragmatism as a "method" in philosophy, and also more narrowly as "a theory of truth"; yet there is nothing one could call a "definition of truth." James's response to Russell, who read James as attempting to give a necessary and sufficient condition for truth, beautifully characterizes the essence of Russell's approach as well as illustrating James's own style of thought:

A mathematical term, such as *a*, *b*, *c*, *x*, *y*, sin, log, is self-sufficient, and terms of this sort, once equated, can be substituted for one another in endless series without error. Mr. Russell . . . seem(s) to think that in our mouth also such terms as "meaning," "truth," "belief," "object," "definition" are self-sufficients with no context of varying relations that might be further asked about. What a word means is expressed by its definition, isn't it? The definition claims to be exact and adequate, doesn't it? Then it can be substituted for the word – since the two are identical – can't it? Then two words with the same definition can be substituted for one another, *n'est-ce pas?* Likewise two definitions of the same word, *nicht wahr*, etc., till it will be indeed strange if you can't convict someone of self-contradiction and absurdity. (*MT,* 148)

Instead of offering a rigorous definition of truth of this kind, the discussion in *Pragmatism* proceeds by means of a number of examples.

In *Pragmatism* two ideas are stressed: (1) truth is agreement with a reality or realities and (2) "truth *happens* to an idea. It *becomes* true, is *made* true by events" (*P,* 97).

James begins his discussion by asking what "agreement" and "reality" mean, in the dictionary definition, when applied to the statement that a true idea is one that "agrees" with reality (*P,* 96). James writes:

In answering these questions, the pragmatists are more analytic and painstaking, the intellectualists more offhand and irreflective. The popular notion is that a true idea must copy its reality. Like other popular views, this one follows the analogy of the most usual experience. Our true ideas of sensible things do indeed copy them.[4]

Shut your eyes, and think of yonder clock on the wall, and you get such a true picture or copy of its dial. But your idea of its works, unless you are a clockmaker, is much less of a copy, and yet it passes muster.... Even though it [your idea of the works] should shrink to the mere word "works," that word still serves you truly. And when you speak of the "timekeeping function" of the clock, or of its spring's "elasticity," it is hard to see exactly what your ideas can copy.

Here we have the idea of a range of cases of which copying is simply one extreme. The idea that it is empty to think of reference as *one* relation is also a central insight of Wittgenstein's; but, without slighting Wittgenstein, one must point out that James already said that here.

James also says something about verification here (*P,* 97): *True ideas are those that we can assimilate, validate, corroborate, and verify. False ideas are those that we cannot.* But James at once points out that that "general statement" is itself vague: "But what do the words verification and validation themselves signify? They again signify certain practical consequences of the verified and validated idea. It is hard to find any one phrase that characterizes these consequences better than the ordinary agreement formula – just such consequences being what we have in mind when we say that our ideas 'agree' with reality. . . . Such an account is vague and it sounds at first quite trivial, but it has consequences which it will take the rest of my hour to explain" (P, 98).

I will examine this lecture ("Pragmatism's Conception of Truth") more closely in Section III. But first I want to look at a passage in *Essays in Radical Empiricism*, where the point that there is not one single relation between an idea (*any* idea) and what it is about is elaborated with the aid of the metaphysics of radical empiricism:

Suppose me to be sitting here in my library at Cambridge, at ten minutes' walk from "Memorial Hall," and to be thinking truly of the latter object. My mind may have before it only the name, or it may have a clear image, or it may have a very dim image of the hall, but such an intrinsic difference in the image makes no difference to its cognitive function. Certain *extrinsic* phenomena, special experiences of conjunction, are what impart to the image, be it what it may, its knowing office.

For instance, if you ask me what hall I mean by my image, and I can tell you nothing; or if I fail to point, or lead you towards the Harvard Delta; or if being led by you I am uncertain whether the hall I see be what I had in mind or not; you would rightly deny that I had "meant" that particular hall at all, even though my mental image might to some degree have resembled it. The resemblance would count in that case as coincidental merely. For all sorts of things of a kind resemble one another in this world, without being held for that reason to take cognizance of one another. (38–9)

In short, mere resemblance never *suffices* for truth. It is what we do with our "images" that makes the difference. "[I]f I can lead you to the hall, and tell you of its history and present uses, if in its presence I feel my idea, however imperfect it may have been, to have led hither, and to be now *terminated*; if the associates of the image and of the felt hall run parallel, so each term of the one corresponds serially as I walk with an answering term of the other; why then my soul was prophetic and my idea must be, and by common consent would be, called cognizant of reality. The percept was what I *meant*, for into it my idea has passed by conjunctive experiences of sameness and fulfilled intention. Nowhere is there a jar, but every moment continues and corroborates an earlier one."

These remarks on the ways ideas correspond to reality presuppose the notion of "conjunctive experiences." (James also speaks of "conjunctive relations," but, according to radical empiricism, relations too are directly experienced.) The most striking aspect of James's radical empiricism is its intention to be close to "natural realism" (ERE, 63ff.). In perception I am *directly acquainted* with external reality – indeed, to speak of my "sensations" and to speak of the external realities the sensations are "of" is to speak of the same bits of "pure experience," counted "twice over" (with two different "contexts"). I have argued that James was the first post-Cartesian philosopher to completely reject the idea that perception requires *intermediaries* (Putnam 1990 and 1994b).

However, James subscribed to the slogan *esse est percipii*. Since one is directly acquainted with reality, impressions are not simply in the mind, and since *esse est percipii*, then all there is are these impressions that are *not* simply in the mind. No doubt, that is why James does not call them "impressions" but "pure experience." Reality just *is* the flux of "pure experience."

In addition, James held that concepts always "build out" the bits of pure experience they describe. For that reason, direct acquaintance is not *infallible*.[5] Even if I see something that looks just like a clock's face, it may turn out that my belief is mistaken – I may be looking at a *trompe l'oeil* painting.

Nevertheless, a vital *part* – if never all – of the "agreement with reality" that James speaks of is verification by direct acquaintance with external realities; and James lashes out at his critics for ignoring this (MT, 104–7). Speaking to what he calls the "fourth misunderstanding" of pragmatism ("No pragmatist can be a realist in his epistemology"), he writes, "The pragmatist calls satisfactions indispensible for truth-building, but I have everywhere called them insufficient unless reality be also incidentally led to. . . . Ideas are so much flat psychological surface (*sic*) unless some mirrored matter gives them cognitive lustre. This is why as a pragmatist I have so carefully postulated 'reality' *ab intitio*, and why, throughout my whole discussion, I remain an epistemological realist" (MT, 106).

Ideas which have not yet been verified may also agree with reality. As we have just seen (ERE, 38–9), James takes the relevant relation(s) to be "conjunctive relations";[6] and as we said, such relations are *given in experience*. The relevant relations are precisely the ones that constitute verifications. The idea that there are elm trees in a certain forest may, for example, be "directly verified" in the future by going to the forest and seeing the elm trees. The fact that the idea "led me" to the elm trees and "terminated in" that direct acquaintance of the elm trees constitutes its "agreement" with the elm trees.

An idea that was never directly verified may also agree with a reality by "substituting" for it (*ERE*, 31–3); for example, the belief that the couch in my office was there at 3AM last Sunday morning leads to as successful a prediction as if I had directly verified it. Compare this with the statement that "Truth lives for the most part on a credit system. Our thoughts and beliefs 'pass', so long as nothing challenges them, just as bank-notes pass so long as nobody refuses them. But this all points to direct face-to-face verifications somewhere, without which the fabric of truth collapses like a financial system with no cash basis whatever" (*P*, 100). Summing up all these sorts of "agreement," James writes, "to 'agree' in the widest sense with a reality *can only mean to be guided straight up to it or into its surroundings, or to be put into such working touch with it as to handle either it or something connected with it better than if we had disagreed. Better either intellectually or practically!" (*P*, 102).

This account of "agreement" led James to link truth to verificatory experiences, and it is necessary to see why James felt constrained to adopt it. James was a direct realist about perception, but not about *conception*. The relation of our concepts to whatever they are said to "agree with" or "refer to" can only be a matter of external relations, according to James. "The pointing of our thought to the tigers is known simply and solely as a procession of mental associates and motor consequences that follow on the thought, and that would lead harmoniously, if followed out, into some ideal or real context, or even into the immediate presence, of the tigers themselves" (*EPh*, 74). Philosophers who think that our ideas possess intrinsic intentionality, he insists, are simply wrong. In the same passage, he even makes the significant slip of equating "our ideas" with mental images: "There is no self-transcendency in our mental images taken by themselves" (*EPh*, 74). (Recall his claim that in the absence of "mirrored matter" ideas are just "flat psychological surface.") Thus, it is *the search for external relations that constitute reference* that leads James to seek particular "conjunctive relations" that can be *observed* to connect our ideas with what they are about.

But this is not the only possible way to think of conception.

Philosophers – and I am one of them – who reject what I have called the "interface conception of conception,"[7] agree that conception frequently involves words and images. But we insist that the words and images which we use in thought are not "flat psychological surface" to which an interpretation has to be added. Words in use are not mere noises, and mental images are profoundly unlike physical images. But the issues are deep, and I do not have space to pursue them here. To round out my account of James's notion of "agreement with reality," I shall instead make two further remarks.

(1) James recognizes that not all of our concepts refer to sensible realities. Unlike the positivists, James was willing to count the objects of "non-perceptual experiences," if their existence should be confirmed, as on an ontological par with the things we can observe by means of the senses (ERE, 10). For example, mathematical notions, ethical notions, and religious notions are not subject to verification either by direct experience or by means of scientific experiments; and James is content to offer separate accounts in each case, without pretending to a single overarching theory of all possible sorts of "agreement with reality." In the case of ethics and religion, James's account is itself pluralistic.[8] In the case of religion, James finds a partial, but very imperfect, analogy between religious experience and observation (VRE) – but there are also purely intellectual factors, and there are ethical requirements, including a need for a picture of the universe that we find sympathetic. The need for trade-offs, if we are ever to find a satisfactory religious world-picture, is the subject of James's Pluralistic Universe. In the case of ethics, there is a utilitarian moment, represented by the idea that we must try to satisfy as many "demands" as possible; but there is also an anti-utilitarian moment, represented by the rejection of the idea that there is any single scale on which demands can be compared. The overriding ideal is to discover "more inclusive ideals" (R. Putnam 1990). (Here James is at his most "pluralistic.")

(2) Verification is a holistic matter, and many factors are involved, success in prediction being only one. Among the other factors that James mentions are conservation of past doctrine (P, 83), simplicity (P, 36), and coherence ("what fits every part of life best and combines with the collectivity of experience's demands, nothing being omitted" [P, 44]). James describes the fluidity of this holistic verification when he writes, "New truth is always a go-between, a smoother-

over of transitions. It marries old opinion to new fact so as to show a minimum of jolt, a maximum of continuity. We hold a theory true just in proportion to its success at solving this problem of 'maxima and minima.' But success in solving this problem is eminently a problem of approximation. We say this theory solves it on the whole more satisfactorily than that theory; but that means more satisfactorily to ourselves, and individuals will emphasize their points of satisfaction differently. To a certain degree, therefore, everything here is plastic" (P, 35). This plasticity provides the space for practical interests to cast their vote, in the way James had in mind when he wrote in the passage from "The Sentiment of Rationality" I quoted earlier, " . . . of two conceptions equally fit to satisfy the logical demand, that one which awakens the active impulses, or satisfies other aesthetic demands better than the other, will be accounted the more rational conception, and will deservedly prevail" (WB, 66).

III   "TRUTH *HAPPENS* TO AN IDEA"

Although James insisted that there is a close connection between verification and truth, he vehemently denied confounding them (MT, 108–9). How then should we understand the statement that "truth *happens* to an idea. It *becomes* true, is *made* true by events. Its verity *is* in fact an event, a process: the process namely of its verifying itself, its veri-*fication*"? (P, 97). It is wrong to take this as a conflation of truth with verification, for the following reasons:

(1) When beliefs are "made true" by the process of verification, they are made true *retroactively.* As James himself puts it:

Ptolemaic astronomy, euclidean space, aristotelian logic, scholastic metaphysics, were expedient for centuries, but human experience has now boiled over those limits, and we call those things only relatively true, or true within those borders of experience. "Absolutely" they are false; for we know that those limits were casual, and might have been transcended by past theorists just as they are by present thinkers. When new experiences lead to retrospective judgments, using the past tense, what these judgments utter *was* true, even tho no past thinker had been led there. (P, 107)

(2) Although any particular verification terminates at a time, "the process namely of [an idea's] verifying itself" is endless. "Experience, as we know, has ways of *boiling over*, and making us correct

our present formulas," he writes (*P*, 106). What we refer to as "verified" claims are "true within those borders of experience" – the experience that we count as having verified them – but whether they are "absolutely" true only future experience can decide. James clearly recognized that "confirmed" is a tensed predicate whereas "true" is tenseless and recognized as well that a statement which is verified (in the sense of being confirmed) may later turn out to be false.

As we saw, James accepted the formula "truth is agreement with reality" – provided that formula is properly understood. His metaphysical commitments caused him to identify the "agreement" in question with *some actually observable "conjunctive relation(s),"* and the only ones James could find are the ones involved in verification processes. So James came to the conclusion that beliefs do not (unobservably) "agree with reality" independently of whether they are verified, but rather *come to agree with reality* as the conjunctive relations in question come into existence. Hence the doctrine that "truth happens to an idea"!

But since reality has ways of making us correct our present formulas, it can only be the entire process of *verification in the long run* that "makes" an idea true. All the elements of James's theory of truth – the Peircean component, the idea that our practical interests play a role, James's conception of "agreement," and the notion that truth "happens" to an idea – have to be kept in mind when one is interpreting any single statement in James's complex text.

I pointed out in Section I that, although Peirce does speak of "the opinion which is fated to be ultimately agreed to by all who investigate," he later glosses this as the opinion which we *would converge to if* inquiry were indefinitely continued, and I asked if James would accept a similar modification. The answer is that he would not. For in Peirce's view, the *counterfactual* "If investigation *had been* indefinitely prolonged, such-and-such a statement *would have been* verified" might be true even though no actually experienced fact supports that counterfactual. A statement may "agree" with reality although the "conjunctive relation" which constitutes that agreement exists only as a counterfactual possibility and not as a "conjunctive experience"; truth does not have to "happen" for an idea to be true, it only has to be the case that "it would have happened if." James's metaphysics has no place for such a claim. (But James does not object to counterfactuals as such. Many counterfactuals actually get verified. But those counterfactuals have had truth "happen" to them; they are not made true by a mysterious kind of potentiality ("Thirdness") but by the "cash-value" of incorporating them in our system of beliefs. Peirce would reply that this insistence on actual bits of "pure experience" as the *sole* constituents of reality is a form of "nominalism," and that nominalism is a profound philosophical error. My concern is not to decide the issue between these two great pragmatists but to bring out the enormous difference in their underlying metaphysical assumptions. James "radical empiricism" has no room for Peirce's "Thirdness."

IV TWO IMPORTANT (AND DIFFICULT) PASSAGES IN *PRAGMATISM* AND *THE MEANING OF TRUTH*

Misreadings of James's views on truth are almost always based upon four paragraphs in *Pragmatism*. Let me quote them in full:

"The true," to put it very briefly, is only the expedient in the way of our thinking, just as "the right" is only the expedient in the way of our behaving. Expedient in almost any fashion; and expedient in the long run and on the whole of course; for what meets expediently all the experience in sight won't necessarily meet all farther experiences equally satisfactorily. Experience, as we know, has ways of *boiling over*, and making us correct our present formulas.

The "absolutely" true, meaning what no farther experience will ever alter, is that ideal vanishing-point towards which we imagine that all our temporary truths will some day converge. It runs on all fours with the perfectly wise man, and with the absolutely complete experience; and if these ideals are ever realized, they will all be realized together. Meanwhile, we have to live to-day by what truth we can get to-day, and be ready to-morrow to call it falsehood. Ptolemaic astronomy, euclidean space, aristotelian logic, scholastic metaphysics, were expedient for centuries, but human experience has now boiled over those limits, and we call those things only relatively true, or true within those borders of experience. "Absolutely" they are false; for we know that those limits were casual, and might have been transcended by past theorists just as they are by present thinkers.

When new experiences lead to retrospective judgments, using the past tense, what these judgments utter *was* true, even tho no past thinker had been led there. We live forward, a Danish thinker has said, but we understand backwards. The present sheds a backward light on the world's previous processes. They may have been truth-processes for the actors in them. They are not so for one who knows the later revelations of the story.

This regulative notion of a potential better truth to be established later, possibly to be established absolutely, and having powers of retroactive legislation, turns its face, like all pragmatist notions, towards concreteness of fact, and towards the future. Like the half-truths, the absolute truth will have to be *made,* made as a relation incidental to the growth of a mass of verification experience, to which the half-true ideas are all along contributing their quota. (*P,* 106–7)

Critics typically cite only the first sentence. Such readers attend only to the idea that "expedience" is what determines truth, although most of this lecture (*P,* lecture 6) is devoted to "agreement" with realities. Thus, Russell quotes James as follows: "The 'true' is only expedient in the way of our thinking. . . .in the long run and on the whole of course." Russell omits "to put it very briefly" and "in almost any fashion" – indications that what we have is a thematic statement, and not an attempt to formulate a definition of "true" – and also substitutes his own notion of what "expediency" is for James's, and ends up saying that James proposed the theory that "true" means "has good effects."

In *The Meaning of Truth,* James complains of an additional misunderstanding: it consists in accusing "the pragmatists" of denying that we can speak of any such thing as "absolute" truth (*MT,* 142–3).

Perhaps such readers take the remark about "the perfectly wise man" to be mocking absolute truth. But what James is telling us is that, while it is true that we will never reach the *whole* ideal set of formulations that constitutes absolute truth, "we imagine that all of our temporary truths" will *converge* to that ideal limit. In his reply to this misinterpretation, James says as much:

I expect that the more fully men discuss and test my account, the more they will agree that it *fits,* and the less they will desire a change. I may, of course, be premature, and the glory of being truth final and absolute may fall upon some later revision and correction of my scheme, which will then be judged untrue in just the measure in which it departs from that final satisfactory formulation. To admit, as we pragmatists do, that we are liable to correction (even tho we may not expect it) *involves* the use on our part of an ideal standard. (*MT,* 142)

On the next pages James is even more explicit:

Truth absolute, [the pragmatist] says, means an ideal set of formulations towards which all opinions may in the long run of experience be expected to converge. In this definition of absolute truth he not only postulates that there is a tendency to such convergence of opinion, to such *absolute consensus*, but he postulates the other factors of his definition equally, borrowing them by anticipation from the true conclusions expected to be reached. He postulates the existence of opinions, he postulates the experience that will sift them, and the consistency which that experience will show. He justifies himself in these assumptions by saying that they are not postulates in the strict sense but simple inductions from the past extended to the future by analogy; and he insists that human opinion has already reached a pretty stable equilibrium regarding them, and that if its future development fails to alter them, the definition itself, with all its terms included, will be part of the very absolute truth which it defines. The hypothesis will, in short, have worked successfully all around the circle and proved self-corroborative, and the circle will be closed. (*MT,* 143–4)

It might be objected, however, that what James is doing here is giving a pragmatist definition of "absolute truth" (in order to reply to those who think that a pragmatist can have no such concept), and that he has quite a *different* theory of "truth" *tout court.*[9] The latter, it might be claimed, just *is* being verified. But such a reading, in addition to ignoring the characterization of truth as "the total drift of thought," "the fate of thought," and "the entire drift of experience,"[10] in James's earlier writings, does not fit the paragraphs just quoted. What is verified is *not* called "true," but only "half-true." And when James writes of such now-refuted doctrines as Euclidean geometry, he writes "we call these *only relatively true,* or true within those borders of experience."

Moreover, in the very next sentence, James adds " 'Absolutely' they are false" – and immediately goes on to write of our newer judgments about these matters "what these judgments utter *was* true," without any use of the qualifier "absolutely." James quite freely equates "true" and "absolutely true"; it is "half-true" that always takes the qualifier.

V A FEW COMMENTS ON JAMES'S THEORY OF TRUTH

One can, I believe, learn a great deal from James. He was the first modern philosopher successfully[11] to reject the idea that our impressions are located in a private mental theater (and thus constitute an interface between ourselves and "the external world"), although one does not have to accept James's whole metaphysics of "pure experience" to follow him here. James emphasized the ways in which *verification* and *valuation* are interdependent, without drawing relativist or subjectivist conclusions, and we should do the same (Putnam 1994). James taught us to see concepts as instruments which serve many different interests. But James's theory of truth is seriously flawed. I will mention just one objection – a fatal one – jotted down by Royce on a copy of James's leaflet, "The Meaning of the Word Truth."[12] The objection is that, on James's account, for a statement about the *past* to be true it is necessary that the statement be *believed in the future*, and that it become "the total drift of thought." In this way, the truth-value of every statement about the past *depends on what happens in the future* – and that cannot be right.

James was aware of the possibility of some such objection, and Perry gives us his answer.[13] What James says is simply that there is a difference between past *realities*, which cannot be changed, and *truths* about the past which are "mutable." Presumably he meant that it is judgments that are true or false (James – reasonably, in my view – would never so much as entertain the Fregean alternative of conceiving of thoughts as entities which exist independently of thinkers); truths do not exist until some thinker actually thinks them. But his claim that the past is immutable (considered as a "reality" and not as a "judgment") is still in tension with his theory, as we may see by considering a contested historical judgment, say that Lizzie Borden committed the famous axe murders. Many believe she was guilty; so the judgment that she was exists, and (since she was acquitted) the judgment that she was innocent was at least entertained as a reasonable possibility. If the immutability of the past means that it is a "reality" that Lizzie Borden committed the murders or a "reality" that she did not, *independently of whether one or the other of these judgments is ever confirmed*, then, if she committed the murders but the judgment that she did never becomes "coercive over thought," on James's theory of truth it will follow that

> Lizzie Borden committed the murders, but the judgment that she did is not true – contradicting the principle that, for any judgment p, p is equivalent to the judgment that p is true.

And similarly if she did *not* commit the murders, but the judgment that she did not never becomes "coercive over thought," we will have a violation of the same principle.

James might reply that the reality is immutable, but what is *true of* the reality is not; but this would totally undercut the reply (the letter to Lane) that Perry reprints.

What led James into this *cul de sac* was his failure to challenge traditional views of *conception*. James decisively rejected the interface conception of perception. And at one point (*ERE*, 10) he even seems prepared to give a parallel account of *conception*, but this was not followed up. Instead, in *Pragmatism* and in *Meaning of Truth* he returned to treating thoughts and ideas as mental shapes, "flat psychological surface," which require *external relations* to connect them to public objects. As we saw, James picked various relations to do the connecting, for example, "leading to" and "substituting for." An idea may lead me to the reality it refers to, or it may substitute for it in the sense that belief in it works as well as if we had perceived the reality in question.

It is easy to see how the problem with the truth of our beliefs about the past results. My ideas cannot "lead me" to past things and events; they are gone. The only way in which an "idea," postulated to be "loose and separate" from what it refers to (*EPh*, 74), can "refer" to the past things and events is by "substituting" for them. But this is just to say that an idea of past events is true if it works now and in the future! ("Works" in the sense(s) appropriate to the "verification process," of course.) This is the way in which James's failure to be as radical in his account of conception as he was willing to be in his account of perception led him to a disastrous theory.

I believe that much of what James wanted to deny should be denied. It is right that we do not have to think of truth as presupposing a mysterious "relation of agreement with reality" – *one and the same relation in all cases* – or an infinite mind able to overcome the limitations of all limited and finite points of view (as in absolute idealism) or some other piece of transcendental machinery, something metaphysical *beneath* our practice of making and criticizing truth claims, which makes that practice possible. James's *Pragmatism* is at its most powerful when it argues just this, and at its least successful when it tries to find the "external relations" which make reference and truth possible.

NOTES

I am very much indebted to Ruth Anna Putnam for close reading and helpful criticism of an earlier draft.

1 §407 in Peirce 1931–60, vol. 5. All my references to this edition will have the form which has become standard, namely, vol. no. paragraph no.

2 Peirce may also be thinking of "The Pragmatic Method" (*EPh*, 123–39). There James writes, "I think myself that [the principle of pragmatism] should be expressed more broadly than Mr. Peirce expresses it. The ultimate test for us of what truth means is indeed the conduct it dictates or inspires. But it inspires that conduct because it first foretells some particular turn to our experience which shall call for just that conduct" (124).

3 It is true that the reference to "fate" is absent. But Peirce himself rather downplays this notion, writing in a footnote to the definition cited, "Fate means merely that which is sure to come true. . . .We are all fated to die."

4 As we shall see, this does not mean that resemblance is ever sufficient for reference.

5 The mutability of knowledge is a constant theme (see, for example, *P*, 107 and lecture 5). Pure experience in itself is neither true nor false, but any conceptualization of it is fallible (*ERE*, 28–9).

6 These are relations which we perceive as *similarities* or at least as *connections*.

7 In recent years we have been urged to think of conceptions as *capacities for representing* rather than as *representations* by John McDowell (1992, 1994), John Haldane (1989, 1992), and myself (Putnam 1994b).

8 James's account of mathematics is in the empiricist tradition. Mathematics deals with internal relations among our ideas which are themselves directly observable by us. I do not think that this account is tenable.

9 This objection was suggested by David Lamberth.

10 Speaking of the propositions "this is a moral universe," "this is an unmoral universe" – for James, these are fundamental moral/religious propositions – James writes (in "The Sentiment of Rationality," one of the essays in *WB*), "It cannot be said that the question Is this a moral world? is a meaningless and unverifiable question because it deals with something non-phenomenal . . . the verification of the theory which you may hold as to the objectively moral character of the world can consist only in this – that if you proceed to act upon your theory it will be reversed by nothing that will later turn up as that action's fruit; *it will*

harmonize so well with the entire drift of experience that the latter will, as it were, adopt it, or at most give it an ampler interpretation, without obliging you in any way to change the essence of its formulation" (WB, 86; emphases added).

11 Thomas Reid and Peirce also opposed it, but, in my view, not successfully (see Putnam 1994b, 468n).

12 Royce's notes may be found in Perry 1935, 2:735–6. The leaflet is reprinted in *MT*, 117–19.

13 See the letter to Alfred C. Lane, reprinted in Perry 1935, 2:477–8.

10   The James/Royce dispute and the development of James's "solution"

In philosophy we have a ... contrast expressed in the terms "empiricist" and "rationalist". . . . The world of concrete personal experiences to which the street belongs is multitudinous beyond imagination, tangled, muddy, painful and perplexed. The world to which your philosophy professor introduces you is simple, clean and noble. . . . It is at this point that my own solution begins to appear. I offer the oddly-named thing pragmatism as a philosophy that can satisfy both kinds of demand.

In a 1900 letter to his colleague – and life-long philosophical interlocutor – Josiah Royce, James confesses: "[W]hen I write, 'tis with one eye on you, and one on the page. . . . I lead a parasitic life upon you, for my highest flight of ambitious ideality is to become your conqueror, and go down into history as such . . . in one last death-grapple of an embrace" (*Sel.Letters*, 192). Indeed, it is arguably the case that much of what James has to say concerning a host of philosophical topics is written with an anxious eye on his ongoing public philosophical debate with Royce. This essay is concerned with one such topic.

The aim of this essay is threefold: (1) to argue for a historical claim: that James's conception of pragmatism is shaped in subtle, and not so subtle, ways by his continuing debate with Royce, and that it is through struggling with criticisms leveled by Royce against his earlier formulations of his doctrine that James arrives at his own idiosyncratic conception of pragmatism; (2) to argue for an interpretative claim: that, once viewed against the background of this debate, it becomes possible to make sense of a number of features of James's thought which have puzzled commentators – most notably, James's late claim that what Royce (and now everyone) calls his "Pragmatic Theory of Truth" is not to be understood as a *theory*; and (3) to provide an overview of how James arrives at his most provocative philosophical claim – that genuine progress in philosophy can only be achieved through the acknowledgment and exploration of the role of temperament in consolidating philosophical conviction – and how that claim bears on James's mature conception of pragmatism.

I ROYCE'S CHALLENGE

The first round of the debate between Royce and James consists of Royce's initial formulation of a sketch for an argument for his favored conclusion – namely, that the doctrine of pragmatism entails the doctrine of absolute idealism. This initial sketch is buried in Royce's lengthy "argument from error," which he develops in chapter 11 of *The Religious Aspect of Philosophy*. Royce's way of putting the implication of his argument that concerns James is to say: pragmatism, insofar as it wishes to confine its account of truth to appeals to the experience of individual knowing subjects, will not be able to succeed in drawing a coherent distinction between truth and falsity. This then prepares the way for Royce's more general objection: pragmatism, insofar as it is unable to furnish a coherent account of truth, is unable to furnish a satisfactory account of what it is to have *objective* knowledge (it offers rather, at best, an account of what it is to have justified beliefs).

Royce claims that he can derive his entire metaphysical position from one indubitable fact, that error exists. The first step is to establish that that fact is indeed indubitable. The second step, the precise execution of which Royce struggles with throughout his career, has a Kantian flavor: to inquire into the necessary preconditions for the possibility of error. Royce argues that only given the possibility (which he takes to be excluded by Jamesian pragmatism) of a certain kind of standpoint ("an absolute standpoint") can the distinction between truth and error be "definitively" drawn. Royce, in order to answer his guiding question "how is the one indubitable fact (that error exists) possible?" says he had to go through "the very heart of skepticism itself" (Royce 1971, 47). The argument proceeds through the heart of skepticism because it provisionally undertakes to doubt everything. Yet even skepticism, insofar as it urges that we can always be mistaken (i.e., be in error), seems to still suggest that error is possible. Can we get around this? Is there some way to deny even this claim, that is, to go beyond conventional skepticism and deny that error exists? Let us try, says Royce. Let's adopt a wholesale skepticism that refrains from making any objective claim, that only countenances what "seems true" – and not what is objectively true. Royce argues that such an extreme form of relativism – that attempts to rule out any appeal to what is "objectively true" – contradicts itself the moment it attempts to formulate itself. The skeptic recommends his view ("that there is only what 'seems true to me' ") to us as true, and thus, in so recommending his theory, presupposes that there is at least one nonrelativistic truth; but the existence of that truth suffices to refute his original thesis. Thus, in arguing that the content of his thesis is true, the relativist (or, as Royce calls him, "the skeptic") contradicts the content of his thesis. The statement "error exists" must therefore be either objectively (or, as Royce puts it, "absolutely") true or objectively ("absolutely") false.

After Royce concludes that "the doctrine of the total relativity of truth" (since it cannot be coherently stated) "has no real meaning," he goes on to point out that "an empiricist view of truth" – one that he clearly identifies with (at least Peirce's early exposition of) pragmatism, and one that he says he, Royce himself, espoused "until recently" – is no better off with respect to the problem of error. He summarizes his own earlier empiricist view as follows:

> [T]he author used to say: "In fact future nature is not given to us, just as the past is not given to us. Sense-data and thought unite at every instant afresh to form a new judgment and a new postulate. Only in the present has any judgment evident validity. And our postulate of causal relation is just a way of looking at this world of conceived past and future *data*. Such postulates avoid being absurd efforts to regulate independent facts of sense, because, and only because, we have in experience no complete series of facts at all, only from moment to moment single facts, about which we make single judgments. All the rest we *must* postulate or else do without them." (Royce 1971, 47)

Royce then goes on to argue that this position is just as vulnerable to the self-refuting consequences of asking itself the question "Does error exist?" as any form of radical skepticism or relativism. For this form of empiricism wishes to assert the following thesis: "all but the immediate content of the present moment's judgment is doubtful." But what is the status of that judgment? It seems either that it itself is open to doubt (in which case it is not clear why we should accept it as true) or it is not open to doubt, in which case it seems to violate its own strictures. Furthermore, if it is true, it is unable to make sense of the grounds of its truth. It is unable to provide a coherent account of the standpoint from which it judges "everything beyond the present to be doubtful": "for in asserting such a judgment it is making a judgment concerning something 'beyond the present' " (Royce 1971, 47). The notion of error it employs (when speaking of "judgments beyond the present" "being in error") presupposes a standpoint which the view requires be an unattainable one. Hence the notion of error it employs, Royce argues, is itself an unintelligible one.

Throughout his subsequent work, Royce further hones his argument for the claim that James's theory of truth comes down to a "what-is-true-for-me" view. Insofar as pragmatism restricts itself to what is verifiable in a single person's experience, Royce argues it is essentially solipsistic; for, strictly speaking, all that is immediately verifiable, in the relevant sense, are statements concerning immediate private experiences. In mounting (what I will call) his "argument from solipsism," Royce seizes on James's incessant talk of accepting truths "on credit":

> Truth lives, in fact, for the most part on a credit system. Our thoughts and beliefs "pass," so long as nothing challenges them, just as bank-notes pass so long as nobody refuses them. But this all points to direct face-to-face verifications somewhere, without which the fabric of truth collapses like a financial system with no cash-basis whatsoever. You accept my verification of one thing, I yours of another. We trade on each other's truth. But the beliefs verified concretely by *somebody* are the posts of the whole superstructure. (P, 100)

Royce seizes on this metaphor of taking the experience of others "on credit" because he sees in it James's attempt to legitimate (from within the narrowly empiricist confines of his early pragmatism) talk about possible experiences which are not part of the pool of one's actual experiences (where the latter are the only experiences that can be put to the test of immediate direct verification). But "a note or other evidence of value is good if it *can* be turned into cash at some agreed upon time, or under specified conditions" (Royce 1969, 697). Royce argues that it is just this condition that James's account of credit values fails to satisfy and hence that the resulting economy must end in bankruptcy.[1]

Royce goes on to mount an additional argument against the pragmatist theory of truth which might be called "the argument from the meaning of 'truth'." James was fond of urging that one of the great virtues of pragmatism – as against absolute idealism (which "offends the common man's sense of reality") – is that it respects the common man's understanding of things. Royce tries to turn this "appeal to the common man" against James. Royce, at a number of junctures, simply calls upon his reader to consult his own intuitions about what he means by the word "truth":

> May we venture to ask ourselves, then: Is this pragmatism a fair expression of what we mean by truth? (Royce 1969, 984)[2]

Royce is willing to concede that the pragmatist does some justice to our intuitions about these matters when he speaks, for example, of true ideas as being those ideas that are successful. Yet Royce is not willing to settle for such a characterization. For everything hinges here on what our views are concerning what makes a successful idea "successful":

> And yet, and yet all this still leaves open one great question. When we seek truth, we indeed seek successful ideas. But what, in Heaven's name, constitutes success? (Royce 1969, 985)

In particular, Royce has his doubts about any characterization of the meaning of the word "truth" that attempts to explicate the nature of this "success" in terms of considerations of expediency:

> Of course, we mortals seek for whatever verification of our truths we can get in the form of present success. But can you express our human definition of truth in terms of any collection of our human experiences of personal expediency? (Royce 1969, 986)

Royce's challenge here is that when James equates the notion of truth with that of expediency he is doing obvious violence to our intuitions concerning the proper usage of the word "true." When we say something is "true," Royce insists, we mean something quite different than "expedient." To reinforce this point, Royce asks us to consider the swearing in of a witness in a courtroom. We ask the witness "to

swear to tell the truth, the whole truth, and nothing but the truth."
Royce asks us to focus on this latter phrase: "nothing but the truth."
What do we *mean* by the word "truth" here? What are we asking the
witness to exclude from his testimony? Among other things, we are
asking him to put aside all considerations of utility or expediency –
particularly those of *personal* expediency. Insofar as the witness fails
to live up to our expectations in this regard, we have grounds for
concluding that either (1) he does not understand the word "truth,"
or (2) he understands the content of his oath and has failed to abide
by it. The pragmatist, Royce contends, cannot do justice to what the
word "truth" means in such a context. For his account of truth blurs
the very distinction we call upon the witness in the courtroom to
keep clearly fixed in his mind's eye.[3] Royce concludes that the pragmatist cannot make sense of the ordinary meaning of the word
"truth" which we all spontaneously understand and rely upon in
such a context (cf. Royce 1969, 988). The distinction (between truth
and expediency) that the pragmatist fails to draw here is one that is
embodied in our ordinary usage and forms an integral part of our
common sense.[4] So, insofar as pragmatism is unable to accommodate this "perfectly universal" and "commonplace" distinction, it
fails to meet its own criterion (of not doing "unnecessary violence to
common sense") for what would count as an adequate account of
truth.

The conclusion that Royce is after with each of these arguments –
one which he aims to put to his own dialectical purposes – is that
pragmatism's own criterion of truth is too narrow to be able to
accommodate the claim that the pragmatist's theory of truth is itself
true:

> The proposition "These are the actual, and, for the purposes of a given
> test, the logically relevant workings of the idea that is to be tested," must
> itself be true, if the empirical comparison of any one of these workings with
> the facts of experience is to be of any worth as a test. (Royce 1951, 117)

Consider the proposition (from James) cited in quotation marks in
the above passage. This proposition is put forward as true; yet it is
not able to accommodate the possibility of an account of its own
truth. For such a proposition to be true on its own account its truth
must be experientially verifiable, and yet its claims outstrip the
possibility of such verification:

The truth of the proposition just put in quotation marks is a truth of a type that no one man, at any instant, ever personally and empirically tests. In every special case it may be, and in general must be, regarded as doubtful. Yet, unless some such propositions are true, Pragmatism becomes a meaningless doctrine; while, if any such propositions are true, there is a sort of truth of which Pragmatism gives no account. (Royce 1951, 117–18)

Either "the whole pragmatist account of truth becomes simply meaningless" or pragmatism stands in need of supplementation:

> In brief, Pragmatism presupposes a certain unity in the meaning and coherence of experience taken as a whole – a unity which can never at any one moment be tested by any human being. Unless the propositions which assert the existence and describe the nature of this presupposed unity are themselves true, Pragmatism has no meaning. But if they are true, Pragmatism presupposes a sort of truth whereof it gives no adequate account. To say this is not to say that Pragmatism gives a wholly false view of the nature of truth, but is only to insist upon its inadequacy. It needs to be supplemented. (Royce 1951, 118)

Without supplementation there is no way that the pragmatist can assert that his own theory of truth is truth; in the absence of such supplementation, it is unclear that we have been offered something that can be dignified with the title "a theory of truth." This specifies the agenda for James's pragmatism: to find a method of stating a pragmatist theory of truth that avoids the problem that it refutes itself the moment the theory's own criterion of truth is applied to the theory itself.

Having established the indubitable fact that error exists, Royce proceeds (in not altogether convincing fashion) to bootstrap the rest of his doctrine out of the slender foundation provided by that single anchor of support. He does this by engaging in a Kantian transcendental inquiry into the conditions necessarily presupposed by the fact that "error is plainly possible in some way." Royce offers a series of arguments to show that all commonsense views of what those conditions could be are clearly inadequate and need to be supplemented by presuppositions that transcend (but do not contradict) anything suggested to us by common sense. Royce then tries to force the following dilemma on James: either (1) you restrict yourself to an analysis of error that remains immanent in human experience and thereby commit yourself to a doctrine which ultimately refutes itself; or (2) you permit your analysis of how we arrive at judgments of error to be supplemented with an account of "the logical conditions" of error – where the only tenable account, Royce claims, will be one which permits itself an appeal to a "higher inclusive thought" – one which is capable of relating the isolated judgment to all other actual and possible judgments concerning the intended object of judgment. It is when he turns to unpacking this notion of a "higher inclusive thought" that Royce pulls his absolute idealist rabbit – that is, the "absolute knower" – out of what at first looks to be a perfectly ordinary hat. For Royce goes on to argue that the intended object of our every thought is "embraced" in a *single* overarching "infinite thought" – and such an "infinite thought" presupposes the existence of an Absolute Being who thinks it. If the pragmatist wishes to render the distinction between truth and falsity (which he presupposes in his theory of truth) intelligible, he must ultimately concede the existence of such an absolute knower as a foundation which underlies the possibility of all judgment – this is Royce's challenge to James.

II JAMES'S INITIAL ATTEMPTS AT A REPLY

James's first reaction to Royce's argument is simply to be dumbfounded by it. He writes to Carl Stumpf in 1887 of Royce's new book:

> The second half is a new argument for monistic idealism, an argument based on the possibility of truth and error in knowledge, subtle in itself, and rather lengthily expounded, but seeming to me to be one of the few big original suggestions of recent philosophical writing. I have vainly tried to escape from it. I still suspect it of inconclusiveness, but I frankly confess that I am *unable* to overthrow it. . . . I can assure you that, if you come to close quarters with it, you will say its author belongs to the genuine philosophic breed. (*Letters*, 1:265)

James goes back and forth for six more years, finally expressing in a letter to D. S. Miller (partly inspired by some of the latter's objections to Royce's view) the resolve to make up his mind on the issue one way or the other:

> . . . with the help of God I will go at it again this semester, when I settle down to my final bout with Royce's theory, which must result in my either *actively* becoming a propagator thereof, or actively its enemy or destroyer. It

is high time that this more decisive attitude was generated in me, and it ought to take place this winter. (*Letters*, 2:18)

James makes a start on this task by contesting Royce's claim that the only way to avoid solipsism is to postulate an "absolute knower." Now, as we saw, Royce (in his "argument from solipsism") presses the following dilemma onto James:

(a) the only way the experiences of others (that temporarily are accepted on credit) are ultimately "cashed in" is through immediate direct verification in one's own experience;

(b) these experiences accepted on credit are verified in some other way (than through direct experience) that does not require ascertaining their directly verifiable cash-value.

If James chooses option (a), Royce will show that his theory reduces to an essentially solipsistic theory that is self-refuting in precisely the way that the " 'true' means 'what seems true to me' " theory is. If James attempts to opt for (b), then Royce will ask: how do you plan to cash in all these credit-values and make good your promissory note? What is this "other way" by means of which we can make out the truth of experiences that are not directly verifiable?

Now the above criticism is no doubt invited by some of James's prose; but, partly in response to these objections, James makes it clear that he wishes to conceive of pragmatic verification in both holistic and intersubjective terms.[5] His frequent appeals to experience are now to be interpreted as appeals to the totality of human experience, including both (diachronic) appeals to the past and future of mankind as well as (synchronic) appeals to the collectivity of human experience. James goes out of his way in a number of places to make it explicit that he fully endorses Royce's claim that any form of radical epistemological individualism cannot supply a coherent foundation for a "theory of the empirical success of ideas." Any appeal, so long as it restricts its scope to the confines of a solitary individual's experience, can never transform itself into an intelligible claim to truth. As James puts it in his discussion of "moral solitude" in "The Moral Philosopher and the Moral Life," a universe in which only one person exists is a universe in which truth does not exist:

In such a universe as that it would of course be absurd to raise the question of whether the solitary thinker's judgments of good and ill are true or not. Truth supposes a standard outside of the thinker to which he must conform. (WB, 191)

The above passage is virtually a paraphrase of one of Royce's central contentions. The sentence summarized what James takes to be the correct moral to be drawn from Royce's "argument from error." Pragmatism, just as much as absolutism, requires "a wider knower" – but not too wide. The crucial question for James becomes: where, if not in the Absolute, does one locate the source of objectivity? – where does one situate the "standard outside of the thinker to which his thought must conform"? His answer to this question is further clarified in the next round of the debate.

James's philosophical ambitions, at this point in the debate, also become somewhat more modest. Against Royce's claim that only one coherent alternative is open to the philosopher, James's philosophical project becomes *to show that there is a coherent alternative to absolute idealism.* His project is no longer to show that this alternative conception is itself true. He takes Royce to have demonstrated that a consistent and forthright pragmatist must acknowledge that the resources needed to cash such a promissory note will forever be beyond his means. His project becomes simply to show that there is indeed a genuine alternative open to the philosopher – that pragmatism remains a "live" option. But, Royce counters: for a hypothesis to be a live option for us, we must at least be able to know what it would mean for it to be true. James is thus still left with the task of responding to Royce's "argument from the meaning of 'truth'."

James's strategy for avoiding Royce's "swearing-in" objection mirrors the rule-utilitarian's attempt to fend off the standard objection to act-utilitarianism (i.e., the objection that utilitarianism must be false since the theory licenses us to commit actions which are self-evidently morally abominable). The strategy (in both cases) is to modify the theory so that it only applies to the justification of practices (rather than individual actions). James claims that the ultimate grounds for the *practice* of honesty – on which our community rightly places a premium – can be fully accounted for in pragmatic terms without in any way licensing an individual engaged in an isolated instance of such a practice to invoke those pragmatic grounds in his own personal deliberations. All that the witness in the witness-box should do (unless he has come across some remarkable ground for impugning our practice as a whole) is just what we all already want him to do – what our practice properly requires of him: "to tell the truth, the whole truth, and nothing but the truth."

If James's formula (those beliefs are "true" which "guide us successfully through experience") is to be understood in terms of what guides each of us *individually*, Royce's argument from solipsism would have force here. For "successfully" would then simply refer to what is "expedient for me." But, as we have seen, James affirms that truth presupposes a standpoint external to the *individual* judging subject. He wants to be able to say to Royce: we do not disagree about the nature of truth, we just disagree about the necessity of postulating the Absolute.[6] The form of the challenge James faces at this point can be put as follows: to formulate an account of the relevant standard (with which a judgment must accord in order to have a claim to truth) so that it satisfies the following desiderata: (1) the standard must remain fully external to each individual thinker,[7] and yet (2) somehow be a function of the collective experiences of the aggregate of individual thinkers. So we find James saying things like this: true beliefs are those which most benefit mankind over the long run, which most conduce toward flourishing individual lives and a harmonious overall social life, and so on. James wants to agree with Royce that "truth supposes a standard outside the thinker," and yet to eschew appeal to a Roycean absolute standpoint "beyond the experience of all possible thinkers," by locating the source of truth in the collective experience of finite judging subjects. James now needs to be able to show how the standard of truth precipitates out of "the agreements of the community." The trick lies in pitching this appeal to "the agreements of the community" at the right level.

In order to sidestep Royce-style objections, James knows he must repudiate all three of the following interpretations of his theory: (1) that his appeal to the community be understood along ethnocentric lines (as merely referring to the norms of *our* culture), (2) that the relevant concept of "agreement" be understood in a conventionalist manner (truth resting on underlying contingent stipulations), or (3) that truth be analyzed in purely communitarian terms (truth as *de facto* consensus) – each of these three alternatives is unmasked by Royce as a disguised version of relativism. James tries to avoid (1) by claiming that the relevant community is the largest possible one (the collective experience of "mankind as a whole over the historical long run"), to avoid (2) by declaring that what is at issue is an "ultimate agreement" regulated by an "ideal standard" which is itself always "liable to correction" (*MT*, 142),[8] and to avoid (3) by introducing the notion of convergence (à la Peirce[9]) toward an "ideal limit."[10] But, despite all this finessing on James's part, Royce can counter that these modifications of his original doctrine still leave the pragmatist no better off with respect to the fundamental problem. For he still lacks the requisite means for genuinely distinguishing what is right from what merely seems right. The appeal to the "convergence of opinion" toward an "absolute consensus" (*MT*, 143) simply postpones the original problem by now identifying "right" (instead of with "what seems right to me") with "what will seem right to all of us in the future." But this will not do. Any adequate theory of truth, Royce maintains, must be able to accommodate the possibility that our entire community may be in agreement about a particular matter and yet be mistaken. Insofar as James's theory is unable to accommodate this possibility, it continues to deprive our judgments of objectivity: it merely substitutes one form of subjectivity for another – the subjectivity of the first-person plural for the subjectivity of the first-person singular. As with the previous example (of the witness), Royce can reply that there remains a question we ought to be able to ask but which the pragmatist tells us we cannot ask. We should be able to ask: "Even though such-and-such a judgment seems true to all of us, all the same, *is* it true?" We have no difficulty understanding the meaning of this question. As long as the pragmatist's theory implies that his perfectly intelligible question lacks intelligibility, it continues to do violence to our commonsense understanding of the meaning of the word "true."[11]

III JAMES'S "SOLUTION": APPLYING THE WILL TO BELIEVE TO PRAGMATISM

In the final round of the debate, James makes a surprising move: he endorses both of Royce's conclusions. He, in effect, ends by agreeing: (a) that the pragmatist cannot speak of the truth of his own "theory of truth," and (b) that, strictly speaking, it is misleading therefore even to call what he offers a "theory." What James does instead is to reexamine the force of Royce's original rationalist refutation of skepticism. In his article "The Pragmatist Account of Truth and its Misunderstandings," James reports Royce's objection, thinly disguising it as that of "a correspondent":

> *Fifth misunderstanding: What pragmatists say is inconsistent with their saying so.* A correspondent puts this objection as follows: "When you say to your audience, 'pragmatism is the truth concerning truth,' the first truth is different from the second. About the first you and they are not to be at odds; you are not giving them liberty to take or leave it according as it works satisfactorily or not for their private uses. Yet the second truth, which ought to describe and include the first, affirms this liberty. Thus the *intent* of your utterance seems to contradict the *content* of it." (*MT*, 107)

This is a lovely summary of Royce's favorite objection against pragmatism. It is also a substitution instance of the argument he employs to demonstrate the untenability of skepticism. What James does at this point is reopen the question whether Royce's original argument really does kill off the possibility of maintaining a skeptical outlook:

> General skepticism has always received this same classic refutation. "You have to dogmatize," the rationalists say to the skeptics, "whenever you express the skeptical position; so your lives keep contradicting your thesis." One would suppose that the importance of so hoary an argument to abate in the slightest degree the amount of general skepticism in the world might have led some rationalists themselves to doubt whether these instantaneous logical refutations are such fatal ways, after all, of killing off live mental attitudes. General skepticism is the live mental attitude of refusing to conclude. It is a permanent torpor of the will, renewing itself in detail towards each successive thesis that offers, and you can no more kill it off by logic than you can kill off obstinacy or practical joking. This is why it is so irritating. Your consistent skeptic never puts his skepticism into a formal proposition – he simply chooses it as a habit. He provokingly hangs back when he might so easily join us in saying yes, but he is not illogical or stupid – on the contrary, he often impresses us by his intellectual superiority. This is the *real* skepticism that rationalists have to meet, and their logic does not even touch it. (*MT*, 107–8)

James emphasizes here that in order for Royce's refutation of skepticism to go through, the skeptic has to assert and affirm a skeptical thesis. He has to formulate it into a proposition and proclaim it as a general truth. If he does so, Royce has him where he wants him. However, what Royce's argument cannot touch is "the live mental attitude" of the skeptic. For this is a scrupulously inculcated habit rather than a proposition (let alone a theory).[12] Hence skepticism as an existentially embodied attitude toward life is not something that is susceptible to being eliminated via "instantaneous logical refutations." The Roycean critic is correct to conclude that the skeptic will never be able to propound his skepticism in the form of a coherent philosophical theory. However, the skeptic does not seek to formulate a philosophical theory, so he should not experience his inability to do so as a cause for concern.[13] James is preparing the way here for the claim that mere logic is similarly unable to kill off the pragmatist's conviction. But a problem remains: The skeptic's "live mental attitude" is said to be immune from refutation only insofar as he refrains from formulating it as an assertible proposition. James, however, does formulate his pragmatic conception of truth, doesn't he? In order to take up this line of defense, James must repudiate his former ambition of formulating "a pragmatic *theory* of truth" – that is, something which must assume a propositional form and the integrity of which turns on its immunity to "instantaneous logical refutations." If he seeks to remain "irreproachably self-consistent," the pragmatist should restrict himself to proposing "a live mental attitude" that he recommends we adopt, cultivate, and embody in the context of our lives:

The pragmatist's idea of truth is ... a challenge. He finds it ultra-satisfactory to accept it, and takes his own stand accordingly. But, being gregarious as they are, men seek to spread their beliefs, to awaken imitation, to infect others. Why should not *you* also find the same belief satisfactory? thinks the pragmatist, and forthwith endeavors to convert you. You and he will then believe similarly; you will hold up your subject-end of a truth, which will be a truth objective and irreversible if the reality holds up the object-end by being itself present simultaneously. What there is of self-contradiction in all this I confess I cannot discover. The pragmatist's conduct in his own case seems to me on the contrary admirably to illustrate his universal formula; and of all epistemologists, he is perhaps the only one who is irreproachably self-consistent. (*MT*, 108)

The "pragmatist's conduct in his own case" should be viewed as "irreproachably self-consistent," because he is not offering a theory but rather a "*conception* of truth" – a proposal concerning how we should lead our lives:

Pragmatists . . . themselves play the part of the absolute knower for the universe of discourse which serves them as material for epistemologizing. They warrant the reality there, and the subject's true knowledge, there, of it. But whether what they themselves say about the whole universe is objectively true, *i.e.*, whether the pragmatic theory of truth is true *really*, they cannot warrant – they can only believe it. To their hearers they can only *propose* it, as I propose it to my readers, as something to be verified *ambulando*, or by the way in which its consequences may confirm it. (*MT*, 108)[14]

James is prepared here both to concede the validity of Royce's claim that the so-called pragmatist theory of truth cannot put itself forward as true (whether what the pragmatists "themselves say about the whole universe is objectively true, i.e., whether the pragmatist theory of truth is true *really*, they cannot warrant") and to declare himself undisturbed by it. He can only "propose" (James italicizes this word) his pragmatist credo to us as something we can "verify" as we go along in life.[15]

James is not offering any arguments which will logically compel us to assent to a particular thesis. He proposes pragmatism not as a theory (something which might be true or false), but as a guide for action (something which might or might not serve us well in "our conduct of the business of living"). But we might ask: So what if he proposes it? Why should we accept it? If James is unable to argue for the truth of his "conception," what rational court of appeal remains open to him?

In the opening lecture of the *Lectures on Pragmatism*, James seems to be urging pragmatism on us on the grounds that it will suit some of our temperaments better than any of the other available alternatives on the philosophical market. He offers us his famous twofold classification of tough-minded and tender-minded philosophies and then appears to suggest that some among his listeners (namely, those who temperamentally incline more toward one of the two extreme sorts of sensibility) will be correct in concluding the pragmatism is not for them. In other words, James seems perfectly willing to concede that some of his readers *should* adopt a philosophy drawn from one of the two enemy camps, if such a philosophy is "best suited" to their particular temperament. This concession to the enemy can seem difficult to square with a further suggestion that is also unmistakably present: namely, that an attraction to either of the standard philosophical options, tough-minded and tender-minded alike, is indicative of a certain deformation and impoverishment of human personality. Under the pressure of our more extreme philosophical impulses, James suggests, we tend to cultivate "a certain blindness in ourselves," stunting our capacities for vision and response. (Where our blindspots lie depends upon which extreme we incline toward.) James freely admits that most *philosophers* belong to one of the two extreme persuasions, but he suggests that this has mostly to do with the way in which the pursuit of philosophy as a professional activity both attracts and produces "men of radical idiosyncrasy" (*P*, 11). He urges that we should not allow this preponderance in philosophy of "very positively marked men" (*P*, 11) to obscure for us the fact that "the healthy human understanding" of the ordinary man or woman – insofar as it remains uncorrupted by excessive exposure to (what he calls) "technical philosophy" – will tend quite properly to incline to a position that lies somewhere between the extremes.[16]

James declares that he is simply making explicit the (usually carefully concealed) fact that temperament plays a decisive role in clinching a philosopher's fundamental convictions:

> The history of philosophy is to a great extent that of a certain clash of human temperaments. Undignified as such a treatment may seem to some of my colleagues, I shall have to take account of this clash and explain a good many of the divergences of philosophers by it. Of whatever temperament a professional philosopher is, he tries when philosophizing to sink the fact of his temperament. Temperament is no conventionally recognized reason, so he urges impersonal reasons only for his conclusions. Yet his temperament really gives him a stronger bias than any of his more strictly objective premises. It loads the evidence for him one way or the other, making for a more sentimental or a more hard-hearted view of the universe, just as this fact or that principle would. He *trusts* his temperament. Wanting a universe that suits it, he believes in any representation of the universe that does suit it. He feels men of opposite temper to be out of key with the world's character, and in his heart considers them incompetent and "not in it," in the philosophic business, even though they may far excel him in dialectical ability. (*P*, 11)

What should strike the reader as far more shocking than James's revelation that temperament often plays a pivotal role in the adoption of a philosophical position is his further suggestion that it is perfectly in order that it should play such a role.[17] This suggestion emerges in the context of his saying what it is that he suspects the majority of his audience (are temperamentally inclined to) want in a philosophy and why it is that they remain unsatisfied by the usual polarized alternatives:

> What *you* want is a philosophy that will not only exercise your powers of intellectual abstraction, but that will make some positive connexion with this actual world of finite human lives. You want a system that will combine both things, the scientific loyalty to facts and willingness to take account of them, the spirit of adaptation and accommodation, in short, but also the old confidence in human values and the resulting spontaneity, whether of the religious or of the romantic type. And this is then your dilemma: you find the two parts of your *quaesitum* hopelessly separated. You find empiricism within humanism and irreligion; or else you find a rationalistic philosophy that indeed may call itself religious, but that keeps out of all definite touch with concrete facts and joys and sorrows. (*P*, 17)

James offers his own "proposal" to those members of his audience who are accurately portrayed in the above description on the grounds that it will furnish them with what, given the nature of their temperament, they cannot help but crave:

> It is at this point that my own solution begins to appear. I offer the oddly-named thing pragmatism as a philosophy that can satisfy both kinds of demand. It can remain religious like rationalisms, but at the same time, like the empiricisms, it can preserve the richest intimacy with facts. (*P*, 23)

James speaks of a particular point in the discussion – namely, the point at which it emerges that alternative philosophies are unable to "satisfy" the "cravings" of his audience – as being the one at which his "own *solution* begins to appear." James's theory is superior to its competitors because it, and only it, can satisfy both kinds of fundamental demand.

What sort of "solution" is this? Isn't it the height of irrationalism to suggest that philosophical positions should be adopted on temperamental grounds? The reason James does not think so is, firstly, because he holds that temperamental grounds, under certain circumstances, constitute legitimate reasons; and, secondly, because he holds that there is a special class of cases in which they constitute the only legitimate reasons. The argument for this view finds its classic expression in the essay "The Will to Believe." James begins by laying down three conditions that must be fulfilled by a postulate in order for the argument of the essay to apply to it: the postulate must involve an option that is (1) *forced*, (2) *living*, and (3) *momentous*. Later on in the essay, James adds a critical (and often overlooked) fourth condition: the option in question must be one which "cannot by its nature be decided on intellectual grounds."[18] Having made it clear that he is only concerned with options that meet these four conditions, James advances his central contention:

> Our passional nature not only lawfully may, but must, decide an option between propositions, whenever it is a genuine option that cannot by its nature be decided on intellectual grounds; for to say, under such circumstances, "Do not decide, but leave the question open," is itself a passional decision – just like deciding yes or no – and is attended with the same risk of losing the truth. (*WB*, 11)

This argument is extended by James, in the final round of his debate with Royce, so as to apply not only to ethical and religious choices but also to the choice of whether one should adopt the pragmatist credo. In order for this extension to be legitimate, however, the pragmatist "proposal" must meet the four conditions on options which are "lawfully decided by our passional nature."

As to the first condition, a choice qualifies (at least according to the letter of James's definition on *WB*, 3) as *forced*, if it involves what James calls "a complete logical disjunction." That is, if it only allows for two mutually exhaustive alternatives. The choice to adopt the pragmatist "proposal" (like most choices) can easily be framed so as to satisfy this condition: either (*a*) one resolves the matter in favor of the option or (*b*) one fails to do so (and thus either by deliberation or by default chooses not to adopt the proposal). In this minimal sense, many options that have essentially no bearing on the practical conduct of our lives qualify as forced. The problem is that, on this definition, choices which anyone would be happy simply to ignore (rather than have to resolve through deliberation) count as forced. James, at subsequent points in his argument, clearly takes himself to be working with a far more restricted notion of what it is for an option to be forced than this. In this more restricted sense, an option counts as forced only if it is one which is in some sense unignorable – one which is forced on us – so that one does not feel able simply to shrug off the question of what to do. (This is, I think, the best way of understanding what James means when he says there is no genuine possibility of not choosing in such cases.) It is therefore important (for the applicability of this condition of the argument from "The Will to Believe" to the pragmatist proposal) that James thinks philosophical questions are experienced by most people as inescapable. The urge to ask philosophical questions and to yearn for answers to them constitutes fundamental aspects of what it is to be human: "philosophy is as indestructible a human function as art is" (*MEN*, 3). Philosophical questions, as often as not, are ones we do not feel able to ignore. We can, of course, leave them unresolved – and often do – but they continue to haunt us.

The choice (as to whether one should become a pragmatist or not) also qualifies as a *momentous* one. This both for an indirect and a direct reason. It is, James argues (particularly in the final lecture of *Lectures on Pragmatism*) indirectly momentous, since the decision to adopt a philosophy can, in turn, indirectly affect (either by underwriting or undermining) important and deeply held (ethical or religious) beliefs concerning how one should live. This already suffices to qualify the choice as a momentous one; but to break off the argument (concerning the applicability of the second condition) at this point would be to understate James's understanding of how philosophy matters.[19] For not only does James think that it is a necessary feature of a flourishing human life that one be exercised by philosophical questions, he holds that even the possibility of a (rational adult) person's experiencing her life as meaningful – and hence as worth living – ultimately rests to some degree upon an underlying philosophical attitude which (either consciously or unconsciously) informs that life. Hence the *Lectures on Pragmatism* begin:

> I know that you, ladies and gentlemen, have a philosophy, each and all of you, and that the most interesting and important thing about you is the way in which it determines the perspective in your several worlds. . . . [T]he philosophy which is so important in each of us is not a technical matter; it is our more or less dumb sense of what life honestly and deeply means. (*P*, 9)

That the choice in question, thirdly, involves a *living* option for most of his readers, James adduces from their evident dissatisfaction with traditional philosophical alternatives and their restless desire to find a philosophy which is genuinely satisfying. (This is, of course, quite consistent with James's thinking that pragmatism may not be a living option for some members of his audience.) The clinching irony comes with the question of the applicability of the fourth condition. For it turns out to have been the great service of Royce to have shown that the pragmatist credo also meets this condition (i.e., that the option of adopting it cannot be decided on intellectual grounds). James therefore finds a way to enlist Royce's carefully tailored argument against pragmatism to his own purpose, now claiming to find a virtue in the very feature of Royce's argument that he had previously most feared (namely, the thesis that any attempt at an intellectual justification of pragmatism can be shown to be self-contradictory).[20]

If the option of adopting the pragmatist "proposal" satisfies all four conditions, the argument from "The Will to Believe" may be extended to it. James is then free to conclude that "our passional nature not only lawfully may, but must, decide" a philosophical question of this sort for us. If we are confronted with an option that is both living and momentous, it would be ludicrous for us *not* to attempt to resolve it in one way or other. If it is a forced option, then we are not genuinely free to leave it unresolved. The only alternatives left open to us are to attempt to resolve it self-consciously and reflectively or unreflectively and by default. Finally, if (as James comes to believe is the case with pragmatism) the option cannot be decided on intellectual grounds, then we are forced to decide it on passional grounds. We should be careful, however, about the sense in which we are "forced" here. It is not that we are now obliged to make a resolute philosophical choice.[21] It is, rather, that whatever choice (or nonchoice) we make in this area is one whose justification rests on passional grounds. ("To say, under such circumstances, 'Do not decide, but leave the question open,' is itself a passional decision.")

But what does James mean when he writes, in his response to Royce, "I propose pragmatism to my readers, as something to be verified ambulando"? In "The Will to Believe" (and in "The Sentiment of Rationality"), James goes on to offer a second argument, building on the first. He argues that there is a further narrowly circumscribed class of beliefs that have the peculiar characteristic that, by virtue of one's having adopted them, they become true – not in the banal sense that one now discovers that they happen to be true – but in the sense that, in the course of allowing the conduct of one's life to be informed by them, one actually brings into being (or at least contributes to bringing into being) the very conditions which make them true. James's way of putting this (in "The Sentiment of Rationality") is to say: "There are then cases when faith (in a belief) creates its own verification" (*WB*, 97). To say that the justification for pragmatism can only emerge for a person *ambulando* means that it can only emerge in the course of living a life informed by the pragmatist credo. James therefore, in his reply to Royce, extends this second argument (also originally tailored so as only to apply to the justification of moral and religious beliefs) to philosophical conceptions as well. There may be no "abstract argumentation" which would allow one to demonstrate that pragmatism is a true theory, but one may (through one's adoption of it) nonetheless be able to bring into being the conditions under which one will be justified *ex post facto* in one's choice. Pragmatism's claim to our allegiance turns on its being able to "earn its way" in "the theatre of life" – its fruitfulness can only *show* itself within a human life and cannot otherwise be demonstrated. A pragmatist therefore is – not just someone who affirms a particular thesis after a chain of argument has convinced him of its truth but rather – a kind of person one *becomes* through a particular way of life.

The procedure by means of which one verifies such philosophical proposals is not only a messy a posteriori business, it is also one which is bound to exhibit in its results a certain degree of agent-relativity. This is an ineliminable consequence of the structure of James's arguments. His first argument decrees that you should adopt a philosophy only if that philosophy arouses a "sympathetic response" in your "passional nature"; it may not. His second argument asks you to look for verification *ambulando*; but, in order for "faith to create its own verification," you first have to be both willing and able to achieve the relevant sort of faith. Whether you are so willing and able will depend in large part on who you are and what sorts of choices are live options for you. So it is starting to look as if James owes us an answer to the question: "Are you only recommending pragmatism to *some* of your readers – namely, those who are most like you?" Some admirers of James no doubt would be pleased to have him answer this question in the affirmative and to let the matter rest at that. Let us reformulate the question so as to bring closer to the surface the difficulty which such a reading of James would pose. How are we to square (1) James's saying that we should adopt pragmatism *only* if it finds a "sympathetic response" in our "passional nature" (thus apparently recommending it only to some of his readers), with (2) his recommending it *to each and every one of us* evidently on the grounds that it is inherently superior to its competitors (in that, for example, it can satisfy two fundamental "kinds of demand" – neither of which should remain unsatisfied – whereas other philosophies can satisfy at most only one)? James needs to be able to reconcile the following two claims: (1) that the criteria upon which each of us should base our choice of a philosophy are, in an important sense, "personal," and so a sound application of those criteria may lead a reader properly to reject pragmatism; and (2) that James himself is nonetheless fully justified in commending pragmatism to that same reader.

James solves this problem by following the spirit, if not the letter, of Royce's most fervent recommendation to him. He supplements pragmatism with grounds only available from a further vantage point – one from which he can, without self-contradiction, commend pragmatism to all of his readers equally without qualification. But the further perspective from which he now asks us to consider the issue is not that of the Absolute, but rather one supplied by his heroes Emerson and Whitman: the vantage point of each person's "unattained but attainable self" (Emerson 1983, 239). Still determined to spurn Royce's Absolute Mind, James can only address his appeal to the sensibilities of finite thinkers. But he is able to distinguish two sorts of appeal: (1) an appeal to each person's actual present self and (2) an appeal to each person's ideal future self. The argument from "The Will to Believe" (in addressing a particular proposal to each of us, as we are presently constituted) must restrict itself to an appeal of the first sort; but James, when he speaks in his own voice, can without inconsistency – and often does – address an appeal of the second sort to his readers (rebuking them for being constituted as they presently are). There is no inconsistency in maintaining (1) that a person's choice of a philosophy should be a function of what is "best suited" to her present temperament; but (2) that human temperament, however apparently inertial, is subject to both criticism and change, and that there is therefore a further vantage point from which our choice of a philosophy is liable to censure, depending upon how well it accords with our latent possibilities for attaining our (Whitmanesque/Emersonian) "higher self."[22]

It is our higher self James must be understood as addressing (if he is to avoid inconsistency) when, for example, he rebukes us for failing to attend to the task of shaping and educating our temperaments. Philosophers, of course, come in for special censure in this regard; for they, above all, try to sink the fact of their temperaments. "There arises thus a certain insincerity in our philosophic discussions: the potentest of our premises is never mentioned" (*P*, 11). By obscuring the role played by individual sensibility in the attainment of philosophical conviction – placing it beyond the reach of criticism – philosophers, James suggests, tend to make themselves the victims of their own temperaments. The implication James draws from his claim that "temperaments with their cravings and refusals" are what "determine men in their philosophies" (*P*, 24) is not the time-honored one (i.e., that the philosopher should learn to transcend the influence of his temperament, permitting himself to be swayed only by "conventionally recognized reason"). James concludes, on the contrary, that what the philosopher needs to learn to do is to take *responsibility* for his temperament. Taking responsibility here requires openly acknowledging the role that temperament plays in consolidating one's philosophical convictions (hence the importance of cultivating a sensitivity as to when in philosophizing one should and should not be speaking in the first-person singular). It also requires subjecting to criticism those aspects of one's temperament which blind one to when and why others recoil, as from "a monstrous abridgment of life" (*WB*, 69), from the very philosophy which so attracts one (hence the importance of identifying the sources of one's feelings of philosophical temptation and compulsion). For most philosophies, James says – like all abridgments – are "got by the absolute loss and casting out of real matter" (*WB*, 69). Pragmatism seeks to redress this hitherto endemic feature of philosophy. It does so by taking as its point of departure the principle that no philosophy is acceptable which – in compensation for its other (metaphysical, logical, or explanatory) virtues – asks us to settle for such monstrous abridgments. "The entire man, who feels all needs by turns, will take nothing as an equivalent for life but the fullness of living itself" (*WB*, 69). James's unqualified recommendation of his pragmatist "proposal" is based on such an appeal to the "entire" person in each of us.

NOTES

This essay is indebted to Stanley Cavell's writings on perfectionism; to conversations about James with Steven Affeldt, Thomas Carlson, Richard Gale, and Hilary Putnam; and to comments on a previous draft by Cora Diamond, Richard Gale, and Ruth Anna Putnam.

1 Here is how Royce summarized the way in which he takes James's financial metaphors to spell bankruptcy:

> If we must, then, conceive recent pragmatism under the figure of a business enterprise, – a metaphor which my colleague's phraseology so insistently invites, – I am constrained therefore to sum up its position thus: First, with a winning clearness, and with a most honorable frankness it confesses bankruptcy, so far as the actually needed cash payments of significant truth are concerned. Secondly, it nevertheless declines to go into the hands of any real receiver, for it is not fond of anything that appears too absolute. And thirdly, it proposes simply and openly to go on doing business under the old style and title of the truth. "After all," it says, "are we not, every one of us, fond of credit values?" (Royce 1908, 346–7)

2 Royce repeatedly admonishes his fellow philosophers for their "thoughtless trust in abstract words" and directs them to attend to those

> matters at once familiar . . . as well as too much neglected in philosophy. When we use words . . . we easily deceive ourselves by the merely abstract meanings which we associate with each of the terms taken apart from the other. We forget the experiences from which the words have been abstracted. To these experiences we must return whenever we want really to comprehend the words. (Royce, 1915, 15–16)

3 Royce outlines his example as follows:

> Well, as to our concept of truth, let us consider a test case by way of helping ourselves to answer this question. Let us suppose that a witness appears, upon some witness stand, and objects to taking the ordinary oath, because he has conscientious scruples, due to the fact that he is a recent pragmatist, who has a fine new definition of truth, in terms of which alone he can be sworn. Let us suppose him, hereupon to be granted entire liberty to express his oath in his own way. Let him accordingly say, using, with technical scrupulosity, my colleague's definition of truth: "I promise to tell whatever is expedient and nothing but what is expedient, so help me future experience." I ask you: Do you think that this witness has expressed, with adequacy, that view of the nature of truth that you really wish a witness to have in mind? (Royce 1969, 987)

4 Here's Royce on how pragmatism offends common sense:

> But I, in answer, insist that common sense well feels this belief to be indeed from moment to moment expedient, and yet clearly distinguishes between that expedience and the truth which common sense all

the while attributes to the belief. The distinction is precisely the one which my fancied illustration of the pragmatist on the witness stand has suggested. It is a perfectly universal distinction and a commonplace one. Tell me, "This opinion is true," and whatever you are talking about I may agree or disagree or doubt; yet in any case you have stated a momentous issue. But tell me, "I just now find this belief expedient, it feels to me congruous" and you have explicitly given me just a scrap of your personal biography, and have told me no other truth whatever than a truth about the present state of your feelings. (Royce 1969, 989–90)

5 See, for example, *P*, 35–6, 44, 83.

6 Thus James denies Royce's frequent claim – as found, for example, in the following remarks in Royce's preface to *The Philosophy of Loyalty* – that he and Royce disagree about the nature of truth:

I have had to engage in a certain polemic regarding the problem of truth, – a polemic directed against certain opinions recently set forth by one of the dearest of my friends, . . . my teacher for a while in my youth; my honored colleague for many years, – Professor William James. . . . But if he and I do not see truth in the same light at present, we still do well, I think, as friends, each to speak his mind. (Royce 1908, x–xi; this preface is not reprinted in Royce 1969)

In reaction to the above remarks, in a 1908 letter to Royce, James claims he and Royce agree on the important thing (the nature of truth); it is merely – James mischievously says – a trifle concerning which they disagree:

Dear Royce, –
. . . I am sorry you say we don't see truth in the same light, for the only thing we see differently is the Absolute, and surely such a trifle as that is not a thing for two gentlemen to be parted by. (Perry 1935, 2:822)

7 Royce puts the challenge as follows:

For the question simply recurs: In what sense are these propositions about my own possible experience true when I do not test their truth, – yes, true although I, personally, *cannot* test their truth? These credits, irredeemable in terms of the cash of my experience, – wherein consists their true credit value? Here one apparently stands at the parting of the ways. One can answer this question by saying: "The truth of these assertions (or their falsity, if they are false) belongs to them whether I credit them or no, whether I verify them or not. Their truth or their falsity is their own character and is independent of my credit and my verification." But to say this appears to be, after all, just the intellectualism which so many of our modern pragmatists condemn. (Royce 1969, 698)

8 This is, of course, just what Royce insists he must say. The question they continue to disagree over is whether James can support his claim that the standard in question is one which is genuinely liable to *correc-*

tion (rather than merely open to revision in accordance with the changing whim of the community).

9 But minus the Peircean claim that we are *fated* to so converge.

10 "Truth absolute, [the pragmatist] says, means an ideal set of formulations towards which all opinions may in the long run be expected to converge" (*MT*, 143).

11 Dewey, who continues to try to refine James's theory (by identifying truth with warranted assertibility under ideal epistemic conditions), eventually (in his *Logic*) accedes to this criticism of Royce's and simply bites the bullet, declaring that he is no longer out to tell us what we mean by "true" but is rather simply scrapping the commonsense notion and offering a revisionist account of truth. Insofar as James's account often resembles Dewey's, some commentators have felt entitled to conclude that James also intends to be in the business of offering a revisionist account of truth. But the preponderance of the textual evidence speaks against the claim that James proposes his theory in this spirit. For he keeps saying to his reader: my account (unlike Royce's) accords best with your own natural understanding – the understanding of the common man; and he keeps saying to Royce: we don't disagree about the nature of truth, we just disagree about the necessity of postulating the Absolute.

12 I am going to pass over the question as to whether this distinction (between asserting something as a general truth and holding it as a live mental attitude) can do the work James wants it to do. (I am inclined to think it cannot.) I am simply interested here in how James, in availing himself of this distinction, believes he has found a way simultaneously (1) to maintain that pragmatism is not a "theory" and (2) to recommend pragmatism to his readers as a "philosophy."

13 One could read James here as saying to Royce: your arguments may short-circuit new-fangled modern (Cartesian) skeptical theory, but not old-style ancient (Pyrrhonic) skeptical praxis.

14 It is quite clear from the context that James is here responding to Royce.

15 If one is to make any sense of this at all, the meanings of both the words "proposal" and "verify" must both be understood in light of the claim that what is at issue here is the adoption – not of a theory, but rather – of a live mental attitude.

16 In a similar spirit, James writes elsewhere: "No philosophy will be deemed permanently rational by all men which (in addition to meeting logical demands) does not to some degree . . . make a direct appeal to *all* those powers of our nature which we hold in highest esteem" (*WB*, 110; emphasis added).

17 This suggestion invites the charge that James conflates the question of

the psychological causes of our beliefs with the question of the normative grounds for their justification. It is thus worth emphasizing that
James himself elsewhere (for example, in the first chapter of *The Varieties of Religious Experience*) attaches great importance to distinguishing a person's "justifiable reasons" for holding a belief from "the causal
antecedents" that may have led to the belief.

18 James would be the first to agree that it would be the height of irrationalism to apply the argument of the essay to most questions (insofar as
they do not meet these four conditions). In particular, scientific questions do not qualify since they do not satisfy the fourth condition; in
such cases James holds (contrary to what most commentators maintain)
that one should wait patiently (even if the matter happens also to be
living, forced, and *momentous*) for it to be decided on "objective intellectual grounds."

19 "Hast any philosophy in thee, Shepherd?" – this question of Touchstone's is the one with which men should always meet one another. A
man with *no* philosophy in him is the most inauspicious and unprofit-
able of all possible social mates (*SPP*, 11).

20 Royce would surely deny that his argument delivers what it is here
advertised as delivering: namely, the requisite materials for satisfying
the fourth condition. From Royce's point of view, the correct conclusion
to draw is that James equivocates in his use of the phrase "X cannot be
decided on intellectual ground," failing to distinguish two very different
sorts of cases: (1) the sort of case in which one is able to understand the
meaning of a question, and to understand what it would be to decide it
on intellectual grounds alone, and then, in the light of this understanding, rejects the possibility of its being so decidable; and (2) the sort of
case in which the very attempt to raise the possibility of deciding the
question on intellectual grounds itself causes us to lose our handle on
the intelligibility of our original question.

21 The argument is insufficiently powerful to yield such a conclusion, especially given the role that an appeal to temperament plays in the argument.
For whether individuals incline toward resoluteness is itself something
which varies with temperament. One can always conclude: "None of the
available options satisfy me." Indeed, by James's lights, very few of us will
ever succeed in being philosophically resolute. Nothing in "The Will to
Believe" argument, taken in isolation, equips James to criticize such ir-
resoluteness. Nevertheless, it is clear that (elsewhere in his writing) he
seeks a vantage point from which he can criticize us for dithering philosophically (and hence, in his view, existentially). I suggest in the closing
pages of this essay that the vantage point presupposed by this dimension

of James's thought cannot be comprehended apart from an examination of (what one might call) his Emersonianism.

22 The perfectionist moment in Emerson and Whitman to which James resonates is also what most attracts him to the philosophy of John Stuart Mill. James's claim that pragmatism is best suited to the temperament of our higher self is, at bottom, a variation on Mill's defense of his own doctrine (which also promises not to leave our true nature "stunted and starved" as other philosophies do) by means of the claim that we only assess the relative merits of the higher pleasures once we have experienced them. The Millian way of formulating James's defense of pragmatism would be to say that once we properly experience the higher satisfactions pragmatism affords we will have a rational basis (not otherwise available) for rejecting our former self's one-sided temperamental affinity for a philosophy that can only satisfy one of our (higher self's) two fundamental "kinds of demand." This helps explain why the book – in which James so frequently quotes Whitman and in which his "own solution" (i.e., that "oddly-named thing pragmatism") is put forward "as a philosophy that can satisfy both kinds of demand" (P, 23) – might be dedicated to Mill.

11 William James on religious experience

At the outset of his Gifford Lectures, *The Varieties of Religious Experience*, William James advises readers that he comes to his subject matter not as theologian nor as historian of religion nor as anthropologist but as a psychologist. James is alluding to his earlier labors, of which *The Principles of Psychology* (1890) and *Psychology: Briefer Course* (1892) are the notable monuments. Whatever varied fortunes these publications met with in James's own times, they have acquired the stature of landmarks, certainly in the history of American psychology but also – less conspicuously perhaps – in the modern history of ideas. Gordon W. Allport, for example, attests to the former fact in his preface to a 1961 reissue of *Briefer Course:* William James's "depiction of mental life is faithful, vital, subtle. In verve he has no equal." The "expanding horizon of James," he adds, contrasts markedly with the "constricting horizon of much contemporary psychology"; and Allport suggests that readers of the book apply the pragmatic test for themselves by asking whether they find their own horizons enlarged, whether they feel the "pulse of human nature."[1]

Allport's comment is applicable in greater or lesser measure to a good deal else in James's authorship and not least to *The Varieties of Religious Experience.* But readers who explore *Varieties* without some familiarity with *Principles* or such earlier essays as "The Will To Believe" (1896) are likely to be surprised, because James's spare identification of himself as a psychologist scarcely prepares them for the broad range of issues that he presents. What they discover is that *Varieties's* twenty lectures and postscript project a complex venture in which multiple and diverse threads of thought weave together to make up a distinctive and often fascinating tapestry, the design of which, however, remains unfinished. This incompleteness is both disappointing and challenging. It is disappointing to readers who wish to have immediately in hand more than the book offers of James's considered conclusions respecting religious experience. It is challenging to readers who are ready to search elsewhere in James's writings for additional evidence of what these views might be. For the purpose at hand, we shall first attend briefly to the reasons for the incompleteness of James's accomplishments in his Gifford Lectures and then to some indications of the complexity of James's project. These indications of complexity will in turn lead us into the substance of the book.

I INCOMPLETENESS AND COMPLEXITY OF VARIETIES

A letter James wrote to Frances Morse on 12 April 1900 reveals something of his developing intentions as the time of the Gifford Lectures approached.

> The problem I have set myself is a hard one: *first,* to defend (against all the prejudices of my "class") "experience" against "philosophy" as being the real backbone of the world's religious life – I mean prayer, guidance, all that sort of thing immediately and privately felt, as against high and noble general views of our destiny and the world's meaning; and *second,* to make the hearer or reader believe, what I myself invincibly do believe, that, although all the special manifestations of religion have been absurd (I mean its creeds and theories), yet the life of it as a whole is mankind's most important function. A task well-nigh impossible, I fear, and in which I shall fail; but to attempt it is *my* religious act. (*Letters,* 2:127)

Among the various implications of these lines, we shall note two. (1) The "philosophy" against which James means to defend "experience" is the philosophy that celebrates complete cosmic unity and clarity from the viewpoint of an "All Knower," a kind of philosophy James had already criticized in his 1898 address, "philosophical Conceptions and Practical Results,"[2] and continued to criticize at greater length in *Pragmatism* (1907) – see, for example, his criticism of the notion of *"the one Knower"* in the chapter "The One and the Many" (71–6) – as well as in *A Pluralistic Universe* (1909) and "A World of Pure Experience" in *Essays in Radical Empiricism* (1912).[3] (2) Again, "experience" in this context stands for, though it is not exhausted by, sensation, perception, feelings, prayer, changes of heart, deliverances from fear, and alterations of attitude. Experience is the cornerstone of James's prospective or pragmatic metaphysical pluralism, which privileges not the "all-form," as do philosophies of the absolute, but the "each-form, which is our human form of experiencing the world" (*PU*, 25–6) and so is far more compatible with the inferences that an empirical study of religious life prompts us to draw. In *A Pluralistic Universe* James asks: "May not the flux of sensible experience itself contain a rationality that has been overlooked . . . ?" (38).

However, James did not accomplish all that his letter to Frances Morse intimates, and the *Varieties* we read is not the *Varieties* he originally planned. His original design had been to devote the second of his two-year course of lectures to his own philosophical assessment of religion, to what on one occasion he called "The Tasks of Religious Philosophy" (*VRE*, 534); but poor health frustrated the realization of that ambition, so that only the twentieth or final lecture together with the author's postscript deal explicitly with his philosophical reflections on religious experience.[4] After completing the whole course, he lamented to F. C. S. Schiller: "99/100 or more of the book is descriptive and documentary, and the constructive part is a mere indication" (547).

Though James could not fulfill his initial plan, *The Varieties of Religious Experience* as we have it is rich and complex. The richness appears in too many places for so brief an essay as this even to mention, let alone examine, but certainly a good example of it is the extended passage on prayer (365–76), which is all the more noteworthy because of the author's disavowal of "any live belief in a conscious spirit of the universe with whom I may hold communion" (492); though James could also write to James Henry Leuba of his own "mystical *germ*. It is a very common germ. It creates the rank and file of believers" (*Letters*, 2:211). The rich complexity of *Varieties* grows in part out of the author's own complicated nature. It is also a function of the distinctive composition of the book; for in *Varieties* we meet with (1) copious firsthand accounts of religious experience – accounts that James calls his *documents humains* – together with (2) James's psychological description and commentary on these accounts and (3) also James's own occasional philosophical assessments of the significance both of the accounts and the psychological commentary. The total effect is that of a never-ending conversation always carried on by several participants. We need, however, to inquire into the specific elements contributing to this effect.

In the order in which these elements appear, the first to announce itself in a subtle but significant way is James's statement at the outset that his treatment of religious experience will be psychological. However, he does not identify the kind of psychology he means to employ. Readers alert to this lack of specificity might expect that the psychology to be applied will be the psychology James himself had already done so much to develop. However, James introduced important changes in his own psychology between *Principles* and *Briefer Course*. One of these requires mention here. It first appears in the fact that James changed his definition of psychology. *Principles* opens with a definition of psychology as "the Science of Mental Life," while *Briefer Course* defines it as *"the description and explanation of states of consciousness as such."* As the "Science of Mental Life," psychology is a relatively open-ended discipline and includes, among other things, some more-or-less elaborated theory of the knowing relation of consciousness to "objects independent of consciousness" or "The Relations of Minds to Other Objects," a major topic of classical philosophical psychology. And *Principles* does in fact explicitly affirm a more-or-less traditional subject/object dualism (*PP*, 1:212–16). But when defined as "the description and explanation of states of consciousness as such," psychology is more restricted and excludes issues of metaphysics, axiology, and theory of knowledge. Indeed, the point of this second definition is to present psychology as an empirical "natural science," which does not purport to be also a "Theory of Knowledge" or a "Rational Psychology."[5] Hence, James's change in the definition of psychology signals a revision of the scope of psychology. Naturally, which of these versions of psychology James intends to put to work in *Varieties* is a matter of great importance. The most plausible hypothesis is that *Varieties* will proceed along the lines of psychology as a natural science "of consciousness *as such*," since the later conception ought theoretically to supersede the earlier. However, we find James saying in the concluding chapter of *Briefer Course*:

When, then, we talk of psychology as a natural science, we must not assume that that means a sort of psychology that stands at last on solid ground. It means just the reverse; it means a psychology particularly fragile, and into which the waters of metaphysical criticism leak at every point, a psychology all of whose elementary assumptions and data must be reconsidered in wider connections and translated into other terms. It is, in short, a phrase of diffidence, and not of arrogance. (*PB*, 400)

Given these remarks, we do well to approach *Varieties* with some caution and attend closely to the text for clues as to whether "metaphysical criticism leaks in." If James stands by his avowal to Frances Morse that he invincibly believes the life of religion as a whole to be humankind's most important function, then metaphysical and other "wider considerations" are likely to exercise a far-reaching influence throughout *Varieties*, no matter how far short it falls of realizing the author's original plan.

We need next to attend to James's philosophical distinction between "existential" and "spiritual" or value judgments. As early as the third paragraph in lecture 1 he states that as a psychologist the natural thing for him is to share with his hearers a *descriptive* survey of human religious propensities, of "religious feelings and religious impulse," drawn from "those more developed subjective phenomena recorded in literature produced by articulate and fully self-conscious men, in works of piety and autobiography" (*VRE*, 12). But almost immediately he explains that he must address not only the question, "What are the religious propensities?" but also the question, "What is their philosophical significance?" The answers to these two kinds of question, he adds, must be made independently of each other and can be combined only subsequently (13). The first question requires by way of answer "existential" propositions or judgments; the second calls for propositions of value or "spiritual" judgments. "[E]xistential facts by themselves are insufficient for determining . . . value"(14). The distinction between existential propositions and spiritual judgments is a matter of urgency for James for at least two reasons. The first derives from his decision to base his descriptions of religious propensities, feelings, and impulses in large measure on the utterances of religious "geniuses" or "pattern-setters" rather than on those who live their religion at "second-hand" or as "dull habit." But such personalities often appear as eccentric and exaggerated, even morbid and pathological. James offers George Fox, founder of the Society of Friends, as an example together with a passage from his journals that makes his point dramatically (16). Plainly he is mindful that his appeal to pathological personalities may prompt readers to be skeptical of the sorts of religious experience he shall be presenting.

The other reason is his philosophical disagreement with those he calls "medical materialists" and their contention that religious experiences are "nothing but" products of hysteria or of a disordered colon or of epileptic seizures.[6] To counter such objections he devotes much of the first lecture to his argument that eccentricity of character or neurological disorders (that is, "natural antecedents") have little, if anything, to do with *the way in which [religion] works on the whole"* (24). On the contrary, James asserts, the value of religious attitudes, beliefs, and ways of life

can only be ascertained by spiritual judgments directly passed upon them, judgments based on our own immediate feeling primarily; and secondarily on what we can ascertain of their experiential relations to our moral needs and to the rest of what we hold to be true. (*VRE*, 23)[7]

In brief, he concludes that the only criteria genuinely applicable in value judgments concerning religious experience are "immediate luminousness," "philosophical reasonableness," and "moral helpfulness" (23).

Just what James means by "immediate luminousness" is not wholly clear, but certainly it applies to experiences so intrusive or compelling in the lives of those who undergo them that an alteration of their sense of self and of their life-world ensues.[8] In the text of *Varieties* James uses the word "experience" rather loosely. At times it seems to mean "[t]hat unsharable feeling which each one of us has of the pinch of destiny . . . rolling out on fortune's wheel" (393). At other times it seems to mean sensible apprehensions of change. James quotes from Jonathan Edwards's well-known "Personal Narrative," which is filled with accounts of sensible apprehensions of change (202). And at still other times it evidently carries yet other meaning; but apparently it always means "knowledge" carrying practical consequences, even though the "knowledge" be by bare acquaintance.

In any case James believes that the criteria he adduces are pragmatic;[9] they are at bottom one and the same with "our empiricist criterion: By their fruits you shall know them, not by their roots." To legitimize the empiricist criterion further, he extracts from Edwards's *Treatise Concerning Religious Affections* the summary sentence: "*The degree* in which our experience is productive of practice shows *the degree in which our experience is spiritual and divine*"

(25). Directly addressing readers, he concludes: "[Y]ou must all be ready now to judge the religious life by its results exclusively, and I shall assume that the bugaboo of morbid origin will scandalize your piety no more" (26).

Evidently, then, James employs multiple methods: the existential or descriptive method *and* the philosophical method. In turn, the philosophical method involves examination and judgment upon the moral usefulness of religious experience *and* the relation of such experience to the rest of what we believe or hold to be true. So we see that the project as outlined in the first lecture is indeed complex and, as we anticipated, involves a good deal more than description of religious propensities. It is not surprising, then, that James introduces into *Varieties* his *own* philosophical judgments of both kinds, namely, judgments about moral usefulness and judgments about the relation of religious experience to the rest of what we believe. And these surface at multiple places prior to this statement of his conclusions in lecture 20. For example, at a point where he compares the implications of the "gospel of healthy-mindedness" with the life-experience of the "sick soul," he corrects, as it were, the philosophical theology professed by advocates of "mind-cure" religion. Whereas their *utterances* tend to be "monistic," their *attitude* toward disease implies no more than that it can be overcome by union with a "higher Presence." "The higher Presence . . . need not be the absolute whole of things"; it need be simply a part, "if only it be the most ideal part" (113, n4). In certain of the healthy-minded James frankly admires their refusal to consecrate evil as necessary to the perfection of the absolute whole of things. For them evil "is emphatically irrational . . . a waste element to be sloughed off and negated." Here we meet with reasons for adopting a pluralistic metaphysics in contrast to a monistic metaphysics. "[P]hilosophical theism," James observes, "has always shown a tendency to become pantheistic and monistic, and to consider the world as one unit of absolute fact; and this has been at variance with popular or practical theism, which latter has ever been more or less frankly pluralistic, not to say polytheistic. . . . I ask you now not to forget this notion [of pluralism]; for although most philosophers seem either to forget it or to disdain it too much ever to mention it, I believe that we shall have to admit it ourselves in the end as containing an element of truth" (112–14).

James's own attitude toward evil, his own moral feeling with respect to philosophies of the absolute, carry very heavy weight in his value judgments when considering certain kinds of narratives and testimonies of religious experience.[10]

II BELIEF IN AN UNSEEN ORDER

While the active presence of James's own philosophizing is plainly evident in the foregoing passage, lecture 3, "The Reality of the Unseen," presents us with material that is more ambiguous. Our question is, once again, whether James is here engaged in a solely descriptive enterprise, a description of consciousness *as such*, or is venturing into territory having possible philosophical significance. (Of course in the normal order of reading we would approach lecture 3 through lecture 2, "Circumscription of the Topic." But the later text also throws light upon the earlier.) James begins by saying that he wishes to call attention to some of the "psychological peculiarities" of belief "that there is an unseen order and that our supreme good lies in harmoniously adjusting ourselves thereto," for it is such "belief that characterizes the life of religion in the broadest and most general terms possible." He generalizes to the effect that "[a]ll our attitudes, moral, practical, or emotional, as well as religious, are due to the 'objects' of our consciousness, the things we believe to exist, whether really or ideally, along with ourselves" (51). Setting aside belief founded upon rationalistic arguments, such as "the proofs of God's existence drawn from the order of nature," he concentrates upon "the existence in our mental machinery of a sense of present reality more diffused and general than that which our special senses yield" (58–9). This latter sense of reality attached both to "abstract objects," such as transcendental ideas of "soul," "God," and "immortality," which despite their lacking sense-content do have a definite meaning for our practice, and to "quasi-sensible realities directly apprehended." Among the latter are feelings of the *presence* of God, and by way of documentation James quotes from an unidentified Swiss writer: "At bottom the expression most apt to render what I felt is this: God was present, though invisible; he fell under no one of my senses, yet my consciousness perceived him" (63). But he also adduces many other similar examples.

Referring to the sense of reality of abstract objects like "God," he observes that its strength can be such that "our whole life is polarized . . . by its sense of the existence of the thing believed in."

It is as if a bar of iron, without touch or sight, with no representative faculty whatever, might nevertheless be strongly endowed with an inner capacity for magnetic feeling; and as if, through the various arousals of its magnetism by magnets coming and going in its neighborhood, it be consciously determined to different attitudes and tendencies. Such a bar of iron could never give you an outward description of the agencies that had the power of stirring it so strongly; yet of their presence, and of their significance for its life, it would be intensely aware through every fibre of its being. . . . The whole universe of concrete objects . . . swims . . . in a wider and higher universe of abstract ideas, that lend it its significance. (*VRE,* 53)

In connection with direct apprehension of quasi-sensible realities, he supplies multiple examples from his *documents humains,* including that of the Swiss writer already mentioned as well as others that he deems to be of a mystical character. "Such," James concludes, "is the human ontological imagination, and such is the convincingness of what it brings to birth. . . . [T]hese feelings of reality . . . are as convincing to those who have them as any direct sensible experiences can be" (*VRE,* 66). Our articulate religious systems of beliefs are persuasive only when our inarticulate feelings of reality have been impressed in favor of the same conclusions. James hastens to add that he does not "yet say that it is *better* that the subconscious and non-rational should thus hold primacy in the religious realm. I confine myself to simply pointing out that [it does] so hold it as a matter of fact" (68).

Clearly, "The Reality of the Unseen" is susceptible of differing readings. It may be descriptive of unusual persons or states only or it may also portend a still-to-be-developed metaphysical significance. Which of these is the case readers must decide for themselves as they follow James's undertaking farther. But several features of this third lecture are especially important. (1) It is here that James introduces his metaphor of the magnetic field. (2) Here also he associates these dumb intuitions of the reality of the unseen with mysticism, a form of religious experience he takes very seriously in *Varieties.* (3) His manner of speaking in lecture 3 is in its tenor though not in its language reminiscent of the distinction he drew in *The Principles of Psychology* between *knowledge of acquaintance* and *knowledge-about.* This distinction requires elaboration. "All the elementary natures of the world . . . must either not be known at all, or known in this dumb way of acquaintance without *knowledge-about*." Whatever we know by way of knowledge of acquaintance only we cannot impart to others. They must make the acquaintance for themselves. "What we are only acquainted with is only *present* to our minds; we *have* it, or the idea of it. But when we know about it, we do more than merely have it; we seem, as we think over its relations, to subject it to a sort of *treatment* and to *operate* upon it with our thoughts. The words *feeling* and *thought* give voice to the antithesis" (*PP*, 1:217–18). The distinction *Principles* makes here is not absolute. Each kind of knowledge appears to be what it is only in relation to the other kind. James went on to develop this distinction in a number of his later publications, notably in *Essays in Radical Empiricism* but also in *Pragmatism* and *The Meaning of Truth*. All in all, *Varieties* is a transitional book, exhibiting description and spiritual judgments, psychology and incipient metaphysics, intertwining in James's mind.

III CHARACTERISTICS OF RELIGION

In the concluding lecture of *Varieties* James asks, "[I]s the existence of so many religious types and sects and creeds regrettable?" His answer is an emphatic "No":

The divine can mean no single quality, it must mean a group of qualities, by being champions of which in alternation, different men may all find worthy missions. Each attitude being a syllable in human nature's total message, it takes the whole of us to spell the meaning out completely. . . . We must frankly recognize the fact that we live in partial systems, and that parts are not interchangeable in the spiritual life (384).

This answer is consistent with the pluralism evident throughout the lectures. Accordingly in lecture 2, "Circumscription of the Topic," James shuns identification of a simple essence of religion and instead sets himself the task of distinguishing multiple signs of religion, all the while keeping in mind that the differences between religious and nonreligious phenomena are vague and variable.

As a starting point, he proposes his well-known formulation: "Religion, therefore, as I now ask you arbitrarily to take it, shall mean for us *the feelings, acts, and experiences of individual men in their solitude, so far as they apprehend themselves to stand in relation to whatever they may consider the divine"* (*VRE*, 34). Following on this flexible definition he moves back and forth between specifications of feelings, acts, and experiences, on the one hand, and specifications of what may be considered as "the divine," on the other; that is, between the "subjective" and the "objective" or "intentional" poles of religious experience. We shall enumerate these subjective and objective features as briefly as possible.

He begins by considering the "divine." Given what we have already noted in "The Reality of the Unseen," this is not as surprising as it might otherwise seem. In any case he takes care to construe the "divine" very broadly. (1) It is "active" (35); (2) "divine" denotes "any object that is god*like,* whether it be a concrete deity or not" (36); (3) "gods . . . overarch and envelop, and from them there is no escape" (36). Thereupon James turns to our human responses to distinguish what counts as religious response. Expressions such as "All is vanity!" (Ecclesiastes 1:2) signify *reactions* on "the whole of life" but do not qualify as religious responses. (4) "The divine shall mean for us only such a primal reality as the individual feels impelled to respond to *solemnly* and *gravely,* and neither by a curse nor a jest" (39, emphasis added). Moreover, (5) religious response is *energetic.* "Energy" and associated terms such as "hot" and "cold" are words James favors throughout, as we shall see. (6) Religious response exceeds the moral frame of mind. Morality involves volitional effort, an "athletic attitude," while in the religious state of mind "the will to assert ourselves and hold our own has been displaced by a willingness to close our mouths and be as nothing in the floods and waterspouts of God" (46). Finally, (7) the religious state of mind is one of happiness. But "religious happiness in no mere feeling of escape. It cares no longer to escape. It consents to the evil outwardly as a form of sacrifice – inwardly it knows it to be permanently overcome." It is "a higher happiness [that] holds a lower unhappiness in check" (48). All this prompts James to conclude: *"Religion thus makes easy and felicitous what in any case is necessary;* and if it be the only agency that can accomplish this result, its vital importance as a human faculty stands vindicated beyond dispute" (49). Thus in his circumscription James proceeds from simple to increasingly complex "states" or "fields" of consciousness. Whether these are indeed predicates of "individual men in their solitude," which James here states them to be, depends on how we construe the individual's relation to the "more," of which he speaks in his last lecture. In any case, it becomes ever clearer he values most the religious attitude that is "two stories deep," that acknowledges the reality of the "negative or tragic principle." For example, later, while commenting on the antagonism between healthy-mindedness and morbid-mindedness, he asserts:

[T]here is no doubt that healthy-mindedness *is inadequate as a philosophical doctrine*, because the evil facts which it refuses positively to account for are a genuine portion of reality; and they may after all be the best key to life's significance, and possibly the only openers of our eyes to the deepest levels of truth (136, emphasis added).

IV TYPES OF RELIGIOUS EXPERIENCE

The ensuing course James follows in *Varieties* moves from healthy-mindedness, with his distinction between an involuntary and a voluntary or systematic healthy-mindedness, to sick soul and divided self, to conversion, saintliness, and mysticism. With the possible exception of the lectures on mysticism, the sequence James adopts conforms to the ideal progression of evangelical religious experience. This sequence provides the bulk of the "concrete data" upon which his own conclusions are based. In the remainder of this essay we shall attend to the divided self, conversion, saintliness, and mysticism, as representing James's whole itinerary. Then we shall consider his final reflections.

Augustine's *Confessions* contains the paradigmatic report of the self divided against itself, yet James's references to Augustine are relatively infrequent and are made only in passing, though he does quote from book 8, in which Augustine describes his two wills as embattled with each other (143–4). He is much more attracted by John Bunyan's spiritual combat, set forth in *Grace Abounding to the Chief of Sinners*, by Leo Tolstoy's *My Confession*, and by the diary of David Brainerd, an eighteenth-century missionary to native Americans. He even compares one of his own experiences to Bunyan's, in an indirect manner;[11] and, as we know from other sources, he, like Tolstoy, considered suicide for an extended period of time.[12] James echoes Tolstoy's words, "Faith . . . is the force whereby we live!" at numerous points throughout *Varieties*. From Tolstoy he cites lines that exhibit several of the classical traits of the self divided and the self converted.

> I remember one day in early spring, I was alone in the forest, lending my ear to its mysterious noises. I listened, and my thought went back to what for these three years it always was busy with – the quest of God. But the idea of him, I said, how did I ever come by the idea? And again there arose in me, with this thought, glad aspirations towards life. Everything in me awoke and received a meaning. . . . Why do I look farther? a voice within me asked. He is there: he, without whom one cannot live. To acknowledge God and to live are one and the same thing. God is what life is. Well, then! live, seek God, and there will be no life without him. After this, things cleared up within me and about me better than ever, and the light has never wholly died away. I was saved from suicide. Just how or when the change took place I cannot tell. . . . I gave up the life of the conventional world, recognizing it to be no life, but a parody on life, which its superfluities simply keep us from comprehending. (154)

One salient feature of Tolstoy's account is that it offers an instance of the practical effects of religious experience. But what is equally if not more striking is the simplicity and restraint of its language. By way of contrast, Brainerd is fervent.

> One morning, while I was walking in a solitary place, as usual, I at once saw that all my contrivances and projects to effect or procure deliverance and salvation for myself were utterly *in vain*. . . . I continued . . . in this state of mind, from Friday morning till the Sabbath evening following, (July 12, 1739,) when I was walking again in the same solitary place . . . *I was attempting to pray; but found no heart to engage in that or any other duty . . . disconsolate, as if there was nothing in heaven or earth could make me happy* . . . then, as I was walking in a dark thick grove, *unspeakable glory* seemed to open to the apprehension of my soul. . . . [I]t was a new inward apprehension or view that I had of *God* . . . it appeared to be *Divine glory.* My soul *rejoiced with joy unspeakable.* . . . I had no thought about my own salvation, and scarce reflected that there was such a creature as myself. . . . I felt myself in a new world, and every thing about me appeared with a different aspect from what it was wont to do. (175–6)

Brainerd's outpouring graphically exemplifies the passage "from a less into a more," "from a smallness into a vastness": the phenomenon of the eruption of a wide extramarginal consciousness into a constricted ordinary consciousness, which James delineates at points to which we shall soon attend. Numerous other voices populate these central lectures, but these examples must suffice as representative of the rest.

It is in lecture 9, the first on conversion, that James defines it as "the process, gradual or sudden, by which a self hitherto divided, and consciously wrong inferior and unhappy, becomes unified and consciously right superior and happy, in consequence of its firmer hold upon religious realities" (157). Of course, in keeping with his general method, he takes due note of counterconversions (147–8), but in *Varieties* his interest is in the former; and it is in lecture 9 that he recurs to the "field of consciousness" metaphor, ostensibly for psychological descriptive purposes only. Alluding to Buddhists and to David Hume's criticism of substantial personal identity, with which in fact he does not wholly agree,[13] James says that "[f]or them the soul is only a succession of fields of consciousness." Appropriating this "succession of fields" model to his own ends, he elaborates that in each successive field is a "focal" subfield containing the "excitement." Such focal subfields are "hot," and from them "personal desire and volition make their sallies," while parts of the field that leave us indifferent or passive are "cold." In the divided self, hot and cold parts oscillate rapidly. But if "the focus of excitement and heat . . . [comes] to lie permanently within a certain system; and . . . if the change be a religious one, we call it a *conversion*, especially if it be by crisis, or sudden" (162). James proposes that such a "hot" place be called *the habitual centre of . . . personal energy.*" Nonetheless, he cautions, while psychology can give a general description of what happens in such alterations of the center of personal energy, it is unable to account accurately for all the single forces at work. In fact, "[n]either an outside observer nor the Subject who undergoes the process can explain fully how particular experiences are able to change one's centre of energy so decisively" (163).

In lecture 10, his second on conversion, James further develops the field-of-consciousness model by returning to the analogy of a magnetic field, which we first met in lecture 3, "The Reality of the Unseen." Now, however, his purpose is to direct our attention to the margins of these fields. Whether mental fields be wide or narrow, each is surrounded by an indeterminate margin resembling a "magnetic field," which influences our attention and our behavior. As our present phase of consciousness with its margins alters into its successor with its margins, "our centre of energy turns like a compass needle" (189).¹⁴ But having said this, he forthwith introduces what he calls the "*extra*-marginal." "The ordinary psychology . . . has taken for granted, first, that all the consciousness the person now has, be the same focal or marginal, inattentive or attentive, is there in the 'field' of the moment, all dim and impossible to assign as the latter's outline may be; and, second, that what is absolutely extra-marginal is absolutely non-existent, and cannot be a fact of consciousness at all." What the ordinary psychology overlooks is "a set of memories, thoughts, and feelings which are extra-marginal and outside of the primary consciousness altogether, but yet must be classed as conscious facts of some sort, able to reveal their presence by unmistakable signs" (190). Along with "extra-marginal" James employs several other terms as synonyms: "ultra-marginal," "subliminal," and "subconscious." This reference to "primary consciousness" and to "conscious facts of some sort" that are outside of it, coming as abruptly as it does, is arresting and leads us to expect more about them from James.¹⁵ But in lecture 10 he offers only scant further comment on their function and importance. Instead he turns to the phenomena of automatism¹⁶ and then adduces more instances of conversion experiences, save that before closing the lecture he makes two significant remarks pertinent to the "extra" or "ultra-marginal" region. (1) A strongly developed ultramarginal consciousness is a "region in which mental work can go on subliminally, and from which invasive experiences, abruptly upsetting the equilibrium of the primary consciousness, may come" (193). (2) James hypothesizes that this ultramarginal consciousness, if fact it be,¹⁷ affords us a possible psychological description of instantaneous conversion, which does not necessarily exclude the validity of the religious conviction that God is directly present in conversion experiences as an "external" and "higher control."

[J]ust as our primary wide-awake consciousness throws open our senses to the touch of things material, so it is logically conceivable that *if there be* higher spiritual agencies that can directly touch us, the psychological condition of their doing so *might be* our possession of a subconscious region which alone should yield access to them. The hubbub of the waking life might close a door which in the dreamy Subliminal might remain ajar or open. (197)

The subjunctive construction in these lines underscores that James is indeed advancing an hypothesis. In fact, it is a double hypothesis: that the subliminal is a possible door opening on a larger reality; and that there may be higher spiritual agencies or the equivalent thereof. But it is an hypothesis he takes with the greatest seriousness. So much is evident in his communication of June 1901 to Henry W. Rankin:

I attach the mystical or religious consciousness to the possession of an extended subliminal self, with a thin partition through which messages make irruption. We are thus made convincingly aware of the presence of a sphere of life larger and more powerful than our usual consciousness, with which the latter is nevertheless continuous. The impressions and impulsions and emotions and excitements which we thence receive help us to live, they found invincible assurance of *a world beyond the sense*, they . . . communicate significance and value to everything. (emphasis added)[18]

But at this point he does not dwell further upon the (double) hypothesis and postpones further discussion of its significance until late in lecture 20 (406–8). For his real interest here lies in the question of the *value* of such possible "higher spiritual agencies." Accordingly, invoking his pragmatic principle, he immediately adds that what matters is the effects such agencies might produce. "[T]he mere fact of their transcendency would of itself establish no presumption that they were more divine than diabolical" (197).

Before we move from James's discussion of conversion to his lectures on saintliness, we should note that his model of consciousness as a wavelike succession of fields with their indeterminate margins thinly partitioned from an ultramarginal region implies that consciousness is not a perduring substantial entity. In this respect the psychology informing *Varieties* recalls James's earlier stream of consciousness model that stresses the transitiveness of consciousness. It also vaguely anticipates his 1904 essay, republished in *Essays in Radical Empiricism*, "Does Consciousness Exist?" in which James challenges the conventional subject/object distinction, rejects its ground assumption that "object-plus-subject is the minimum that can actually be," and proposes that subject and object, consciousness and content, are two additive moments of pure experience (*ERE*, 5–7).

James's lectures on saintliness (11–13) and on the value of saintliness (14–15) follow naturally on his inquiry into conversion. Saintliness is the ideal though uncertain outcome of conversion; in it spiritual emotions form the new center of personal energy. It is in these pages that he explicitly brings his "spiritual judgments" on religious experience to bear. Among these some of the more notable are: (a) religions "approve" themselves so far as they minister to vital needs; "[n]o religion has ever yet owed its prevalence to 'apodictic certainty' " (266); (b) religious institutions are prone to becoming interested chiefly in their own dogma and corporate ambitions (268–9); (c) every saintly virtue is liable to corruption (272); (d) charity, for all its tenderness, is essential to the evolution of society (285–6); (e) the truth in asceticism is that "he who feeds on death that feeds on men possesses life supereminently . . . and meets best the secret demands of the universe" (290). But we must leave these judgments without further comment except to note the summary spiritual proposition that "on the whole . . . the saintly group of qualities is indispensable to the world's welfare" (299).

The place James's lectures on mysticism occupy in *Varieties* suggests that they are the culmination to which all of his previous inquiry leads. But in certain respects they also furnish readers with the most direct view of the premises upon which the entire sequence of the lectures depends.[19] So much is indicated by the opening declaration: "One may say truly, I think, that personal religious experience has its root and centre in mystical states of consciousness" (301). Similarly, James writes in his letter to Rankin: "The mother sea and fountain-head of all religions lie in the mystical experiences of the individual, taking the word mystical in a very broad sense."[20] James turns to mysticism following his lectures on the *value* of saintliness, in order to inquire into the *truth* of religion (300). This turn from value to truth at first seems startling, especially to readers who remember his earlier statement that religions approve themselves by ministering to vital needs (266) and who are familiar with the principle enunciated in *Pragmatism* that "truth is one species of good" (*P*, 42) and other such statements as "True is the name for whatever idea starts the verification-process, useful is the name for its completed function in experience" (*P*, 98). But James softens the apparent inconsistency, when at the conclusion of lecture 17 on mysticism he advances the judgment that the higher mystical states "point in directions to which the religious sentiments even of non-mystical men incline. They tell of the supremacy of the ideal, of vastness, of union, of safety, and of rest. They offer us *hypotheses*, hypotheses which we may voluntarily ignore, but which as thinkers we cannot possibly upset. The supernaturalism and optimism to which they would persuade us may . . . be after all the truest of insights into the meaning of life" (339).

Saint Teresa is one of the mystics upon whom James depends for this hypothesis, which by this point has acquired an unmistakably metaphysical character. Others are Al-Ghazzali, Jacob Boehme, and Saint John of the Cross. A few lines from Teresa convey something of what so much seizes James's ontological imagination.

In the orison of union the soul is fully awake as regards God, but wholly asleep as regards things of this world and in respect of herself. During the short time the union lasts, she is as it were deprived of every feeling, and even if she would, she could not think of any single thing. Thus she needs to employ no artifice in order to arrest the use of her understanding: it remains so stricken with inactivity that she neither knows what she loves, nor in what manner she loves, nor what she wills. In short, she is utterly dead to the things of the world and lives solely in God. (324)

But not all moments of transport qualify as belonging to high mysticism of this sort. Accordingly, James distinguishes between "sporadic" and "methodical" mysticism, though both spring from the same "transmarginal region of which science is beginning to admit the existence" (337–8). Among the former he includes a wide range of phenomena that are mystical-like, ranging from ephemeral sensations of the deeper significance of life prompted by witnessing the transformation of landscape in changing light or hearing music to the lyrical naturalistic pantheism of Walt Whitman's poetry. He even alludes to his own experiment with nitrous oxide, which sufficiently impressed him as to ascribe to it metaphysical significance.

One conclusion was forced upon my mind at that time. . . . [O]ur normal waking consciousness . . . is but one special type of consciousness, whilst all about it, parted from it by the filmiest of screens, there lie potential forms of consciousness entirely different. We may go through life without suspecting their existence; but apply the requisite stimulus, and at a touch they are there in all their completeness. . . . No account of the universe in its totality can be final which leaves these other forms of consciousness quite disregarded. (307–8)[21]

Proceeding much in the manner he followed in his "Circumscription of the Topic," James lists four marks of mystical experience: *ineffability, noetic quality, transiency,* and *passivity.* However, in the face of the verbal eloquence provided by Teresa and other classic mystics, he qualifies this attribution of "ineffability"; evidently, ineffable means for him nonconceptual. He concedes the utterances of mystics exhibit a "distinct theoretic drift," toward optimism and toward monism (329–30). And although he asserts that regardless of "clime or creed" there is an "everlasting and triumphant mystical tradition" that testifies we become one with the Absolute (332), he also concedes that among mystical states there are such significant differences that, if we take them as evidential, we must conclude that the "wider world" on which they open is of mixed constitution, just as is this world. "It would have its celestial and its infernal regions . . . its valid experiences and its counterfeit ones" (339). We have to put them to the test of use, for that wider world "contains every kind of matter: 'seraph' and 'snake' abide there side by side. To come from thence is no infallible credential" (338).

We may summarize then: Mystical states are utterly authoritative for their subjects; "they are absolutely sensational in their epistemological quality," exhibiting the sense of presence on which James dwelled in lecture 3 – "they are face to face presentations of what seems immediately to exist" (335–6). No authority emanates from them to others who stand outside of them (335). "They break down the authority of . . . rationalistic consciousness, based on the understanding and senses alone. They show it to be only one kind of consciousness (335). "What comes [from them] must be sifted and tested, and run the gauntlet of confrontation with the total context of experience" (338). In brief, the mystic state is like Tolstoy's faith state; men live by them, but the truths they proffer are fallible.

V   JAMES'S CONCLUSIONS

In his reflections on prayer (lecture 19, "Other Characteristics"), which provide a preview of the conclusions at which he finally arrives, James says that prayer is "the very soul and essence of religion . . . [i]t is religion in act" (365–6). If the prayerful consciousness be deceitful, then religion is not genuine. In his further reflection, James adds that we find in the prayerful life the "persuasion that . . .

energy from on high flows in to meet demand, and becomes operative within the phenomenal world. So long as this operativeness is admitted to be real, it makes no essential difference whether its immediate effects be subjective or objective. The fundamental religious point is that in prayer . . . spiritual work of some kind is effected really" (376). These comments on prayer make a bridge to James's own conclusions in lecture 20. Among his conclusions there are two of a general sort that are continuous with the themes we have so far followed and of which we must take notice.

The first is James's reaffirmation of the thesis that we apprehend religious experience most vividly when we seek sympathetically to discern its characteristics in individual persons. The way in which James reiterates and underscores this point is to insist that a "sense of a self" must always belong to a *"full* fact." An "object" minus such a sense is hollow. Religion and religious experience is of this kind: "A conscious field *plus* its object as felt or thought of, *plus* an attitude towards the object *plus* the sense of a self" (393). This means to James that religion is "egotistic." "To describe the world with all the various feelings of the individual pinch of destiny, all the various spiritual attitudes, left out from the description – they being as describable as anything else – would be something like offering a printed bill of fare as the equivalent for a solid meal. Religion makes no such blunder. The individual's religion may be egotistic, and those private realities which it keeps touch with may be narrow enough; but at any rate it always remains infinitely less hollow and abstract . . . than a Science which prides itself on taking no account of anything private at all" (394).

The second of James's general conclusions we must note is a broad hypothesis that takes him and the reader beyond "egotistic" religion. It depends on our accepting the "subconscious self" as a real entity and on our agreement that the "germinal higher part" of ourselves is *"conterminous and continuous with a more of the same quality"*; a more that works outside of us and that we can *"get on board of and save* [ourselves] *when all our lower being has gone to pieces in the wreck"* (400). On its hither side, this "more" is the subconscious continuation of our conscious life (403), and it constitutes *"a wider self through which saving experiences come,* a positive content of religious experience which . . . *is literally and objectively true as far as it goes"* (405). On its farther side – and this is

James's personal hypothesis or overbelief – it is "an altogether other dimension of existence from the sensible and merely 'understandable' world. We belong to it in a more intimate sense than that in which we belong to the visible world, for we belong in the most intimate sense wherever our ideals belong" (406). This other dimension produces real effects, regenerative change, and different conduct on our part. Hence, James believes we have no philosophical excuse for calling this other dimension unreal, and he himself is ready to call it God. Moreover, a god that enters only into a religious person's experience falls short of fulfilling the requirements of a real hypothesis. A satisfactory god "needs to enter into wider cosmic relations in order to justify the subject's absolute confidence and peace" (407). Consequently, in following out his own overbelief to conclusions he holds as appropriate, James ventures again into the realm of "truth" as distinct from value (401, n23). "What is this but to say that Religion, in her fullest exercise of function, is not a mere illumination of facts already elsewhere given. . . . But it is something more, namely a postulator of new *facts* as well. The world interpreted religiously is not the materialistic world over again, with an altered expression; it must have, over and above the altered expression, *a natural constitution* different at some point from that which a materialistic world would have" (407–8). So it is that James's final hypothesis or overbelief brings readers to the brink of a pragmatic metaphysics of religious experience that James did not, could not, finish in *The Varieties of Religious Experience*. "We and God have business with each other; and in opening ourselves to his influence our deepest destiny is fulfilled. The universe, at those parts of it which our personal being constitutes, takes a turn genuinely for the worse or for the better in proportion as each one of us fulfills or evades God's demands" (406–7).

NOTES

1 G. W. Allport, "Introduction," *Psychology: Briefer Course* [abridged] (New York: Harper and Row, 1961), xiii, xxiii.
2 See *P*, appendix 1, 257–70.
3 See, for example, *ERE*, 30. "A World of Pure Experience" originally appeared in 1904.
4 See Ignas K. Skrupskelis's history of "The Text of *The Varieties of Reli-*

gious Experience" in *VRE*, 520–54. James wrote the lectures in two stages, reporting progress with the second set of ten in a diary entry dated 14 November 1901, well after his delivery of the first course of ten (545).

5 See Michael M. Sokal's "Introduction," *PB*, xxxiii–xxxvi; also 9–11.

6 Of course James's pragmatic position contravenes *all* arguments from origins, including those made by dogmatic theologians.

7 A passage in *Talks to Teachers on Psychology: and to Students on Some of Life's Ideals* sheds some further light on James's conviction that value judgments are based on immediate feeling primarily. "Our judgments concerning the worth of things, big or little, depend on the *feelings* the things arouse in us. Where we judge a thing to be precious in consequence of the *idea* we frame of it, this is only because the idea itself is associated already with a feeling. *If we were radically feelingless, and if ideas were the only things our mind could entertain,* we should lose all our likes and dislikes at a stroke, and *be unable to point to any one situation or experience in life more valuable or significant than any other"* (132).

8 The pertinent sentence is open to more than one reading: "*Immediate luminousness,* in short, *philosophical reasonableness,* and *moral helpfulness* are the only available criteria" (*VRE*, 23).

9 Later in *Varieties* James invokes C. S. Peirce to justify his pragmatic procedure in assessing religious beliefs (350–1).

10 We see the effects of this attitude also in other essays and books by James, not least in *Pragmatism*.

11 James disguises the passage quoted as French in origin. In fact, it describes an experience of his own. See *VRE*, "Notes," 447.

12 See Lewis 1991, 185; also *Letters*, 1:129.

13 For James's judgment on Hume's notion of self see *PP*, 1:332–6. "As [substantialist philosophers] say the Self is nothing but Unity . . . so Hume says it is nothing but Diversity" (333).

14 James uses the magnetic field and compass needle metaphor again in *A Pluralistic Universe.* "Every bit of us at every moment is part and parcel of a wider self, it quivers along various radii like the wind-rose on a compass, and the actual in it is continuously one with possibles not yet in our present sight . . . may not we ourselves form the margin of some more really central self in things which is co-conscious with the whole of us?" (131).

15 In fact we do learn something more about "primary consciousness" in lecture 19, "Other Characteristics," where in commenting on inspiration James proposes that personality "has" an A-region and a B-region. The latter corresponds to the subliminal or transmarginal region and is

functionally equivalent to the "secondary consciousness" that James does not mention but that his "primary consciousness" implies. This B-region is "obviously the larger part of each of us" (381). It is the region in which religious inspiration transpires, and James regards inspiration as a species of automatism. See 376–81.

16 James's interest in automatism is well documented. See *VRE*, 191–9; also note 16 above; and his 1901 essay, "Frederic Myers's Service to Psychology" and 1903 review of Frederic W. H. Myers's "Human Personality and Its Survival of Bodily Death" among other entries in *Essays in Psychical Research*.

17 That James does take the ultramarginal or subliminal region as an hypothesis of great, even metaphysical, importance is evident in his letter to Henry W. Rankin of 16 June 1901, written just prior to his delivery of lecture 10. I quote from this letter below; see *Letters*, 2:149–50. Ralph Barton Perry quotes from James's Gifford Lectures notes: "Remember that the whole point lies in really *believing* that through a certain point or part in you you coalesce and are identical with the Eternal"; see Perry 1935, 2:331. See also the passage from a letter to F. C. S. Schiller, 24 April 1902, quoted in *VRE*, 547.

18 See James's letter to Rankin, as cited above in note 17.

19 I hold the lectures on mysticism to be part of the whole inquiry into religious experience and not to be on a separate topic. In his introduction to *VRE* John E. Smith argues that religious experience and mysticism are distinct phenomena (xliii–xliv).

20 See the letter to Rankin cited above in note 17.

21 Compare these lines with James's 1910 autobiographical essay, "A Suggestion about Mysticism" in *Essays in Philosophy*. See especially the statement, "The feeling – I won't call it belief – that I had had a sudden *opening*, had seen through a window, as it were, distant realities that incomprehensibly belonged with my own life, was so acute that I cannot shake it off to-day" (160).

12 Interpreting the universe after a social analogy: Intimacy, panpsychism, and a finite god in a pluralistic universe

The last decade of William James's life was his most productive and distinguished, beginning in 1901–2 with his hugely successful Gifford Lectures, *The Varieties of Religious Experience*, and seeing the publication of virtually all of his strictly philosophical writings, with the notable exception of *The Will to Believe*. Although his output in this period was voluminous in pages and expansive in topic, James expressed dissatisfaction throughout the decade with his failure to produce a systematic work explicitly on metaphysics.[1] From *Varieties* itself, which was to have had a philosophical complement, until the final effort, posthumously published as *Some Problems in Philosophy*, nearly every project of James's harbored both the hope and the disappointment of this desire to found and defend his radically empiricist *Weltanschauung* in a thoroughgoing manner.

In 1907 when an invitation to lecture at Oxford from the Hibbert Trust Committee arrived, James appears to have been more interested in working on a book to fulfill his promise for a metaphysics than in offering yet another series of public lectures. He found himself nonetheless unable to resist the temptation to attack philosophies of the absolute one last time.[2] Originally titled "The Present Situation in Philosophy" and delivered in 1908, the lectures include a mixture of rousing polemical refutation and spirited constructive exposition, thus manifesting both interests. Given this fact, *A Pluralistic Universe* (the published form of the lectures) can be seen to offer an important vantage on the developing details of James's philosophical position, one which follows by several years – and, as I argue, a good deal of development – his oft-considered 1904–5 flurry of articles introducing radical empiricism formally on the philosophical scene.[3] Although *Pragmatism* and *Essays in Radical Em-*

piricism have received more attention in connection with James's metaphysics, in what follows I want to explore a central thematic line – that of intimacy and sociality – from James's Hibbert Lectures as a means of elaborating some of the details of James's philosophical world-view.

What follows is divided into four sections. In the first section, I examine what James seems to understand by "intimacy," arguing that it has three distinct uses: (1) a phenomenological use that focuses on intimacy as an affect or feeling; (2) a metaphysical use wherein intimacy is related to the factual relations that, according to radical empiricism, constitute the world; and (3) an ideal notion of intimacy-in-the-making that James construes on the model of sociality or reciprocity. Following this schematic overview of the criterion of intimacy, the next three sections look at James's particular commitments that develop from or correspond to each of the renderings of intimacy. In the second section, then, I take up James's idea of substituting intimacy for rationality as a criterion in philosophy, relating it to the phenomenological sense of intimacy. The next section considers James's commitment to a moderate form of panpsychism ("pluralistic panpsychism"), connecting it to the metaphysical conception of intimacy. In the final section, I turn to James's understanding of supernaturalism, religious experience, and theism, linking this view of religion to James's ideal rendering of intimacy as sociality. At the conclusion, it will be clear how central the criterion of intimacy in all its forms is to James's mature philosophical world-view.

My exploration, it should be noted, presupposes the interpretive claim that, more than any other work, *A Pluralistic Universe* represents the most coherent, developed, and fully integrated articulation of James's philosophical world-view.[4] Although I cannot adequately defend this claim here, many of the issues at stake should be illuminated through the argument that follows.

I THE COMPLEX CRITERION OF INTIMACY

A Pluralistic Universe opens with a chapter on "The Types of Philosophic Thinking," in which James seeks to clarify his vision of the nature and goals of philosophy, and to survey the range of recent philosophical work. Regarding the nature of philosophy, James focuses on the human character of the philosopher, arguing that particular philosophies are "the expressions of a man's intimate character" (*PU*, 14). Philosophers derive their world-views from analogies to their own experiences, he argues: ". . . the only material we have at our disposal for making a picture of the whole world is supplied by the various portions of the world of which we have already had experience" (*PU*, 9). "All follow one analogy or another . . . ," he continues later, contending that "Different men find their minds more at home in very different fragments of the world" (*PU*, 10). In spite of these substantive, empirical differences, to James's mind all philosophies nonetheless spring from a common desire: "We crave alike to feel more truly at home with [the universe], and to contribute our mite to its amelioration" (*PU*, 11). Thus notwithstanding the wide divergence in philosophical views, for James all philosophy can be seen as similar in its reference to actual human experience and, ultimately, human interests.

Although striking for its aesthetic characterizations of philosophy, lecture 1 is more arresting for its classificatory endeavor. James begins by distinguishing materialistic and spiritualistic philosophies in general, claiming in a passage reminiscent of *Pragmatism* that each proceeds from a different philosophical temperament and yields a world-view of a different character. James then goes on to express a preference for spiritualistic over materialistic philosophies, since the outcomes of the latter are more foreign, James thinks, while those of the former prove more intimate.

James then proposes two more distinctions within spiritualistic philosophy itself, leaving materialism aside apparently as a noncontender. The first of these divides spiritualistic philosophy into two subspecies, dualistic theism and pantheism. Dualistic theism is deemed more foreign by James, since it "makes us outsiders and keeps us foreigners in relation to God," while philosophies of the pantheistic kind are seen to attain a "higher reach of intimacy" through their inclusion of human beings in the divine (*PU*, 17, 16). Within pantheistic philosophies, James finally locates the critical pairing for his own argument, namely, the division between the monistic subspecies of philosophies of the absolute and his own pluralistic view – radical empiricism. James's ultimate goal in his Hibbert Lectures is to demonstrate that radical empiricism is more intimate than rationalistic philosophies of the absolute. From this overview it is also clear that "intimacy" is in some sense the central criterion for James's distinctions among the types of philosophic thinking. In order to add content to this notion, in the following subsections I explore James's three distinct uses of the notion of intimacy mentioned above and chart their interconnections.

Intimacy as a phenomenological affect

In distinguishing between materialistic and spiritualistic philosophy in lecture 1, James notes that materialism derives from or corresponds to a cynical temper, thus defining the world "so as to leave man's soul upon it as a sort of outside passenger, or alien." By contrast, spiritualistic philosophies for James come out of a sympathetic temper, and "insist that the intimate and human must surround and underlie the brutal" (PU, 16). On this basis, one might well characterize James as offering a psychological – even a genetic – explanation for the differences among philosophical world-views.

The major distinction James draws in these passages, however, has to do not with the views' origins but rather with their experiential consequences.⁵ Materialism (and dualistic theism), according to James, leads human beings to experience their relation to the world as alien, while spiritualistic philosophies on the whole allow for a more intimate experience and self-understanding (PU, 18–19). The principal difference between materialistic and spiritualistic philosophies, as sketches or world-views, then, depends on what we might call the "phenomenological" character of the experiential relation that the philosophical view casts between particular human beings and the rest of the world.

This notion that differences in intimacy are the critical differentiators among philosophies is closely related to several central components of James's radically empiricist Weltanschauung, most notably his nondualistic metaphysical thesis of pure experience. In this thesis, stated most overtly in the 1904 article "Does Consciousness Exist?" James claims that everything in the world can be understood to be composed of "pure experience," a plural sort of "stuff" that has as many natures as there are things experienced (ERE, 4, 14). Upon close consideration of the articles now comprising Essays in Radical Empiricism, one can see that James has at least two different aims in proposing his thesis of pure experience. First, James is interested in developing a metaphysical concept that can facilitate a logically satisfying and empirically adequate understanding of the dynamic relations among the components that make up the world (including thoughts, things, and the epistemic and energetic relations that interconnect them). Second, James is interested in pursuing a "radical" empiricism – a philosophy that excludes everything we cannot experience, but more importantly, includes in some fashion all that we do experience. Therefore, James is also interested in propounding a metaphysics that can account directly for concrete, first order characteristics of lived experience and human sensory life. This desire is, in great part, what is behind his choice of the "double-barrelled" term "experience" as the basic element in his philosophy (see *ML*, 331).

This "first order" application of the term "pure experience" appears in the 1904–5 essays when James speaks of pure experience as "the *that* which is not yet any definite *what*," or "the instant field of the present" (*ERE*, 46, 13). On my interpretation, this concrete usage should be understood to be the phenomenological analogue to the metaphysical deployment of the notion of pure experience as the basic element of all that is real.[6] "Pure experience," then, is a fundamentally complex category, susceptible both to conceptual, *metaphysical* treatments (typified by their second order, broader perspective) and to *phenomenological* or affective renderings (identifiable by their sensory or concrete characteristics).

Turning back to *A Pluralistic Universe*, it is now possible to see James's bias for intimacy as a phenomenological characteristic in a somewhat different light. Whereas on a first reading James's distinction comes across as arbitrary, ascribable perhaps only to *his* psychological temperament, on a second reading one can see James drawing his distinctions according to a particular philosophy's adequacy in accounting for the phenomenological concreteness of our actual, lived experience. His preference for intimacy at the phenomenological level can thus be understood to be consistent with (and even dependent on) both his thesis of pure experience and his methodological commitment to a radical form of empiricism. Intimacy at the phenomenological level, then, pertains to a view's adequacy to concrete, first order, lived experience.

Intimacy as metaphysical relationality

Although references to temperamental differences and an appeal to experience are relatively common themes in James's work, the centrality of the appeal to "intimacy" in *A Pluralistic Universe* is novel, at least in print. A distinction between intimacy and foreignness appears first in James's corpus in his discussion of conjunctive relations in the 1904 essay "A World of Pure Experience." There, elaborating on what one might call the factual thesis of radical empiricism (namely, that relations, both conjunctive and disjunctive, are themselves facts of the same order as the things related), James treats conjunctive and disjunctive relations as differing one from another by degree on a spectrum of intimacy and, by implication, foreignness:

Relations are of different degrees of intimacy. Merely to be "with" one another in a universe of discourse is the most external relation that terms can have, and seems to involve nothing whatever as to farther consequences. Simultaneity and time-interval come next, and then space-adjacency and distance. After them, similarity and difference, carrying the possibility of many inferences. Then relations of activity, tying terms into series involving change, tendency, resistance, and the causal order generally. Finally, the relation experienced between terms that form states of mind, and are immediately conscious of continuing each other. The organization of the self as a system of memories, purposes, strivings, fulfillments or disappointments, is incidental to this most intimate of all relations, the terms of which seem in many cases actually to compenetrate and suffuse each other's being. (*ERE*, 23–4)

Striking for its recasting of the long-standing problem of the status and character of relations, this discussion in 1904 is nonetheless ambiguous in terms of its import. James speaks of "withness" in a "universe of discourse" as the pole of foreignness, while treating certain states of mind of the self as being maximally intimate. He thus appears (perhaps inadvertently) to consider relations only in a narrow, merely cognitive (as opposed to metaphysical) sense, leaving open the question of whether states of mind are all that there is, and thus leaving undetermined questions concerning the application of the criterion of intimacy.[7]

The article in which this passage occurs focuses on epistemological issues – specifically, the cognitive relations involved in cases where knowing is a relation between "two pieces of actual experience belonging to the same subject" (*ERE*, 27). James's language seems both tailored to his topic and perhaps still infused with terminological habits from his own dualistic psychological writing. However, based on the metaphysical thesis of pure experience discussed above (and presented in James's article just prior to this one), one would be mistaken to take James as a subjectivist concerning cognitive relations in particular, or relations as a general class. For an empiricism to be radical, James writes, "*the relations that connect experiences must themselves be experienced relations, and any kind of relation experienced must be accounted as 'real' as anything else in the system*" (*ERE*, 22). Thus although relations of intimacy may phenomenologically appear to be subjective, according to radical empiricism and its nondualistic thesis of pure experience, the relations being experienced are themselves objective. Metaphysically speaking, then, degrees of intimacy correspond to degrees of conjunction, while relative foreignness maps onto disjunctive relations.

This metaphysical extension of the term "intimacy" is, in fact, unambiguous in *A Pluralistic Universe*. There, in the context of treating intimate relations, James discusses "human substance" and "divine substance," "the order of the world," "the substance of reality," and "the world" and "the universe" as such (*PU*, 20–1). It follows that intimacy concerns not only the phenomenological affects that can be discerned through considering the subject; in addition intimacy refers directly to the concrete characteristics of factual relations, conjunctive and disjunctive, which are constitutive of all of reality as such (inclusive of thoughts and things). Intimacy as a criterion, then, demands a philosophy that is both phenomenologically and metaphysically responsive to experience.

Intimacy as the ideal of sociality

In addition to this radically empiricist demand that philosophies take up the world as we actually experience it, both phenomenologically and metaphysically, James also invokes intimacy in another sense in *A Pluralistic Universe* – a dynamic use of intimacy more closely related to what he means by sociality. Intimacy in this sense is an ideal – something we want the world to become more thoroughly – in this case, the ideal specified by sociality. Although James criticizes his philosophical opponents both on logical grounds and on the adequacy of their conceptions to our concrete experience, James also argues that radical empiricism, as a form of pluralism, is preferable to its contenders in that it advances the intimacy of the world at this ideal level. In his 1905–6 Seminar on Metaphysics, in fact, James offered this characterization of his whole world-view of radical empiricism, noting that "It frankly interprets the universe after a social analogy" (ML, 367). If the metaphysics of radical empiricism provides a means of understanding the first appeals to intimacy, what are we to make of James's appeal to sociality as an ideal?

In lecture 1 of *A Pluralistic Universe* James introduces sociality when distinguishing forms of theism. Dualistic theism, he argues, "makes us outsiders and keeps us foreigners in relation to God . . . his connexion with us appears as unilateral and not reciprocal. His action can affect us, but he can never be affected by our reaction. Our relation, in short, is not a strictly social relation" (PU, 17). Sociality is specified here as reciprocal relation, indicating James's preference for a particular sort of dynamic interactivity within the world. Thus where intimacy referred directly to the factual, relational aspects of the world, sociality further specifies intimacy as an ideal with regard to the *character* of dynamic relations within the world thus composed.

When subsequently returning to the general difference between materialistic and spiritualistic views, James digresses concerning sociality and intimacy again, clarifying further what he means by sociality as an intimate ideal:

From a pragmatic point of view the difference between living against a background of foreignness and one of intimacy means the difference between a general habit of wariness and one of trust. One might call it a social difference, for after all, the common *socius* of us all is the great universe whose children we are. If materialistic, we must be suspicious of this socius, cautious, tense, on guard. If spiritualistic, we may give way, embrace, and keep no ultimate fear (PU, 19).

"Socius," which also appears in *Principles*, means an ally, partner, or even a family member with whom one is closely and actively related (PP, 1:301). Interpreting the universe after a social analogy thus implies two things, in addition to the earlier forms of intimacy discussed. First, it indicates that James favors a philosophy in which all our dynamic relations in the world are cast (metaphysically) as reciprocal rather than merely relational. Second, James thinks that accepting such a view of reality is itself productive of further affects of intimacy and habits of trust. Interestingly, although in *Principles* James had implied that an adequate socius could only ever be "ideal" in the sense of "not real," in 1906–8 James implies that a spiritualistic view can, at least potentially, provide for the possibility for an adequate socius in the empirical world.

It should be noted that this appeal to sociality as an ideal is not of the same order as James's critique of his rivals from the perspectives of phenomenological and metaphysical intimacy. When attending to the actual world of experience, James finds the facts at hand enough to discredit philosophies of the absolute (and other contenders) in relation to radical empiricism. Hence where intimacy in the first two senses for James is fully realist in valence, sociality involves a fusion of real and ideal elements, since it is as yet only partially produced, and thus is still ideal in its full form. The overwhelming appeal of philosophies of the absolute lies in their claim to express, if not also realize, the optimism and intimacy of the sympathetic temper. If radical empiricism is to aspire to the mantle of spiritualistic philosophy, it too must be able to set intimacy forward as an ideal that should – but more importantly – can be worked toward. The following three sections, on rationality, panpsychism, and the finite conception of god, explore James's systematic response to this aspiration.

II RATIONALITY

Comprehending James's complex notion of intimacy – as a phenomenological affect, a variable, concrete, and independent feature of real metaphysical relations, and ultimately, as an ideal for human action – is crucial to developing an understanding of some of his more peculiar philosophical commitments evidenced in *A Pluralistic Universe*. Perhaps the most striking of these is James's surprising suggestion near the close of his lectures that philosophy might be better served overall if the criterion of intimacy were to replace that of rationality in philosophy. "It would be a pity if the word 'rationality' were allowed to give us trouble here," he writes:

It is one of those eulogistic words that both sides claim – for almost no one is willing to advertise his philosophy as a system of irrationality. But like most of the words which people use eulogistically, the word "rational" carries too many meanings. . . . It would be better to give up the word "rational" altogether than to get into a merely verbal fight about who has the best right to keep it.

Perhaps the words "foreignness" and "intimacy," which I put forward in my first lecture, express the contrast I insist on better than the words "rationality" and "irrationality." *(PU,* 144–5)

What James "insists on" by this point in the text is not merely the phenomenological affect of intimacy discussed. In addition, he seems to have in mind the normative reintroduction into philosophy of the concrete (and variably intimate or foreign) characteristics of actual experience. In this concreteness, James finds both conjunctive and disjunctive relations to be fundamentally real and in flux, with some bits of reality "compenetrating" one another, while others are just with or next to one another. "The immediate experience of life solves the problems which so baffle our conceptual intelligence," he writes, excoriating the intellectualist understanding of relations (shared by materialism and philosophies of the absolute) on which all relations among the metaphysical parts of reality are understood to be separate things, added by thought *(PU,* 116). "If we hold to Hume's maxim," he writes, ". . . that whatever things are distinguished are as separate as if there were no manner of connexion between them, then there seemed no way out of the difficulty save by stepping outside of experience altogether" *(PU,* 119). Radical empiricism, in taking concrete, lived experience as its fundamental *metaphysical* component, "insists" that this intellectualist view of relations be set aside in favor of a view on which the concrete intimacy we experience as part of the relation itself can also be seen to figure philosophically as a fundamental part of reality.

What, one might ask, is the connection between recognizing the reality of conjunctive, intimate relations and the philosophical notion and ideal of rationality? Not surprisingly, given James's notion of intimacy as both phenomenological and metaphysical, there are two connections to be followed here. At a metaphysical level, James is, in a sense, pursuing something similar to Hegel's dictum that "the rational is actual and the actual is rational," only substituting intimacy for rationality. By this I mean that the factuality of relations, which James presents as basic to radical empiricism, provides a metaphysical hook for phenomenological or affective intimacy. This hook is similar to Hegel's notion of the absolute, which is conceived of as a metaphysically basic component of reality that itself is *productive* of rationality. What is different is that while rationality and the absolute strike the reader as having an all-or-nothing character (as James himself notes), intimacy, like all relations, inevitably seems to involve matters of degree. More or less intimate, then, is the analogue to more or less rational in philosophy for James.

Rationality, however, is not merely or perhaps even most basically a feature of the world; more commonly, it is understood to apply to a specific subset of that broader group of "pure experiences" – namely, our conceptions. James's use of intimacy as the basic criterion in philosophy is less perplexing when one recalls that for him rationality has an affective aspect. James first wrote about rationality in detail in 1879 in "The Sentiment of Rationality," reprinted in *The Will to Believe*. There, James approached rationality psychologically, characterizing it as involving "fluency" or "unimpeded mental function" (*WB*, 57–8). On this view, we *sense* rationality (and its lack) much as we sense our other affective states. What was unclear in that early essay, which still subscribed to mind/matter dualism, is how James could or would account for the sentiment of rationality ever having any correlation to the way the world itself is, as distinct from how it merely feels.[8]

When James raises the issue of rationality again in 1908, the philosophical context is quite different. By this time James has articulated a formally monistic metaphysics of pure experience. One form of intimacy that philosophy must aspire to, on James's view is a feeling that the world as we experience it and the ideas we have of that world must themselves be intimately related, or at least capable of intimate relation. In James's radical empiricism, and particularly on his functional account of the verification of objective reference ("knowledge about"), this amounts to the claim that our philosophical ideas must be able to find their verification by exhibiting expected continuities with the details of the concrete world as we actually experience it.[9] Objective reference, for James, involves "leading" through "definitely felt transitions" to concrete, pure experiences "meant," whenever verification is in question (*ERE*, 28–9). This leading is the phenomenological analogue of a metaphysical relation of continuity, which, as I have argued, involves a relatively high degree of intimacy. In the context of verifying a conception, then, this intimate experience of leading can be taken as a phenomenological mark of truth or "rationality," or, as James puts it in *Varieties* (in a different context), of "the sentiment of reality." James's desire to replace rationality with intimacy as the basic criterion in philosophy, then, can be understood to be both founded on, and an elaboration of, his radically empiricist commitments to the reality of relations and the interrelated phenomenology, metaphysics, and epistemology of concrete pure experience.

III   PLURALISTIC PANPSYCHISM

Interpreters of James disagree widely as to whether, and to what extent, he endorsed some form of panpsychism.[10] This is particularly odd, since James allies his view directly with panpsychism on two occasions in *A Pluralistic Universe*, which was the last "new" (i.e., not compiled) book he published (*PU*, 141, 143). Further, James's unpublished manuscripts and lecture notes clearly demonstrate an overt interest in, and ultimately commitment to, some form of the view (e.g., *MEN*, 6, 43, 48, 55; *ML*, 223, 278, 308, 403). Biographically, James's developing panpsychist ideas coincide with his metaphysical work on radical empiricism. It should not be surprising, then, that James's interest in panpsychism can be substantively related to his advocacy of intimacy in philosophy, both at the level of developing an intimate metaphysics of relationality, and in enabling the social ideal of intimacy as reciprocity.

Much of the disagreement about, and even lack of interest in, James's panpsychist leanings derives from a lack of clarity about what panpsychism is as a philosophical position, and why it is even an issue. In the late nineteenth century panpsychism was a common view, shared in principle by many of James's colleagues. At a minimum panpsychism involves the claim that all elements that make up the universe have an inner psychical aspect or disposition. Panpsychism is not simply the claim that matter is intrinsically active (hylozoism); rather, panpsychism involves the inherently evaluative claim that the psychical component is "higher" or more valuable than the nonpsychical component (if there is one). Thus on this view the universe is intrinsically animated, at least potentially, all the way down to (and up from) its parts.

In the late nineteenth century the issue of panpsychism became acute when philosophers like James found themselves dissatisfied with accounts of the continuity of experience, consciousness, and thought that had emerged out of both materialistic and idealistic philosophical views. The problem was, on the one hand, to account for the independence of objects in the world, while on the other, to explain plausibly (and logically) how they could be interconnected (or "dialectical") in thought or experience.

Panpsychism admits of various interpretations. Among those common in James's day, I will distinguish a strong and a weak version before identifying a third, moderate version that is James's own. On the strong view (held by Gerhardus Heymans and Charles Strong), every individuable element in the universe is understood, at its philosophically most basic level, to be self-experiencing or self-conscious, in addition to whatever other relations or characteristics it may have (including its physical characteristics and causal relations, since strong panpsychism retains a fundamental mind/matter dualism). This psychical activity is understood to be causally basic and efficacious, thus rendering the physical order subservient to psychical activity. This view, which James calls "idealistic panpsychism," intends to account for both the radical independence of objects (things-in-themselves) and the dialectical (relational) character of experience without proposing two separate realms of experience, ignoring the successes of the physical sciences, or ruling out some form of idealistic philosophy (ML, 396).

A weaker version of panpsychism (held by Friedrich Paulsen) holds that, although every element in the universe must have an inherent psychic aspect or disposition, this aspect is always subordinate in terms of activity to the material characteristics of the object in question. On this view, individuable elements are understood to be self-conscious or self-experiencing; however, this psychic state is not seen as basically responsible for the existence or activity of the element, as is the case with the strong version. Self-consciousness, and indeed any form of psychic or mental activity, then, is epiphenomenal to material activity. "Epiphenomenalism," as James called it, thus attends (albeit weakly) to the dialectical character of experience that materialism tends to leave unexplicated, but, unlike strong panpsychism, it remains thoroughly committed to the priorities of classical dualistic materialism over idealism (ML, 396).

Between idealistic panpsychism and epiphenomenalism there is much room to maneuver, and maneuver James does through the 1900s. The history of James's commitment to panpsychism is foggy, since he only infrequently referred to his view by that name. As time goes on in James's career, however, the references grow more clear regarding his own affinity. The first published mention is early, in the 1881 "Reflex Action and Theism" where James notes (as he also does seventeen years later) that modern thought seems to be converging on panpsychist conclusions (*WB*, 12; cf. *PU*, 141f.). More notable are his two references in the *Essays in Radical Empiricism* sequence, where he mentions panpsychism as an open question and refers positively to Strong's view by name (*ERE*, 43, 95). After *A Pluralistic Universe*, the only other published mention is in the 1909 "Confidences of a Psychical Researcher," where James again notes convergence on the view (*EPR*, 374).

When one turns from published to unpublished materials, James's commitment to and understanding of panpsychism becomes much more evident. The references also date from the early 1880s, and generally indicate a growing interest in the doctrine, particularly from *Varieties* onward (e.g., *MI*, 146, 198, 278, 308; *MEN*, 6, 43, 48, 55, 176, 223). Although James appears to have concurred with his colleagues' analysis as to why panpsychism was philosophically mandated, once he turned to his metaphysics of radical empiricism (with its nondualistic pure experience), he found himself unsatisfied with the explicit mind/matter dualism of all the panpsychist positions he knew.[11] This may, in fact, account for why James so infrequently used the term in print.

James's ultimate solution seems to have been to develop a moderate form of panpsychism, "pluralistic panpsychism," that eschews the fundamental mind/matter dualism of his colleagues in favor of both a pluralistic metaphysics of pure experience and a correspondingly pluralistic notion of causality. The textual references for the outlines of this view are somewhat meager. Although the locution "pluralistic panpsychic view" appears in *A Pluralistic Universe*, James's extant corpus only provides serious philosophical discussion of the emerging details of such a view in two places: in a 1905 notebook passage, "Heymans Book"; and the following year, in the notes for his 1906–7 "General Problems of Philosophy" (*MEN*, 223; *ML*, 403).

In the first of these manuscripts, James is interested in modifying

strong panpsychism according to his formally monistic and nonre-
ductive thesis of pure experience. Specifically, given James's view
that the mental/physical split is secondary and not metaphysically
basic, he is at pains to make sense of the claim that all activity,
specifically causal activity, is inherently psychical. According to
radical empiricism, whether an experience (object) in the world is
considered mental or physical depends not on a preexisting metaphysical hierarchy but rather on the sorts of activities and effects
the particular experience is related to in the wider field of experience. Causal activity, then, is not singular but rather plural in
nature – all experiences (potentially) produce effects, though not
necessarily effects that can be grouped together as similar. Further,
actual concrete experiences often admit of multiple contributing
causal conditions, some of which may be of differing sorts. The
claim that psychical causality is primary (or more real) thus proves
too reductionistic for James's radically empiricist and pluralistic
program. Ultimately, James finds strong panpsychism unable to account for both the existence of and the interaction among physical
and mental systems at a secondary level, once pluralistic pure experience, with its many and varying "natures," is taken to be metaphysically primary (see ERE, 14).

James's notebook does indicate that he was headed toward a solution at this point, one which parallels his solution to the mind/matter
split in radical empiricism. In 1904–5, James had accounted for the
commonsense mental/physical split by speaking of the "sorting out"
of pure experiences into different systems of associates (principally
mental and physical) on the basis of their mode of interaction (ERE,
69–70). In 1905–6 James draws another functional distinction, this
time between physical and mental causation: "Energetic [physical]
action is simply transeunt action – 'psychic' causation is simply immanent action" (MEN, 223). These two sorts of action are thus distinguishable on the basis of their modes of functioning. In addition to
operating separately, forms of causality can also combine in effecting
a single experiential change; for example, perception is, according to
James, both mind and brain conditioned. "When to the immanent
kind the transeunt kind is added," he writes, "experience is of physical things" (MEN, 223). Psychic activity and physical activity, then,
are ultimately distinguishable and distinguished (analogously to
pure experiences themselves) on the basis of concrete degrees of

experiential continuity and discontinuity in relation to the broader stream of experience. Further, although these forms of activity are distinguishable, like the varying relations of intimacy and foreignness discussed above, it is not necessary, ultimately, to claim that they are different in kind. Thus the reductive edge of strong panpsychism (as well as that of materialism) can by bypassed in favor of a more pluralistic view, while nonetheless keeping alive panpsychism's notions of interaction and dynamism, as well as its openness to novel mental influences.

James's second important discussion of panpsychism occurs in his notes for a course in which Paulsen's "epiphenomenalist" text was required reading. (James's own system was not presented in this course.) In these notes James distinguishes "idealistic panpsychism" from "epiphenomenalism," developing the details of each position. Late in the manuscript, after considering in detail the advantages and disadvantages of each view, James poses the general question "whether panpsychism should be interpreted monistically or pluralistically," indicating directly both the rhetorical and the metaphysical features of pluralistic panpsychism that he would expand a year later in *A Pluralistic Universe*. "Is there one *all-inclusive purpose* harbored by a general world-soul, embracing all sub-purposes in its system?" he writes, "Or are there *many various purposes*, keeping house together as they can, with no overarching purpose to include them? In other words, are the different parts of matter 'informed' by diverse souls that obey no one unifying principle, but work out their mutual harmony as best they can?" (*ML*, 403). Although the class read Paulsen as a text, it is clear from this quotation that James was more intrigued by strong panpsychism. In addition, it is evident that, whatever metaphysical reasons he had, James was also drawn to some form of panpsychism precisely as a means to provide an intimate – and ultimately more social – alternative to the overbearing all-knower of philosophies of the absolute (such as those of Royce and Bradley). Panpsychism, interpreted moderately and pluralistically, offered James the metaphysical means to render intimate goals and interests potentially efficacious and real in the universe. At the same time, however, panpsychism opened the way for James to pursue his spiritualistic and empiricist ideal of a "piecemeal," but inherently social universe. Thus for James, providing a pluralistically panpsychist explanation of the (causal) activity and the nature of pure experience is a means not only of furthering his metaphysical conception of intimacy but also of rendering philosophically plausible the ideal of interpreting the universe after a social analogy.

IV FINITE GOD(S)

Thematically, the text of *A Pluralistic Universe* represents the majority of James's interests from the last decade of his life, taking on the absolute, exploring metaphysical and epistemological issues such as the compounding of consciousness, attempting to provide a pluralistic, empiricist alternative to materialism and idealism, and taking seriously the facts of religious experience and parapsychological phenomena. As I have interpreted the text so far, all of these issues can be understood to be of a piece, at least insofar as they seek to understand the universe as intimately interconnected with and through our lived experience, and ultimately open to becoming more intimate through our own activity. Near the end of the Hibbert Lectures, James appears to address the ideal of intimacy, as he calls for philosophical action that would advance the cause: "Let empiricism once become associated with religion, as hitherto, through some strange misunderstanding, it has been associated with irreligion, and I believe that a new era of religion as well as of philosophy will be ready to begin" (*PU*, 142). What might he mean by this, and how does it elaborate his intimate ideal of sociality?

When James came to give the Hibbert Lectures in 1908, he had behind him the empirical endeavors of *Varieties*, his psychical research, and the metaphysical and epistemological reflections known as radical empiricism and pragmatism. Although similar in subject, the differences between James's first treatment of religion and the Hibbert Lectures are significant. Despite his original intentions for the Gifford Lectures, in 1902 James did not publicly offer a metaphysical system with which to account for his "piecemeal supernaturalism," "the wider self," or his claim that religion postulates "new facts" (*VRE*, 406–8). In fact, although *Varieties* has numerous indications to the contrary, the overt approach to its subject is from the perspective of dualistic psychology.

In 1908, by contrast, James presents his views on religion against the background of a radical and pluralistically panpsychist empiri-

cism, which takes as basic both the reality of dynamic relations –
conjunctive and disjunctive – and the continual introduction of
novelty through the various causal activities of the parts that make
up the world. This background implies that the relational structure
of religious experience and the objective notion of the "wider
self" – which James could only claim to have explained psychologically in *Varieties* – can and should now be read metaphysically. On
this interpretation, the relational character of religious experience
can be understood as an objective function within the fabric of pure
experience, rather than a merely subjective one in the mind of the
experiencer. Further, the "wider self" and "the more" can be taken
to refer not merely to a subjective subconscious region but also to a
real "superhuman consciousness" (see *PU,* 130–1). This superhuman consciousness would go well beyond any individual system of
experience, interconnecting various systems concretely through factual, dynamic, conjunctive, and thus intimate, relations. Whether
these conclusions are warranted, of course, depends for James on
the concrete, empirical facts; but the *philosophically* real possibility of these conclusions, he thinks, need not be looked upon as
skeptically as before. This, it appears, is what he means when he
demands that we let (radical) empiricism become associated with
religion (*PU,* 142).

James's treatment of religion in the Hibbert Lectures quite literally begins where he left off in *Varieties.* Quoting directly from his
own Gifford Lectures on the "wider self" and the "more," he describes his own panpsychist metaphysics at the phenomenological
level (*PU,* 131, 139; *VRE,* 400, 405). "Every bit of us at every moment
is part and parcel of a wider self," he writes, "it quivers along various
radii like the wind-rose on a compass, and the actual in it is continuously one with possibles not yet in our present sight" (*PU,* 131).
When directly addressing religious experience, James characterizes
the religious person as "continuous, to his own consciousness, at
any rate, with a wider self from which saving experiences flow in . . .
we inhabit an invisible spiritual environment from which help
comes, our soul being mysteriously one with a larger soul whose
instruments we are" (*PU,* 139). Such are the phenomenological facts,
James thinks, of religious experience.

Given the characterization I have offered of James's metaphysical
commitments, it should be relatively clear how radical empiricism

as an intimate, spiritualistic philosophy will account for religious experience. But what of James's understanding of the nature of the superhuman consciousness, with whom we are "mysteriously one" and whose "instruments we are"? James's last Hibbert lecture is sketchy, offering little argument, tending instead to trace general ideas. Of God, however, James draws two conclusions: first, God should be understood to be finite (and not necessarily singular); and second, our activity should be taken to contribute to God's in making the world more ideal.

James advances the first of these claims on two fronts. Throughout the book he argues, both from within idealism's conceptual system and from the perspective of his own radical empiricism, that God as the absolute is not logically necessitated. Once "intellectualism's edge is [so] broken," the fate of the absolute is subject, like other conceptions, to verification among empirical facts (*PU*, 130). Such facts as free will, evil, and religious experience, James thinks, certainly do not indicate an infinite being, but rather one that is finite. Concerning the character of such a finite being, James argues that we should provisionally conclude that a superhuman consciousness is like other systems of consciousness of which we know more (e.g., human beings). That is, we should postulate at least that God has an environment, is in time, and works out a history (*PU*, 144).

The conclusion that any superhuman consciousness must be finite is, James thinks, adequate to the facts both phenomenologically and conceptually. Among other things, it allows us both to include all of our experiences of the world, good and bad, and to satisfy our conceptual (logical) consciences. "Let God but have the least infinitesimal *other* of any kind beside him," he writes, "and empiricism and rationalism [spiritualistic philosophy] might strike hands in a lasting treaty of peace" (*PU*, 141). James's pluralistic conclusion, however, also has an ideal component that is not of the factual order: its invocation of a social analogy in depicting the superhuman/ human relationship.

As I discussed above, James objects to dualistic theism in lecture 1 on the grounds that it does not interpret our relations with the divine as reciprocal, social relations. At the close of *Varieties*, James had concluded hopefully that "the faithfulness of individuals here below . . . may actually help God in turn be more effectively faithful to his own greater tasks," suggesting a God who was finite in some respect, and thus minimally, if not reciprocally, dependent on us (*VRE*, 408). Concluding his Hibbert Lectures, James returns to this theme, casting our faithfulness as a more concrete, empirically demanding task that approaches reciprocity, at least in terms of the import of our contributions. "[T]he incompleteness of the pluralistic universe," he writes, " . . . is also represented by the pluralistic philosophy as being self-reparative through us, as getting its disconnections remedied in part by our behavior" (*PU*, 148; *VRE*, 408). Our sociality with a finite superhuman consciousness is, then, directly related to our actually contributing to the continuity and intimacy of the pluralistic universe in a contingent, rather than a necessary, future.

There is a second sense in which our relations with superhuman consciousness are understood as both social and ideal. In the opening lecture James identified the common socius of us all as "the great universe whose children we are" (*PU*, 19). In speaking of the finite God, James takes up the same inclusive notion, writing that: "We are indeed internal parts of God and not external creations, on any possible reading of the panpsychic system" (*PU*, 143). Thus not only are our own efforts required for the life of the superhuman consciousness but also, on this pluralistically panpsychic system, our life is in fact part of that life. The intimate ideal of a common socius, it follows, is to be achieved in the concrete streams of experience of individuals, which are, at the same time, constitutive of the broader stream of the life of us all. It seems only a short step to comprehending the necessity of reciprocal and thoroughly social relations among human beings, if our intimate philosophical ideal is to be realized.

V CONCLUSIONS

Through a close look at several themes in *A Pluralistic Universe*, I have attempted to discern and outline James's desire for and understanding of an intimate and social philosophical world-view. The obvious question that remains is why one should ultimately prefer the intimate view over the foreign. James's radical empiricism commits him to the view that philosophy (and science) is always faced with the case of "life exceeding logic," with novelty, some of which is in principle unpredictable (*PU*, 148). Coupled with James's recognition of the empirical reality of free will and the influence of ideas and thoughts on the world (through their inclusion as both objects in and functional operators on the world), this commitment to novelty implies that philosophical conceptions themselves are not just passive representations, but rather active contributions to and participants in the future course of history. Pursuing sociality and intimacy as ideals, then, appears to be justified (until the facts prove otherwise) on the basis of the claim that philosophers and their ideas themselves must be "taken up" into the world they treat (*PU*, 21, 143).

This argument alone, however, does not make it *necessary* to pursue either spiritualistic philosophies in general, or a pluralistic view like radical empiricism in particular. At the close of his lectures, James admits that there is, in fact, no logically coercive reason to accept his view: "This world *may*, in the last resort, be a block-universe; but on the other hand, it *may* be a universe only strung-along, not rounded in and closed. Reality *may* exist distributively, just as it sensibly seems to, after all" (*PU*, 148). But since the world actually appears to be amenable to being changed, even "remedied," by our behavior, James sees no "rationality" in the idea that we as human beings would aspire to a world that was less intimate at any of the three levels I have considered. Such a view, then, counsels (although it certainly does not necessitate) a preference for intimacy and sociality among our guiding philosophical ideals, since it is through these that the concrete streams of our lives might themselves be rendered more ideal.

NOTES

1 See, for example, his letter to F. C. S. Schiller, 20 April 1902 (*Letters*, 2:165); his letter to Theodore Flournoy, 30 April 1903 (2:187); and his letter to Henry James, 6 October 1907 (2:299).

2 See his letter to Henry James, 6 October 1907 (*Letters*, 2:299), as well as "The Text of *A Pluralistic Universe*," *PU*, 214–15.

3 By "developing" I mean more worked out than the presentation of the views in his 1904–5 journal articles. As for the flurry of articles, "Does Consciousness Exist?" "A World of Pure Experience," "Humanism and Truth," "The Pragmatic Method," "The Thing and Its Relations," "The Experience of Activity," "The Essence of Humanism," "How Two Minds Can Know One Thing," "Humanism and Truth Once More," "Is Radical Empiricism Solipsistic?" "The Place of Affectional Facts in A

THE CAMBRIDGE COMPANION TO WILLIAM JAMES

World of Pure Experience," and "La Notion de Conscience," all appeared between September 1904 and June 1905, eight in *The Journal of Philosophy, Psychology and Scientific Methods*, two in *Mind*, and one each in *The Psychological Review* and *Archives de Psychologie*. "The Pragmatic Method" was the only article written prior to the publication period.

4 This view is defended in Lamberth (forthcoming). See particularly chapters 2 and 5.

5 James makes a similar distinction in the opening of *The Varieties of Religious Experience*, where he distinguishes origins from values, and charts the corresponding existential and spiritual judgments (*VRE*, 13). It is interesting to compare this section of *A Pluralistic Universe* to the opening passage in *Pragmatism*, where James makes so much of temperament (*P*, 9–26).

6 For a more in-depth explanation of this reading, see Lamberth, chapter 2. My reading of pure experience as both metaphysical and phenomenological seeks to avoid the position taken by a number of interpreters who understand James simply to vacillate between a neutral monism and the idea of an unanalyzed experience. See, e.g., Ford 1982, 76–7; Wild 1969, 161; Bird 1986, 95; and Myers 1986a, 308.

7 The argument of "Does Consciousness Exist?" and "A World of Pure Experience" is overtly intended, however, to forward a metaphysical view in which experience is the most basic component. Since the two articles are primarily focused on epistemological questions (particularly the status of cognitive relations), James's language sometimes leaves open certain metaphysical questions that one would expect him – given radical empiricism's methodological restriction to experience – to foreclose.

8 One can read "The Sentiment of Rationality" from the perspective of radical empiricism, providing the simple answer that the distinction between how it feels and how it is is not severe, mediated as it is by the notion of pure experience. My point, however, is that James himself did not yet subscribe to this view, and thus must be read as a metaphysical dualist, even if a somewhat hesitant one.

9 There are two distinct classes of knowing for James, namely, direct acquaintance and knowledge about. Direct acquaintance is characterized by immediacy (though not certainty), bridging two systems of associates through one experience. Knowledge about, by contrast, is a mediated form of knowing involving the functional substitution of one part of experience for another. These functions themselves are dynamically interrelated, in that knowledge about is verified through its leading to direct acquaintance, while direct acquaintance itself is understood to give way to knowledge about as immediacy fades (or is broken) phenomenologically. See Lamberth, chapter 2, for more detailed analysis.

10 Perry sees James as wavering, but not ultimately subscribing to panpsychism (Perry 1935, 2:394–5). Among recent interpretations, only Ford (1982) and Spriggs (1993) claim directly that James is a panpsychist (75f.; 137.). Myers (1986a) finds that James himself never endorses such a view (612), while Levinson agrees with Perry that he wavers but concludes that any commitment to panpsychism makes no difference to his overall view (Levinson 1981, 177f.).

11 This turn to radical empiricism's nondualistic metaphysics of pure experience occurs in 1895 and is clear in "The Knowing of Things Together" from that year, well before the publication of the essays known by that name. See Lamberth, chapter 3, for a sustained demonstration and exploration of this interpretation.

13 Moral philosophy and the development of morality

In "The Moral Philosopher and the Moral Life" (*WB*,* 184–216),
William James offers a general survey of moral philosophy and its
central problems. Its main interests lie in answering what James
calls the "casuistic" question of the "measure of the various goods
and ills which men recognise," and in the role which religious belief
may play there. In that standard context of a justification for moral
principles, he veers toward a utilitarian view but is also critical of
any such philosophical task. But before he discusses that question
he also identifies and answers two others; first a "psychological"
question about the "historical origin of our moral ideas" and second
a "metaphysical' question about the "meaning of the words 'good,'
'ill' and 'obligation' " (185). The apparent contrast between those
two questions is, however, blurred in James's answers to them. For
even the metaphysical question, it seems, has more to do with the
origins of moral discriminations than with what we should understand as an account of the meanings of those moral terms. This
raises a general problem about James's enterprise in those two initial
sections which I want to consider in this essay.

That problem can be made more pointed in two related ways. For
first, and positively, James's discussion concerns the reality of moral
properties and so current issues about moral realism or moral naturalism. Second, and negatively, it faces the difficulty of explaining
how a "genetic" question about the origin of moral properties can
legitimately throw light on their nature.[1] In order to explore these
issues I first outline the central claims that James makes in discussing those initial questions; second I consider two more recent
related accounts, due to Jonathan Bennett and Mark Johnston, of
the character of moral properties (Bennett 1971, 94–102; Johnston

260

1989);[2] and finally, I assess the extent to which James's account contributes to these issues.

I JAMES'S ACCOUNT

James contrasts his own position with a number of others. He makes it clear from the start that moral skepticism is to be rejected, and begins his discussion of the psychological question by criticizing two opposed schools of a priori intuitionism and a posteriori evolutionism. His view of these is that they oversimplify moral considerations, even though it appears later that there is room for some contribution from each of them. At this early stage, however, he notes the contrasting merit of an empiricist utilitarianism which stresses the role that simple bodily pleasures and relief from pain play in the matter. But even utilitarianism is regarded as oversimple since it makes no room for what are called "secondary affections" which cannot, James thinks, be explained merely by "association or utility." Features such as "the love of drunkenness, bashfulness, or susceptibility to musical sounds," among others, are described as "brain-born" in origin (*WB*,* 186). Further light is cast on his view when he says: "The feeling of the inward dignity of certain spiritual attitudes, as peace, simplicity, . . . and the essential vulgarity of others as querulousness, anxiety . . . are quite inexplicable except by an innate preference of the more ideal attitude for its own sake" (187). He adds, typically: "The nobler thing tastes better, and that is all we can say" (187). It seems that the "secondary affections" are innate preferences which are to be explained in terms of physiological brain structures.

The reference to a manifest "taste" in such cases gestures toward the notion of a "moral sense" and offers some role for intuitionism as James himself goes on to explain. For he draws a distinction between strictly moral responses, in which we regard some action as wicked, for example, and others where we describe behavior as "mean" or "vulgar." The former need a reference to consequences, the latter have an immediate reference instead to feelings of distaste or repugnance. Such feelings would prevent us from accepting a utilitarian bargain which trades the general happiness for the endless torture of one person, and they reveal weakness in the empiricist position. That weakness is further underlined in the claim that all the " . . . higher, more penetrating, ideals are revolutionary and present themselves less in the guise of effects of past experience than in that of probable causes of future experience" (WB,* 188–9). Ideals cannot all be explained in terms of pleasures and pains, and do not "merely repeat the couplings of experience" (189).

The upshot of the discussion is that none of the licenced schools of moral philosophy is adequate. Intuitionism places too much reliance upon an a priori conscience, though it is right to stress both our immediate responses to some moral circumstances and the revolutionary, prospective, development of moral ideals. Utilitarianism is right to place weight on simple bodily pleasures and reliefs from pain and on consequences but, like evolutionism, places too much weight on past experience and too little on the development of moral ideals.

Apart from the reference to innate preferences James says little overtly in the first section about the historical question of the origin of moral discriminations and in the second, metaphysical, section, little overtly about the semantics of moral terms. It is, however, in that second section that he embarks on a series of thought experiments which seem to be designed to throw further light on the origins of morality. Since it is quite clear that the experiments tell us nothing about its historical origins, a question remains about the cash-value of the experiments. We might say that in the first section James at least offers a psychological, and physiological, explanation of the origins of some moral discriminations, namely, those he calls "secondary affections"; while in the second he offers instead an account of the metaphysical origins of moral properties. But what are "metaphysical origins"? Before attempting to answer that question let us consider how the experiments are conducted.

James begins with a description of a universe in which he believes no moral properties arise. This is a purely physico-chemical world in which no sentient life exists. At the next stage the universe is complicated by the addition of a solitary sentient being. James allows that here "there is a chance for goods or evils really to exist"; what is good is good for that being who is the sole arbiter of such values. In such a moral solitude, as he calls it, the creature may not live an unproblematic life. It may have to make choices, to weigh competing demands at a time or over time, and may come in various degrees to regret those choices. All these features mimic the moral world we inhabit, but James is also clear that it will lack one aspect of our world. For in such a solitude he thinks that there can be no question of the truth or falsity of moral judgments. The reason for this is that "Truth supposes a standard outside of the thinker to which he must conform; but here the thinker is a sort of divinity subject to no higher judge" (WB,* 191). We might say, echoing Wittgenstein (1953, § 202), that since what *seems* right *is* right, there is no scope for a public morality in which the ascription of truth or falsity might properly be made.

With the addition of other sentient creatures the moral solitude develops into either what James calls a "moral dualism" or a "moral universe." In the former the inhabitants lead separate, indifferent, moral lives, while in the latter those lives are not indifferent. James's reference to indifference is ambiguous and covers, for example, the case where the creatures have no conscious or sympathetic relation to each other even though they compete, and cases where there is some recognition of the competition, whether sympathetic or not. That latter, richer, situation evidently marks a closer approach to our own moral world with its plural demands, its competition for scarce resources, and a recognition of these issues which motivates the philosophical search for conciliatory rational ideals. That latter development heralds James's "casuistic" question, but before he considers that he returns to the earlier rejection of skepticism.

For he notes that a plural moral universe, with no criterion for resolving disagreements or weighing competing ideals, will yield only an "ancient skepticism" in which the agent is the measure of its moral view. The earlier rejection of moral skepticism is now linked to a rejection of this position. Although James is modest about the practical role of moral philosophy, he nevertheless clearly believes that the general task of providing a rational order for divergent ideals cannot be abandoned. If he is antiskeptical in that context, however, he also endorses a further skepticism. For he thinks it only a superstition to believe in an ". . . abstract moral order in which the objective truth resides" which might be associated with theism (WB,* 194). Such a commitment may have some part to play in morality, as his own later discussion shows, but it cannot establish that objective order. James refers explicitly to the Euthyphro problems (10b–1b).[2] as a decisive ground for rejecting such a theistic appeal. Instead the direction toward which we must look for an understanding of morality is our human world and not some super-natural existence. "Whether a God exist or no God exist . . . we form at any rate an ethical republic here below" (198).

Just as James rejects a supernatural moral order presided over by a theistic God so he also rejects a crude naturalism. Moral properties do not exist as inhabitants of a supernatural realm but neither do they exist as natural phenomena like the aurora borealis. There is for James a residual subjectivity in our moral discriminations, and it is this which he seeks to capture before passing on to the casuistic issue. Here are some quotations from this section:

. . . nothing can be good or right except so far as some consciousness feels it to be good. (WB,* 192–3)

. . . that betterness must be lodged concretely in someone's actual percep-tion. It cannot float in the atmosphere for it is not a sort of meteorological phenomenon like the aurora borealis. . . . Its esse is percipi. (193)

The only reason . . . why any phenomenon ought to exist is that such a phenomenon actually is desired. (195)

. . . we have now learned what the words "good," "bad," and "obligation" severally mean. They mean no absolute natures, independent of personal support. They are objects of feeling and desire which have no foothold or anchorage in Being apart from the existence of actually living minds. (197)

These suggestions lead James to the formulation of his view that every obligation requires a demand and every demand brings an obligation, and of his own ideal prescription to satisfy as many de-mands as possible at the least cost. It is in this way, too, that he represents his discussion as a contribution to the meaning of moral terms, for the suggestion is that their meaning can be understood only by reference to these origins. Such a claim, however, is at best unclear, since the specification of the relevant meanings is too gen-eral, and we might see it more as an account of the metaphysical status of moral properties. For the general upshot of his discussion is that moral properties are essentially dependent upon sentient living minds and exist, or have reality, only in relation to that dependence. It is in this way that his thought experiments raise, and seek to answer, problems about the "mind-dependence/independence" of moral properties, which anticipate more recent debates about the status of moral and other mind-dependent properties. James's experiments are intended to guide us toward a proper appreciation of the dependence of moral properties on personal feelings, what he calls "personal support," and so to explain the idea that they are residually "subjective." We have seen, however, that such a claim remains unclear. James rejects certain forms of subjectivism as he rejects certain forms of objectivism. Just as James's association of truth with expediency does not licence us to believe what we please, so the association of what is right with what is expedient does not licence us to do as we please. A Protagorean relativism is rejected as firmly as an objective supernaturalism and a naive naturalism.

James's account gestures in this way toward the larger scale project of elucidating that residual subjectivity, although he offers little more than a sketch of it. It initiates a search for those factors which provide the complex base from which our moral discriminations emerge. I have suggested that such an account could not plausibly or usefully be understood as an account of the *historical* origins of those moral properties. Even James's nominal reference to historical origins in the "psychological" question points more toward the physiological bases of moral properties than their history. A nominally better way of expressing the project would be as an inquiry into the emergence or provenance[3] of moral properties, but those descriptions, like the earlier references to metaphysical status or metaphysical origins need elucidation too. The positive question which James's experiments leave behind is simply whether in his sketch there are any clues to throw light on current issues about mind-dependence especially in relation to moral properties. In order to make some progress in understanding the project, I compare it in the next section with two more recent accounts.

II TWO RECENT FORMAL ACCOUNTS

James's thought experiment seems strongly to contrast with some recent discussions of the status of moral properties, and this may suggest that James's discussion has no contribution to make at all. In order to assess that claim I want to consider two related recent accounts of such issues. These are Jonathan Bennett's discussion of the distinction between primary and secondary qualities, and a similar but revised version of values, or moral properties, due to Mark

Johnston. Bennett did not consider how his account of secondary qualities might throw light on values, but later commentators have attempted to use the account in order to assimilate the two cases and to draw conclusions about the nature of moral properties.[4] Johnston offers an extensive revision of Bennett's account, classifies values as dispositional and response-dependent, and canvasses what he calls a "qualified realism" about them. I outline and comment on both accounts before returning to James's position.

Bennett's original discussion was guided by the idea that secondary, but not primary, qualities are dispositional, relational, and mind-dependent. These characteristics are revealed by analyzing ascriptions of secondary qualities as hypotheticals. The claim

(1) X is red

is equivalent to

(2) If X stood in relation to a normal human he would have a sensory idea of kind K.

I shall not consider in detail how adequate such a form may be, but it is intended to capture the idea of a causal disposition in X, in virtue of its primary qualities, to produce in percipients a certain mind-dependent response. Color qualities on this view are not simply inherent in objects. They can be ascribed to objects as powers or dispositions, but they are dependent on primary qualities and on mind-dependent, sensory responses on the part of normal human percipients. The argument for such an analysis rested on an illustrated difference between color- and size-blindness. In any such systematic distortion the latter will be more significant than the former and at the limit will result in an inability to conceive of the physical world as normal observers do. Physical science underlines that difference in selecting its explanatory vocabulary from among the primary qualities.

I identify four general difficulties which Bennett's account faces. These are:

(i) That it seeks to mark a difference of kind on the basis of a difference of degree.

(ii) That it leaves open the form and the status of the hypotheticals in the analysis.

(iii) That its treatment of specific cases is questionable.

(iv) That it is unclear in its primary appeal to science and to metaphysics.

(i) The argument from color- and size-blindness at least initially demonstrates only a difference of degree of importance in the two cases. Someone who has monochrome vision, for example, can probably navigate the world adequately, but, the suggestion is, size-blindness will be more serious. But even if such a claim is true it will need additional support to draw Bennett's conclusion about a radical difference of status between color and size properties. The degree of seriousness in such cases may not remain uniform, since some very minor size-deficits may actually be less serious than some color-deficiences. Even the added premise that at the limit size-problems will prevent an understanding of the physical world contains dangers. For it may need to be supported by appeal to science's selection of its explanatory vocabulary and will then raise difficulties in connection with (iv).

(ii) It will be evident that the hypothetical form which Bennett uses is unspecific and perhaps incomplete. We should need, strictly, to know more about the circumstances of the interaction, what restrictions are to be placed on the normal percipient, and how exactly to characterize the sensory effect. But these will be minor problems compared with that of the status of the hypotheticals. Here the difficulty is that although Bennett treats (2) as an analysis of (1), he describes the relation between them as that of "equivalence." So weak a relation will make it hard to draw the required distinction between secondary qualities, for which the analysis is available, and primary qualities, for which it is not available. Since our knowledge of primary qualities must also be based on a causal transaction between the objects and our senses, we can formulate parallel hypotheticals for primary qualities. It has always been recognized as a difficulty for a hypothetical analysis of dispositions that such hypotheticals can be formulated even for intuitively nondispositional properties. It seems that the relation between (2) and (1) would need to be strengthened for secondary qualities in order to distinguish them from primary qualities.

(iii) Bennett offers a number of illustrations of properties with different combinations of the three features of being dispositional, relational, and mind-dependent. Many of these might be queried, but I note one salient case which begins to cast doubt on the classification. We have an intuitive picture of a relational, mind-dependent disposition from such a property as being hallucinogenic ascribed to a drug. We think of this as a property causally related to chemical features of a substance and arising from a person's relation to it, namely, absorbing it into the bloodstream and having certain sensory experiences. Being red is importantly different from this, for the sensory response in the former case is not direct; even if the drug has a distinctive taste, it does not taste hallucinogenic. This reflects two problems already noted first about the specification of the sensory response and second about the required contrast between hypotheticals for primary and secondary qualities. In the case of the color we seem forced to specify the sensory response in terms of the quality of being red, while in the other case we seem forced to describe the response in independent terms. Moreover if we allow both being red and being hallucinogenic to be relational mind-dependent dispositions, then this may make it correspondingly difficult to deny this of the primary qualities. Relational mind-dependent dispositions may cover so wide a range that they cannot be distinguished from categorical mind-independent properties.

(iv) On the face of it Bennett's argument seemed designed to explain science's selection of primary qualities by means of certain general aspects of our experience. We might say that the metaphysics of experience served to show why science selects those qualities. And yet, at various stages in the argument, it also seemed as though that scientific selection acted as a premise. If that were so, then the illustrative case from ordinary experience would be redundant and could not be used without circularity to explain that selection. This indicates a dilemma. If the argument relies solely on the metaphysics of ordinary experience, then it is open to the queries raised already; but the appeal to science will make the argument potentially circular. It is unclear whether the argument moves from metaphysics to science or the other way round.

Two of these problems have a general significance. If the account were to work adequately, then there has to be some way of distinguishing genuinely categorical, primary qualities from genuinely dispositional, secondary qualities. One way of doing this within the hypothetical framework would be to support the idea that the relevant hypotheticals are *necessarily* related to the secondary qualities but not to the primary. This would be to concede, realistically, that the same forms *can* be constructed for both even though their relation to the original claims will differ. A second general issue arises from the suggestion that mind-dependence is not itself a well-defined relation but covers a wide range of diverse cases. The existence of such a range may make it difficult or impossible to draw a clear line between what is mind-dependent and what is not, and indicate that the distinction is too crude to be serviceable. We may have to recognize that mind-dependence is of different types or even of different degrees, and that such differences do not support any one clear distinction between the dependent and the independent. A more careful and more subtle subdivision of the diverse properties within that range would help to clarify the issue. That might be recommended not merely on the grounds of an Austinian interest in detail but also as one way, as it happens Austin's way,[5] of rejecting a crude traditional mind/body dualism.

Those weaknesses in Bennett's account are in principle remediable and Johnston's account of values as dispositional properties aims to remedy many of them. His revisions are directed not only at the formal account of "mind-dependent" dispositions but also at the metaphysical conclusions that might be drawn from such an account. He is, for example, rightly skeptical of conclusions about the real or unreal character of secondary qualities so understood, and is careful to characterize his preferred conclusion about values as a "qualified realism." I shall focus, however, mainly on his account of "response-dependence" (R-dependence) as a revision of Bennett's formal treatment of secondary qualities.

For Johnston R-dependence can be understood in these terms: If C is a concept then it is a necessary condition for C's being R-dependent that one of the following biconditionals be a priori true:

(3) X is C iff in K Ss are disposed to produce X-directed response R.

or

(3') X is C iff X is such as to produce R in Ss under conditions K.

The difference between (3) and (3') is that between cases where S's response is of an intentional kind and those where it is more purely causal. The latter cases would include, for example, those where James would characterize the effects as simple bodily feelings.

Johnston concedes some flexibility in these forms when he requires for R-dependence that "something of the following (biconditional) form" should hold a priori. In this respect his version matches a similar flexibility in Bennett's account, but in other respects Johnston makes it clear that his formulae differ significantly from Bennett's in at least the following ways:

(i) In requiring that the biconditionals should be a priori true Johnston acknowledges the problem of distinguishing between similar forms for both R-dependent and R-independent concepts. Although that requirement is only a necessary condition for R-dependence, so that some R-independent properties may meet it, still any property which fails it will be R-independent.

(ii) Although the biconditional is to be a priori it is not to be understood as an analysis of the relevant concept C. One way of reinforcing this would be to say that it does not provide a definitional or semantic account of C, but gives the metaphysical status of such a concept as one essentially related to subjects' responses. Johnston regards it as an advantage in such an account that it need not always avoid circularity, as it would have to do if it were an analysis. But he also makes it clear that his account must avoid the triviality of so adjusting the variables that the requirement would be met by any property whatever. The biconditionals must be a priori but neither analytic nor trivial.

(iii) Johnston, like Bennett, offers a number of illustrative examples of both R-dependence and R-independence. The "nauseating," the "titillating," and the "credible" would all be examples of the former, while such concepts as "conjunction," "much," and "successor" are examples of the latter. There are problems to raise here just as there were in Bennett's examples, but intuitively the former R-dependent group appear plausible. Like "hallucinogenic" they fit better into the genuinely dispositional group than "red" seems to do.

Johnston's account offers a necessary revision of the earlier account, but still faces similar difficulties of formal and material kinds. The formal point arises from uncertainty in the range of variables in the biconditional. We know that the variables have to be so construed that the formulae will be a priori but not trivial, and yet it is not clear how this is to be achieved. It is not clear, for example, whether we might not be forced to allow such an a priori connection even for those concepts which we expect intuitively to be *R*-independent without committing a purely formal triviality. There is no guarantee that we will be able to draw the required distinction between *R*-dependent and *R*-independent concepts even if we avoid a construal of the variables which renders the formulae trivially true a priori. In a similar way, although Johnston rightly requires that the biconditional should be a priori true for *R*-dependent cases it remains unclear how we determine this, or whether we can clearly distinguish *R*-dependence/independence in these terms.

It may be said that these points are remediable details, and it is true that they are so far faults of incompleteness. But some of them already indicate potentially more serious obstacles. It may really be difficult to draw the required distinction between *R*-dependent and *R*-independent cases even if we avoid trivializing the formulae and even if we have a clear criterion to distinguish what is a priori from what is a posteriori. The material difficulties reinforce this anxiety in the following way. Suppose that we contrast the three claims:

(4) The waterfall is 500 feet high.
(5) The waterfall is very high.
(6) The waterfall is impressive.

Intuitively we would expect (4)'s predicate to be *R*-independent and (6)'s to be *R*-dependent. It is not initially clear whether we should expect (5)'s to be *R*-dependent or *R*-independent. However, in each case we can formulate corresponding biconditionals as

(4') The waterfall is 500 feet high iff competent *S*s who measure it in appropriate conditions regard it as around 500 feet high.

(5') The waterfall is very high iff competent *S*s who compare its height with that of others in the neighborhood (some appropriate region) put it in the upper quartile of the range (some appropriate standard).

(6') The waterfall is impressive iff competent *S*s who in appropriate circumstances observe the waterfall are (suitably) impressed; or judge it to be impressive.

It might be objected that the references to "competence," "adequacy," "appropriateness," and "suitability" are just of the sort to reduce the requirement to triviality, but the intention here is that these should be specified even if it is not wholly clear how to do so. If it is then claimed that the specifications will prevent the biconditional from being a priori true, the question arises why this should be different in the R-dependent and R-independent cases. Similarly, it might be objected that whereas (4′) specifies a verification test for the original claim this is not so for (6′). Johnston draws briefly a distinction between the content of such claims and their verification, but this seems insufficient to answer the difficulty. Johnston himself insists that the right-hand side of the biconditional is not an analysis of the content of the left-hand side; the biconditional offers no such analysis even in R-dependent cases. So one who thinks that (4′) and (6′) might both be a priori true is not committed to any verificationist account of content.

Is there any good reason to claim that (6′) is a priori true while (4′) is not? It seems plausible to argue that there is a necessary connection of some sort between the clauses of the biconditional even in the case of (4′). It is at least difficult to see how the contrast is to be made out in these cases; and even more difficult in the case of (5′). Nor can it plausibly be said that (5′) invokes some standard in terms of which the comparison might be made, while this is not true of (4′) or (6′). Clearly (4′) does invoke standards of measurement of some sort, and standards are also involved, perhaps less obviously, even in (6′). We would not be inclined to think a five-foot-high waterfall impressive merely because it impressed Ss who had never seen a waterfall before. Of course in this case, as in the others, there remains the unresolved question not only about the appropriate standards by which Ss might judge, or respond, but also about the number, or proportion, of Ss required to make the a priori connection with the original claim.

These material difficulties follow the tracks of the earlier formal flexibility. They suggest that in each case there will have to be some reference to the standards by which the response is to be assessed as well as to the circumstances of the response and the response itself. For there is hidden complexity in the responses even of the intuitively R-dependent concepts. Even for such a plausible candidate as "nauseating" there will be differences to draw between its ascription to food and to tastes; between its reporting an occurrent response and its reflecting a general judgment; and between its literal and figurative uses.[6] Even here the earlier problem about different types, or degrees, of R-dependence arises again. The problem will be more serious the further one moves from the intuitive to the more problematic cases such as those of value or moral value themselves. It is, of course, not difficult to find natural responses associated with moral judgments, but they are themselves complex and do not seem to exhaust the grounds for such judgments. In James's category we find references to immediate responses such as feelings of inward dignity or of vulgarity, and of distaste or repugnance, which we may link with feelings of approval or disapproval. But if James's catalog is accurate then such responses play only one part in the complex derivation of those judgments.

I make these points to suggest not that Johnston's account is to be rejected but that it is incomplete and in need of further exploration. I leave open the possibility that in the light of such further exploration R-dependence might be rejected, but the more likely result is that R-dependence will be established on a clearer and more restricted basis. Whether in that case moral properties will be included in such a restricted range remains to be seen. I shall, however, not pursue that question directly but instead consider whether a comparison between Johnston's account and James's project throws light on the issue. In two respects such a comparison seems promising. For Johnston's account gives us an explanation of the metaphysical status of moral properties, which concerns neither their historical origins nor their semantic analysis, while James's project seemed to need just such an alternative. Moreover, it has been suggested that Johnston's account is determinedly formal and is open to some queries as a consequence. It is evident, by contrast, that James's account is not formal but material, and this raises the question whether it might not be used to complement that formal treatment. In order to examine these possibilities I return finally to James's account.

III JAMES'S ACCOUNT REVISITED

James offers no more than a brief sketch of his project and it consequently faces a number of problems. Some of these concern the methods to be used in conducting the thought experiments, and some concern his summary conclusions from them. It would not be possible here fully to justify his procedure or to carry out the project;

but I shall offer some suggestions both of method and substance to gain a clearer picture of it.

The principal ingredients in James's account of the emergence of moral properties can be summarily listed as follows:

(i) Simple bodily pleasures and pains. Direct emotional responses to events.

(ii) "Brain born" innate preferences built into our physiology which James calls "secondary affections."

(iii) Biological goals, such as survival, which may apply not only to individuals but also to groups or species.

(iv) Complex acquired preferences and desires.

(v) Explicit goals and longer term benefits and harms.

(vi) Scarcity of resources and competition for them.

(vii) Assessment of consequences, and the ability to act.

(viii) Requirements for the ascription of truth and falsity to moral judgments.

(ix) Explicit "ideals" which express a conscious strategy for resolving social problems, such as those arising from (vi), including some ranking or weighting procedure for the relevant factors.

Such a list seems on one side to be unremarkable, and yet it deserves some immediate comment, for it may also seem to be both unsystematic and incomplete. Although from James's point of view the list is important in identifying items which can be included under his generic title of a "demand," it is evident that many of the items overlap. It may well be that some factors listed under (iii) should also appear under (ii). Even if items listed under (ii) and (iii) as innate or instinctive can be contrasted with the acquired preferences of (iv), still many of the latter may be specific realizations of the former. The distinctions between (iv) and (v) on one side, and between these and (ix) on the other, will seem to be at best blurred. It may be said that no room has been made for such obvious factors as access to information, or ability to process it, which may be characterized as determinants of belief, and thought essential in the ability to express moral judgments. It may be queried whether James is justified in drawing a line between a nonmoral and a moral universe at the point of sentience, rather than at the boundary between what is living and what is not, or between what is conscious and what is not. And it may be objected that James has given no guidance about the procedure to be followed in the associated thought experiments. In what follows I make some attempt to answer some of these difficulties, but I shall not resolve the problems of overlap between headings. James's procedure is unsystematic but the overlaps are of less importance than the requirement that salient factors are not left out.

James evidently envisages a procedure in which we ask of items in the list whether if they were absent from some world it would still be possible to imagine a scope for moral judgment. But this immediately raises two problems. For philosophers sometimes resist any appeal to imagination as inadequate; and in this case it is so far unclear what it is to imagine a scope for moral judgment. The first point can be answered by insisting on an adequate check for any imaginative conclusion. The experiment would certainly be worthless if it rested on nothing more than an appeal to individuals' imaginative powers; but so long as it is possible to check any such appeal the objection is defused.

More serious is an ambiguity which arises over the nature of the imaginative exercise. There are two related projects which James does not distinguish. In the first we ask whether in some world it would be possible for the *inhabitants* to construct moral judgments, and in the second we ask whether it would be possible for us to make such judgments about that world. Both projects are viable and might have some interest, but it seems to be the latter rather than the former which James principally envisages. One reason for this is that the former question could be answered only if the inhabitants themselves were invested with sufficient apparatus, such as information gathering and processing, to make such judgments. But the latter question would not necessarily involve this, for we have the requisite apparatus and we might think that moral judgments can be made about the inhabitants of some world even if they were themselves incapable of making them. James encourages such an approach by drawing the line between a nonmoral and a moral universe at the point of sentience, and also by omitting from his list any reference to belief. For sentience by itself makes no reference to information gathering or processing. Such a reference would be necessary for the former project but not for the latter, even if we accepted that creatures with such developed abilities had more of a call on our moral sensibilities than those without them.

A further restriction arises over the likely outcome of the experiment. Merely to say that without any of the listed factors moral properties would find no application seems weak. We would be left with the bare physico-chemical world which James dismisses quickly as morally unproductive. Of course harms might be said to arise even in such a limited world, as when we speak of the storms harming a coastline, but nobody would seriously think that this provides enough of a basis for moral judgment. Nothing would be lost if we replaced the notion of harm in such a context with the more apposite one of "damage," and its correlative "repair," without allowing an entry for moral properties. A stronger conclusion would be to claim that some, or all, of the separate factors are necessary for the introduction of moral properties, but it seems impossible to treat any of the listed factors as strictly necessary in that way. James's simple bodily sensations, and even the immediate emotional responses, are not necessary for moral judgment. Swift's rational horses might evade such features without preventing an appeal to moral properties. Scarce resources and competition are again not strictly necessary, for moral considerations can arise even without them. Even in conditions of abundance the use of resources will introduce moral issues, and in any case harms and benefits can arise independently of resources. The one factor which seems difficult to avoid, as James himself emphasizes, is the generic notion of a demand or of a goal, but that precisely covers the wide range of other types of factor none of which seem individually necessary.

Consequently, the upshot of the experiment cannot realistically be a list of separately necessary and jointly sufficient conditions for any specific moral property. What might be expected is only that certain combinations may in some world be sufficient for the introduction of some moral property, and that the headings will include all the relevant type factors of that kind. The resulting picture will not provide clear criteria for the application of any specific moral property, but rather a pool of resources from which the natural base for any moral property has to be chosen. What we can expect to find is that certain combinations of such factors will approach more or less closely to the moral universe which we inhabit. A world of barely sentient living things with no consciousness and a restricted activity, which might identify a world of plant rather than animal life, will diverge strongly from ours even though there may still be room for moral judgment. But a world of sentient, conscious, competing animals whose activities are not so restricted will approximate more closely to our world. James himself indicates such a conclusion in the contrasts he draws between a moral solitude, a moral dualism, and a genuinely moral universe, for these are represented as successive approximations to our own moral condition.

Among the listed factors some, such as the appeal to different biological goals, will plainly be realized in divergent ways and give rise to a pluralistic moral universe. Others, such as the incidence of conflicting demands, will also directly involve a pluralistic account. It is partly for that reason that James declines officially to formulate any single overarching moral principle and in the end appeals only to the general satisfaction of competing demands at the least cost. Such a relation between a pool of natural factors and a divergent moral development can respect a general supervenience which insists only that whatever natural base is chosen in some world for some moral property must yield the same moral property wherever that descriptive base reappears in that world.[7] But that formal compatibility tells us nothing about the criteria to be used for specific moral properties and contains some unclarity about the range of descriptive properties from which such criteria might be drawn. That kind of unclarity, however, does not arise in James's account since he does no more than list the salient type factors in the pool, and offers no account of the formal relations between them and their associated moral properties.

James's account differs also from another more recent interest. Some philosophers have also constructed lists of type factors from which moral judgments derive, but their interest has often been simply to reflect the ground for moral judgments in an existing society. Lukes for example, lists such items as "scarce resources, competition, egoism, desires, ends, conceptions of 'good' and 'self,' rationality, information, ranking, dispute-resolving, co-ordinating, and damage-remedying" as among the determinants of our choice of moral criteria (Lukes 1987, 98–109). But the inclusion of moral features such as a conception of "good" or of "self" would yield a circularity in James's project. His interest lies in outlining how a conception of "good" might itself arise rather than in using that conception to determine the application of moral properties.

It might, however, be objected that even James includes in his list what he calls "ideals" under (ix), which may seem to indicate already some explicitly moral factors. It is true that James's list indicates a natural progression from more primitive to more sophisticated worlds to which moral judgment might be applied, so that some of the headings indicate only a change from implicit to consciously recognized demands. The reference to ideals and to their rank order marks the most sophisticated development in the hierarchy which approximates most closely to our plural moral world. Still it remains true that if those ideals are themselves consciously "moral" then at this point James's project would overlap with that of Lukes and be in danger of circularity. We seem to have to draw, on James's behalf, a distinction between factors which serve to introduce moral discrimination and those which already embody it. Like the earlier distinction between the two projects of introducing moral properties, as it were from the inside or from the outside, this related distinction identifies two different, but viable, aims. Officially, as I have represented it, James's aim is to list nonmoral factors which serve to introduce moral discriminations rather than to list factors, moral or nonmoral, which determine our specific moral judgments or principles.

The issue will then turn on the question whether the notion of an "ideal," as James understands it, is an explicitly moral notion, but it seems that we can distinguish between ideals which are explicitly moral and others which are not. A principle which in some way determines the outcome of competing demands in a situation of scarce resources may not be itself a moral principle but may only determine an outcome in what we regard as a morally salient situation. There is an ambiguity here in the way we use the term "moral." In one way it indicates an item which belongs to an explicit moral system or consciousness; in another it indicates only an item which we think calls for a moral consideration, or response, even though it is not itself yet part of an explicit moral system. James's official interest is in identifying items which belong in that second category, that is, items which call for a moral response but do not themselves qualify as such a response. The point can be put in another way. Responses to conflict or competition, for example in a zero-sum game, may determine what is a prudent but not necessarily a moral outcome. In James's project to close the list at the point where prudence shades into morality is to evade the charge of circularity. But prudence can be expected to have a structure similar to that of an explicit morality for it can also be represented as governed by principles or ideals. It may have been such a thought which prompted James's view that the right is after all no more than the expedient. Such a claim, in the context of the project of explaining the provenance of moral properties, is not so shocking as it might initially appear. It may there be understood not simply to recommend considerations of expediency but rather to suggest how more purely moral considerations arise out of expediency or prudence.

IV CONCLUSION

A comparison between James's discussion and Johnston's helps to clarify both projects. There are three respects in which James's account matches Johnston's, and one evident, major respect in which their procedures differ. Johnston provides a formal model in terms of which to understand James's inquiry into the origin of moral properties. Both accounts, moreover, converge over the issues of naturalism and subjectivity, although neither endorses those doctrines without qualification. The major difference between them is that Johnston's account is primarily formal while James's is exclusively material.

Earlier the question arose whether James's inquiry might not collapse into either a historical account of the origins of moral properties or a semantic analysis of them. Neither option would be satisfactory for James. He patently does not offer a historical account and his claim to discuss the meaning of moral terms in the metaphysical question is open to question. Johnston's account is presented neither as a historical nor an analytic enquiry, but instead as a sophisticated model of what I called the "metaphysical status" of moral properties. It gives a sense to those earlier unclear references to the "metaphysical origins" or the "provenance" of moral properties. It indicates an essential, a priori relation between those properties and subjects' responses to features of their environment. James's discussion aims at the same goal, and his conclusions match it.

James embarks on his project in order to show how morality develops out of, and can be understood only in terms of, the natural situation in which agents find themselves. To that extent he is a confirmed naturalist, even though he revises some of the traditional empiricist and utilitarian ways of articulating such a view. That position is matched by Johnston's account of R-dependence, where moral properties depend essentially upon what is given in the environment and on our normal or standard responses to it. So long as those responses, like the environment itself, are regarded as part of the natural world, then both accounts are naturalistic. One of the strongest motives in James's project was to restrict the scope of provenance of moral properties to what he called "the ethical republic here below." His account identifies that ethical republic with the natural phenomena from which moral properties develop.

The obverse side of that naturalism is that it rests on a residual subjectivity. James rejects strong forms of moral subjectivism and skepticism, but he accepts that moral properties rest essentially on the "demands" of sentient creatures, of "actually living minds." Moral properties in that way depend on what he calls generally "personal support." The account of moral properties as R-dependent makes the same point that some such degree of subjectivity is ineliminable. In both cases it is a subjectivity qualified in its essential reference also to "objective" features of the inhabited world. Johnston's commitment to what he calls "qualified realism" makes a similar point. Such a commitment amounts to no more than the weak denial that moral concepts are independent of concepts of our responses, and James's account would endorse that conclusion. For him, it seems, moral properties are real in just the way that any properties with that provenance are real.[8]

Yet Johnston's account is formally sophisticated in a way that James's is not. James makes no use of the apparatus of hypotheticals which marks the classification of moral properties as dispositions. He offers no formal explanation of the way in which objects acquire moral properties through their influence on subjects and their consequent responses. Nor does he offer any explicit answer to the question how his project can avoid the unwelcome alternatives of a historical or analytic account. It is nevertheless not difficult to see how James's project might fit into, and complement, Johnston's formal account. If Johnston's R-dependence has the merits of a formal approach, it has also some corresponding weaknesses. R-dependence requires a clear distinction between categorical and dispositional properties, and an adequate criterion to distinguish a priori and a posteriori hypotheticals. Those hypotheticals themselves depend upon a wide range of substitutions for the variables which, at the limit, may threaten the distinction between R-dependence and R-independence. Because James has no such formal apparatus he is not vulnerable to those problems. Even if it turned out that the formal apparatus was unsatisfactory in the case of moral properties, this would not prevent James's account of a natural base for such properties from being correct. It would still be necessary to fit that account into some formal framework, and James makes a contribution on the material side to that project.

NOTES

1 Both traditional and recent philosophers have used this genetic idiom. Hobbes's account of the origin of a social contract provides a traditional example, and Grice's accounts of an intentional theory of meaning and of the development of such concepts as belief and truth provide recent examples. James uses the device in other contexts, too, in his pragmatic account of truth and his discussions of the emergence of consciousness.

2 The issue is discussed also in Johnston 1989.

3 Interestingly Johnston uses this term in "Dispositional Theories of Value" (1989, 171). It is a natural term to use to indicate something different from both historical origin and analytic derivation. James often uses the term "emergence" in such contexts.

4 Some discussion of those later issues is given in Dancy 1993, 156–63.

5 Austin 1962. There is a comment on this aspect of Austin's views in my entry "J. L. Austin" in Dancy and Sosa 1992, 34–6.

6 The first distinction I have in mind is obvious, and the other two can be exemplified in the following pairs: (1) That is nauseating (but not actually now causing nausea)/ That is nauseating (me now). (2) It is nauseating (that is, causing, or liable to cause, nausea)/ It is nauseating (that is, it tastes unpleasant, revolting, etc., but is neither causing nor liable to cause nausea). Of course we also use the term in still more extended, figurative ways which have nothing to do with taste.

7 I do not consider more complex accounts of supervenience because James's position seems not to involve them. For a discussion of supervenience and what he calls "resultance" in the moral context see Dancy 1993, 73–82.

8 Different forms and accounts of moral realism are given in Brink 1989; Dancy 1993; and McNaughton 1988.

14 Some of life's ideals

In the preface to *The Will to Believe* James described his "philosophical attitude" as a "radical empiricism," empiricism because he regarded all claims concerning matters of fact as hypotheses subject to revision in the light of subsequent experience, and radical because he extended this empirical attitude to metaphysical hypotheses. Specifically, "unlike so much of the halfway empiricism that is current under the name of positivism or agnosticism or scientific naturalism, it does not dogmatically affirm monism as something with which all experience has got to square. *The difference between monism and pluralism is perhaps the most pregnant of all the differences in philosophy"* (WB, 5; emphasis added). Although he uses the expression "radical empiricism," this view is not yet the doctrine that he later advocated as radical empiricism.[1] Yet he was already a pluralist in more than one sense.

In this essay I am interested in the kind of pluralism that James intended to foster in "On a Certain Blindness in Human Beings" and "What Makes a Life Significant," but not only in those essays. He characterized this pluralism in the preface to *Talks to Teachers* as follows. "The truth is too great for any one actual mind, even though that mind be dubbed 'the Absolute,' to know the whole of it. The facts and worths of life need many cognizers to take them in. There is no point of view absolutely public and universal. Private and incommunicable perceptions always remain over, and the worst of it is that those who look for them never know *where"* (TT, 4; emphasis in the original). This view coheres with fallibilism. If one is keenly aware that one's own point of view is limited, one should be prepared to learn from others, to have one's perspective widened, or even radically changed, by listening to them. Conversely, if one is prepared to alter one's beliefs in the light of experience, that experience should include what one hears from others. These are not logical entailments, but what reasonableness requires. However, to recognize that our deepest moral convictions may be overthrown by later experience is *not* to warn us against acting on them – on the contrary, moral progress depends on persons who heroically risk life and reputation for a "larger ideal whole than [established rules] permit" – it is simply to call upon us to be prepared to modify our own ideals or the manner in which we attempt to realize them if "the cries of the wounded" inform us that we have made a "bad mistake" (*WB*, 156, 158).

Reflecting on "The Sentiment of Rationality" early in his philosophical career, James found it incredible that "working philosophers would pretend that any philosophy can be, or ever has been, constructed without the help of personal preference, belief and divination" (*WB*, 77); near the end of his life, he found that philosophical systems are "just so many visions, modes of feeling the whole push, and seeing the whole drift of life, forced on one by one's total character and experience, and on the whole *preferred* – there is no other truthful word – as one's best working attitude" (*PU*, 14–15). This, then, is one sense in which James's philosophy is pluralistic; by arguing that one's philosophy can be no more than a "vision . . . forced on one by one's total character," he legitimizes a plurality of world-views each of which balances in one way or another our needs for the explanatory and unifying power of classifications, for appreciation of the multiplicity of particulars in all their diversity, and for making sense of our practical impulses. But this Jamesean pluralism is not an "anything goes" subjectivism. James points to the views of Spinoza and Hume as two examples of philosophies that fail to have adherents because, so he says, they ignore one or the other of these needs completely.

However, when James wrote that the most consequential difference in philosophy is that between monism and pluralism, he had in mind not the plurality of philosophies embraced by persons of different temperaments but a particular metaphysical view embraced by him, namely, the view that pluralism is "the permanent form of the world . . . the crudity of experience remains an eternal element thereof. There is no possible point of view from which the world can appear an absolutely single fact. Real possibilities, real indetermination, real ends, real evil, real crises, catastrophes, and escapes; a real God, and a real moral life, just as common sense conceives these things, may remain in empiricism as conceptions which that philosophy gives up the attempt either to 'overcome' or to reinterpret in monistic form" (WB, 6–7). For James, belief in real possibilities – belief both in our ability to make choices that are not determined by events that occurred before we existed and in a future whose shape depends at least to some extent on these choices – was an indispensable prerequisite of psychological well-being.[2] Moreover, James could not understand how one could be motivated to act for good even at great cost to oneself, unless one believed that there are real goods and real evils. And he did not believe that there would be real goods and real evils in a deterministic world.[3] I cannot pursue this metaphysical issue here.

Neither can I discuss James's attempt to reconcile his claim (in "The Moral Philosopher and the Moral Life") that "nothing can be good or right except so far as some consciousness feels it to be good or thinks it to be right . . . " (WB, 147) with his view, just mentioned, that there are real goods and real evils. He takes it that an objective moral order results from the fact that we make claims upon one another and are able to recognize these claims. He holds that a world consisting of but "two *loving* souls" doomed to extinction would "have as thorough a moral constitution as any possible world" (WB, 150; emphasis added). One hears here echoes of Kant, but there is a difference. For Kant, a preexisting morality *requires* that we make the ends of others our own; for James morality *presupposes* that we have done that and are continually doing so. Only then will we seek resolution when claims or ideals conflict, only then can one speak of a point of view that transcends that of any one thinker. James did not think that he had to refute the moral skeptic (although he responds to moral skepticism elsewhere), and this is not the place to ask whether his, or indeed anyone's, position is an adequate answer.

What is of interest here is that we cannot in this world satisfy all claims, and that gives rise to what James calls the "casuistic" question. The upshot of his lengthy discussion of the casuistic question is this: "In the casuistic scale, therefore, those ideals must be written highest which *prevail at the least cost,* or by whose realization the least possible number of other ideals are destroyed" (WB, 155;

emphasis in the original). One must, *qua* philosopher, seek an inclusiveness that will do justice to some extent even to the ideals that are destroyed. What those ever more inclusive ideals are can be determined only through social experiments, judged "by actually finding, after their making, how much more outcry or how much appeasement comes about" (*WB*, 157).

James is a consequentialist: the empirical consequences of actions or of policies are what ultimately determines the rightness or wrongness of those actions or policies and guides subsequent choices. But James, though he greatly admired John Stuart Mill, is not a hedonist, nor any other kind of reductive utilitarian. While acknowledging that many of our ideals are connected more or less remotely with bodily pains and pleasures, he maintains that many others, especially the higher ones, have other sources. "The elementary forces in ethics are probably as plural as those of physics are. The various ideals have no common character apart from the fact that they are ideals" (*WB*, 153). Once again, James is a pluralist.[4]

I shall not pursue this topic here. For I am, in this essay, interested not in James as an ethical theorist but in James as a moralist and public philosopher. Of course, that distinction must not be taken too seriously. Even in his most theoretical writings on ethics – in "The Moral Philosopher and the Moral Life" or in the *Principles of Psychology* – the voice of the moralist is heard. In the former, implicitly, he advocates the strenuous moral life as well as, explicitly, the pursuit of ever more inclusive ideals. In the latter, having claimed that as one becomes aware that one's essence is like that of other human beings,[5] one will adopt some version or other of a universalizing principle, he illustrates the point with a supposedly irrefutable argument for the admission of women to Harvard Medical School, based on the premise that women are human beings and, therefore, entitled to all the rights of human beings.[6]

James, the moralist, addressed students who were idealistic, and, especially the women, wondering whether their lives would have, could possibly have, any significance. Being college bred, they were, moreover, inclined to overvalue "culture and refinement," to look down upon, to be "blind" to what might give significance to the lives of the uneducated. James, aware that he too tended to suffer from this blindness, understood it to be not only a moral failing, not only to impoverish the blind themselves, but to provide excuses for United States imperialism and generally to constitute a basis for antidemocratic tendencies.

In "What Makes a Life Significant" James concluded after much reflection on various kinds of lives – the sheltered, refined, and cultured life at Chautauqua; the exposed, daring lives of construction workers on high scaffolds; the dullness of the lives of day laborers that might yet be redeemed if chosen in the name of some ideal – that no single factor can "redeem life from insignificance. Culture and refinement alone are not enough to do so. Ideal aspirations are not enough, when uncombined with pluck and will. But neither are pluck and will, dogged endurance and insensibility to danger enough, when taken alone. There must be some sort of fusion, some chemical combination among these principles, for a life objectively and thoroughly significant to result" (*TT,* 165).

Let us begin with culture and refinement. Not only are they not sufficient to make a life significant, one may wonder whether they are, strictly speaking, necessary. On the one hand, unless one is completely downtrodden (by poverty, illness, an implacable foe, or depression), one will seek to add some beauty, some adornment, to one's abode or one's person; one will celebrate certain events (births, comings of age, harvests, etc.) in a narrower or wider community. On the other hand, sometimes when life is intensely significant and precarious (climbing Mount Everest, plotting to assassinate a dictator), one gives no thought to these "frills." In the coves of squatters in North Carolina, James claimed not to find "a single element of artificial grace to make up for the loss of nature's beauty"; yet he came to understand that the ugliness they had created was for them "a symbol redolent with moral memories and sang a very paean of duty, struggle, and success" (*TT,* 134). That may have sentimentalized what was, after all, a very hard and minimal existence; it also leaves out what may well have been present: efforts to make the cabin "beautiful" (say, with a picture torn from a magazine) and the consolations of a simple faith.

Literature, both imaginative and otherwise, art, and music broaden one's vision, deepen one's understanding, enliven one's imagination. Science has not only changed our lives, it has changed our understanding of ourselves and the world around us. High culture is not merely an enjoyable addition to lives that would otherwise be drab, however "significant"; it alters those lives, it increases their significance by broadening and enriching the ideals that animate them.[7] But one would suffer from the blindness James wanted to cure, if one denied that lives untouched by high culture may be significant.

I have considered the relevance of culture and refinement to the significance of a life from the standpoint of the individual who lives that life. James addressed the same question from a social perspective when he spoke to a group of alumnae of women's colleges about "The Social Value of the College-Bred." In that essay he introduced Americans to the term "intellectual" as a term of pride, to the idea of an educated class with its own class consciousness.[8] "In our democracy," he wrote, "where everything else is shifting, we alumni and alumnae of the colleges are the only permanent presence that corresponds to the aristocracy in the older countries. We have continuous traditions, as they have; our motto, too, is *noblesse oblige*; and, unlike them, we stand for ideal interests solely, for we have no corporate selfishness and wield no powers of corruption" (*ECR*, 110). We intellectuals are to guide the human ship through "gales of passion" and "currents of interest" toward truth and justice. We are to be the social critics, the molders of public opinion, and we are to do this in a disinterested manner. James understood a liberal education to be a study of the various ways in which human beings have sought perfection, "and when we see how diverse the types of excellence may be, how various the tests, how flexible the adaptations, we gain a richer sense of what the terms better and worse may signify. Our critical sensibilities grow both more acute and less fanatical" (*ECR*, 108). For James, tolerance for a great variety of ideals is itself a governing ideal. The inclusive ideal that we are to seek is not to be achieved by fashioning a society in which all think alike, but rather by finding through sensitivity and mutual respect a way of harmonizing a variety of ideals. One thinks of the grand symphonies of the late nineteenth century, say Bruckner's, rather than the singing in unison of the National Anthem.

A college education, James believed, helps one to recognize goodness when one encounters it. Of course, one could not be an intelligent voter, nor one who influences public opinion in a beneficial direction, if one were not able to recognize goodness, whatever goodness may be relevant, in a candidate. But the point is not merely political. Educators worry about role models, or more often about the lack of role models for certain groups (women who want to go into science or politics, inner-city youths who want to go to college, and so on). We do not speak very often of role models in connection with being a decent human being; James, I am convinced, would have done so.[9] He realized also that most of us know only a few good human beings, that we come to meet varieties of goodness in literature and biographies that we might never encounter otherwise; hence, once again, the relevance of culture.

But, one might ask, do we need role models for being decent human beings? Here culture and refinement make contact with another necessary condition of the significant life, "pluck and will," that is, with character. When one confronts a significant moral choice, James wrote, what is at issue is not so much what one shall now choose to do as what kind of person one "shall now resolve to become" (PP, 1:277). That requires not only the ability to picture to oneself vividly what one is about to do and its immediate consequences for oneself and others, but also the ability to visualize the kind of person one will be, will have become, if one pursues this path rather than that, commits oneself to this ideal and not that one. Role models, positive and negative, real or fictional, help in this task. Nevertheless, "culture and refinement" are of secondary significance only. "The solid meaning of life is always the same eternal thing – the marriage, namely, of some unhabitual ideal, however special, with some fidelity, courage, and endurance; with some man's or woman's pain" (TT, 166).

While one will unhesitatingly agree with James when he says that there is nothing so despicable as a person who professes many lofty ideals but fails to do anything to bring them about, there is more to character than pluck and will. There is, in fact, an intimate connection between character and ideals. "Character" is a rather flexible term. Is one's shyness, for example, a part of one's character? Surely, it is relevant to what kind of life's work one will choose for oneself. To be sure, one may be required to make a heroic effort to speak up in defense of victims of injustice in spite of one's terror, but one is not required to become a trial lawyer or a politician if one finds addressing strangers painful. Different people are able to hear the cries of different wounded, different characters find different causes appealing, different talents and weaknesses lead their possessors to adopt different projects, different long-range commitments result from different passions. Having a certain type of character, or becoming that type, may itself be one's ideal. For James, being a person who has "pluck and will," who leads the morally strenuous life, who succumbs neither to "a nerveless sentimentality" nor a "sensualism without bounds" is such an ideal (*WB*, 132).

For the sake of this ideal, James believed in and defended the pluralism of real possibilities; for the sake of this ideal, he advises, "Keep the faculty of effort alive in you by a little gratuitous exercise every day" (*TT*, 52). Here it is important to note not only the emphasis on effort but also the word "little." James was as opposed to the inability of Americans to relax as he was to any tendency to pamper oneself. Both, he thought, were a danger to the individual and to the nation.

However, the ideal of (moral) heroism is a secondary ideal; whether a resolute determination in the face of major obstacles or temptations is really a good thing depends on the first-order ideals it serves. Nothing appears to be easier than being heroic when one's country is engaged in fighting a war, and persuading oneself that one's country is right. But this is not the heroism James had in mind, nor was he blind to his country's faults. Let us, therefore, consider ideals as the third necessary condition of a significant life.

What is an ideal? James emphasizes two features; first, that ideals are "intellectually conceived," and second, that "there must be *novelty* in an ideal – novelty at least for him whom the ideal grasps." But novelty, hence ideals, "are relative to the lives that entertain them" (*TT*, 163; emphasis in the original).

An ideal is any idea, any project or commitment, that guides one's life, or a major part thereof. James, we saw, thought one might have ideals without having the will to try to realize them; but for the sake of simplicity, I shall understand having an ideal to include being motivated by it at least to some extent. Not every passing desire is an ideal, nor are all our actions guided by our ideals. We sacrifice without even a murmur thousands of passing desires to our more lasting projects, and even the most interesting life is shot full of routine activities and habitual actions. Finally, even when actions require thought, such as driving a car or writing a check, the thought may not be related to any ideal. James calls an ideal an intellectual fact to make two points: that one is aware of having the ideal, and that having that ideal is part of one's self-conception. James, for instance, was aware of himself as, among other things, a mug-wump.[10] Ideals may be quite inarticulate commitments – to clear a cove – or well articulated long-range goals – James's commitment to a world without war.

In "The Moral Equivalent of War" James proposes a national con-scription for a war against nature. Ignoring our modern sensibilities that cringe at the idea of a war against nature, I want to note that the essay attempts to meet two problems: that we are pugnacious and love glory, and that certain virtues fostered in war are needed for national survival. The moral equivalent, the conscript army against nature, will satisfy the longing for a fight fairly fought and won, and it will instill such virtues as courage, persistence, and putting the collec-tive interest above one's own. It will also, James said, teach the gilded youth the realities of a life of hard physical labor. James himself was ever and anon struck by the fact that the physical labor of others provided the foundation on which a life of the mind, such as his, rested.[11] He appreciated the unsung heroism of the laboring masses (see, e.g., *TT*, 154–5), but that raises the question of what benefits working class youths were to derive from this sort of national service. Perhaps, by its mingling of classes, it was to make for less blindness and more tolerance all around; perhaps rich and poor alike would come to understand, as he wrote elsewhere, that "no outward changes of condition in life can keep the nightingale of its eternal meaning from singing in all sorts of different men's hearts. . . . If the poor and the rich could look at each other in this way, *sub species æternitatis*, how gentle would grow their disputes? what tolerance and good hu-mor, what willingness to live and let live, would come into the world!" (*TT*, 167).

But here – at the end of "What Makes a Life Significant" – James has been carried away by his own eloquence, carried away, I believe, because he genuinely believes in tolerance. There is, however, a difference between letting others live their lives as long as they don't interfere with one's own, or coming to mutually agreed upon com-promises when conflicts loom, and tolerating oppression. James saw this clearly in the case of the U.S. occupation of the Philippines. What was wrong was precisely that the United States did not let the Filipinos live as they wished, and James objected repeatedly and vociferously.

The second feature of an ideal, according to James, is that it contains novelty. This raises a host of problems, none of which are adequately addressed by James. We must ask why ideals must contain novelty, if indeed they do. We must ask how an ideal contains novelty. We shall discover that in order to answer these questions we need to consider more carefully what is meant by a significant life. In the end I shall conclude that it is not clear how an ideal contains novelty, that some ideals, nevertheless, seem rather obviously devoid of novelty, and that lives animated by the latter ideals might nonetheless be significant.

Why must an ideal contain novelty? One's first thought might be this. While one person's boring routine may be another's exciting variety, whenever one feels that one's life consists of nothing but ever the same old thing, what pulls one out of this malaise is finding some new interest, project, or commitment. That leads to the further thought that a significant life cannot be a life consisting of nothing but routines. Whether one imagines spending eight hours a day at an assembly line, performing the same motion over and over again, or one imagines being confined to one's bed by a lengthy illness, what strikes one has horrifying is the sheer boredom of such a life. Surely, one wants to say, a significant life cannot be so boring, it must contain some novelty. But real novelty, not the vicarious novelty that might come through reading books, would seem to require that one's life be animated by some ideal that brings the novelty with it. But we have now shifted from the thought that one needs a new idea (new ideal) to redeem a boring life to the quite different idea that each ideal must contain novelty.

What does that mean? It cannot mean that a life animated by an ideal cannot be a life of extraordinary regularity. The life of a religious contemplative, though following a set daily, weekly, and annual pattern and devoid of external novelty, is a life suffused by an inner significance as few more active lives are. Moreover, the inner life of prayer, study, and reflection, a life of intense mental activity, may be full of its own kind of novelty. But the ideal itself is not novel, and those who embrace it may well resist novelty not only in their rituals but in the circumstances of their lives and in the society of which they are a part. That would worry James because it would be an obstacle to humanity's progress toward more and more inclusive ideals. One need only think of resistance to peace between Israel and the Palestinians by certain types of orthodox Jews and their Islamic counterparts. But, clearly, one may be deeply religious and yet actively promote peace and other forms of social progress; conversely, resistance to social change is not confined to those with strong religious commitments. In any case, James recognized that one cannot tell from the outward form of a life whether or not it is animated by an idea; even the hard, impoverished, and hopeless lives of day laborers may, for all we know, be animated by ideals, for example, by the ideal of providing for one's family. But are these novel ideals, or do they contain novelty in some other sense?

An ideal may contain novelty in at least these two ways. First, an ideal may be of such a kind that a person living in pursuit of it will inevitably encounter novelty, although the ideal itself is not novel. I am thinking of the ideals that animate explorers and experimentalists, people who want to add to their own and to humanity's knowledge by deliberately seeking new experiences, whether by going to new places or by producing new conditions in a laboratory. More generally, the search for knowledge is an ideal that has novelty built into its very core. Perhaps this is why Peirce thought that it was the only ideal one could pursue no matter what; from which he concluded that "the rule of ethics will be to adhere to the only possible absolute aim, and to hope that it will prove attainable" (Peirce 1931–60, 5.136).

Of course, James would have objected, rightly, that one's adherence to the growth of knowledge can be as conservative, as much an obstacle to social progress, as clinging to a long-established social order or inherited values. Moreover, I believe that James would have objected to the very idea of an absolute aim, for that implies a kind of infallibility. Thus I disagree with Edward H. Madden, who has argued that James has one fundamental moral commitment – maximizing need satisfaction – and that this commitment is "as absolute as the commitment of any other moral philosopher" (WB, xxxiii). I believe that any ascription to James of so specific an absolute commitment is ultimately misleading, for it ignores James's antireductionism and his pluralism. In contrast, his own formula, "There is but one unconditional commandment, which is that we should seek incessantly, with fear and trembling, so to vote and to act as to bring about the very largest total universe of good which we can see" (WB, 158), is compatible with his antireductionism – the good is left unspecified – and with his pluralism, for we do not all see now the same largest total universe of good. James seeks the more inclusive *ideals* (note the plural!), but any formulation that speaks of maximizing satisfactions (or minimizing pain) ignores the fact that for James there is no common measure by which one might compare ideals.

One's ideal may contain novelty in a second sense; one may envisage changing the world, changing the way the world would go without one's intervention. Often this is what James had in mind. The squatters in the mountains of North Carolina are changing the face of the particular cove they have chosen to clear. The anarchist Swift writes about the misery of the unemployed in an effort to bring about a more just world. James reads excerpts from Swift's writings to his audience of complacent gentlefolk to open their eyes to a kind of evil that need not persist and to the shallowness of a Leibnizian optimism (P, 21–2).

It is not always easy to tell, however, whether another person's ideal promotes or resists change. In 1894 and again in 1898, James opposed bills that would have criminalized the practice of medicine by anyone who did not have a degree from a reputable medical school or had not passed an examination. In a letter to the *Transcript* James explained his opposition as based on three grounds: it would interfere with the liberty of citizens to choose their healers; it would not guarantee more effective treatment; it would tend "to obstruct the progress of therapeutic knowledge" (ECR, 145).[12] Four years later, testifying before the Massachusetts State Legislature, he argued in words that must by now sound familiar, "Our State needs the assistance of every type of mind, academic and non-academic, of which she possesses specimens. There are none too many of them, for to no one of them can the whole of truth be revealed. Each is necessarily partly perceptive and partly blind. Even the very best type is partly blind. There are methods which it cannot bring itself to use" (ECR, 60). Though from the point of view of orthodox practitioners James resisted change, for which he was roundly condemned, his own rationale was exactly the opposite; he saw himself as defending progress.

Matters are even less clear when we turn to the novelty in the cove-cultivator's ideal. The cove-cultivator wants to change the face of the earth; the advocate of national parks wants to keep it unchanged. Their ideals may collide concerning a particular piece of real estate. The cultivator wants to change the face of the land; the conservator wants to change the course of human endeavor, divert it from dominating nature toward leaving nature alone. Whose ideal contains novelty?

What I have tried to suggest with these examples is simply that it is quite unclear what "containing novelty" means, though one is also tempted to say that there are ideals that do not contain novelty in any obvious sense. Finally, it will not do to say that while there may be ideals that do not contain novelty, the lives that those ideals animate are not significant. To say so would, I think, simply betray the blindness that James was eager to combat.

This, however, reveals an ambiguity in the phrase "making a life significant." When James asks whether the life of a day laborer, a worker in the subways, or the Austrian peasant women whom he sees on market days might be significant, he gives two types of answer. He says both that they deserve monuments because our whole civilized life rests on their backs, depends on their toil, and that we do not build them monuments because they endure drudgery, hardship, and even danger not for any lofty ideal but for the bare necessities and most modest of luxuries (some tobacco, beer, or coffee). He seems to suggest that the lives of those whose labor supports our "culture and refinement" are significant from our point of view, that is, to us, but not from theirs, that is, to them. But who, after all, denies that their lives are significant? Not they, for all that we can know, but we, because *we* despise the ideals that animate these toilers.

The point of "On a Certain Blindness in Human Beings" is precisely that we are blind to what makes other lives significant to those who live them. While we might think that cultivating a cove in North Carolina has significance also on a larger scale – that it might be comparable to raising chickens and cows, collecting eggs and churning butter so that on market day one can come to the city to supply it with food – that is not the point James wants to make. For his next example is taken from Stevenson's description of boys with bull's-eye lanterns. Having lit the lantern hidden under one's coat was a source of the sort of excitement of which James writes that wherever it is, "there life becomes genuinely significant" (*TT*, 134). From an external, adult point of view, one is tempted to object that the boys enjoy this particular pleasure only in the fall, that even in that season it takes up a small part of their day, that surely what is of long-range significance to their lives is what they learn in the schoolroom. But that would be to miss the point; the boys go to school, do their chores, eat their meals, and so forth, all for the sake of that time with the lantern. That is their animating ideal. Their state of mind is best understood by comparing it, as James does, to that of someone who has fallen in love. And just as the lover discovers ever new features in the beloved, so one discovers ever new features in an ideal to which one commits oneself, however "familiar" or "old" that ideal may be.

The boys' ideals are fleeting and divorced from the rest of their daily activities, but that is not essential. Intellectuals can most easily imagine ideals similar to their own, ideals that fill large parts of each day and shape years of one's life. Both kinds of ideals may be utterly opaque to outsiders, who may indeed, as James said in the preface to *Talks*, not even know where to look for the significance in these alien lives. In fact, one might be blind to the ideals that make another's life significant to that other in two distinct ways. One may not know what the ideal is – as a stranger would not know that the boy is carrying a lit lantern under his tightly buttoned coat – and substitute for that unknown ideal some contemptible ideal of one's own devising, or one may know what the ideal is but consider it contemptible. James falls victim to one or the other form of this blindness when he explains why we do not build monuments to laborers.

Yet James recovers, he remembers that ideals (and their novelty!) are relative to the lives they animate. Thus keeping out of the gutter is not an ideal for us (we are not conscious of it as an aim, nor would the attempt or the experience be novel), but "for many of our brethren it is the most legitimately engrossing of all ideals" (163). Still, one is tempted to wonder how that can be an ideal. James seems to think once again of the day laborers whom he had mentioned earlier in the essay. Then he had suggested that some of them might be animated by ideals, both the simple one of supporting a wife and child (to keep them out of the gutter?) and more complex ones – seeing it as a religious duty, or engaging in it temporarily to enlarge one's sympathetic understanding of different lives – but he also thought the more usual laborer's life was barren and ignoble because it was not animated by any "ideal inner springs" (*TT,* 162). I believe that James allows us to witness his own continual struggle against being blind to the possible values of nonintellectual lives. He shares our inability to know where to look for "the private and uncommunicable perceptions," that is, moral perceptions, perceptions of duties and ideals, that animate those leading lives very different from our own (*TT*, 4).

Finally, let us consider what makes a life significant to an onlooker, or to humanity, or at any rate to some other people. When James wants to build monuments to workers in the subway, he has that sense of significance in mind. Here I want to say, just in passing, that lives may be significant in this sense even though those who live these lives may be wracked by self-doubt, and even though the significance of their lives is not appreciated by their contemporaries. Every starving artist illustrates the second point; and that lack of recognition is one, though not the only, source of self-doubt.

When James insisted that an ideal must contain novelty, he may have taken this external point of view. A life has significance for humanity if it is for the most part (not exclusively; moral holidays are not only permitted, they are important) animated by an ideal that will change the world. James was a child of his time, imbued with a belief in progress that is perhaps impossible for us. New inventions, new conceptions in the arts and sciences seemed, on the whole, to make human lives better. In particular, James treasured novelty in social arrangements that would allow more diverse ideals, hence more individuals, to flourish. Because intolerance of one kind or another, a blindness to the value of lives different from our own, continues to be a major obstacle to human flourishing. James's unflagging devotion to the ideals of plurality and tolerance is as relevant and as inspiring as it was a century ago. James's epistemological pluralism, his understanding that there is no point of view from which the whole truth can be grasped, supports the demand for a moral pluralism, for there is also no point of view from which the whole moral truth can be grasped, no ideal that includes all others. Indeed moral progress consists largely in the extinction of ideals of domination and exclusion by ideals of equality and inclusion.

James's belief in progress was dealt a serious blow by the American occupation of the Philippines, though not a fatal one. James argued forcefully and frequently against American imperialism, as in this letter to the *Boston Evening Transcript*.

Here was a people toward whom we felt no ill will . . . . Here was a leader who . . . appears as an exceptionally fine specimen of the patriot and national hero. . . . Here were the precious beginnings of an indigenous national life. . . . [Yet] we are now openly engaged in crushing out the sacredest thing in this great human world – the attempt of a people long enslaved to attain to the possession of itself, to organize its laws and government, to be free to follow its internal destinies according to its own ideals. . . . We are destroying the lives of these islanders by the thousand. . . . We are destroying down to the roots every germ of a healthy national life in these unfortunate people and we are surely helping to destroy for one generation at least their faith in God and man.

James knew that the justification offered for the imperialist policy was the old cant of the "white man's burden," and continued, "Could there be a more damning indictment of that whole bloated idol termed 'modern civilization' than this amounts to? Civilization is then the big, hollow, resounding, corrupting, sophisticating, confusing torrent of mere brutal momentum and irrationality that brings forth fruits like this!" (*ECR*, 154–8).

An ideal that makes the life it animates significant from the social point of view must "contain novelty" in the quite straightforward sense of envisaging a social order that differs from the existing one in being more inclusive, in leaving room for more individuals to have more freedom to pursue their own destinies as they see fit, provided they accord that same freedom to everyone else. But not all ideals are social, and in the case of personal ideals it is neither descriptively nor normatively correct that they must contain novelty. The enormously important social ideal of tolerance that has inspired all the writings of James I have considered here entails, I believe, tolerance for personal ideals even if they lack novelty.

I have spoken of tolerance because that is the term James used. But what is at stake here is more than tolerance, it is a form of respect. Once one is aware of the ideal that makes another's life significant, one does not merely tolerate it, one respects it, and that is why one seeks to include that ideal in one's own.[13]

NOTES

1 Radical empiricism, as developed in the essays in *ERE*, adds to the radical demand that metaphysical theses be treated as hypotheses the asser-

tion that the objects of experience stand in relations that are themselves experienced. Here the latter, technical doctrine and with it the notion of pure experience will be ignored except to mention in passing that radical empiricism is not only a more radical empiricism but also a more radical pluralism than that advocated/defended in the essays in *The Will to Believe* and in the two essays from *Talks*. For pure experience is not a general stuff of experience, rather "there are as many stuffs as there are 'natures' in the things experienced" (*ERE*, 14). In other words, his ontology is more appropriately seen as a neutral pluralism rather than a neutral monism.

2 In 1870 James recovered from a mental crisis by convincing himself that free will need not be an illusion and deciding, according to his diary, to "assume for the present – until next year – that it is no illusion. My first act of free will shall be to believe in free will" (quoted in Lewis 1991, 204).

3 The arguments for this position are spelled out in "The Dilemma of Determinism" (*WB*, 114–40). Here I shall simply take note of it.

4 I have discussed James's ethical theory at length in Putnam 1990.

5 "They agree with us in having the same Heavenly Father, in not being consulted about their birth, in not being themselves to thank or blame for their natural gifts, in having the same desires and pains and pleasures, in short in a host of fundamental relations" (*PP*, 2:1266).

6 "A gentlemen told me that he had a conclusive argument for opening the Harvard Medical School to women. It was this: Are not women human? – which major premise of course had to be granted. Then are they not entitled to all the rights of humanity? My friend said that he had never met anyone who could successfully meet this reasoning" (*PP*, 2:1266n). Perhaps the most impressive example of James's ability to weave his sociopolitical concerns into even quite abstract arguments is his reading from the writings of an anarchist journalist during the first lecture on pragmatism (see *P*, chapter 1). Those readings described in horrifying detail the sufferings of the unemployed.

7 In a similar vein, James wrote, "Education, enlarging as it does our horizon and perspective, is a means of multiplying our ideals, of bringing new ones into view" (*TT*, 163).

8 One of the causes James had embraced was that of the French Jew Alfred Dreyfus, who had been unjustly convicted of treason. Those who fought for and finally won Dreyfus's pardon and exoneration were known as *les intellectuels*.

9 Agnes Heller, in the preface to her *A Philosophy of Morals*, argues that all "original" moral philosophers have had a particular model of the good person in mind. Her own model is that of her father (Heller 1990).

10 (A political independent, first, someone who had left the Republican Party in spite of its abolitionist credentials when it became thoroughly corrupt, and later an antiimperialist.) Describing his oration at the unveiling of the monument of Robert Gould Shaw, colonel of the black 54th Massachusetts regiment, James wrote to his brother Henry, "I brought in some mugwumpery at the end, but it was very difficult to manage it" (*Corresp.*, 3:9).

11 He wrote to his brother Henry, "[W]hen one sees the great West one also feels how insignificant in the great mass of manually working humanity the handful of people are who live for the refinements" (*Corresp.*, 3:39).

12 James was, however, in favor of a bill that would prevent those who had not passed a state examination from referring to themselves as physicians or using "doctor" before or "M.D." after their names, because people have a right to know "who is regular and who is irregular" (*ECR*, 149).

13 Of course, this last comment leads us back to what James calls the "casuistic question," the search for ever more inclusive ideals. It raises the problem of conflicting ideals, and, finally, the question of what one is to do about those who embrace intolerance as an ideal. This is not the place to pursue these vitally important questions.

15 "A shelter of the mind": Henry, William, and the domestic scene

> Men always have attempted and always will attempt to make their minds dwell in a more reasonable world, just as they always have sought and always will seek to make their cities and their homes more beautiful. (*MEN*, 3)

> If his hand comes in contact with an orange on the table, the golden yellow of the fruit, its savor and perfume will forthwith shoot through his mind. . . . The voice of the violin faintly echoes through the minds as the hand is laid upon it in the dark. (*PP,** 1:556)

I

When Henry James writes of "the house of fiction" in his preface to the New York edition of *The Portrait of a Lady*, he teaches us to range analogically among domestic sites. He asks us to consider the relations, between, on one hand, the temporary home where he sits writing the novel – "I had rooms on Riva Schiavoni, at the top of a house near the passage leading off to San Zaccaria; the waterside life, the wondrous lagoon spread before me, and the ceaseless human chatter of Venice came in at my windows" – and, on the other hand, the conceit of the artist's process of building, his "edification." Describing "the house of fiction," he writes, "The spreading field, the human scene, is the 'choice of subject'; the pierced aperture, either broad or balconied or slit-like and low-browed, is the 'literary form'; but they are, singly or together, as nothing without the posted presence of the watcher – without, in other words, the consciousness of the artist" (James 1984, 1070, 1075). Furthermore, by writing such a preface, Henry James asks us to reconsider *The Portrait of a Lady* as a novel of houses: Gardencourt, the Archer residence in Albany, Osmond's apartment in a Tuscan villa, Palazzo Roccanera, Pansy's convent.

Serialized beginning in 1880 in *The Atlantic Monthly*, a magazine that published some popular fiction even as it attempted to maintain its credentials as magazine for the intelligentsia, *The Portrait of a Lady* would have been read by an audience willing to pay for the familiar tale of popular domestic fiction. Such stories usually featured an orphan girl, thrust into the world, who must live by her wits and Christian values, and ultimately win for herself through marriage a home where she can fulfill the Victorian American cultural fiats of purity, domesticity, piety, and submissiveness.[1] Isabel would have been recognized as one of a sisterhood of potentially bestselling heroines who inhabited the private sphere of home and hearth, the genteel haven from the brutalities of the marketplace. As William Veeder has so amply demonstrated, even Isabel's deviations from the domestic, sentimental commonplace – she is wealthy not poor, a naive Romantic not a pious Christian, an emigré not a loyal daughter of upstate New York and so forth – cannot fully distinguish her from the heroines of popular fiction. They, too, seemed to sell better when they tested the limits of formula, when they bore witness to the inconsistencies and hypocrisies of a prescribed genteel American womanhood, so long as their "message" eventually reaffirmed Victorian social codes. Indeed, at novel's end Isabel intends, however ambiguously or temporarily, to return to her responsibilities as Gilbert Osmond's wife and Pansy's stepmother.

If Henry James's "house of fiction" figures, then, the novel as genre, the rooms in Venice where he wrote for three weeks, the houses within *Portrait,* and the idealized American household of magazine fiction, it perhaps also meant to him just "home." With what meanings does James fill that word? One of the most intense soundings of the term may be found in his correspondence as he arranges to buy Lamb House, the dwelling in Rye he had been renting. In August of 1899 he writes to William, who has cautioned him against paying more for the property than it is worth:

My whole being cries aloud for something that I can call my own – & when I look round me at the splendour of so many of the "literary" fry my confrères . . . & I feel that I may strike the world as still, at 56, with my long labour & my genius, reckless, presumptuous & unwarranted in curling up (for more assured peaceful production), in a poor little $10,000 shelter – once for all & for all time – *then* do I feel the bitterness of humiliation, the iron enters into my soul & (I blush to confess it), I *weep*! (*Corresp.*, 3:78)

Henry James yearns for a home as mark of literary achievement, as literary workshop, as haven whose "thick old walls never give the faintest shudder & keep out the cold as well as the violence" (*Corresp.*, 3:48), and as family retreat, "Lamb House," he writes William, "is *Yours* utterly – interminately – absolutely – for *all* the time you are in Europe" (*Corresp.*, 3:94). Henry would be both masterly genius and angel in the house for visiting family members; when Alice Gibbens James visits him, he reports to William, "beautiful sunsets, net frugal dinners, evenings as peaceful as the afternoons" (*Corresp.*, 3:132). The domestic "Là-bas," the ordinary transformed by sheltering love to the beautiful and blissful, has been achieved.

William James, too, writes within and against the Victorian American culture of sentimental domesticity; his audiences, like those of Henry, learn to expect from him the familiar with a twist, the domestic and sentimental made to yield the profound, the erudite, the surprising. To trace William's rewriting of sentimental domesticity within his works of psychology and philosophy is to link them to a whole series of creations lying, it appears, precisely outside the realm of academic disciplines and the concerns of technical philosophy. Perhaps appearances deceive. James's life and thought have been generally viewed as masculine in character; he is a neurasthenic who is saved by manly activity, an advocate of the outdoor life and moral strenuousness, a son who transforms his father's intellectual legacy. Meliorism, voluntarism, pragmatism all have to do with action implicitly gendered masculine; willing (rather than submitting), building (rather than being or dwelling), having one's say (rather than remaining silent) in nothing less than the universe itself. I wish to present a different James, one who learned from his mother and wife; a man always attracted to effeminate languor, private intensities, and life indoors within a specifically domestic, even sentimental, scene.

It is by now a truism that nineteenth-century Americans imagined experience as divided between women's private sphere of home and hearth, and men's public sphere of marketplace and professionalism. But William James, more than most men of his day, lived, thought, and worked in both; indeed, wholly separate spheres did not exist for him. Within his home, he blurred the lines between motherly and fatherly roles. He worked long hours at home in a study, often with his children present. At Harvard and, indeed, nationally and internationally, he was recognized by students and colleagues as exceptionally nurturing, tenderhearted, and modest even as he stood his ground. Yet William James's domesticity, his participation in "woman's" culture, should matter to us only if it be reflected in his intellectual work. It is such a presence – of the feminized and domestic within his thought – that I will sketch. Let us consider then, four principal domestic tableaux: William James as he establishes the problematical nature of domesticity in "The Sentiment of Rationality"; James as he self-consciously participates in the domestic and popular culture of his day; Elizabeth Stoddard, a domestic novelist of the day, as she grapples with and "solves" similar dilemmas of domesticity; and James's own solution, bearing a family resemblance to that of Stoddard, as he presents it in "On a Certain Blindness in Human Beings."

We begin with one of the most noted passages in William James's works, the disguised account of his spiritual and emotional crisis in *The Varieties of Religious Experience*, which opens:

Whilst in this state of philosophic pessimism and general depression of spirits about my prospects, I went one evening into a dressing room in the twilight to procure some article that was there; when suddenly there fell upon me without any warning, just as if it came out of the darkness, a horrible fear of my own existence. Simultaneously there arose in my mind the image of an epileptic patient whom I had seen in the asylum, a black-haired youth with greenish skin, entirely idiotic, who used to sit all day on one of the benches, or rather shelves against the wall, with his knees drawn up against his chin, and the coarse gray undershirt, which was his only garment, drawn over them inclosing his entire figure. He sat there like a sort of sculptured Egyptian cat or Peruvian mummy, moving nothing but his black eyes and looking absolutely non-human. (*VRE*, 134)

Like popular women writers who, often publishing pseudonymously, paradoxically announced in a public voice the principle that woman's voice should be heard only in the private sphere, James veils his words.[2] He bases *Varieties* on the value of personal testimony but denies his own, presenting autobiography as the "translated" words of a French correspondent.

The force of the passage develops precisely in its deviation from the domestic everyday: what should be an ordinary experience in that most ordinary of places, a dressing room, becomes a twilight experience of hallucinatory seizure, infectious madness. The epileptic youth has become a thing on a shelf rather than a person in a chair; the very sign of madness is simultaneous proximity to and utter distance from the securities of home. The asylum where James has seen the idiotic creature travesties a domestic haven, just as, for the space of this vision, James's closet is home and not home. Sympathy, that most powerful of domestic virtues, here intensifies into horror; such fellow-feeling makes of a man a small child: "for months I was unable to go out into the dark alone" (*VRE,* 135). He needs the security of home now more than ever, and, as if by imagistic power, his mother makes an appearance: "My mother in particular, a very cheerful person, seemed to me a perfect paradox in her unconsciousness of danger, which you may well believe I was very careful not to disturb" (*VRE,* 135). As a man James must shelter her from the horror he knows; but he also may, like every male in genteel America, claim refuge in woman's sphere. His mother's cheerfulness and light are, with the Bible ("if I had not clung to scripture-texts. . . . I think I should have grown really insane"), the signs of his salvation (*VRE,* 135).

To this plot of entitlement – the beset male may expect the domestic presence of the cheerful female – James adds a sensational twist: it is an interior cataclysm, not the vagaries of the marketplace, that has caused the speaker to cling to his home. But home, usually the locus of sincerity in contrast to the slippery morality of the public sphere, here becomes a theater. James has seen the huddled figure as "a sort of sculptured Egyptian cat or Peruvian Mummy" (*VRE,* 134): within the mind within the closet within the house lurks the intense strangeness beauty, and danger of the aesthetic, of life captured and slain into art.

This metamorphic quality of the ordinary, its tendency to appear now as a maternal, domestic haven, now as a darkened theater of imagination, plays itself out not only in James's primary work of the sensationalistic margins, *The Varieties of Religious Experience,* but also throughout his oeuvre. Home is an important context in which to consider James's thought.

James's commentators have from the first recognized his interest in "human life in the everyday world" (*P*, xxvii), his insistence that the amateur and the professional philosopher alike assent to philosophical beliefs on the basis of temperament, his warnings against ignoring "everyday" experience. But the everyday world is always *an* everyday world; the ordinary is perhaps the most time- and place-bound of all concepts. Morton White has clarified James's notion of the ordinary world of human feeling by tracing a philosophical narrative from Lockeian intuition, to Jonathan Edward's "Sense of the Heart," to the Scottish Common Sense philosophers as they were transformed by the Transcendentalists, through Emerson's "sentimental" Reason. William James then takes his place in a line of American philosophers who have granted sentiment a decisive role in theories of knowledge, metaphysical belief, and ethics. The representative passage of this intellectual heritage would be, for our purposes in establishing the importance of domestic culture in James's work, these words from Emerson's "American Scholar":

What would we really know the meaning of? The meal in the firkin; the milk in the pan; the ballad in the street; the news of the boat; the glance of the eye; the form and gait of the body; – show me the ultimate reason of these matters; show me the sublime presence of the highest spiritual cause lurking, as always it does lurk, in these suburbs and extremities of nature. (Emerson 1983, 3)

About these homely matters we know by feeling. Let us turn to one of William James's own essays about knowledge and feeling, "The Sentiment of Rationality" (*WB*, 57–89), to explore with him the philosophical venue of the human heart.

II

William James writes to the woman he hopes to marry, Alice Howe Gibbens, that he feels most intensely alive, most himself, when he experiences an "active tension" within and trusts outward things "to perform their part without any guarantee that they will." The absence of guarantee he feels as a "sort of deep enthusiastic bliss, of bitter willingness to do and suffer anything, which translates itself physically by a kind of stinging pain inside of my breast-bone." This mood or emotion is "to me as the deepest principle of all active or theoretic determination."[3] At letter's end he apologizes, as well he might, for his aridity and awkwardness; nevertheless he stands by his plan to make intellectual epistolary love, to describe his inner feelings as relevant both to his philosophy and to his acceptance by Alice.

Courting as a philosopher, James philosophizes soon after as a family man in "The Sentiment of Rationality" (*WB*, 57–89). James here explores such topics as the nature and types of rationality; the contrasting temperaments of idealists and materialists; and the power of personal belief, in certain circumstances, to create truth. Yet at the same time he confronts a troubling contradiction at the heart of domestic life in genteel America: home is the haven that men wish for, but it is also the site of emasculation, of a peacefulness that might anaesthetize or even permanently cripple its male inhabitants.[4] The domestic and sentimental entwine as a leitmotif of the essay; through its philosophical music and its rhetorical patterns James returns us repeatedly to the site of the middle-class home.

Philosophical thought, James tells his audience, is inseparable from the ordinary experience of actual people. We recognize a rational world-view by the "ease, peace, and rest" it brings (*WB*, 57). Such peacefulness and simplicity are aesthetically pleasing – "the relief of the musician at resolving a confused mass of sound" – and domestically prudent – "the passion for parsimony, for economy of means in thought, is the philosophic passion par excellence" (*WB*, 58). Yet this desire for simplification meets a conflicting desire for "distinguishing" which "loves to recognize particulars in their full completeness." Purely "theoretic rationalism" fails because it oversimplifies; we must consider rationality in its "practical" aspects as well.

Simple conceptions here just won't do. We must leave the "insipid spaciousness" of theoretic rationality, a shelter that is no shelter, and pass into the "teeming and dramatic richness of the concrete world" and acknowledge the complicated feelings of the entire man. Here we find ourselves squarely in the world of custom. "The daily contemplation of phenomena juxtaposed in a certain order" (*WB*, 66) which allows us to understand objects by what they have been and will probably become is now the very source of "whatever rationality the thing may gain in our thought" (*WB*, 67). Every acceptable philosophical conception must "banish uncertainty from the future," must make us feel at home. "When we take up our quarters in a new room, we do not know what draughts may blow in upon our back, what doors may open, what forms may enter, what interesting objects may be found in cupboards and corners," he tells his audience. But after a few days "the feeling of strangeness disappears" (*WB*, 67). Just as we inhabit rooms and grow to feel the balm of familiarity, so rational conceptions practically considered must also save us from the strange and unpredictable.

As if with a dawning horror, James, safely tucked into the bed of home truths and predictable outcomes, suddenly sits upright. Too much reassurance, he counsels, is bad. The familiar and the customary now must play a different role: they must invite us to act upon them. Materialism, by denying that there is an eternal aspect under which we may consider our purposes, makes us feel *unheimlich*, unhoused, in the universe. Materialism allows us to act, but not to feel that our acts matter in the great scheme of things. Yet idealism, with its sentimental, intimate relation to the world, seems to obviate the need for action, as we dwell in our egos and minds, sure that our minds and absolute mind are of one substance. Idealist "atonement" encourages utter passivity. In choosing between tough-minded materialism and tender-minded idealism, James explains, we find ourselves either distanced from a sympathetic home or paralyzed deep within one.

Neither alternative suits him; James wants both to rest at home and to live intensely, physically, strenuously. He embraces domestic security, but he must seek risk and challenge. Lest we underestimate his masculine striving (which we might well do, since he appears to characterize the rational, whether theoretical or practical, as a homecoming), he closes with one last dichotomy. Do we wish to be moral skeptics (alarmingly foppish, epicurean, and superficial) or moral absolutists (energetic, if tragically rigid)? As between the skeptic's anaesthesia and the absolutist's energy, James would clearly have us choose the latter, but also run risks, *make* truth in an as yet unfinished universe that defies the determinist's tragic view. Yet even this repudiation of the effeminate and foppish he couches in effeminate terms. Any acceptable philosophy, he explains, must not disappoint our "dearest desires and most cherished powers" (*WB*, 70). The case for masculine spontaneity and power, the personal contribution "x" that the meliorist makes to the mass of mundane phenomena, is made in the very bastion of the heart, the private sphere of home and hearth. "All that the human heart wants is its chance," he insists: a plaintive enough call to action (WB, 89). Can the promptings of the heart, that throbbing organ of sentimental American popular culture, ever send men up mountains to tax their endurance and prove themselves against the universe? Will a philosophy that takes seriously the feeling person forever be a trap?

Having explored the domains of sentiment and custom for their philosophical "cash-value," James has opened a philosophical space which threatens him as a cultural prison. It is to James's reactions to this impasse that we turn, and in order to do so we must begin by viewing his problem as a wider phenomenon of mid- and late-nineteenth century American culture.

III

William James came to writing in a richly varied milieu. We might focus on his widely documented family situation or on the influence of contemporary academics at Harvard and elsewhere (Kuklick 1977). Or, widening our explorations further still, we might examine James's position in the larger culture, focusing on James this time as a public philosopher who attempted to meet his anxious and listless society on the ground of its most pressing needs by creating "a discourse of heroism" (Cotkin 1990, 11).

In these varied approaches to the culture of letters in which James gradually found his way, his domestic circumstances, still considered part of "woman's sphere," tend to fade away, as if into one of the vague auras he describes in Principles of Psychology. As one of James's biographers has stated – and he might speak for virtually every other commentator – "This is primarily a story about men, not because women are unimportant, but because the sources tell it that way" (Feinstein 1984, 16). Although "the" sources have long included William's sister, Alice, evidentiary anxiety prevails.[5] We know a great deal about James's living quarters, clothing, travel, illnesses, and family members (indeed, his correspondence with Henry is overwhelmingly slanted toward what we might label "domestic" issues), but the "so what" question intrudes. How are we to make useful connections between ordinary life at home and the life of the mind? That we would want to make such connections an essay such as "The Sentiment of Rationality" suggests.

We might well begin, as Cotkin has, with the general social malaise of the period. He sees James's "solution" (however problematical) in an exploration of strenuous experience that reads culturally as the rigors of outdoor life, martial energies redirected to peaceable ends, and a certain posture of lively feistiness toward the universe or, more modestly, toward one's own ennui. But here I would point also to James's search for a renewal of failing energies within the domestic scene itself, and specifically within that scene's potential for intense, aesthetic experience. The American genteel home traps men and women alike, but James considers more than traditional masculine routes of escape. His pragmatism, a method predicated upon action and testing, might be, as well, a product of turn-of-the-century decadence.

In support of this contention I do not turn directly to the record of his domestic life but instead pose William James both in and against another culture of letters, that of the so-called "domestic" novelists of the nineteenth century.[6] Elizabeth Stoddard, a New England novelist, provides my test case, in part because Henry read her works and reacted violently to them, and in part because, like William the Harvard professor and the transcontinental popularizer, she situated herself between "high" and "low" cultures, ultimately blurring the distinctions between them. Since we have no evidence that William ever read Stoddard, this is emphatically not a study in sources; rather it is an exploration of the intersection of various cultures of letters – philosophical, literary, regional, popular, domestic – whose very shifting limits constitute their most vivid revelatory value.[7]

The record of domestic fiction I seek to explore synecdochically through Stoddard indisputably places matters of hearth and home in the foreground. That these women wrote fiction (and not, say, sociology, history, or psychology) only strengthens their value as commentators on the American scene. How better to understand what mass audiences wanted and needed to hear about their courtships, houses, marriages, children, work, and deaths, than to examine the short stories and novels they bought in huge numbers?[8]

Rather than dismissing (feminine) sentimentality as part of the debasement of American culture against which James had to speak out in a discourse of (masculine) heroism, we might instead consider James's self-conscious participation in it. We might also pause to notice that such culture, described and recreated in popular fiction of the day, is never purely platitudinous or formulaic. It may embrace an idealized status quo, but it can also criticize, explore, and even undermine it.

To understand William James's view of domestic matters, we ask, then, how he saw himself in relation to the "low" culture of domestic discourse. Immediately we notice that, like authors of domestic handbooks and like many a domestic novelist, he speaks directly, in familiar, even avuncular, tones to audiences whom he wishes to convince of the legitimacy of certain ways of taking their humble experience. We recognize that James's essays usually began as public lectures for a general audience; that he deliberately popularized his ideas on religion and ethics; that, as Cotkin argues, he spoke therapeutically as well as scientifically of discipline, habit formation, and even metaphysics. Indeed, his commitment to such popularization of his ideas – like the domestic novelists, he spoke and wrote to support his family – actually stood in the way of his ever working out a technical philosophy for an audience of experts (MEN, xxvi).

Furthermore, James's personality, if not his metaphysics, was tender: people felt drawn to him, believed he cared about them and their problems. Witnesses agree upon his gift of intimacy; even adjusting for hagiographical tendencies, we notice that reports of former students depict James as wise, modest, sympathetic. One of them writes of his teaching, "Always happy turns of intriguing phrases, a glow of warmth and meaning. . . . We were always thinking together. That sort of 'teaching' made us like the subject and love the instructor." He adds that James often inveigled students into "participating in the gracious hospitality of a perfect home. He was the consummate artist at living" (Starbuck 1943, 128–9). So popular was he that in 1904 he declined one hundred invitations to speak (P, xvi). Grateful readers and audience members wrote to him directly.

Part of James's appeal would have been the comfort of hearing new ideas patiently explained in familiar terms and framed by traditional values. In book reviews and occasional essays he describes the home as man's haven, "one tranquil spot where he shall be valid absolutely & once for all," and the proper wife as subordinate to her husband (ECR, 253–4). His own correspondence reveals that he in fact lived the ideal, that the premier domestic prize of the comely, intelligent, strong, and pure helpmate was actually his. When William, beset by nerves, fatigue, and ambition, leaves Alice in Cambridge with small children and a tight budget while he travels abroad, she writes: "You must not come home before spring. For your own sake it is a world of better that you should stay. Wait till things are settled and you have done the work you desire to unhindered by the interruptions you would groan under here. . . . I am happy to think of you in comfortable lodgings seeing these men you like" (Houghton, 22 December 1882). Alice attends the deathbed of Henry, Sr., and then writes a letter to William expressing grief, hope, and love worthy of the idealized heroine of popular fiction. Sentimental: yes, but genuine precisely in her ability to report and evoke the tender emotions. William James could speak directly to a general audience of domestic concerns popularly conceived because he knew them intimately and associated them seamlessly with his work as a philosopher.

Yet at the same time, he denigrated his "squashy popular-lecture style" (quoting Evans 1929, 378), resented speaking before crowds of Chautauqua visitors, and registered the cost of his public persona; "I have also just been offered 1500 dollars worth of lecturing in California. . . . All this means hard labor & is inseparable from a social jigging which is rank poison to my nature" (Corresp., 3:2). William James had managed to situate himself within genteel domestic and popular culture – he married well, sold well, and, at least compared to his earlier periods of mental strife, even slept and ate well. Yet he also sounded the limitations of such culture, yearned for more, sought to contribute to the "high" stream of philosophical achievement. The problem he posed in "The Sentiment of Rationality," the intrinsic conflict within domestic forms as he knew them, he would address and even put to rest. And he would do so in an essay he himself labeled "popular," "On a Certain Blindness in Human Beings." To appreciate the message there, let us make a brief detour through Stoddard's The Morgesons.

IV

In 1865 Henry James submitted a (never published) review of Elizabeth Barstow Stoddard's novels The Morgesons and Two Men to the

North American Review. About *The Morgesons* Henry feels negative
in a positive way. It is a "thoroughly bad novel" but an "uncommon" failure. Its incoherent dialogue and lack of narrative exposition are causes of a "lively irritation of the critical senses." Although the story is "abortive," it "contain[s] several elements of
power." This is a book written with "undoubted sincerity," "amaz-
ing ignorance," "shrewdness," and "imagination" (Henry James
1984, 614–17, hereafter *AW*). It is both worthless and promising.

We can in retrospect see that James complains of just those elements in Stoddard that we recognize as marks of the master he is to
become: the novel's dramatic method (Stoddard never explains)
which requires hard work of the reader; the mysterious quality of
the heroine; and the emotional violence of the social scenes. Even
though Stoddard has "enough imagination to equip twenty Mr. Trol-
lopes," she "amuses herself in talking what we feel bound to call
nonsense."

The Morgesons is a female *Bildungsroman* that tells the story of
Cassandra Morgeson, daughter of a shipbuilding merchant and a
pious mother, in Surrey (Mattapoisett), Massachusetts in the early
nineteenth century. Stoddard's narrator chronicles Cassandra's three
forays from home – one to her maternal grandfather's Calvinist
household where she is sent to quell her wildness, one to a distant
relative's house who awakens her sexually, and finally one to Belem
(Salem) where she learns of the twisted values of the New England
aristocracy and finds her husband-to-be, the rakish Desmond. Stoddard periodically brings Cassandra home to depict her ambiguous
relationship with her sister Veronica, a strange young woman indeed, Cassandra's Ligeia-like alter ego. By novel's end, the proud and
impetuous Cassandra has, like any good domestic heroine, chastened and married the Byronic suitor. She is surrounded by needy
family members whom she evidently plans to nurture to the end of
her days. The romantic heroine – Cassandra communes with the
sea, her source of wisdom and strength – has been appropriated by a
formulaic domestic plot.

To recount plot alone would be to overlook the principal stylistic
sources of the novel's meaning. Nonsequiturs and half-explained
events abound. Secretiveness prevails: every character has a mysterious obsession only imperfectly understood by herself and half-
hidden from others. Family members circle about, stating their in-

ability to know one another, but they also melodramatically issue psychological bulletins on people or situations: "stir up Adelaide, she is genuine, has fine sense, and half despises her life; but she knows no other, and is proud" (167).

Certainly the novel has a nightmarish, almost submarine quality. Henry James writes of it, "if the reader threw down the book with the sensation of having been dreaming hard for an hour, he was yet also sensible of the extraordinary vividness of the different episodes of his dream. He arose with his head full of impressions as lively as they were disagreeable" (AW, 614). Stoddard infuses *The Morgesons* with romantic energy by viewing the domestic scene so intensely that it metamorphoses into the grotesque. The household reveals dark powers as Stoddard presses on the everyday life of the Morgeson household until it yields mystery and violence. She places her characters in proto-surrealist frames of mind: they share their dreams, dream aloud, sleepwalk, practice the art of *frottage*, and even hypnotize themselves before hallucinating. By staring hard at what is most familiar, Stoddard moves beyond gothic topoi to induce and figure forth the strange in the very stronghold of the sentimental. Her revolutionary approach to the domestic must have pleased her as she realized that such a performance might even "pass" as Victorian domestic fiction, and thus sell well. Even better, it might enable her to recapture not just her New England childhood but also the curious life she led as a writer among professional *littérateurs* in New York City. Like William James, Stoddard dwelled uneasily but fruitfully within a domestic culture that she wished at once to celebrate, exploit, and escape.

When, in 1853, Elizabeth Drew Barstow, daughter of a New England shipbuilding family gradually falling on hard times, married Richard Henry Stoddard, the "genteel" poet, she also joined, for better or worse, a literary movement that managed to decline during every moment of its ascendence. Richard Stoddard and his circle of close friends, Bayard Taylor, Edmund Clarence Stedman, and George H. Boker, wrote an elitist poetry of idealized and ultimately vapid loveliness, a failed *l'art pour l'art*, at the same time as they contributed to, and even helped to edit or publish the popular magazines of the day, such as *Harper's Monthly, The Century, The Atlantic Monthly, The North American Review, The Nation, Scribner's.*[9] These poets, literary institutions, and aesthetic articles of faith operated off-balance, as if a mild earthquake rumbled perpetually beneath them. The genteel poets wondered whether they were feminized artists or men of business, whether they were most themselves when they tailored literature to middle-class standards and a largely female market, or when they praised Swinburne, Rossetti, and Poe, and maintained that the didactic had no place in literature.

The genteel circle conveyed to Elizabeth Stoddard a sense of deep artistic insecurity masked by a fervent literary professionalism. Her husband and his friends fell ever deeper into a gap between what Santayana would later characterize as the opposing aspects of the American mind: practical, energetic, and aggressive on one side, languorous, intellectual, and feminized on the other. As she came to consider herself an artist, Elizabeth transformed the genteel *agon* into the very style and substance of her fiction: one might say that the genteel poets lived and wrote defensively and hypocritically, while Elizabeth lived and wrote with a sense of irony so acute that it issued in a genuinely experimental prose.

Well connected in the publishing community of mid-century America, the genteel poets gave Elizabeth the practical means of publishing her writing. An intimate brotherhood that regarded itself as a family, the genteel poets unintentionally gave her the means of thinking of art in deeply domestic terms: a quest for Beauty which could take place within the confines of the domestic scene. What the genteel poets put asunder – the "serious" poetry they wrote at home in carpeted and book-lined studies, and the popular literature they most publicly wrote, edited, or published – Elizabeth Stoddard joined together, writing three novels which from the James brothers' day to ours defy comfortable literary categorization or evaluation.

Elizabeth Stoddard traveled the Möbius strip of their two "private" lives: that of her immediate family (Richard, three children – only one of whom survived childhood – brother Wilson, and father) and that of her extended literary family. Her letters reveal a woman who was helpmate and virago in the former, subordinate poet and peer of the "great" in the latter, but the two could never be separated. It is no wonder she experienced these varied roles, at times conflicting, at times synergistic, most powerfully as shifting moods, not fixed positions. Within the course of each of her longer letters we can watch her ringing the changes on her own personality. "My whole life and interest are in the different forms of art – and the *artist* belongs to his work," she writes in summation.¹⁰ It is precisely work, woman's work and man's work, public work and private, that the genteel poets put into question. If she cannot distinguish her domestic self from her position within a culture of letters, we can hardly blame her. The two lives are almost one, both as they are presented to her by others and as she sets about manipulating them. She writes in her journal,

I think I thanked God when I walked out this afternoon for suddenly feeling virile. By virile I mean that I came to myself for an instant, the kingly power asserted itself. It is very pretty here, my dear old pictures never looked better than they do on the yellow or buff paper, behind the glass door of the closet are some of the familiar illustrated books, my vases, boxes, boxes, [sic] ornaments are round me, but how I have labored to place them . . . .
It is all done newly[,] when the books are arranged, I shall be ready to write my book, and the method of my life will be tantalizing, unique, picturesque, unsocial, sad, incomplete. (Stoddard 1984, 348)

As the "method of her life," so the method of her art. To arrange her home is to allow herself to feel "virile," ready to write. To write of beauty is to write of domesticity, for Stoddard believes the "artist belongs to his work," and the notion of "work" is for her intriguingly, frustratingly, and fruitfully resistant to the separate categories of art and life. She would create as a genius, *sui generis*, but the very concept of genius would place her among literary peers who regarded themselves as a family. Her first novel showed her roots in American middle-class culture of home and hearth, but also conveyed a sense of her rootlessness and poverty in New York City, her sense of never having arrived, of having no home. Like many families, her genteel kin both served and failed her. But, as artists of the *l'art pour l'art* persuasion, they always did so in the name of beauty.

In essence, Stoddard created an aesthetic solution to the problem of negotiating a way between public and private forms of expression, elitist and popular ambitions, resistance and capitulation to the cult of true womanhood. *The Morgesons* is a sentimental and domestic novel that works its potentially revolutionary transformations precisely within the confines of the genteel household. Refinements of dress and interior decoration lose their power as tropes of respectability and take on an unsettling imaginative quality. Because Stoddard read Friedrich Schiller, and indeed quoted him among the epigraphs to her third novel, she was able to imagine a return to savagery that would reinvigorate people and lead them to an aesthetically conceived freedom. In Schiller's narrative savage man finds in beautiful, outward, artificial forms – "his dwelling, his furniture, his clothing" – a pattern for a recreation of himself as a set of harmonious qualities; he moves from the arrogance of brute strength to the "triumph of form" in the aesthetic, and from there to morality, the "simple majesty of Law" (Schiller 1965, 136). The violence in Stoddard's novels to which Henry James reacted so acutely is a fictional savagery which turns to domestic forms for its source of energy.

Thus the dilemma of William's "Sentiment of Rationality" – the attraction to the securities of home which might cripple American achievement with a vast yawn – has been faced and solved by Stoddard, another writer for whom the popular and the domestic posed a special problem. Home may be "just" home, but precisely within its enclosures a world of Schillerian savage energy may metamorphose to beauty. "In passing the hand over the sideboard or in jogging the coal-scuttle with the foot, the large glossy dark shape of the one and the irregular blackness of the other awaken like a flash" (*PP*,* 1:556), William writes, some twenty-five years after Henry expressed a most troubled fascination with *The Morgesons*. And, as if looking ahead, Stoddard's Poe-like twinning of Veronica and Cassandra testifies to the importance of transitions and relations, of fluxional relations among people, as being more real than the people themselves.

Although fiction was not William James's form, domesticity was intrinsic to his productivity as a thinker yet threatening to his fondest philosophical ambitions. We have reason to believe that his "tough-minded" and "tender-minded" types are revisions of Schiller's "sentimental" and "hard-hearted" in his "On Naive and Sentimental Poetry."[11] And James considers in *Principles of Psychology* that "many of the so-called metaphysical principles are at bottom only expressions of aesthetic feeling" (*PP*,* 1:672). He periodically attacks traditional philosophical aesthetics as a grim science that misses the point of beauty; in a review of Henry R. Marshall's *Pain, Pleasure and Aesthetics* (1894) he notes approvingly that the author expands the concept of beauty to include the actual experiences of people feeling pleasure, hinting, it seems, at a nascent *Varieties of Aesthetic Experience* (*ECR*, 490). Like Stoddard, James wishes to include everyday experience in the continuum of aesthetic experience which might begin with a tramp in comfort and culminate in appreciation of Michelangelo or Beethoven (*ECR*, 337–8).

William James attempted to resolve his troubling relation to the domestic in his essay "On a Certain Blindness in Human Beings." He states that in the essay lies "really the perception on which my whole individualistic philosophy" is based (*TT*, 244). Like Stoddard, James claims within this "rather popular" work an aesthetic way not beyond, but *into* the domestic that simultaneously asserts its conservative and popular roots and exposes its transformative potential. To Dr. G. C. Ferrari he writes that the volume in which the essay is included "is better loved by me than any of my other productions, especially [valued is] the Essay on a certain blindness" (*TT*, 256). Here is the William James who believes that the tender can subsume the strenuous. That he "loved" both his essay and the essay by Robert Louis Stevenson he quotes at length within it; that it sold extremely well; that he believed his individualistic philosophy to be based on its insights; that in form it pays lip service to logical development but in performance early on gives way blissfully to a stream of metamorphosing tableaux and echoing images; that these tableaux, however exotic (James takes us all the way to Patagonia), are presented within a context of homemaking: all of these matters testify to James's realization over the years that domesticity, aesthetically comprehended, provides an opportunity, not a trap. The heroic and the energetic may be located within the tender heart of domestic security.

V

In "On a Certain Blindness in Human Beings" James preaches the message of tolerance and respect for others. The world we know and appreciate is the world each one of us makes; we cannot expect ever to experience the world as another "knows" it to be. Rather than developing an epistemological argument, James instead chooses to paint with words the most familiar and individual form of world making: homemaking. As he figures forth the major tableaux of the essay – scenes from Patagonia, Russia, North Carolina, Brooklyn, and Scotland – James meditates upon aesthetic practice as the surest route to one's truest self: one's imagination in intimate and changing relation with the universe.

James displays repeatedly in "On a Certain Blindness" the site of homesteading, of claiming and arranging the world, of arriving at that "custom" he has introduced in "The Sentiment of Rationality." Yet each time that he rehearses the domestic imperative – to claim the here and now and make it fit for human habitation – he expands its realm and abstracts its goals. Eventually he portrays something like the ideal habitation he describes in an 1873 letter to Henry: "How people can pass years without a week of that *Normal* life I can't imagine. Life in which your cares and responsibilities and thoughts for the morrow become a far off dream, and you *are* simply, floating on from day to day, and 'boarded' you don't know how, by what Providence, washed clean without and within, by the light and the tender air" (*Corresp.*, 1:215). Here is a lodging that invokes the world of dream and irresponsibility in the open air; the very ether claimed as home.

It is remarkably similar to the close of James's essay, in which W. H. Hudson has gone (manfully) exploring in the wilds of Patagonia. No domestic acedia for him. The land he explores provides an antithesis to the genteel parlor: it is an unformed "grey waste, stretching away into infinitude, a waste untrodden by man" (*TT,* 147). Hudson "explores" without object or motive; indeed, he rides about for hours at a slow pace in "aimless wanderings," open to every sensation. The summit of a hill reveals undulating grey sameness to the very horizon. But the narrative takes a turn: Hudson finds a grove on a hill that looks different from neighboring hills; he makes a "point of finding it and using it as a resting place every day at noon" (*TT,* 148). As the habit forms, he begins to conceive of his special site as tidy, "that particular clump of trees, with polished stems and clean bed of sand beneath" (148). It is a place of repose from which he would watch and listen in a strange and elating state of suspense. Hudson believes that he has *"gone back"* (149); like Stoddard and William James, he is interested in the "mental state of the pure savage."

Home is now a bed of sand at the end of the earth; the explorer who energetically strikes out from his "insipid existence" at home now lies in utter languor which is simultaneously savage. But what a savagery: he is "in perfect harmony with nature" (149). His daily drama played out for irrational reasons has taken him home to a sheltered grove and to all of nature, home to the concentered self and to the egoless being of a "wild animal." Like Baudelaire's dandy-savage of *The Painter of Modern Life,* Hudson practices "the central-ization and vaporization of the self."

James has prepared us to grasp intuitively the limit at which do-mesticity opens upon the imaginative habitation of the cosmos in the long passage he quotes from Stevenson's "Lantern Bearers." The tin bull's-eye lanterns hidden inside the coats of Scottish boys surely offer James a powerful metaphor for the hiddenness of the human heart, but as "some golden chamber" at the heart of life, the image of the lantern (romantic emblem of the imagination itself) echoes Ste-venson's emblem of the "warm, phantasmagoric chamber of [man's] brain, with the painted windows and the storied walls" (*TT,* 137). Both insist upon the imaginative quality of every site of deep secu-rity. The boys who hide the lanterns gather in "some hollow of the links" or in the "belly of a ten-man lugger" (135) in order to escape the blasting winds. Their secret lantern-bearing fellowship within sheltered spaces is practical (they seek shelter from the cold), utterly and importantly whimsical (Schillerian play matters), and ever dra-matically and aesthetically conceived: lanterns for lanterns' sake.

A theme with variations, "On a Certain Blindness" is also a col-lage of essay, poetry, fiction, and travelogue. By quoting volumi-nously, James adopts the voices of his chosen writers; as he points to the morals of these borrowed passages, he also lets them speak for themselves and contradict the logical scheme of his essay, which aims to document the solitude of the human heart as a first step in urging us to overcome barriers. Not only does Whitman, for exam-ple, celebrate his oneness with, rather than distance from, members of the crowd: "Just as you feel when you look on the river and sky, so I felt"; but by quoting at length, James causes us to lose track of where his voice ends and Whitman's or Tolstoy's or Stevenson's begins. He *is* these others; their vision is his vision, Patagonia, Brook-lyn, Russia are his worlds. Even the ugly cabin in North Carolina is his; who more than the tender William could understand the home-steader who wishes only to gather his family safely about him?

What, then, have we sketched? We might consider it a prologue to a future study of William's participation in domestic culture. Like Henry James and Elizabeth Stoddard, William places tremendous emphasis on the domestic as subject, style, and enabling circum-stance. Henry stakes upon the ownership of Lamb House his right to be and to thrive as an artist. Stoddard feels a feminine virility, a power welling up from within the heart of domesticity itself, which enables her to find within the home the very condition of her artistic expression, and to chronicle this discovery in the fiction she writes. Domestic contradictions fascinate both Henry James and Elizabeth Stoddard: home is the place of confinement and freedom both; the ordinary, that which is "given," is also the strange, the aesthetically intense, the artificial. William James, too, explored domesticity in his work, wove it as spur and obstacle, image and theme, solution and problem, into the very substance of his intellectual life. Home as found, home as made: between these two possibilities William sets his thought in motion.

Within the "painted windows and the storied walls" of the mind, William comes home to freedom, beauty, and even truth. Taking into account Emerson's sentimental Reason, Stoddard's domestic beauty decadently construed, Henry's supple revisions of the domestic commonplace, and William's insistence on the ordinary, the everyday experience of real people, we might perhaps begin to rethink the importance of domesticity to pragmatism itself as a method of imaginatively determining the truth. James assures us, "If I am lost in the woods and starved, and find what looks like a cowpath, it is of the utmost importance that I should think of a human habitation at the end of it, for if I do so and follow it, I save myself" (P, 98).

NOTES

1 See Welter 1966 for a discussion of the cult of true womanhood in nineteenth-century America. For the fullest discussion of James's transformation of popular fiction, see Veeder 1975.

2 For discussions of the problems inherent in the very process of publishing for nineteenth-century American women, see Wood 1971 and Kelley 1984.

3 William James to Alice Howe Gibbens, 7 June 1877, James Family Collection, Houghton Library. Hereafter cited in the text as "Houghton."

4 For accounts of American malaise and fear of emasculation, see Lears 1981, Cotkin 1990, and Lutz 1991.

5 For Alice's place in William's story, see Strouse 1980, Yeazell 1981, and Lewis 1991.

6 By now a formidable body of criticism exists that defines, describes, and

critically places this body of literature. All such efforts must take into account the work of Baym 1978. See also Baym 1984, Kelley 1984, Harris 1990, Brown 1990, and the bibliographies within these books, which give the many scholars in this field their due.

7 See Brodhead 1993 for the phrases "cultures of letters" and "scene of writing," that appear throughout my essay. Brodhead argues that "American literary history should be rethought as the history of the relation between literary writing and the changing meanings and places made for such work in American social history" (1–2). I find his claims especially compelling in considering a writer such as William James, who straddles literary and philosophical cultures.

8 In fact, the phenomenon of the "best-seller" was created to satisfy this market; see Geary 1976.

9 For an excellent overview of the genteel poets, see Tomsich 1971.

10 Stedman Collection, Columbia University Library.

11 See Weigand 1952 for the evidence linking James's terms to Schiller's thought.

16 The influence of William James on American culture

"The turning was due to William James." W. E. B. Du Bois here recalls, in his autobiography *Dusk of Dawn* (1940), that his favorite Harvard professor encouraged him to move from studying philosophy to history and social problems (Du Bois 1986, 582). But, more important, this short sentence neatly distills James's catalytic impact not only on Du Bois but on two generations of Harvard students. The act of turning is James's most characteristic move, be it found in the turning or troping of words as "in itself an act of power over meanings already in place," or as it animates the pragmatist's emblematic stance (Poirier 1987, 17). In James's famous words, the pragmatist "turns his back resolutely ... upon a lot of inveterate habits dear to professional philosophers. He turns away from abstraction ... from verbal solutions, fixed principles, closed systems, and pretended absolutes and origins. He turns toward" facts, action, and power (*P*, 31).

A remarkable number of American intellectuals responded to James's invitation to turn. He directly influenced two generations of his Harvard students: Du Bois, Gertrude Stein, Walter Lippmann, the sociologist Robert Park, the philosopher Alain Locke, Robert Frost, the jurist Learned Hand, and the cultural philosopher Horace Kallen. He also shaped the thinking of young contemporary admirers like the socialists Harold Laski, William English Walling, and Randolph Bourne, and, of course, younger pragmatists – John Dewey, George Herbert Mead, and Charles Cooley – and psychologists James Mark Baldwin and John B. Watson. His writings on the experience of religious belief influenced a variety of later theologians, including Reinhold Niebuhr, Norman Vincent Peale, and Mordecai Kaplan. In sum, the problem in assessing James's impact is where to draw the line, since his influence is felt in modern literature, sociology, political theory, psychology (including the experimental and behaviorist), philosophy (not only pragmatism but also phenomenology), and theology. Thus the present essay must of necessity be radically selective. The attempt here is to disclose how some of his most creative students play variations on a major Jamesean theme – his effort to reinstate what prevailing orthodoxies overlook, fear, and despise.[1]

I

James is always turning from the settled and assured to that "zone of insecurity in human affairs" we call the present. And he faces the fact of contingency in an exultant, Nietzschean spirit. Indeed, he invokes "Nietzsche's *amor fati!*" in 1910 to praise the "voice of defiance" he finds in the pluralistic mysticism of his friend Benjamin Paul Blood who declared: "Simply, *we do not know*. But when we say we do not know, we are not to say it weakly and meekly, but with confidence and content" (*EPh*, 189). Sympathetic to Blood's embrace of mysticism and his relegating of reason and knowledge to the "secondary," James was adamant about the ineradicable openness of reality. In sentences that his friend Henri Bergson loved, James declared in *Pragmatism* that "for rationalism reality is ready-made and complete from all eternity, while for pragmatism it is still in the making . . . the universe is still pursuing its adventures" (*P*, 123).

In this dynamic world, pragmatism prospered by being on the move, pausing only to invite. This stance is as radically prospective as Whitman's "I stop somewhere waiting for you" – the evaded conclusion that ends "Song of Myself." Pragmatism was not a philosophy – "it does not stand for any special results" – but a method, one that beckons and has room for all, or at least all who are willing to get dirty – to immerse themselves in the "tangled, muddy" mess of "concrete, personal experience" (*P*, 17). Such immersion was part of James's effort to reorient philosophy from its traditional perspective, as "essentially the vision of things from above," to a radically descendental one – lying "flat on its belly . . . in the very thick of its sand and gravel" (*PU*, 125).

James rarely missed an opportunity to mock proprieties and pieties of the haute-bourgeois world in which he uneasily lived and taught as a "sort of Irishman among the Brahmins," in Santayana's words (94). Thus James makes genteel "refinement" his consistent target of scorn. "A philosophy that breathes out nothing but refinement," that is, intellectualist philosophies, "will never satisfy" the pragmatist temper because refined philosophy reduces experience to epistemology, to an affair of knowledge. This is "the world to which your philosophy-professor introduces you" – a world "simple, clean, and noble. . . . Purity and dignity are what it most expresses." But this philosophy ignores that our immediate encounter with experience is prior to reflective translation (and division) into concepts or language, and in this precognitive dimension "we are like fishes swimming in the sea of sense" (P, 17–18, 63). Rather than pursuing a "refined object of contemplation," pragmatism seeks to teach us to think like fishes swimming in a sea of sense. But this plunge into gross experience is not an abandonment to primitivism but rather coincides with the procedures and subject matter of the natural sciences, which experiment among the things of raw experience. James lauds science as "dispassionate method" rather than "a certain set of results" and warns that to regard its findings as definitive is to be unscientific. For science, "like life, feeds on its own decay. New facts burst old rules" (WB, 236). "Our science is a drop, our ignorance a sea" (WB, 50).

James's Whitmanesque invitation to turn from stuffy and doctrinaire classrooms of philosophy and to open oneself to the shocks of the ordinary, functions as a "ferment," to borrow one of his favorite words. Like his revered Emerson, James worshipped genius, not passively, nor for its own sake, but for its "fermentative influence" upon our own thinking. There is no more compelling testimony to the power of James's own fermentative genius than the number of brilliant figures that he helped propel into the tumult of a new century where the cherished certitudes provided by positivism and rationalism were buckling under pressure of unprecedented social change.

Pragmatism seemed to offer a way to be at home with this homelessness. James described a "loose universe," a "tramp and vagrant world, adrift in space," where experiences lean on nothing but other finite experiences, "but the whole of them, if such a whole there be, leans on nothing . . . finite experience as such is homeless. Nothing outside the flux secures the issue of it" (P, 125). What is particularly

compelling about this world without foundations is James's insouci-
ant attitude toward it: he describes the "radical pragmatist" as a
"happy-go-lucky anarchistic sort of creature" who doesn't mind the
looseness at all. Whereas most professors of philosophy would be
scandalized by such a world – not only would it discomfit their dogmatic temper but also "would not be *respectable*, philosophically" –
James is more than "willing to live on a scheme of uncertified possibilities" amid reality in flux. And he inspires his students to join
him in this world. Seven years after *Pragmatism*, Walter Lippmann
caused a sensation with *Drift and Mastery*, for it seemed to emerge
out of James's evocative pages to capture the mood of a generation at
once fearful and exhilarated at the prospect that "no mariner ever
enters upon a more uncharted sea than does the average human
being born into the twentieth century" (Lippmann 1985, 112). "We
are homeless in a jungle of machines and untamed powers that
haunt and lure the imagination." We will see below how Lippmann's proposals for how one might live in a "tramp and vagrant
world" at once extend and turn James's ideas in new directions.

II

James's thought comprised the crucial American contribution to the
international matrix of early modernism. Along with Nietzsche, Bergson, Freud, Shaw, Ibsen, and Dostoevsky, it was James whom the first
self-conscious American cultural avant-garde – the young intellectuals of the generation of 1910 – adopted as a hero in their revolt
against Victorian and Puritan culture. This generation, composed of
prewar cultural critics (often called "the Lyrical Left") and Green-
wich village bohemians, toppled the authority of the genteel tradition, so dubbed by James's colleague George Santayana, and chal-
lenged the assumption that the university is the sole domicile of the
intellectual. James's distaste for the intellectual orthodoxies of academic life was vigorously affirmed by other iconoclastic figures such
as Santayana and Thorstein Veblen. Together they inspired Lyrical
Leftists like Bourne and Lippmann, along with others such as Van
Wyck Brooks, Max Eastman, and Lewis Mumford, to emancipate
themselves from the genteel spirit of Anglo-Saxon culture still linger-
ing in the groves of academe. This younger generation fashioned ca-
reers outside its often suffocating confines, becoming eminent public

intellectuals, occasionally taking temporary academic appointments but on the whole remaining unaffiliated. These thinkers helped create the dominant twentieth-century image of the American literary intellectual as a freewheeling figure whose natural habitat was the critique. This icon reigned triumphant until the 1970s when according to some scenarios, American academe absorbed and domesticated this glamorous figure of incorrigible independence.[2]

Perhaps more than anyone, William James inspired the venerable American romantic tradition that makes the intellectual virtually synonymous with radical individualism. Indeed, James was the first American to use the word "intellectual," importing the French term in 1907 that had been coined in 1898 to deride Zola and the other Dreyfusards who had intervened against the rabid nationalism of the Right. "We ought to have our own class consciousness: 'Les Intellectuels!' " announced James. Representing "ideal interests only, for we have no corporate selfishness and wield no powers of corruption," the intellectual whom James conceived must always "work to keep our precious birthright of individualism and freedom from . . . institutions. *Every* great institution is perforce a means of corruption – whatever good it may also do. Only in the free personal relation is full ideality to be found" (quoted in Matthiessen 1962, 633, 635). His hero Emerson could not have said it better.

At this point we encounter one of the striking paradoxes that inform James's life and thought. His stature as a powerful impetus to cultural modernism coexisted with an animus toward modernity that he expressed in his quasi-anarchist dismissal of collectivities. He railed against "bigness and greatness in all their forms" – from scientism to imperialism to academic professionalism. Yet James's protest against "all big organizations . . . all big successes and big results," and his championing of the idiosyncratic and the small ("only small things can be veracious and innocent") constitutes less an engagement with history and its constraints than a stubborn refusal to interrogate their workings (quoted in Perry 1935, 2:315). This refusal is often overlooked thanks to James's incomparable moral eloquence and passion. His rhetoric of heroism acquired its elan from the urgency of his embattled defense of the individual, including the dark-skinned alien that American foreign policy sought to colonize. He enshrines tolerance of otherness – respect for particularity and multiplicity – as the guiding moral standard for the always precarious American democratic tradition. Thus he condemns the McKinley–Roosevelt administration's predatory expansion of the American empire as morally indefensible. But as an alternative to imperialism, all he can offer is the empty hope that the country will once again "possess its ancient soul" by emancipating itself from our destructive "belief . . . in a national destiny which must be 'big' at any cost" (*ECR*, 157). Although James likely knew that America from its origins had conceived of itself as an empire and had equated expansionism with freedom and prosperity, he chose instead to ignore history and to lodge his moral protest as a responsible intellectual standing for "ideal interests solely."

James's resolute idealism is rooted in a self-confessed, and self-imposed, sense of political "impotence" that is (temporarily) relieved by expressing moral outrage.[3] The Jamesean cultural critique, in short, functions as a therapeutic. Perhaps because intellectuals as a social class are predisposed to status anxiety and disaffection, this dialectic of impotence and therapy (by venting moral outrage against modernity) became deeply attractive to succeeding generations of American public intellectuals. In this context James's legacy is mixed: despite his contempt for smugness and certainty, he perpetuated the idealist premises of genteel cultural criticism. His celebration of individual voluntarism helped make him a beloved figure by the last decade of his life, for he uplifted an audience in need of spiritual solace to confront the bewilderments of modernity. James's exuberant earnestness not only survives but thrives even in our own antiromantic, antihumanist age of relentless parody and vertiginous irony. This testifies both to his compelling personal example and our own need for solace. Especially for some on the academic left, who find little sustenance in the allegedly ascetic, carcereal vision of Foucault, James is venerated as a public intellectual of exemplary moral conscience.[4]

The reverence his students had for James was inspired as much by his moral stature, "gallant spirit," and "gay passion for ideas" (Bourne 1977, 347) as by the particular substance of his thinking. Of those influenced by him, a number carefully revised his subjectivist and moralistic fervor. Take the case of Du Bois. At Harvard he treasured James's friendship and found his "realist pragmatism" a compelling alternative to the "sterilities of scholastic philosophy" (Du Bois 1968, 133). Yet Du Bois in 1954 looked back upon his doctoral dissertation published as his first book, *The Suppression of the African Slave-Trade* (1896), as sharply attenuated in its historical understanding in part *because* of his Harvard training. However liberating, James's pragmatism promoted what Du Bois called "the New England ethic of life as a series of conscious moral judgments" (Du Bois 1986, 1315). For instance, James would urge in *Pragmatism* that "the way of escape from evil . . . is by dropping it out altogether, throwing it overboard and getting beyond it, helping to make a universe that shall forget its very place and name" (*P*, 142). This attitude could be of little help in Du Bois's confrontation with the evil of slavery: "I was continually thrown back on what men 'ought' to have done to avoid evil consequence. My book's last admonition was 'to do things at the very moment when they ought to be done'. . . . I still saw slavery and the trade as chiefly the result of moral lassitude." Du Bois notes that had he acquired a knowledge of Marx and Freud (as he later did) his conclusions would have been "less pat and simple"; doubtless he would have grasped that "slavery was a matter of income more than of morals" (Du Bois 1986, 1315). Du Bois's creative appropriation of James's pragmatism will be discussed later. Here let us examine how another James student, Walter Lippmann, turned his professor into an enthusiastic modernist by erasing his ambivalences toward modernity.

III

Drift and Mastery negotiates the passage from a Victorian to modern universe. At one point Lippmann quotes from Matthew Arnold's *Dover Beach:* "nor certitude, nor peace, nor help for pain; / And we are here as on a darkling plain." Where has the certitude for which Arnold cries out gone, Lippmann asks. He considers the answer of Harvard professor Irving Babbitt, who blames Romanticism and the French Revolution for shattering divinely sanctioned authority. Babbit urges a return to "eternal forms of justice and moderation," a return, says Lippmann, "to the Golden Age of the classics" (Lippmann 1985, 111). Although he dismisses Babbitt's nostalgic antimodernism as a fairy tale that imagines it possible to "wipe out the memory of the last hundred years," he concedes that Babbitt has located the "spiritual problem." "We have no authority to lean upon. . . . We drift. . . . Never before have we had to rely so completely upon ourselves" (118, 111).

Mastery, of course, is Lippmann's antidote to drift. And as he starts elaborating what he means by mastery, we will see that he adroitly manages to impart a Jamesean flavor to ideas that he turns in a direction rather different from that his mentor was willing to go. That direction is science, and Lippmann enthrones it as the engine of mastery, the key instrument of domination and control. As soon as we start reflecting "the thing we call science begins," for reflection substitutes "conscious intention for unconscious striving" (148). In words that Dewey and a whole generation of progressive social thinkers would articulate in their own versions, Lippmann declares that "rightly understood science is the culture under which people can live forward in the midst of complexity. . . . Custom and authority will work in a simple and unchanging civilization, but in our world only those will conquer who can understand. There is nothing accidental then in the fact that democracy in politics is the twin-brother of scientific thinking" (151). Not only would James have qualms over Lippmann's rush to crown science as a panacea, but his student's enthusiasm for controlling and conquering would likely strike James as smacking of the imperialism that he abhorred.

But just when Lippmann seems on his way to becoming a technocratic mariner smugly guiding his craft on modernity's uncharted seas, the Jamesean legacy reasserts itself. Lippmann hastens to assure us that science is not the inhuman, sanitized, positivist attitude most people mistake it for. He borrows James's critique of rationalism to indict those scientists who come to regard their "rigorous, classifying method where each color is all one tone" as more important than "the blendings and interweavings of reality" (159). Urging skepticism of classification and concepts, Lippmann quotes James ("Use concepts when they help, and drop them when they hinder understanding") and then defends him as a model scientist who was unfairly ridiculed for his psychical research into the existence of ghosts. The attack on James was ignorant, "for the attitude of William James toward 'ghosts' was the very opposite of blind belief. He listened to evidence. No apostle of authority can find the least comfort in that. For the moment you test belief by experience you have destroyed the whole structure of authority" (161).

The rest of *Drift and Mastery* (some twenty pages) continues in this Jamesean vein, distinguishing the desire for control from absolute objectivity, and equating science with the "creative imagination" of the "working artist" who disdains routine and instead nurtures invention and possibility: "To escape from barren possibilities: this must be the endless effort of a democratic people" (172–4). In his first book *A Preface to Politics* (1913), Lippmann had also opposed the routineer to the inventor as two modes of the politician. He celebrates the latter by praising him in Jamesean terms as imbued with initiative and originality, who bends things to human use, and who concurs with Nietzsche's imperative: " 'Let the value of everything be determined afresh by you' " (Lippmann 1962, 183–4).

The exciting sense of possibility that Jamesean pragmatism offered helped ignite the vaulting ambition of Lippmann's first two books. Lippmann was convinced that a new century requires a "new sense of political values" infused with "contemporary insight" so that the mind is kept "flexible and adapted to the movement of real life" (29). Such suppleness was of course part of the lesson of pragmatism. In applying that lesson, Lippmann's books inadvertently expose James's own vagueness about the uses of that suppleness. The source of that vagueness inheres in his construction of pragmatism as a method rather than a philosophy. James uses the method to propagate tolerance for people and experiences ordinarily stigmatized by various rationalist orthodoxies. He widens the boundaries of the known, revelling in the drift of pluralistic indeterminacy. In Lippmann's hands the method is also in the service of freedom, but freedom construed as the product of an elite's control of technology and surplus energies. In *A Preface to Politics*, for instance, he ingeniously linked "the sublimations of the Freudian school" to James's advocacy of a "moral equivalent of war" as two strategies that redirect rather than render taboo recalcitrant impulses. "Every lust is capable of some civilized expression." A gang of juvenile delinquents is potentially a "force that could be made valuable to civilization through the Boy Scouts." For Lippmann, "the work of statesmanship is . . . finding good substitutes for the bad things we want. This is the heart of a political revolution" (42–3, 67). Before long Lippmann would become an intimate of Woodrow Wilson and the ultimate political insider; his *Public Opinion* (1922) would urge the authority of the expert as the savior of democracy.

IV

In 1914, "the applied pragmatic realism" of *Drift and Mastery* swept up the Deweyan social critic Randolph Bourne and many others. But with the coming of war in 1917, Bourne's enthusiasm for Lippmann waned as the latter became an avid supporter of Wilson's bloody crusade for peace. When Dewey came out in support of war, Bourne felt betrayed by his former Columbia professor, disillusioned with Dewey's "keen sense of control over events" and hostility toward "any attitude that is not a cheerful and brisk setting to work" (Bourne 1977, 341). Working through his sense of betrayal, Bourne wrote a series of articles that amounted to a profound critique of pragmatism's fetish of control. He scoffed at the smug certainty of the "realists": "How soon their 'mastery' becomes 'drift' " (330). In turning from Dewey and Lippmann, Bourne turned toward the spirit of William James: "If William James were alive would he be accepting the war-situation so easily and complacently?" Would he join the hysteria against dissenting opinion and be "excommunicating from the ranks of liberal progress the pitiful remnant of those who struggle 'above the battle' " (337)? What Dewey's prowar stance crystallizes for Bourne is "the inadequacy of his pragmatism as a philosophy of life." Bourne invokes James to remind himself that pragmatism can mean more than a philosophy of scientific method, adaptation, and adjustment. And the memory of James also reminds him that when the pragmatic method is in other hands it can imbue even war with a "creative" note of "spiritual adventure" or "poetic vision" (336, 343). By this last phrase Bourne means all that escapes the rule of adjustment, all that enables a philosophy of control "to get beyond itself" and confront the "quality of life as above machinery of life" (342). "If your ideal," says Bourne, is "adjustment to your situation ... then your success is likely to be just that and no more. You never transcend anything. You grow but your spirit never jumps out of your skin to go on wild adventures. ... Vision must constantly overshoot technique" (344).

Bourne's Jamesean critique of pragmatism as a technique of control was not without impact. But it occurred posthumously since he perished in the influenza epidemic of 1918. In the postwar years Dewey's philosophy decisively widened in a Bournean direction. By

1925, Dewey had come to recognize that despite science's prodigious power and achievement, experience remained fundamentally hazardous and precarious (Dewey 1958, 40–1). His two late masterpieces *Experience and Nature* (1925) and *Art as Experience* (1934) honor these qualities and associate them with art and, implicitly, with the "poetic vision" that Bourne had earlier found fatally absent. To understand what experience is, said Dewey, the philosopher must go to esthetic experience, for it is "freed from factors that subordinate an experience as it is directly had" to something more refined – an object of knowledge (Dewey 1980, 274). The opening chapters of *Experience and Nature* contain some of Dewey's most eloquent, even lyrical, writing. For in returning to a Jamesean theme – that "what is really 'in' experience extends much further than that which at any time is *known*" – his prose takes on a measure of Jamesean passion for reinstating all that intellectualism would relegate to an inferior order of existence or explain away altogether – the obscure and vague, the dark and twilight, potentialities, and possibilities (Dewey 1958, 21).

Dewey in effect recovers the "unclassified residuum" that James had first named and sought to preserve in the realms of philosophy and in his antiimperialist politics (*WB*, 222). This residuum plays havoc with the "ideal of every science," namely, to create a "closed and complete system of truth." In early and late essays James had criticized one such system – Hegel's "logic of identity" for its sacrifice of contingency and particularity to abstract laws. James also sought to save the residuum from Theodore Roosevelt's racist imperialism. In 1899 James denounced him as an "arch abstractionist" and accused him of in effect practicing, in his nativist demand of one hundred percent Americanism, an Hegelian politics of identity that "swamps everything together in one flood of abstract bellicose emotion" (*ECR*, 164). By 1907, under the sway of Bergsonian vitalism, James dramatically renounces identity logic in *A Pluralistic Universe* and will attempt to think in "non-conceptualized terms," for concepts "cut out and fix and exclude everything but what we have fixed" (*PU*, 113). Embracing the severe consequences of his logic, James must take a vow of silence: because "words can be the names only of concepts," all one can say is "I say no more: I must leave life to teach the lesson" (*PU*, 132).

V

James's sensitivity to the excluded and his resistance to the disciplin-
ary imperative of identity made his thought particularly congenial
to African-American intellectuals. Under the regime of Jim Crow
they struggled daily with the yoke of identity in its congealed form
of racist stereotype, which brutally circumscribed freedom and
democratic participation. In white America, "nature's law" seemed
to decree, noted Du Bois, that "the word 'Negro' connotes 'inferior-
ity' and 'stupidity' lightened only by unreasoning gayety and hu-
mor" (Du Bois 1992, 726). Because James's impact on black figures is
a dimension of his influence that has been insufficiently recognized,
I will spend my remaining pages tracing several connections.

Pauline Hopkins's magazine novel – *Of One Blood* (1903) – offers
striking evidence that James's sponsorship of the unclassified residuum spoke directly to black intellectuals. The fictional protagonist of
her science-fiction fantasy is Reuel Briggs, a brilliant black Harvard
medical student specializing in mesmerism and multiple personalities. He is first observed reading a treatise entitled *The Unclassified
Residuum*. Hopkins not only borrows the phrase from James but
quotes from the essay in which it originally appears – "The Hidden
Self" (1890) – which was reprinted as part of "What Psychical Research Has Accomplished" in *The Will to Believe* (1897). Briggs himself embodies an "unclassified residuum": he is a mulatto (he passes
for white) scientist who will cast off his American identity and travel
through time and space to reunite with his African ancestry. His
obvious model is Du Bois. In an 1897 *Atlantic* essay, Du Bois had
theorized a "double consciousness" unique to black Americans. (In
The Souls of Black Folk Du Bois would revise and republish this essay
in the same year that Hopkins published *Of One Blood*.) Du Bois drew
in part on James's notion of a "hidden self," "subconscious" and
"buried." This also inspires Hopkins's Africanist fantasy. James
speaks of this " 'subliminal' self" as capable of making "at any time
irruption into our ordinary lives. At its lowest, it is only the deposi-
tory of our forgotten memories; at its highest, we do not know what it
is at all" (*WB*, 237). It is accessible by hypnosis and manifests itself
telepathically. Hopkins turns James's notion of a hidden self (actually
a notion that James himself shared with psychologists like Alfred

Binet, author of *On Double Consciousness*) into a metaphor of the recovery of "forgotten memories" – the black American's buried African self. She also literalizes the metaphor; at one point Briggs speaks of "the undiscovered country within ourselves – the hidden self lying quiescent in every human soul" (448). Africa is at once the "undiscovered country" and "hidden self" that Reuel Briggs is transported back to, as he rediscovers the Ethiopian city of Meroe and his own ancestry as an African king.[5]

In the first decade of the twentieth century, pragmatism, along with Franz Boas's anthropology, stood virtually alone among behavioral and social sciences as an intellectual weapon against the theory and practice of white supremacy. Pragmatism refused absolutist systems and purified essences, the modes of thought often employed to defend racialist assumptions and racism. Like Boasian contextualism, pragmatist pluralism dismissed "all the great single-word answers to the world's riddle, such as God, the One . . . Nature" and "*The* Truth," as "perfect idol[s] of the rationalistic mind!" (*P*, 115). Bourne would add White Anglo-Saxon Protestantism to the list of idols. Bourne, who thought Boas and Dewey his greatest teachers at Columbia, was the first to lambaste the WASP ideal in the name of a cultural and ethnic pluralism that rejected the coerced synthesis demanded by the "melting pot ideal." Bourne advocated a "trans-national" cosmopolitanism inspired by Horace Kallen, a devoted student and friend of William James. Kallen, like another James student, the sociologist Robert Park, found particular inspiration for pluralism in James's "On A Certain Blindness in Human Beings" (1899). The urgency of James's plea for "the significance of alien lives" was rooted in the immediate context of imperialist aggression. But its argument was ontological: because humans are innately self-absorbed in pursuing their own affairs, we are all afflicted by blindness to the feelings of others. Only when we confront squarely the fact of human selfishness can respect for difference grow.

From the nineteen-twenties to the forties, Kallen, along with Boas and his colleague Melville Herskovits and his students Ruth Benedict and Margaret Mead, as well as Dewey, Park, and George Herbert Mead, formed the nucleus of the cultural pluralist movement in the United States. Although they were not a formal group, together their writings and activism constituted the most intellectually vigorous and prestigious defense against nativist intolerance and scientific racism. Like any legacy of ideas, James's pluralism was given particular inflections by those who appropriated and extended his thought. Kallen and another Harvard student influenced by James, Alain Locke, the African-American philosopher and cultural critic, had an illuminating disagreement about the meaning of Jamesean pluralism; and to this split in the ranks I now turn.

VI

Kallen is best known for coining the phrase "cultural pluralism" in 1915 in his influential essay "Democracy Versus the Melting Pot" (reprinted in his book *Culture and Democracy in the United States*, 1924). James's philosophical pluralism, Kallen would recall, encouraged him to accept "the reality of manyness" and to refuse "to accept the proposition that the many are appearance and only the one is reality" (Kallen quoted in Sollors 1986, 265). Kallen began to formulate the notion of cultural pluralism as early as 1905 when, as a teaching assistant for William James, he encountered the brilliant black undergraduate Alain Locke. According to Kallen, Locke was "very sensitive, very easily hurt" and insisted that "he was a human being and that his color ought not to make any difference. . . . We are all alike Americans." But Kallen thought Locke mistaken and told him: "It *had* to make a difference and it *had* to be accepted and respected and enjoyed for what it was." Two years later Kallen met Locke again in England, at Oxford, where Locke was the first black Rhodes scholar and Kallen was on a fellowship. They continued their earlier conversation about "how the differences made differences, and in arguing out those questions the formulae, then phrases developed – 'cultural pluralism,' 'the right to be different' " (Kallen, quoted in Sollors 1986, 269).

According to Kallen, in short, cultural pluralism is born of his adamant insistence, resisted by Locke, on Locke's ineradicable racial difference. In other words, from its birth Kallen's pluralism possesses an element of separatism and purism in its effort to honor difference. Appropriately enough, Alain Locke years later would criticize this quality of purism, and recent historians have pointed to it as a major defect in the model of cultural pluralism. Kallen's purism derives from his belief that "what is inalienable in the life of mankind is its . . . psycho-social inheritance. Men may change their

clothes, their politics, their wives, their religions, their philosophies, to a greater or lesser extent: they cannot change their grandfa-
thers" (Kallen 1924, 122). This commitment to the permanence of
ancestral endowments immune to cultural and historical change
informs his famous metaphor of pluralistic America as an orchestra
of harmonious diversities in a "democracy of nationalities." "As in
an orchestra every type of instrument has its specific *timbre* and
tonality, founded in its substance and form . . . so in society, each
ethnic group may be the natural instrument . . . and the harmony
and dissonances and discords of them all may make the symphony
of civilization" (Kallen 1924, 125).

As Werner Sollors has noted, Kallen's metaphor emphasizes static
separatism and "unhistorical ethnic persistence," whereas the "melting pot image is eminently dynamic and accommodates the continuous processes of assimilation and ethnogenesis. . . . At the root of
cultural pluralism is a notion of the eternal power of descent, birth,
natio, and race" that Kallen shares with his racist opponents (Sollors
1986, 261). A question that emerges for us, if not for Sollors, is
whether Kallen's essentialist cultural pluralism is derived from William James. Or did Kallen simplify James? The latter seems the case.
After all, James called his pluralism and his empiricism radical because they insist on the reality of relations as distinct from the
atomism posited by traditional pluralism and empiricism. Even
though James describes pluralism as an "each-form" of reality in contrast to monism's "all-form," the former's eachness is not atomistic
but exists in "inextricable interfusion" with "its very next neighbors" (PU, 146).

This is from *A Pluralistic Universe* which James delivered as the
Hibbert Lectures at Oxford during the academic year 1907–8, just
when Kallen and Locke were on campus. Given their shared interest
in questions of identity and difference, they doubtless found James's
lectures immensely stimulating. Yet judging by their later work,
Kallen and Locke came away from the Hibbert Lectures with very different understandings. If we take his 1915 essay on cultural pluralism
as evidence, Kallen largely ignored James's renunciation of the logic
of identity and his emphasis on the experience of "immediately-felt
life" as nothing but "overlap" – "all shades and no boundaries" –
where margins and centers are in perpetual exchange (PU, 130).
Probably Kallen was already preoccupied with the weight of ancestral

of experience in flux, no longer chopped up into static concepts. Instead, like the guild socialist Harold Laski, Kallen would allude in 1915 to James's depiction of the pluralistic world as a "federal republic." But Kallen's republic is teleological, implicitly ruled by separatism and immutability, for he describes it as a "democracy of nationalities, cooperating . . . in the enterprise of self-realization through the perfection of men according to their kind" (Kallen 1924, 124).

Unlike Kallen, Locke entered into what is radical in James's pluralism – skepticism toward identity and the exclusionary bias of concepts. Thus *A Pluralistic Universe* proved a fertile stimulus to thought. When Locke in 1925 conceptualized "the new Negro" (he edited the landmark anthology of that same name) he sought to avoid making it simply another easily classified cultural commodity. A decidedly pragmatist logic informs his anthology's opening declaration that "in the last decade something beyond the watch and guard of statistics has happened in the life of the American Negro and the three norms who have traditionally presided over the Negro problem have a changeling in their laps. The Sociologist, the Philanthropist, the Race-Leader are not unaware of the New Negro, but they are at a loss to account for him. He simply cannot be swathed in their formulae" (Locke 1993, 3). William James would have cherished the existence of this elusive changeling, this defiance of categories, including separatism.

"The fiction is that the life of the races is separate," notes Locke in *The New Negro;* the fact is that New York has witnessed a "richly fruitful" "reopening of intellectual contacts" (1993, 10). Locke regards such evidence of "mutual understanding" as a sign that the Negro is successfully repairing a "damaged group psychology . . . and warped social perspective" (10). Part of this healing process includes increased self-respect and self-reliance as part of a resurgent race pride – a "deep feeling of race is at present the mainspring of Negro life." But this feeling is "radical in tone but not in purpose." For the purpose of restoring race pride is that blacks will affirm their Africanness not as separatist but as part of America's pluralist democracy that is obstructed when any of its channels are closed. Locke calls this "attempt to build . . . Americanism on race values [a] unique social experiment, and its ultimate success is impossible except through the fullest sharing of American culture and institutions" (11–12).

This "new phase of things is delicate," warns Locke, and his own delicate balancing of racialism and democracy avoids dichotomies by straddling the edge between assimilation and antiassimilation. In other words, Locke's acute sense of the African-American as defined by simultaneous relations refuses the atomism of Kallen's brand of cultural pluralism. In a later essay, "Who and What is 'Negro'?" (1942), Locke makes this explicit when he urges that we "must abandon the idea of cultural purism": the "Afro- or Negro-American [is] a hybrid product" who is becoming "progressively even more composite and hybridized" as he interacts with the "common cultural life" (Locke 1989, 213). As if answering Kallen's bullying insistence in 1905 that race "*had* to make a difference," Locke declares that "to be 'Negro' in the cultural sense, then, is not to be radically different, but only to be distinctly composite and idiomatic, though basically American" (213). In opposing Kallen's purism, Locke's stress on the hybrid and simultaneous is closer to James's spirit of pluralism. By conceiving identity as an open process of reciprocal influence, Locke partakes of the dynamism that James's "each-form" enjoys as it allows for the "taking up and dropping of connexions" between parts. Rather than monism's "through-and-through unity of all things at once, [the] each-form [is] at all times in many possible connexions which are not necessarily actualized at the moment" (*PU*, 146).

VII

Although of different generations and often rival "Race Men," W. E. B. Du Bois and Alain Locke shared a commitment to James's radical, that is, impure, pluralism. Both Locke and Du Bois, each of whom did postgraduate work in Berlin before obtaining his Harvard doctorate, constructed racial identity as mobile and fluid. Like Pauline Hopkins, Du Bois uses James's research into possible hidden selves within the psyche as an inspiring metaphor to recast radically the ways identity is conceived. With his poetic genius, Du Bois turned skepticism of stable selfhood into an indelible image of the black American's anguished psychic striving:

The Negro is a sort of seventh son, born with a veil, and gifted with second-sight in this American world, – a world which yields him no true self-consciousness, but only lets him see himself through the revelation of the other world. It is a peculiar sensation, this double-consciousness, this sense of always looking at one's self through the eyes of others. . . . One ever feels his two-ness, – an American, a Negro; two souls, two thoughts, two unreconciled strivings; two warring ideals in one dark body, whose dogged strength alone keeps it from being torn asunder. The history of the American Negro is the history of this strife. (Du Bois 1986, 364–5)

Of this epochal passage from the opening pages of *The Souls of Black Folk* (1903), Du Bois's biographer, David Levering Lewis, says: "Henceforth, the destiny of the race could be conceived as leading to neither assimilation nor separatism but to proud, enduring hyphenation" (Lewis 1993, 281). Virtually from its publication, Du Bois's notion of double consciousness has been recognized as setting the terms by which African-American identity is understood in the twentieth century. Like James's "stream of consciousness," Du Bois's "double consciousness" has become a touchstone of modern thought, continually reorienting conventional thinking and generating new.[6] But the resonance of Du Bois's phrase is not only prospective but retrospective. It reverberates with earlier usages from literature and medicine, including Goethe, Emerson, William James, and other psychologists' research into multiple personality disorders, research that the popular press reported on in the nineteenth century.[7]

Scholarly work on Du Bois's relation to James has largely been confined to the latter's influence on "double consciousness." But the impact of Du Bois's beloved professor was not merely local and contained. Nor was it restricted to Jamesean psychology. Du Bois called himself "a devoted follower of William James at the time he was developing his pragmatic philosophy" (Du Bois 1968, 133). And he seems to have internalized pragmatism as a method and style of thinking, for it tapped and channelled what Du Bois called his restless "anarchy of the spirit which is inevitably the goal of all human consciousness" (Du Bois 1986, 652). He shared this spirit with James, that self-described "anarchistic sort of creature" who cherished "a world of anarchy . . . with an 'ever not quite' to all our formulas, and novelty and possibility forever leaking in" (quoted in Perry 1935, 2:700). Du Bois construed Jamesean pragmatism, with its pluralistic immersion in indeterminacy and chance, as in effect a philosophical anarchy whose lesson to Du Bois the social scientist was that "he could not stand apart and study *in vacuo.*" Abandoning the insulation of a spectator theory of knowledge (to borrow Dewey's phrase), Du Bois opened himself to a "certain tingling challenge of risk" (Du Bois 1944, 57, 58).

Du Bois's decidedly Jamesean phrase is apt for it describes the visceral commitment of his writing during twenty-four years (1910–34) as editor of the NAACP journal *The Crisis*. He calls his work in that quarter century "sociology" that was inspired by "Jamesean pragmatism." I have been quoting from a remarkable yet seldom cited 1944 career retrospective, "My Evolving Program For Negro Freedom." It charts the various "re-adaptations" he has been improvising over the course of his career. His pragmatist sociology counts as the most dramatic revision for it set Du Bois "in the midst of action" and "continuous, kaleidoscopic change of conditions." The hectic pace of the "hot reality of real life" rendered his "previous purely scientific program" (his Atlanta University studies) old before it was even analyzed (Du Bois 1944, 56). Driven by journalistic immediacy, Du Bois's pragmatist sociology attempts not to discover physical laws of action but instead to "measure the element of Chance in human conduct." At the helm of *The Crisis*, Du Bois "faced situations that called – shrieked – for action" if "social death" was to be averted, and that left no time for the patient testing of scientific observation. Yet neither could he simply work "fast and furiously" by "intuition and emotion"; thus Du Bois seeks to be responsive to the raw unfolding of events while simultaneously pursuing "ordered knowledge" of the race problem which "research and tireless observation" would supply (57). Du Bois is working in the grain of pragmatist science as James construed it: his effort is to practice science as immersion in and reflection upon gross experience, rather than science as preoccupied with technical verification and a specious objectivity.

Summing up his pragmatist stance, Du Bois writes: "I was continually the surgeon probing blindly, yet with what knowledge and skill I could muster, for unknown ill" (Du Bois 1944, 58). This is a metaphor of crisis, of authority stripped of authority and flirting with chaos as it confronts the hazards of unmastered experience in a "tramp and vagrant world, adrift in space." These are James's words describing the pragmatist universe where Du Bois reconstructed authority with the permanent risk of chaos built in. Above all, pragmatism inspires in Du Bois a mode of conduct that precisely accords with the mobility of his "double consciousness" of "unreconciled strivings," a tension Du Bois internalizes as the structure of his vision. Sociologist, historian, novelist, essayist and poet, Du Bois's is a career of turnings, of finding freedom in moments of transition, of moving between. Skeptical of the preordained, preferring to improvise under pressure of changing historical circumstance, Du Bois declared that "no idea is perfect and forever valid. Always to be living and apposite and timely, it must be modified and adapted to changing facts" (Du Bois 1986, 364, 776).

He not only theorized this historicism but acted upon it. Indeed Du Bois made the above statement to explain one of the most controversial decisions of his career – his 1934 effort to revise the raison d'etre of the NAACP: commitment to racial integration and opposition to segregation. This sacred goal of 1910 must be interrogated in the light of what history reveals – that the net result of the campaign against segregation "has been a little less than nothing" (Du Bois 1986, 1241). To reinsert himself in the moving present, that "zone of insecurity in human affairs," as James called it, Du Bois was willing to expose himself to predictable (and ahistoricist) charges of betraying his own identity as valiant fighter for equality. The NAACP ousted him after he attempted to unsettle its identity from within by urging voluntary economic segregation. While fully aware that he was "touching an old and bleeding sore in Negro thought," Du Bois hoped to turn segregation from a traditional "badge of servitude" into one of self-respect (777). A surgeon blindly probing, Du Bois is willing to risk the pain of reopening wounds, ripping off scabs of habit grown indurate, of boundaries and identities grown sclerotic, all in an effort to reinstate the rawness of experience pregnant with possibility and potential. In taking upon himself the "tingling challenge of risk," Du Bois turned James's legacy into a way of being free in a world determined to encage him.

NOTES

1 In *The Principles of Psychology* James speaks of his effort to "restore . . . the *vague* to its psychological rights. . . . The passing and evanescent are as real parts of the stream [of consciousness] as the distinct and comparatively abiding" (1:452). This registers an animating concern of James's psychology, pragmatism, and social activism. In showing the influence of this particular Jamesean legacy, I have used a criterion to make selections – how well known the connection is to James. Thus, for instance, Gertrude Stein's relation to James is sufficiently well known not

to need rehearsal here; a number of excellent studies of their relation already exist. For provocative recent treatments see Ruddick 1990 and Poirier 1993.

2 The best known presentation of this scenario is Russell Jacoby's (1987). I discuss James's relevance to Jacoby's argument in Posnock 1989.

3 James notes that "the impotence of the private individual, with imperialism under full headway as it is, is deplorable indeed. But every American has a voice or a pen and may use it" (ECR, 158).

4 See Frank Lentricchia's influential "The Return of William James" in Lentricchia 1989.

5 Pauline Hopkins's use of William James was first discussed in Otten 1992. He writes that "in validating countercultural science, James also seems to validate those moments in black letters in which basic assumptions about identity become open to question" (242). See also Sundquist 1993.

6 For recent testimony to the continued vitality of the phrase see Early 1993, which convenes a group of African-American writers to respond to Du Bois's phrase.

7 For a useful summary of the intellectual history attached to the phrase see Bruce 1992. For a brilliant reading of the phrase in the context of the first chapter of The Souls of Black Folk and in Du Bois's career as a whole see Holt 1990.

17   Pragmatism, politics, and the corridor

In *Pragmatism*, William James says of the pragmatic method that it

lies in the midst of our theories, like a corridor in a hotel. Innumerable chambers open out of it. In one you may find a man writing an atheistic volume; in the next someone on his knees praying for faith and strength; in a third a chemist investigating a body's properties. In a fourth a system of idealistic metaphysics is being excogitated; in a fifth the impossibility of metaphysics is being shown. But they all own the corridor, and all must pass through it if they want a practicable way of getting into or out of their respective rooms. (*P,* 32)

James identifies this method with the principle according to which "to develop a thought's meaning, we need only determine what conduct it is fitted to produce: that conduct is for us its sole significance" (*P,* 29). That is, if we want to know what, if anything, a given theory means, we must figure out what it tells us to *do:* a difference that makes no practical difference *is* no difference. This principle is a "corridor" from concept to concept or theory to theory in that it provides a concrete way of entering or understanding a given thought or theory, and of stepping outside of it to test it and compare it with others.

James's version of pragmatism also contains a theory of truth. This theory, according to which "true" names "whatever proves itself to be good in the way of belief" (*P,* 42), is certainly the more famous of these ideas, and its elaboration is one of James's distinctive contributions to the pragmatic movement. According to what we can call Jamesean pragmatism, then, the "corridor" is a means of evaluation and, crucially, of escape. Theories and concepts are to be entered by comprehending the conduct they call for, and exited once

343

and for all if they consistently lead to bad or unproductive conduct, or to no conduct at all. Theories to rest in, "true" theories, lead, *ceteris paribus* and in the long run, to profitable things and better living.

This philosophical theory has its perplexities and deceptive simplicities, but I think that it is fundamentally straightforward and comprehensible, and that the truly hard work of understanding pragmatism is understanding the opposition. Or, at least, that the difficult thing is understanding pragmatism in relation to its opposition, and seeing how this comparatively simple set of ideas mounts a challenge to very complex philosophical thought. Therefore I attempt, in the following discussion, to explain the lucid in terms of the more obscure. I describe some of the Marxist political criticisms of Jamesean pragmatism that are offered in passing by Antonio Gramsci and in detail by Gramsci's adherent Cornel West, and I offer a response. I hope that along the way I make clearer the nature of the pragmatic corridor among theories, and the uses that corridor may have even for political thinkers.

I PRAGMATISM, REALISM, IDEALISM

At bottom, what both Gramsci and West criticize in James's pragmatism is what they criticize in other, more traditional philosophies, namely a relative lack of engagement with concrete, down-to-earth political and social conditions. This may seem surprising: James's philosophy displays such a real-world, brass-tacks focus that readers have sometimes perceived it to be unprincipled and unreflective, and therefore "unphilosophical." James was determined to offer theories of meaning and truth that accorded with the ways real people – "geologists, biologists" and philologists, for example – actually do develop ideas and beliefs (*P*, 34).

Moreover, James begins *Pragmatism* with an allusion to politically based criticisms that can be made of unpragmatic philosophical views. He refers to a pamphlet called *Human Submission* by "that valiant anarchistic writer Morrison I. Swift": Swift tells of John Corcoran, a clerk who lost his job due to illness, and who, after having spent his little savings and having been fired from a temporary job shoveling snow, returned home to find his wife and children had been evicted and were without food. Corcoran poisoned himself the next day. Swift deplores the "guileless thoroughfed thinkers" Royce and Bradley for their rationalist idea that human suffering like this contributes to the absolute goodness of the world, and James agrees that the well-ordered principles of rationalist moral philosophy and epistemology can be no more than a distraction from the painful and tangled experiences of life in "our civilized régime" (*P*, 20–3).

Nevertheless, the pragmatist may still be hopelessly disengaged from the real world if pragmatism is a kind of idealism. Idealism was the original philosophical target of Marxism: it was Hegel whom Marx "stood on his head" and attacked for a kind of otherworldly unrealism.[1] And if one thinks of pragmatism as a method of interpreting and criticizing beliefs and ideas solely in terms of their goodness or satisfactoriness to us human believers, it is easy to conclude that, despite James's critique of Royce and Bradley, pragmatism must itself be a kind of idealism, insufficiently appreciative of the concrete and coercive world beyond thoughts, language, and desires. I think that Gramsci and West do something like this, and that this is why they ultimately reject James's pragmatism. Let us therefore consider the connections among pragmatism, realism, and idealism, before we try to assess the criticisms of Gramsci and West.

Beliefs are made true, on a realist philosophical picture, by a relationship to facts and objects that are "external" and mind-independent. "Idealist" philosophers look "inward" to the contents of the mind for the truth-makers (or -maker, as the case may be), but not to facts or objects that depend on what any concrete individual person thinks. Both realists and idealists distinguish between true and false beliefs about the world without reference to individual beliefs and believers: both kinds of philosophers have taken it for granted that the point of individual beliefs – a point beliefs can and often do fail to serve – is correct representation of these individual-belief-independent entities (or, in the case of Hegelian idealists, of a single, individual-belief-independent, mind-of-God-like Entity). However, James attacks this idea, and he thus challenges both realism and idealism in all their rationalist and empiricist varieties.

He does this when he criticizes the Hegelian idea of truth as existing *ante rem* or "before the things" (cf. *P*, 104–7). James complained that Hegelians regarded truth as a relation that somehow existed as a "*tertium quid* intermediate between the facts *per se*, on the one hand, and all knowledge of them, actual or potential, on the other" (*P*, 322). He offered in response a naturalistic picture of truth as a "function" or a "habit" that existed *in rebus* or "in the things" – the "things" here being true beliefs themselves.[2] For James, truth exists inside "truths" or beliefs as a function or habit of delivering good experienced consequences. It is not a set of reserved slots waiting patiently for beliefs to come along and fit in: truth comes and goes with the concrete beliefs that contain it and the individual persons who, through interactions with the world and each other, generate those beliefs. It is an internal function of human beliefs, a thing some beliefs sometimes *do*.

James thinks that we have a tendency to treat "-th" words like "strength" and "truth" as names of abstract things separable from their instantiations and sublimely unaffected by the pressing, changing circumstances that make them valuable. But truth, says James, is no more an abstract and fixed "relation" than strength is an independent abstract quality. It's obvious that without particular persons involved in various concrete events of heavy lifting, no strength would ever come into being; and, equally clearly, no one cares about strength except insofar as it makes further similar concrete events possible. Analogously, without individual believers, their beliefs, and the concrete events in which some of those beliefs meet the reality we experience and are "verified" by the encounter, no truth would come into existence. At least no truth of the kind we care about, the kind that actually helps us in life, would come to be. That kind of truth exists only *inside* the individual beliefs or "truths" we believers generate, residing there as a timebound, mutable "habit" those "truths" have of getting verified or being useful. To adapt the terminology of Donald Davidson and Richard Rorty, true beliefs are not "made true" by any external, abstract, rationalistically discoverable relation to the world (see Rorty 1986).

Thus, pragmatism, like Marxism, originates in a clash with Hegelian rationalism. The main motivation for the above argument is the defense of the individual person, individual experiences, and individual freedom from the "vicious abstractionism" that James associated with the Hegelian view of truth: James thought that Hegelian monistic idealism declared genuinely separate individuals and individual experiences unreal, and thus denied the power of individuals to react freely to their unique experiences and actually make the world better. The world could not possibly be made better on the Hegelian view because it was "simple, clean and noble": its ultimate goodness could be logically – and, James thought, speciously – demonstrated along with its total unity (cf. *P*, 17–18). James wanted to attack this picture of the world by challenging its picture of truth as a rationally knowable relation independent of individual belief and experience, and showing how individuals and their discrete experiences in time were prerequisites of the very existence of truth.

However, James did not attack Hegel's idealistic story by offering a traditionally realistic one in response. Instead, he criticized the whole realism-versus-idealism debate. That was (and is still) a debate about what kinds of objects are represented by our true ideas, beliefs, and words. James's response to both realists and idealists is, in effect, that this is the wrong question. Truth, our goal in thinking and speaking, is best understood not as representation of any kind of objects, but rather as usefulness in solving problems. The goal of improving our search for truth, of ending meaningless disputes and integrating our different views of things, is best served by this pragmatic conception.

Marx, like James, criticized not only idealism but the whole philosophical conflict between realism and idealism, and he, too, did this by paying more attention than idealist philosophers had to the way problems are actually solved in the "material" world of nature and human action. The famous eleventh of his "Theses on Feuerbach" – "The philosophers have only *interpreted* the world in various ways; the point, however, is to *change* it" – sounds a clearly pragmatic note. Marx deplores empty, abstract philosophical theorizing, and calls for discussion of conditions and practices in the public world, with the goal of changing those conditions and practices if they are confused or "contradictory." Despite this, however, the critiques of pragmatism offered by the "philosophers of praxis" Gramsci and West parallel Marx's criticism of Hegelian idealism. Let's now turn to consider those critiques.

II GRAMSCI AND THE PRAGMATISTS

Gramsci and West both applaud the efforts of all the pragmatists to challenge traditional philosophy's ahistorical tendencies. These tendencies, in the views of both Gramsci and West, lead philosophy to neglect or even to help hide the injustices of the political world. And West holds that his own view, "prophetic pragmatism," takes pragmatism to a still higher level of political engagement. But Gramsci associates the name of James with a philosophical effort to reform "language" that is bound to fail; and West thinks that James's version of pragmatism is an immature, naively optimistic view that pays too much attention to the individual and her or his beliefs. These criticisms, on closer examination, resemble the Marxist political critique of idealism. Let's try to see whether they are fair.

Gramsci thinks of philosophy as "a cultural battle to transform the popular 'mentality' " (Gramsci 1971, 348). Gramsci emphasized the importance of this kind of cultural battle to Marxist political ends. He is one of the Marxists who transformed the concept of "ideology," originally a negative term for capitalism's distorted picture of the social and moral world, into a label for all forms of social and cultural consciousness, including Marxism itself. The Gramscian theoretician accordingly sees her or his struggle with political society as in part a contest of wills and ideas. Gramsci is not a practitioner of "crude economism": he does not take simple class-based self-interest to be at the bottom of all political actions and all thought (163ff.). He recognizes the ability of a dominant class to rule through moral and intellectual leadership and intelligent compromises with lower-class allies. This "hegemony" includes the exchange of philosophical ideas, an important aspect of ideology in which not only intellectuals but all thinkers and users of language engage to some extent. This kind of leadership, information exchange, and compromise results in the consent of the governed, and Gramsci ultimately interprets the special historical role of the proletariat as the expansion of this consent, or the development of a "regulated" society, and the diminution of "political" constraint.[3]

James's pragmatism is, on Gramsci's theory, only one of "a number of idealist currents" that have absorbed Marxist elements, reflecting the efforts of "pure" intellectuals to "moderate an excess of speculative philosophism with . . . historicist realism," this in the interest of maintaining hegemony (389–90). Of James's commitment to think in terms of practical differences, Gramsci says: "one can see from this the immediacy of the philosophical politicism of the pragmatists. . . . The pragmatist . . . wishes to tie himself immediately to practice" (372–3). And this immediate connection to action establishes pragmatism as an " 'ideological party' rather than a system of philosophy" (372). It makes pragmatism, like the Marxist "philosophy of praxis," a way of motivating action in the social world.

However, the similarities end with the connection to action. Gramsci takes pragmatism to be chiefly an effort to reform language in order to avoid illusory philosophical disputes, and thus presumably to remove, in a quasi-positivist way, the hindrances that philosophical confusions and religious hangovers can offer to rational and moral action. But Gramsci thinks that this effort at linguistic reform has to fail because it still reflects insufficient engagement with the public world and insufficiently revolutionary political goals. Pragmatism manifests "the absence of a critical and historicist conception of the phenomenon of language," and this leads to "errors in both the scientific and the practical field" (451). When pragmatists direct us to avoid empty disputes by understanding concepts in terms of practical consequences, they only "theorise abstractly about language as a source of error." This "abstract" theorizing will be unhelpful because "Language is transformed with the transformation of the whole of civilisation," and the pragmatic theory will not foster widespread social change.

Gramsci thinks, curiously enough, that because of pragmatism's Anglo-Saxon Protestant historical origin, German and Italian philosophers – both idealist and Marxist – have made and will make all the serious cultural contributions in this struggle. In Catholic countries, religion and the practical everyday culture have been so firmly separated that philosophers, who are thinkers from the religious side of the line, cannot think of themselves as dealing immediately with the practical: they deal with "higher" issues. There is no such split among the Anglo-Saxon Protestants, and so:

the Italian or German type of philosopher is more "practical" than the pragmatist who judges from immediate reality, often at the most vulgar level, in that the German or Italian has a higher aim, sets his sights higher and tends . . . to raise the existing cultural level. Hegel can be considered the theoretical precursor of the liberal revolutions of the nineteenth century. The pragmatists, at the most, have contributed to the creation of the Rotary Club movement and to the justification of conservative and reactionary movements. (373)

Thus, in Gramsci's view, pragmatism is an idealism that is not ideal-ist enough to be realistic: it is an attempt to make a cultural change that cannot succeed because it is focused too closely on the concrete and the particular, and therefore can't contain the grander moral or social vision necessary for genuine change.

III WEST'S GRAMSCIAN CRITIQUE

In his book *The American Evasion of Philosophy*, West claims affini-ties with Gramsci and his criticisms of the historical pragmatists. In setting out his own view, West offers a kind of pragmatist manifesto: *"The goal of a sophisticated neo-pragmatism is to think genealogi-cally about specific practices in light of the best available social theories, cultural critiques, and historiographical insights and to act politically to achieve certain moral consequences in light of effective strategies and tactics"* (West 1989, 209; emphasis in the original). Thus, the contemporary pragmatist should leave behind the old goal of demolishing traditional philosophy and instead take on present-day political evils.

The transcendentalizing philosophical theories of the Western tra-dition have come under a wave of criticism in both America and Europe. West describes this wave as a burgeoning rejection of arm-chair philosophizing in favor of new theories that address concrete social, political, and moral issues from perspectives informed by literary theory, economics, sociology, and the rest of the humanities and social sciences. West locates himself within this movement, and he announces a new, politicized pragmatism that offers a "heteroge-neous genealogy," or a historicist theory that recognizes practically significant differences not only among individuals but among people *in different political groups.*

West acknowledges that democratic ideals do and should operate both in pragmatic epistemology and pragmatic politics, but he points out that, for example, "not one [of the original pragmatists] viewed racism as contributing greatly to the impediments for both individuality and democracy" (147). He bitterly accuses pragmatists like James of "pandering to middle class pieties" (66), and of blind-ness to "the plight of the wretched of the earth, namely, the majority of humanity who own no property or wealth, participate in no demo-cratic arrangements, and whose individualities are crushed by hard labor and harsh living conditions" (147–8). Pragmatism both argues for and depends on the freedom and problem-solving abilities of individuals. When confronted with hard political facts about the lives of many of the world's inhabitants, pragmatism can seem naive and trivial, especially if its account of the origin and justification of beliefs and language neglects to mention explicitly those social ills. A sophisticated pragmatism, West thinks, will stop treating people simply as believers and language users with particular small problems to solve in a piecemeal way, and start focusing on them as objects or imposers of larger-scale domination.

West sees James and the other pragmatist philosophers as, in Gramsci's term, "organic intellectuals": they destabilized the moral status quo, and both reflected and energized a constituency capable of producing social change. They didn't write as disinterested users of pure reason: their status as particular members of a particular social group was explicit in their writings, as was their contagious personal desire for changes in the way that group lived. They were, however, too individualistic and indifferent to the deepest problems of the human beings around them to be really effective. They refused to join radical political associations, and they remained fearfully and myopically committed to the fundamental structures of "civilized" America.

In particular, James was fundamentally motivated by a desire to put "distance" between his views and "the working class, women, and people of color" (62). The centerpiece of West's evidence for this is James's "crucial and peculiar" lecture "The Social Value of the College-Bred." There James says that:

The sense of human superiority ought, then to be considered our line, as boring subway is the engineer's line and the surgeon's is appendicitis. . . . The best claim we can make for higher education is . . . it should enable us to know a good man when we see him. . . . [I]n our democracy, while everything else is so shifting, we alumni and alumnae of the colleges are the only permanent presence that corresponds to the aristocracy in older countries . . . and, unlike them, we stand for ideal interests solely, for we have no corporate selfishness and wield no powers of corruption. We ought to have our own class consciousness. "Les intellectuels!" (ECR, 108–10; see West 1989, 62)

West takes this passage to reveal clearly a patrician and discriminatory attitude that colors James's pragmatism generally.

West's response to these remarks is, to say the least, hasty. He deprecates their "elitism" (62), though it seems clear that James is declaring college-educated persons to be an "aristocracy" only in that they are the best at *recognizing* the best men and women, and not at all in that they themselves *are* necessarily the best. West asks about this educated class, "no selfishness? no corruption?" But James says only that there is no "corporate" selfishness on the part of this group, probably meaning that few interests will be shared by all the different persons who manage to get college degrees; and James says that they wield no *powers* of corruption, intending no doubt to imply that they will lack the law-giving power of old-world nobility. And as for the idea that working people, people of color, and women are intentionally excluded from this aristocracy, even supposing James knew of no working-class people who had ever managed to scrape through and get degrees from any college, he knew of at least one person of color in the group, for his student W. E. B. Du Bois already had his Ph.D by the time James gave this speech; and it's hard to see how James could have intended to exclude women by giving this address to the American Association of *Alumnae* as they were meeting at Radcliffe.

Still, whatever the psychology *behind* James's pragmatism, West wants also to do as Gramsci did, and locate impediments to revolution in pragmatism itself. West thinks that James's theory of truth, with its "conservative" attachment to the body of prior beliefs, constitutes a "gradualism" and reflects "a preoccupation with continuity" that "minimizes disruption and precludes subversion" (65). West cites James's claim in *Pragmatism* that any true account of a new experience will, as an essential part of its "working," getting "verified," or being true, always "[preserve] the older stock of truths with a minimum of modification, stretching them just enough to make them admit the novelty" (*P*, 35; see West 1989, 65). West seems to think that this commitment to (most aspects of) the epistemic status quo will hinder efforts to destabilize the political status quo – or at least that it will unless we politicize this story more, and take account of the hidden political conditions that shape both the individuals who seek truth and the prior truth-stocks they start out with.

"The older stock of truths": this is equivalent, for James, to the initial set of beliefs with which we begin our inquiries. This is in turn the same as what we usually think and affirm about things in the world, or the way we conceive of things. That is, it is our "philosophy," or our conceptual system; and "our conceptual system" is also as good a way as any to think of our "language." Gramsci acknowledges something like this set of equivalences when he says that "Language also means culture and philosophy (if only at the level of common sense)" (Gramsci 1971, 349). When we recognize this, it is easy to see that Gramsci and West both make what is at root the same point: if pragmatism is ever really to leave behind sterile philosophical debates and cease being a minor obstacle to serious and beneficial change, it must leave behind its insular obsession with language – established truths, older beliefs – and look to a more inclusive political reality.

IV POLITICS AND THE WORLD BEYOND BELIEF

The sophisticated pragmatist, in West's view, will never lose sight of the extralinguistic conditions that pull the strings of our language-games and control the formation of our beliefs. Language does not constitute or control "modes of production" or other extralinguistic determinants of power. We language users have needed structuralists, poststructuralists, and politically minded pragmatists to help us to awareness of the "materiality" of language, or its location among the rest of the things that get moved around by economic, physical, and political forces. Now that we have this awareness, we can begin to look past language or our previous "truths" to the enduring powers that control our "transient vocabularies" (see West 1989, 209).

Of course, prophetic pragmatists also know better than to be realists or foundationalists: they recognize human fallibility, and refuse to take any particular vocabulary or set of beliefs as fundamentally justified by a direct, unmistakable relation to reality. But though our attempts to know the physical and social world in detail are always error prone, we can still turn to our best-developed social theories and try to use them to motivate *action*, interventions in the public world that will both test those theories and begin to ameliorate our bleak political situations (209–10). Antifoundationalism should not turn into a fixation on language: the task of a mature pragmatism may include the critique of linguistically induced false consciousness – as exemplified, perhaps, in idealistic or non-"prophetically" pragmatic tendencies to understand the human cognitive relationship to the world in vaguely mentalistic terms of beliefs and language, rather than in material terms of power relations – but that is the only relevance of language or truth to our new pragmatist project.

However, the Jamesean pragmatist will respond to this that there simply is no relief from the skewings and warpings of prior "truths" or language, which must figure even in the accounts of the world offered up by revolutionary political thinkers. In the view of the pragmatist, *all* consciousness is "false" in the sense that it is at least partly linguistic, or at least partly a product of humanly verified "truths." It is never a pure reaction to the extralinguistic world of things and facts.

James makes this point when he describes the "reality" we know and speak of in our truths as consisting of three parts, one of which comprises "the *previous truths* of which every inquiry takes account" (*P,* 118; emphasis in original). The other parts, if such things really do exist out beyond the realm of truth, constitute the "core" of reality, the mutely existing stuff that we knowers wrap up in organizations and classifications of our own making. These other parts of reality are described as "sensations" and their relations, though James construes "sensations" broadly enough so that this "core" of perceived things might turn out to be what "scholasticism" identifies as "matter" (cf. *P,* 120). James has nothing final to say about either the existence of this primal stuff or the extent to which we can theorize philosophically about it: he insists only that the final true account of it will be, like the final true account of anything else, "the one that proves most satisfactory" (*P,* 120). But while he provisionally holds that it is out there, James says that this primal core is not the only thing we have to answer to when we set out to say true things about reality. Sensations and relations would not even come to our attention if not for the "previous truths" or prior beliefs in which they arrive prewrapped.

James says that

Every hour brings its . . . own facts of sensation and relation, to be truly taken account of; but the whole of our *past* dealings with such facts is already funded in the previous truths. It is therefore only the smallest and recentest fraction of the first two parts of reality that comes to us without the human touch, and that fraction has immediately to become humanized in the sense of being squared . . . to the humanized mass already there. As a matter of fact we can hardly take in an impression at all, in the absence of a preconception of what impressions there may possibly be. (*P,* 119)

Thus, paradoxically, unless we have already sorted perceived things and their essential and accidental relations into our own categorical schemes for our own convenience, we are unlikely ever to notice them in the first place; and even if we do somehow attend to an "aboriginal" reality on its own, we find it "absolutely dumb and evanescent." If we try to say anything about it, we ultimately wind up appreciating and discussing a substitute for it that has been "peptonized and cooked for our consumption" by our prior categorizations and beliefs (*P,* 119–20).

This does not entail that our own beliefs and categories are the only things in the world for us to know. Again, James assumes, absent any good reason to say otherwise, that the human contribution amounts to only one part of the real world. But he asks, "Does the river make its banks, or do the banks make the river? Does a man walk with his right leg or with his left leg more essentially? Just as impossible may it be to separate the real from the human factors in the growth of our cognitive experience" (*P,* 120). And if it is impossible to do this, the idea of a reality beyond those "human factors" is empty. There is then nothing in our experience that we can isolate as an item located behind or apart from our human arrangements of categories, concepts, and beliefs, or what Gramsci calls our "language." There may *be* such items, but they have nothing to say for themselves. They can't point themselves out, and we can't pick them out, so all attempts to rest our talk on them become idle.

Thus, when Gramsci and West criticize James for worrying too much about language and not enough about the dark, enveloping political powers that lie behind human beliefs, they draw an empty distinction. When they focus their attention on the political, "material" world, what they see there is indistinguishable from the language and beliefs that so interest James.

To put this another way, Gramsci and West are offering a new "language," a new vocabulary and set of claims that, in their view, finally stops obscuring what really goes on in the world of action. In support of their new language they offer us not more talk but the full political world. The pragmatists have so far failed to appreciate fully the language-independence of that world, and so Gramsci and West proceed to use a new language that is, they think, better connected to extralinguistic reality, especially in that it is better suited to provoke and promote *action*. But how can they tell that this new language has this better connection to the world beyond language? Why do they say it does? And why should we believe them, and adopt their way of looking at things?

There are three possible ways of answering these demands for justification. First there is silence, reflecting the fact that claims concerning the relationship between language and the world can be *justified* only in language. There are, of course, efficient ways besides offering justifications to get an audience to talk a certain way or accept certain claims: there is active demonstration of the new claims, for example, not to mention the weeding-out of dissenters with imprisonment or executions. These approaches are compatible with Gramsci's idea that "the whole of civilisation" must be transformed through action before a new way of looking at things will be adopted. But the idea that these methods will *always* be possible, or even always work, is not compatible with Gramsci's idea that "hegemony" is needed to get people's cooperation. If there really is sometimes a need for the exchange of philosophical ideas, surely it will surface in this particular context. And, moreover, if extralinguistic reality is, as James says, "like a client who has given his case to a lawyer and then has passively to listen in the courtroom to whatever account of his affairs . . . the lawyer finds it most expedient to give" (*P*, 118), wordless demonstrations will be among the realities that have nothing to say for themselves, and they will thus be subject to "expedient" interpretations that don't support the new way of looking at things. Thus, entirely wordless action is unlikely to be the right way to address these questions.

The second possible response is a justification of the new language *in the old language*; it is an attempt to account for the unfamiliar idea that, say, epistemology might have something to do with social problems by, for example, pointing to familiar epistemological or political problems and explaining how they can be solved or made less pressing by drawing this kind of connection. This is basically James's own procedure in his philosophical writings, and it reflects his idea that previous truth must be dealt with when we account for reality in new ways. This is as "conservative" a way of proceeding as James would require. James says that new beliefs must involve a "minimum of modification" to the old intellectual order, but, of course, a "minimum" need not be a small amount. James is not here declaring allegiance to the status quo: he is only indicating our real, general aversion to new theories that gratuitously disregard our hard-won previous beliefs, and suggesting that, according to our own actual procedures, our best new theories will *engage* with our old ones.

Finally, the Gramscian might deal with questions about the justification of his new views by explaining the relation between his new language and the world *in the new language*, ignoring all our old ideas about the mind and the world, and taking for granted his new ideas about the downtrodden and the intellectual world that abets their oppression. Only this third approach requires a response from the Jamesean pragmatist, who will quickly point out that this justification begs the question. Of course Marxists, like everyone else, see their beliefs as the best possible accounts of the world beyond beliefs: otherwise those particular thoughts would not be their *beliefs*. Still, Gramsci and West cannot justify either their new beliefs or their political actions by appeals to objects or obligations that entirely transcend familiar beliefs and concepts, except, again, circularly. James's pragmatism does allow one to appeal to the world beyond language in justification of what one says and does, because pragmatism does not "idealistically" deny the existence of a belief-transcendent world. Nevertheless, James trivializes any possible result of any such gesture by pointing out that the world beyond language and belief cannot reach out and appropriate any descriptions of it. Explanations or justifications of a new way of speaking must come in some human language or other, must take some set of beliefs for granted; and unless those justifications come in more or less familiar terms, they are not really justifications.

Notice, moreover, that this claim about the unavailability of the world beyond "language" is not simply a point about human fallibility. The most unregenerate metaphysical realist would usually insist on the ever-present possibility of human error concerning what the world beyond our present set of categorizations and beliefs is really like. James, however, is not urging simply that we might be wrong, but rather that it would not make any difference if we were right.

James's pragmatism holds that both our world-views and their justifications originate in a world whose "non-linguistic" features are not distinguishable in any principled way from its "linguistic" ones, and that thus even the most wildly *successful* gesture beyond the humanized realm of language and belief is futile and empty. No such gesture could justify anything we might say, and we can get all the justification we could ever have without any such gestures.

Still, perhaps West would respond that although appeals to the world beyond our transient vocabularies may be philosophically trivial in this sense of "question-begging," they may still be important in a more pragmatic or strategic sense: they may be indispensable as a means of motivating change. West thinks we need a way of upsetting the complacency that afflicts our inward-looking little communities, and opening those communities up to the influence of outsiders and "others" of all varieties. He might say, echoing Gramsci, that, for this vital political project, we need *theory*, not just more minor, tinkering, convenient changes in our talk. In that theory we must put language in its comparatively unimportant place and think of it as a surface phenomenon, though the subsurface conditions may be more complicated than previous grand theorists thought they were.

If we do not think of language and belief this way, we may lack motivation to question our familiar and anodyne social homilies, and we may not work hard for change. There are diversely arrayed groups of human beings – women, residents of the developing world, Americans of African descent, and others – who are coming in from the margins to describe, from their unique perspectives, hidden contours of the natural and social world. Those persons' voices hold the world's best hope for producing better and fairer ways of speaking and acting in the future, and we cannot listen carefully and with full seriousness to what they have to say unless we pull ourselves out of our philosophical self-absorption. The prophetic pragmatists and philosophers of praxis will therefore keep their eyes on the public world of objects, persons, and societies; pragmatic overemphasis on language or conserved prior "truth" threatens insularity and political stasis.

But should Jamesean cognitive conservatism, rightly understood, really incline one to complacent political conservatism? I cannot see why: "conservative" pragmatism in no way lessens our urgent moral responsibilities to the miserable. You don't have to look "beyond language" to see what an absurd state the world is in; you don't have to think that truths do more than help us keep our other truths organized in order to see that right now, politically, economically, and morally, we are in dire need of some new truths. When the Jamesean looks out on all those victims of injustice, she is made aware that something must be done, and that along the way some unfamiliar thoughts must be had and assimilated; but what lets her know this is not the world beyond truth, language, and belief, but rather the dissatisfaction she feels with the relationship between her new observational beliefs (new experiences prewrapped in very familiar categorizations) and all those other, older beliefs that she is trying to hang on to. She knows that some of her beliefs and classifications are going to have to go, but which ones?

This problem may seen too solipsistic to allow any nonarbitrary solution. Fortunately, however, among the Jamesean's new observational beliefs will be the realization that some of those suffering human beings are producing their own views of the world using their experiences just as she does. She will be able to see that their in-some-ways-unfamiliar beliefs may be a rich source for her to plumb in search of new ideas, as long as those outsiders share with her enough familiar ideas so that she can understand them and take them seriously. (Unfortunately, once in a while we find people suffering because they are deranged, developmentally disabled, or massively and irremediably self-deceived: they are then unable to participate in this process.) Serious consideration of ideas need not lead to their adoption, of course, and a Jamesean will disagree strongly with some of the ideas expressed by people outside her particular community of believers. She may even find that, after agreeing with the outsiders at first, she must later change her mind, if their ideas do not work out any better than hers did. (They may turn out to have been too close to their own problems.) But in no case is she prevented from agreeing with those outsiders and working with them to change political circumstances by her indifference to the world beyond language. Her "critical edge" will come not from that world, but instead from her own convictions and from *human voices* that she has not heard or listened to before.

This does represent a tinkering, reconstructive, individual-problem-solving approach to philosophy. No appeal is made to a world that transcends individual concerns and local efforts to cope using language and thought. But there is no reason to believe Gramsci's and West's claims that this approach cannot let us see far enough to address pervasive moral and political problems, or that it cannot result in suitably grand or radical theories of the social world. We can be especially brief in dealing with Gramsci's culturally chauvinistic version of this idea: although James's pragmatism is not a "scientism," or a view that takes the methods and assumptions of the natural scientist to be the only ones that can lead to genuine truth, James did model his general method of "marrying" new truth to old and looking to practical consequences on the procedures of working natural scientists (cf. *P*, 34–5), and science, of course, has had no shortage of radical revolutions or generalization-filled theories over its history. Revolutionary scientific ideas succeed if they *work*; and, likewise, if a radically new moral or political generalization *works* for us in some practical way, if it engages with our older beliefs and pulls its weight in the truth-process, then it too will be a pragmatic "truth."

What's more, James famously insists that there is just as much room in a pragmatic outlook for "tender-minded" moral and religious abstract theorizing as there is for "tough-minded" scientific attention to particulars (see *P*, 9–26, for example). It's just that if an abstract theory turns out to be *irrelevant*, as a practical matter, to those – and especially to *us* – particulars, that is cause to reject the theory. This is, of course, just the kind of thing that Marxists say in criticism of Hegelians and "philosophers" generally. It is not the rejection of all abstract thought, but only of abstract thought without consequences in the world of experience and practice. Jamesean melioration and cognitive conservatism thus need have no more to do with the end of moral and political radicalism than Marx's, Gramsci's, or West's own views.

V CONCLUSION

Nothing in the foregoing is meant to depreciate West's or Gramsci's projects of making philosophy worldly and making the world philosophical, or introducing political issues into our thoughts about thought. Nor have I intended only to carp at the scholarship of these two authors: Gramsci was a physically infirm political prisoner with no access to a library when he wrote about James, and West's main goals in discussing James are social and motivational rather than philosophical. Instead, my target has been the negative idea that bringing specific historical and social issues into philosophy is the "sophisticated" pragmatic objective, and that pragmatist interest in belief and language reflects only insularity and complacency. If it is foolish and vain to overlook politics in the attempt to study language and thought, it is equally foolish and vain to overlook language and thought in the attempt to study politics. Hence the search for Jamesean "truth," a search that is as much a matter of trying to see how we can organize and reconcile our thoughts as it is of pointing out material wrongs and having material effects on them, is still a reasonable thing to think about and a decent thing to try to carry on.

It is, of course, compatible with maturity and political commitment to be reflective about the ways in which preconceptions affect even potentially revolutionary thought and activity. Such reflection can make us harder to stampede into transformative actions that leave us less "empowered" rather than more. And it can make us less hardheaded in our political theorizing, and thus better able to appreciate or criticize intelligent alternatives.

Moreover, the most trenchant social critique by itself will not always produce needed change, even if it provokes some people to radical social activism, because that activity and change may provoke even more people to counterrevolution. Sometimes, in political matters, it will be enough to call attention to material circumstances no one has noticed or thought about; but sometimes the other side will have a different story to tell about those circumstances, and an abiding commitment to that story. What will be urgently needed then is *common ground on which to argue, and a way to find that common ground.* Pointing still more indignantly to a hidden world beyond the old beliefs, and insisting that our opponents try harder to match their thoughts up to that world, may not do the job: people who care about the oppressed have found, in some such cases, that ostensible evidence from that world can be shrugged off as a mere artifact of the way ideologues and bleeding-heart victimologists look at things. Which is to say, they have discovered that the "material" world, considered apart from language or prior beliefs, is ultimately immaterial to the justification of new belief and action.

If we human beings are going to decide thoughtfully and undogmatically what to say and do about our moral and political condition, if we are going to quit preaching to our various choirs and start building genuine consensus and cooperation, we shall sometimes need another touchstone besides "material reality" to use in evaluating competing moral and political views. That is, we'll need a corridor among those views, a way to take whatever prior beliefs we may share, combine them with our new experiences, and use the combination as a practical, flexible way of deciding what to believe and do. There will often be no other feasible way to proceed, even in bad and steadily worsening social circumstances. And that is why, even in a time when new ideas, direct advocacy, and straightforward calls to action are sorely needed and in short supply, we can still make use of a Jamesean pragmatism that takes no sides intransigently, and that thus may help all of us, even the skeptical and the confused, to pick thoughtfully the sides we want to take.

NOTES

I am indebted to Ruth Anna Putnam for extensive comments on an earlier draft of this paper.

1 In the second chapter of West 1991 there is a helpful discussion of the young Karl Marx's renunciation of his own earlier "Young" or "Left" Hegelianism in favor of more "radically historicist" and politically aggressive views.

2 James's picture of Hegelianism may not accurately represent anybody's actual position: James had mixed feelings about his own comprehension of Hegel and blamed Hegel's "abominable habits of speech." Hegel's views may also have changed through his different works.

In any case, this account does at least reflect James's understanding of transcendentalist tendencies in especially the Hegel of the *Science of Logic* and the *Lesser Logic* and James's view of his American Hegelian opposition, especially Josiah Royce. Cf. lectures 2 and 3 on Hegel and the Hegelians in *PU*.

3 A detailed discussion of these issues can be found in Mouffe 1979.

18 James and the Kantian tradition

One of the most interesting and problematic threads in the literature on James concerns the relationship between his philosophy and Kant's. It is difficult to imagine at first two philosophers farther apart than Kant and James. Kant was a lover of unity and systematicity, and exalted the absolute and necessary features of our experience; James had little patience with philosophical systems, thought there was much less unity to the world than often imagined, and denied there were any utterly indefeasible elements in our experience. These deep differences are undeniable. It is perhaps then no surprise when we find Richard Rorty arguing that James's pragmatism is part of what he thinks of as "the anti-Kantian revolution" (Rorty 1979, 7). Elsewhere he writes:

No other American writers have offered so radical a suggestion for making our future different from our past, as have James and Dewey. . . . Logical empiricism was one variety of standard, academic, neo-Kantian, epistemologically-centered philosophy. The great pragmatists should . . . be taken as . . . breaking with the Kantian epistemological tradition altogether. (Rorty 1982, 160)

This is a powerful claim. Nevertheless, it is my intention – quixotic as it may be – to defend the idea that James may be best read as a sort of Kantian.

James himself would shudder at the suggestion that there are significant similarities between his views and Kant's. He insisted that: "As Schiller, Dewey, and I mean pragmatism, it is *toto coelo* opposed to either the original or revived Kantism. . . . [I]t is irreconcilable with anything in Kant, – only the most superficial resemblance obtaining" (Perry 1935, 2:469–70).[1] James was of course familiar with Kant's views, but contrary to the mainstream of philosophy in

363

his day, he argued that "the true line of philosophic progress lies . . . not so much *through* Kant as *round* him." Kant, he claimed, "bequeathes to us not one single conception which is both indispensable to philosophy and which philosophy either did not possess before him, or was not destined inevitably to acquire after him through the growth of men's reflection upon the hypotheses by which science interprets nature" (*P*, 269).

One might argue that this last clause would allow James to dismiss *any* philosopher, and I must admit that there is a certain embarrassment in the face of James's hostility to Kant. But like many others, I think James is mistaken in his assessment of Kant's work and its relationship to his own philosophy.

This belief was apparently shared even by some of his friends and colleagues. James once reported that Munsterberg had been "poohpoohing my thought," saying "I seem to be ignorant that Kant ever wrote, Kant having already said all that I say" (*Letters*, 2:267–8). Similarly, James Ward informed him, "All the worth I see in pragmatism is to be found – don't kick – in Kant, in his 'primacy of the practical reason,' and in his showing that there is 'room for faith' " (Perry 1935, 2:655).[2]

Contemporary writers have also seen the affinities between James and Kant. Echoing Ward, Wiener points out one focus for the comparison:

William James in his own empirical way did what Kant tried to do in an a priori way, namely, to show the limits of science in order to make room for faith. . . . That neither physical nor biological science sealed man's fate or destined him to passive resignation in a closed universe was one of the chief moral and metaphysical conclusions of James's great psychological work. (Wiener 1949, 99)

And this view is again put forward by Murphy in his highly suggestive article "Kant's Children: The Cambridge Pragmatists":

It was Kant who was the dominant influence upon the pragmatists. . . . If . . . we look to the origin of pragmatism in American philosophy, it is clear that the concept was introduced as part of an idealistic interpretation of science and in the interests of harmonizing science with religious and metaphysical views. . . . His determination to protect the freedom and originality of the mind led James to emphasize the activity and constructive action of the mind in a manner which is profoundly indebted to Kant and the idealists. (Murphy 1968, 9, 14–15, 19)

Another perspective is offered by Aiken:

There is . . . something distinctly Kantian about James's principled distrust of inclination, of "doing what comes naturally." And it is precisely this Kantian belief that what is right or obligatory always cuts against the grain of inclination which, together with his equally Kantian sense of loyalty to the right as he conceived it, provide the unifying clues to many otherwise paradoxical aspects of James's thought and character. (Aiken 1962, 241)

But the boldest claims about James's relation to Kant are made by Kuklick in *The Rise of American Philosophy:*

Harvard pragmatism was a form of neo-Kantianism whose adherents drew from a set of connected technical doctrines. . . .

Rather than being the least neo-Kantian of the major Cambridge thinkers, James was the most serious neo-Kantian of the group: in his thought the ambiguities and ambivalences of the Kantian position were most apparent.

Was James, then, a Kantian? There is much to be said for James's denial. The whole of the nineteenth century's emphasis on change and development and the impact of Darwin mediated between him and Kant. But equally clear was James's debt to idealism: his evolutionary Kantianism was clear. (Kuklick 1977, 257, 334, 272–3)

But James's "evolutionary Kantianism" is *not* clear; each aspect of this synthesis stands in need of explication.[3] It is not even very clear what might be meant in characterizing James as a Kantian at all. It might be thought that James's Kantianism is to be made out in terms of a direct influence of Kant's thought on James. But it is not at all clear what the essential nature of, nor how extensive, such an influence must be to warrant the appellation.

That there was some influence is undeniable. James had studied Kant, of course, but far more significant were the indirect sources of Kantianism. First among these were Renouvier and Lotze, and his colleagues Peirce, Munsterberg, and Royce; but there were also the German psychophysicists Helmholtz and Fechner, as well as the American transcendentalists, who owed much to Kant via Coleridge. It would be an interesting and profitable task to try to sort out the myriad ways in which James's views might be traced via these intermediaries to Kant.[4]

However, in this exploration I want to take a different tack. I do not intend to offer a partial pedigree for James's pragmatic idealism – I will neither claim nor deny that it *descended* from Kant's metaphysics via a Darwinian epistemology. My analysis is offered as physiology, not phylogeny, and I take it as obvious that these are related in a variety of complex ways. For me, to characterize James as a Kantian is simply to note a family resemblance.

But it is often much easier to perceive a family resemblance than it is to state what it consists in, especially when the resemblance reflects the deep structure of the views in question rather than superficial verbal agreement on particular philosophical problems. A strategy is suggested by Kant's observation:

The field of philosophy . . . may be reduced to the following questions:

    1. What can I know?
    2. What ought I to do?
    3. What may I hope for?
    4. What is Man?

The first question is answered by *Metaphysics*, the second by *Morals*, the third by *Religion*, and the fourth by *Anthropology*. In reality, however, all these might be reckoned under anthropology, since the first three questions refer to the last. (Kant 1974, 186)

Thus Kant thought that our philosophical inquiries must be approached via investigation into the nature of humanity, as it conditions these three subject domains. This has sometimes been called Kant's "transcendental humanism": it is our given human nature which determines for us what are the most reasonable philosophical positions for us to hold.

Although James substitutes "psychology" for Kant's "anthropology," this transcendental humanism is a primary ground of their resemblance. They share as well some fundamental commitments regarding the constraints of human nature which then yield similar responses to Kant's questions. And often where they differ, the differences may be traced to the impact of Darwinian thought on James.

Let us examine the responses of Kant and James to these fundamental questions.[5]

I   WHAT CAN I KNOW?

In Kant's time, the paradigm of knowledge was to be found in Newton's physics. In reducing the complexity of the sensible world to a few fundamental laws, Newton had apparently shown that it was possible to anticipate the structure of physical events with certainty. But such judgments would seem to be problematic, for as Hume had argued, insofar as it is derived from our contact with independent objects, our experience of the world can only show that objects have stood in certain relations, not that they *must* so stand. And if the judgments of natural science are problematic, how much more so must be the judgments of metaphysics, which seem to extend the claims of reason beyond the bounds of any possible experience. How can these judgments be possible a priori?

Kant's solution was, of course, the transcendental idealism of his *Critique of Pure Reason*: "nothing in *a priori* knowledge can be ascribed to objects save what the thinking subject derives from itself" (Kant 1968, Bxiii). Scientific reason does not give us knowledge of relations obtaining among objects independent and separable from us but merely characterizes our sensible experience. Knowledge is a construct, made by taking up sensation into the a priori forms given by "the natural constitution of our reason" (Axiii).

The deterministic world of Nature is as much an invention as a discovery, constructed through the scientists' activity of projecting their hypotheses onto the data of the senses.

Reason has insight only into that which it produces after a plan of its own. ... Reason, holding in one hand its principles, according to which alone concordant appearances can be admitted as equivalent to laws, and in the other the experiment which it has devised in conformity with these principles, must approach nature to be taught by it ... [as] an appointed judge who compels the witnesses to answer questions which he himself has formulated. (Bxiii)

Thus the claims of scientific reason are to be justified not through their derivation but by their consequent fit with experience. An immediate corollary is that the domain of the a priori is exhausted in giving the determinate conditions of sensible experience, as fixed by the natural constitution of our reason. As Kant noted, "Can something be discovered through metaphysics? Yes; regarding the subject, but not the object" (as quoted in Cassirer 1981, 152).

So Kant's philosophy forever debars us from the very goal of traditional metaphysics – the security of certain knowledge of God, freedom, and immortality – since such claims cannot be justified by appeals to experience. In this lies Kant's real break with the tradition. In his view, not only is this security not possible, it is undesirable, for the very possibility of a moral life is contingent on showing the limitations of our theoretical knowledge. If the theoretical propositions of natural science stood on a par with the practical propositions concerning freedom, then reason would stand in conflict with itself, for we cannot reconcile the determinism of natural necessity with morality's presupposition of freedom. But we suffer no real loss here, for:

Morality does not, indeed, require that freedom should be understood, but only that it should not contradict itself, and so should at least allow of being thought, and that as thus thought it should place no obstacle in the way of a free act (viewed in another relation) likewise conforming to the mechanism of nature. . . . This, however, is only possible in so far as criticism has . . . limited all that we can theoretically *know* to mere appearances. (Bxxix–xxx)

"I have therefore found it necessary to deny *knowledge*," Kant continues, "in order to make room for *faith*."

In James's time, the sciences still provided the paradigms of knowledge, of course, but Darwin's theory of evolution through spontaneous variation and natural selection offered as well a general model of the means by which knowledge itself is constructed. James's friend and mentor, Chauncey Wright, argued, "our knowledges and rational beliefs result, *truly and literally*, from the survival of the fittest among our original and spontaneous beliefs" (Wright 1877, 116n). The idea of an evolutionary epistemology is deeper and richer than a simple commitment to a thoroughgoing naturalism. When the Darwinian separation of the source of characteristics from the mechanism of preservation is extended to mental evolution, the result is a new critique of empiricism. Beliefs need not be derived inductively from our experience to have meaning, for whatever their origin, they meet the test of experience ex post facto.

James developed this idea in his critiques of Spencer, whose error, he thought, lay in characterizing mental evolution as a merely passive "adjustment of inner to outer relations" (Spencer 1872, 1:387). James wrote in lecture notes:

[W]e can give no clear scientific description of the facts of psychology . . . without restoring to the inner, at every step, that active originality and spontaneous productivity which Spencer's law so entirely ignores . . . he repeats the defects of Darwin's predecessors [who] thought only of adaptation. They made the organism plastic to its environment. . . . Darwin almost wholly discards this. . . . He means to emphasize the truth that the regulator or preserver of the variation, the environment, is a different part from its producer. (Perry 1935, 1:478)

With his evolutionary view of mental development, James adopts Kant's "Copernican" emendation of empiricist epistemology: Knowledge, as the product of the interaction of the knower and his environment, finds its justification in part through the contribution of the knower.

For James, our experience consists in a variety of sensible qualities or "feelings," some of which may correspond to particular nonmental facts. But the mental realm also includes *interests* which do not straightforwardly represent particular external objects, but rather postulate "certain ideal ends." While "[c]orresponding itself to no actual or outward thing; referring merely to a future which *may* be, but which these interests now say *shall* be; purely ideal, in a word, they judge, dominate, determine all correspondences between the inner and the outer" (*EPh*, 11). Insofar as cognition is conditioned by these interests, not derived from our sensible experience, they represent "the real *a priori* element in cognition" (*EPh*, 11n).

Thus James acknowledges the fundamental tenet of Kant's transcendental idealism: essential reference must be made to an a priori conceptual element given through the spontaneity of our mental endowment. For both Kant and James, the world of our experience is a construct, the product of our mental activity. For James, however, its structure is the result of the natural evolution of the mind, which has over the course of time carved the world of experience from the raw material of experience, and which might have chosen a different world:

[T]he mind is at every stage a theater of simultaneous possibilities. Consciousness consists in the comparison of these with each other, the selection of some, and the suppression of the rest by the reinforcing and inhibiting agency of Attention. . . . But this is far from meaning that it implies nothing but passive faculty of sensation. As well might one say that the sculptor is passive, because the statue stood from eternity within the stone. So it did, but with a million different ones beside it. . . . We may even, by our reasonings, unwind things back to that black and jointless continuity of space and moving clouds of swarming atoms which science calls the only real world. But all the while the world we feel and live in, will be that which our ancestors and we, by slowly cumulative strokes of choice, have extricated out of this, as the sculptor extracts his statue by simply rejecting the other portions of the stone. (*EPs*, 51–2)

James continues with this corollary: "Other sculptors, other statues from the same stone! Other minds, other worlds from the same chaos!"

In the context of James's evolutionary view of the a priori, this claim has two different aspects. The first concerns his rejection of the rationalistic emphasis found in Kant's theoretical philosophy. For Kant, the structure of experience was fixed through the essential nature of theoretical reason. But for James the categories of our experience are determined by a priori elements of *interest*, and in his view the interest of theoretical reason in the unification of sensible representations is but one interest among others; it has no indefeasible claim over its challengers.

The interest of theoretic rationality . . . is but one of a thousand human purposes. When others rear their heads it must pack up its little bundle and retire till its turn recurs. The exaggerated dignity and value that philosophers have claimed for their solutions is thus greatly reduced. The only virtue their theoretic conception need have is simplicity, and a simple conception is an equivalent for the world only so far as the world is simple; the world meanwhile, whatever simplicity it may harbor, being also a mightily complex affair. (*EPh*, 56)

Thus James in his own way follows Kant in limiting knowledge to make room for faith:

I myself believe that all the magnificent achievements of mathematical and physical science – our doctrines of evolution, of uniformity of law, and the rest – proceed from our indomitable desire to cast the world into a more rational shape in our minds than the shape into which it is thrown by the crude order of our experience. The world has shown itself, to a great extent, plastic to this demand of ours for rationality. How much farther it will show itself plastic no one can say. Our only means of finding out is to try; and I, for one, feel as free to try conceptions of moral as of mechanical or logical rationality. If a certain formula for expressing the nature of the world violates my moral demand, I shall feel as free to throw it overboard, or at least to doubt it, as if it disappointed my demand for uniformity of sequence, for example; the one demand being, so far as I can tell, quite as subjective and emotional as the other is. (*WB*, 115–16)

While James's denial of Kantian rationalism of course marks a major difference between their views, the distance between them here should not be exaggerated. James would recognize that the interest of theoretic rationality is necessary for any systematic experience of objects, and might even allow that in relation to the unification of the manifold of sensations it entails a unique set of theoretical categories.[6] However, the influence of Darwin has shifted James's attention from an abstract and universal Reason to the concrete reasoning individual in the natural order. From this point of view, although the evolution of consciousness and the capacity to reason have contributed greatly to the survival of the human species, other characteristic interests also influence our cognition and ground our actions – thereby determining the structure of our experience. What James objects to is Kant's identification of himself with his faculty of theoretical reason. For him, nothing less than the "whole man" can be the proper subject of philosophy: "Pretend what we may, the whole man within us is at work when we form our philosophic opinions. Intellect, will, taste, and passion co-operate just as they do in practical affairs" (WB, 76).

The second aspect of James's claim "Other minds, other worlds from the same chaos!" is also grounded in his Darwinism; it rejects Kant's view that philosophy considers the particular only in the universal. In lecture notes from this period James writes:

Darwin's doctrine shows no essential difference between individual characters & generic ones to exist. Any difference is a diff. of a real kind – even an accidens is one. Nature a continuum from wh. we carve as we please, and in carving always rethink some eternal tho't. The full plethora is God's way of thinking. The character of the individuals in their totality are the only ones *realized*. The rest are abstractions. (Houghton, bMS Am 1092.9 (4423), published in part, *MEN*, 196–7)

On a separate sheet he notes: "Each individual is a kind with one example." According to Darwin, each individual can be taken to represent a real kind, insofar as it is distinguished from others through spontaneous variations that might prove to have adaptive value and thus be propagated through that individual's offspring. Yet each of its offspring might in turn be distinguished by spontaneous variations – *must be* so distinguished, for as James notes, on this view *any* difference is a difference of a real kind.[7]

Thus the array of interests that determines the a priori structure of experience may vary for each individual – "other minds, other worlds" applies distributively, each individual determining "his own world."

The truth appears to be that every individual man may, if it pleases him, set up his private categorical imperative of what rightness or excellence in thought shall consist in, and these different ideals, instead of entering upon the scene armed with a warrant – whether derived [through evolution] from the polyp or from a transcendental source – appear only as so many brute affirmations left to fight it out upon the chess-board among themselves. They are, at best, postulates, each of which must depend on the general consensus of experience as a whole to bear out its validity. The formula which proves to have the most massive destiny will be the true one. But this is a point which can only be solved *ambulando*, and not by any *a priori* definition. . . . Our respective hypotheses and postulates help to shape the course of thought, but the only thing which we all agree in assuming is, that thought will be coerced away from them if they are wrong. (*EPh*, 17,20)

However, this can only be true within limits; it is bounded by the extent of determination of the structure of sensible experience through interest and by the extent of variation determined by the course of natural evolution. While the question of our convergence can only be solved *ambulando*, the hypothesis of James's "empiricist pluralism" (*WB*, 208) is that it will remain "a pluralistic restless universe, in which no single point of view can ever take in the whole scene." (*WB*, 136).

II WHAT OUGHT I TO DO?

Kant believed that as physical beings in the natural order, we are impelled by nature to perform certain actions, but the possibility of moral action is the possibility of freedom. In acting morally, we act according to a law not given in the physical world, but by pure practical reason – we say that something *ought* to be so even if it is not, was not, or never will be so. We try, through our actions, to change the world and bring it into conformity with this law.

I entitle the world a *moral world,* in so far as it may exist in accordance with moral laws; and this is what by means of the freedom of the rational being it *can be,* and what according to the necessary laws of morality it *ought to be.* Owing to our here leaving out of account all conditions . . . , this world is so far thought as an intelligible world only. To this extent, therefore, it is a mere idea, though at the same time a practical idea, which really can have, as it also ought to have, an influence upon the sensible world, to bring that world, so far as may be possible, into conformity with the idea. The idea of a moral world has, therefore, objective reality . . . as referring to the sensible world, viewed, however, as being an object of pure reason in its practical employment, that is, as a *corpus mysticum* of the rational beings in it, so far as the free will of each being is, under moral laws, in complete systematic unity with itself and with the freedom of every other. (Kant 1968, A808–B836)

Pure practical reason is the objective law of freedom: to act under the idea of freedom is to overcome one's nature by choosing from among the acts to which we are inclined only those which are consistent with a similar choice for all, subjugating one's interests to the universal form of the moral law. The subjugation of interest to the moral law is a categorical imperative – an obligation grounded in reason – and only insofar as we follow this categorical demand can we be said to act freely.

Kant refers to this goal of the systematic unity of all rational beings in the free pursuit of their interests as "the kingdom of ends." In it we abstract "from the personal differences between rational beings, and also from all the content of their private ends . . . to conceive a whole of all ends in systematic conjunction (a whole both of rational beings as ends in themselves and also of the personal ends which each may set before himself)" (Kant 1964, 101; Ak. 433).

Moral worth lies in the attempt to act under this ideal, not in whatever consequences accrue in the physical world: since all natural events are subject to universal law, other factors may intervene and morality may fail of complete effect. The moral life is thus a struggle to overcome inclination and make the moral law the highest determining factor in all one's choices. In spite of our individual failures to act morally, nonetheless:

[H]istory . . . permits us to hope that if we attend to the play of freedom of the will in the large, we may be able to discern a regular movement in it, and that what seems complex and chaotic in the single individual may be seen from the standpoint of the human race to be a steady and progressive though slow evolution of its original endowment. (Kant 1963, 11; Ak. 17)

Even though it lay at the center of his thinking, James never offered a full characterization of his moral philosophy. It grew gradually out of his early experience and must be teased out of remarks in various essays written at various times.

Like Kant, James's early training as a scientist had led him to think of the natural order as deterministic. His study of physiology in Berlin in 1867 apparently precipitated a depression which lasted for several years. To a friend he wrote in March of 1869:

> I'm swamped in an empirical philosophy. I feel that we are nature through and through, that we are wholly conditioned, that not a wiggle of our will happens save as the result of physical laws; and yet, not withstanding, we are *en rapport* with reason. How to conceive it? Who knows? (*Letters*, 1:152–3)

And in his diary for 1 February 1870, he noted, "Today, I about touched bottom, and perceive plainly that I must face the choice with open eyes; Shall I *frankly* throw the moral business overboard, as one unsuited to my innate aptitudes, or shall I follow it, and it alone, making everything else mere stuff for it?" (Perry 1935, 1:322). By "moral business" James apparently meant the attempt to overcome his selfish nature through free application of his will. Ultimately he decided in its favor, for his diary entry for 30 April reads:

> I think that yesterday was a crisis in my life. I finished the first part of Renouvier's 2nd Essay, and saw no reason why his definition of free will – the sustaining of a thought *because I choose to* when I might have other thoughts – need be the definition of an illusion. At any rate I will assume for the present – until next year – that it is no illusion. My first act of free will shall be to believe in free will. (*Letters*, 1:147–8)

Thus James found in Renouvier's neo-Kantian doctrine of freedom a way to reconcile his scientific understanding with the possibility of free will, and therefore morality: "Liberty is the centre of gravity of [Renouvier's] system, *which henceforth becomes a moral philosophy*" (*ECR*, 266; emphasis added).

For James, "an act has no ethical quality at all unless it be chosen out of several all equally possible" (*EPs*, 50), and thus it is the commitment to freedom which makes for a moral philosophy. But like Kant, James thinks the reasoning must run from the presumed validity of the moral judgment to freedom. In a letter to Renouvier he writes:

I believe more and more that free will, if accepted at all, must be accepted as a postulate in justification of our moral judgment that certain things already done might have been better done. This implies that something different was possible in their place. . . . So, for entirely practical reasons, I hold that we are justified in believing that both falsehood and evil to some degree *need not have been.* (Perry 1935, 1:682–3)

The standpoint of moral judgment assumes that the merely theoretical ideal of a deterministic natural order is false and that freedom is real, for a moral judgment assumes that something that has been done to ill effect could have been done otherwise and better. To act morally, for James, is thus to act under the postulate of freedom.

It is at the same time to act under some ideal end set by human desire. Ethical judgments "presuppose some Good, End or Interest" and accordingly they are independent of the natural order assumed by science, because "goal[s] cannot be posited at all so long as we consider the purely physical order of existence" (*EPs,* 43).

[T]he words Use, Advantage, Interest, Good, find no application in a world in which no consciousness exists. Things there are neither good or bad; they simply are or are not. Ideal truth to exist at all requires that a mind also exist which shall deal with it as a judge deals with the law, really creating that which it only professes to declare. (*EPs,* 44)

The ideal truth at the basis of ethics, that some thing is *best,* is "an ultimate, arbitrary expression of feeling, an absolute fiat or decree" on the part of consciousness.

A letter from James's depressive period indicates more of the determinate content of his own moral ideal:

All I can tell you is the thought that with me outlasts all others, and onto which, like a rock, I find myself washed up when the waves of doubt are weltering over all the rest of the world; and that is the thought of my having a will, and of my belonging to a brotherhood of men possessed of a capacity for pleasure and pains of different kinds. . . . And if we have to give up all hope of seeing into the purposes of God, or to give up theoretically the idea of final causes, . . . we can, by our will, make the enjoyment of our brothers stand us in the stead of a final cause. . . . (*Letters,* 1:130–2)

Another letter of the same period restates this view of the end of moral action: "if one can set out with the supposition of harmony among phenomena as the *summum bonum,* and look upon the world as a progressive development, I don't know whether such ['an optimistic'] faith be not the best. It seems to be so practically at any rate" (Perry 1935, 1:160–1).

James, like Kant, sees the moral life as a struggle to overcome the motives to action provided by our natural inclinations:

> [T]he strongest mere traction lies in the line of the sensual impulse. The moral [motive] appears in comparison with this, a still small voice which must be artificially reinforced to prevail. Effort is what reinforces it . . . [a]nd if a brief definition of moral action were required, none could be given which would better fit appearances than this: It is action in the line of greatest resistance. (*EPs*, 119–20)

Moral action requires the subordination of certain sensual desires to the demands of a higher ideal and entails effort to overcome the motives provided by ordinary pleasures and pains. But there can be no guarantee that the action will actually ensue: "whether the act do [sic] follow or not upon the representation is a matter quite immaterial so far as the *willing* of the act represented goes. . . . In a word, volition is a psychic or moral fact pure and simple, and is absolutely completed when the *intention* or *consent* is there" (*EPs*, 107).

The aim of "ethical philosophy," James says, "is to find an account of the moral relations that obtain among things, which will weave them into the unity of a stable system, and make of the world what one may call a genuine universe from the ethical point of view" (*WB*, 141). The task of the ethical philosopher is the task of practical reason, the search for unity amidst the diversity of ideals chosen by given individuals. Thus James continues:

> So far as the world resists reduction to the form of unity, so far as ethical propositions seem unstable, so far does the philosopher fail of his ideal. The subject matter of his study is the ideals he finds existing in the world; the purpose which guides him is this ideal of his own, of getting them into a certain form. (*WB*, 141–2)

The moral philosopher is seeking to use reason to establish some unity amidst the diversity of given moral ideas; he tries to establish an ethical philosophy without determining the content of the particular ideal which any given individual ought to follow.

James thinks that there is only one possible way to provide an impartial measure, one which abstracts from the content of any particular ideal:

Since everything which is demanded is by that fact a good, must not the guiding principle for ethical philosophy (since all demands conjointly cannot be satisfied in this poor world) be simply to satisfy at all times *as many demands as we can?* That act must be the best act, which makes for the *best whole*, in the sense of awakening the least sum of dissatisfactions. In the casuistic scale, therefore, those ideals must be written highest which *prevail at the least cost*, or by whose realization the least possible number of other ideals are destroyed. (*WB*, 155)

In seeking the form of the highest ideal through the application of reason to ethics, we must try to respect each individual's ends as our own and satisfy as many of her demands as we can. Since we ought to act under the ideal with the most authority, we ought to choose to act under that ideal which is closest to the unattainable goal of the preservation of all purposes. However, since for James the interest of reason is only one interest among others, he cannot agree with Kant that the demand of this rule of practical reason is *necessarily* binding on all individuals. Only insofar as reason determines an ethical ideal through its own goal of unity amidst the diversity of given ideals is acting morally acting in accord with pure practical reason; individuals might still act morally, from James's point of view, if they follow lower ideals. But luckily, there are some persons who follow the demand of pure practical reason, for they serve as the source for societal progress:

Since victory and defeat there must be, the victory to be *philosophically* prayed for is that of the more inclusive side – of the side which even in the hour of triumph will to some degree do justice to the ideals in which the vanquished party's interest lay. The course of history is nothing but the story of men's struggles from generation to generation to find the more and more inclusive order. *Invent some manner* of realizing your own ideals which will also satisfy the alien demands – that and that only is the path of peace! Following this path, society has shaken itself into one sort of relative equilibrium after another by a series of social discoveries quite analogous to those of science. (*WB*, 155–6; emphasis on "philosophically," added)

. . . The pure philosopher can only follow the windings of the spectacle, confident that the line of least resistance will always be towards the richer and more inclusive arrangement, and that by one tack after another some approach to the kingdom of heaven is incessantly made. (*WB*, 156–7)

James thus envisions Kant's kingdom of ends as the product of an evolutionary process determined by the spontaneous ideals of freedom, equality, and unity; "little by little, there comes some stable gain; for the world does get more humane, and the religion of democracy tends toward permanent increase" (TT, 156).

III WHAT MAY I HOPE FOR?

"Hope" expresses an element of uncertainty that would have been unsettling to Kant's peers, operating in the context of a rationalist Christian theology with its emphasis on the absoluteness of God's existence and life after death for the faithful. However, the upshot of his Critique is that theoretical reason warrants only agnosticism: although the very ideas of God and immortality are immanent in the natural structure of reason, only experience could yield actual knowledge of the existence of God and the immortal soul, and our sensible experience is clearly inadequate to fund these concepts. But this is not to deny the existence of God or a future life; it only states the limits of merely theoretical reason. But there is a prima facie tension between the practical and theoretical applications of reason.

While pure practical reason demands that we make our actions conform to the moral law, theoretical reason tells us that nonetheless all our actions and their effects within the sensible world are completely determined by other natural events. There can be accordingly no *guarantee* from the theoretical standpoint that actions in accord with the moral law will lead to the satisfaction of our deepest desires. But there would be little motivation to do our duty if happiness in accord with morality was not at least possible. Moreover, the hope of religion is hope for a state in which happiness and morality *necessarily* coincide. But this would be impossible without a God who guarantees that this state *must* come in a life hereafter.

Accordingly, Kant offers a *moral* argument for the existence of God and immortality:

[With respect to morality] it is absolutely necessary that something must happen, namely, that I must in all points conform to the moral law. The end is here irrefragably established, and according to such insight as I can have, there is only one condition under which this end can connect with all other ends, and thereby have practical validity, namely, that there be a God and a future world. . . . Since, therefore, the moral precept is at the same time my maxim . . . , I inevitably believe in the existence of God and in a future life, and I am certain that nothing can shake this belief, since my moral principles would thereby be themselves overthrown, and I cannot disclaim them without becoming abhorrent in my own eyes. (Kant 1968, A828–B857)

We are justified in acting with a moral certainty that God exists and that he will guarantee future happiness in accord with present virtue. This moral certainty falls short of *knowledge*, however; we can draw no theoretically valid conclusions from these postulates. We assume their truth "for the purposes of framing a conception of the possibility of the final end morally prescribed to [us], . . . for the direction of our energies toward the realization of that end" (Kant 1952, 121, 124; Ak. 453, 455). The virtuous individual, struggling to approximate the seemingly impossible demands of the moral law, feels "a pure moral need for the real existence of a Being, whereby . . . morality gains in strength" (113; Ak. 446).

James agreed with Kant that the idea of God arises naturally, given to us by nature of our mind, but also that this was insufficient to ground claims of his existence:

My thesis . . . is this: that *some* outward reality of a nature defined as God's nature . . . is the only ultimate object that is at the same time rational and possible for the human mind's contemplation. . . . Theism, whatever its objective warrant, would thus be seen to have a subjective anchorage in its congruity with our nature as thinkers. (WB, 93–4)

James also rejected the pretensions of rational theology to offer proofs of the existence of a deity: "the attempt to demonstrate by purely intellectual processes the truth of the deliverances of direct religious experience is absolutely hopeless" (VRE, 359). And concerning the soul he concluded, "So far, no one can be compelled to subscribe to it for definite scientific reasons" (PP, 1:329). He added, nevertheless, "The reader who finds any comfort in the idea of the Soul is, however, perfectly free to continue to believe in it; for our reasonings have not established the non-existence of the Soul; they have only proved its superfluity for scientific purposes" (PP, 1:332). For James, as for Kant, the grounds of faith are found in our practical needs; "Infra-theistic conceptions, materialism and agnosticisms, are irrational because they are inadequate stimuli to man's practical nature" (WB, 106). Accordingly, he offered his own moral argument for the existence of God and a future life.

James argues that "For a philosophy to succeed on a universal scale it must define the future *congruously with our spontaneous powers"* (*WB*, 70). Our volitional nature sets for us, over and above our theoretic concern for unity and simplicity, certain demands that call equally for satisfaction. We try to see the world in terms of ideal should-be's, and we are dissatisfied with any conception that leaves our desires hopelessly frustrated. In order for a conception of the universe to be rational, it must give us reason to believe that our deepest aspirations might be satisfied through our personal action.

The monstrously lopsided equation of the universe and knower, which we postulate as the ideal of cognition, is perfectly paralleled by the no less lopsided equation of the universe and the *doer.* We demand in it a character for which our emotions and active propensities will be a match. (*WB*, 71)

A view of the world that satisfies purely theoretical requirements will be incomplete and irrational, unless it also accords with the demands made in the name of practical rationality. We are impelled by our own nature to adopt a view of the universe which will give us reasons for action in ways consistent with our ideals.

Nothing could be more absurd than to hope for the definitive triumph of any philosophy which would refuse to legitimate . . . the more powerful of our emotional and practical tendencies. Fatalism, whose solving word in all crises of behavior is "all striving is vain," will never reign supreme, for the impulse to take life strivingly is indestructible in the race. Moral creeds which speak to that impulse will be widely sucessful in spite of inconsistency, vagueness, and shadowy determination of expectancy. Man needs a rule for his will, and will invent one if one not be given to him. (*WB*, 74–5)

What we need is a view of the world which will appeal to our active powers and allow us to pursue life in "the strenuous mood."

This view, James believes, must be theistic, for "in a merely human world without God, the appeal to our moral energy falls short of its maximal stimulating power" (*WB*, 160). If there were a God – one who is sympathetic to my ideals – the thought of this God, working his best to satisfy my ideals, affords me the belief that if I but put my own shoulder to the wheel, their demands may yet be satisfied. "When . . . a God is there, . . . the infinite perspective opens out. . . . The imperative ideals now begin to speak with an altogether new objectivity and significance, and to utter the penetrating, shattering, tragically challenging note of appeal" (*WB*, 160). For the sake of living a strenuous life in pursuit of a moral ideal, we *need* a God.

Thus James, like Kant, suggests that from the practical point of view, God may be *postulated* for the sake of morality:

It would seem, too – and this is my final conclusion – that the stable and systematic moral universe for which the ethical philosopher asks is fully possible only in a world where there is a divine thinker with all-enveloping demands. . . . In the interests of our own ideal of systematically unified moral truth, therefore, we, as would-be philosophers, must postulate a divine thinker, and pray for the victory of the religious cause. (*WB*, 161)

We are therefore justified in acting with *moral* certainty that God exists beyond the bounds of the world of natural science. "[W]e have a right to believe the physical order to be only a partial order; . . . we have a right to supplement it by an unseen spiritual order which we assume on trust, if only thereby life may seem to us better worth living again" (*WB*, 49).

Unlike Kant, James apparently did not see his moral argument for the existence of God as equally supporting a faith in immortality. Nonetheless, his sympathies seem to run in that direction. In a letter to Stumpf he wrote: "I never felt the *rational* need of immortality as you seem to feel it; but as I grow older I confess that I feel the practical need of it much more than I ever did before; and that combines with reasons . . . to give me a growing faith in its reality" (Perry 1935, 2:345).

Just what the character of James's "practical need" for immortality is, is unclear, but further perspective is gained from his answers on a questionnaire on religious belief:

Do you believe in personal immortality?
Never keenly; but more strongly as I grow older.
If so, why?
Because I am just getting fit to live. (*Letters*, 2:214)

Presumably when James says that he is "just getting fit to live" he has reference to his contributions toward furthering his moral ideal. Compare his remark in the *Principles of Psychology*:

The demand for immortality is essentially teleological. We believe ourselves immortal because we believe ourselves *fit* for immortality. A "substance" ought surely to perish, we think, if not worthy to survive; and an insubstantial "stream" to prolong itself provided it be worthy, if the nature of Things is organized in the rational way in which we trust it is. (*PP*, 1:330)

It seems likely that James's "practical need" for immortality is founded in the view that the "worthy" individual – "fit" for immortality – through the continuation of life after death, might still be able to contribute to the progress of the world toward moral perfection.

I hope that I have succeeded in showing just what it might mean to characterize James's philosophy as an "evolutionary Kantianism." It is to recognize that the heart of Kantianism is to be found in the "Copernican turn" of transcendental humanism: the search to establish what are the most reasonable philosophical views for us to hold through examination of our nature as autonomous rational individuals. It is to see that as a consequence of an examination of our epistemological situation, our views of reality are necessarily conditioned by our finite human limitations, and as such cannot exhaust the realm of possibility. It is to see that as a consequence of our capacity for self-determination, the first virtue of the ideal human community is democratic respect for the pluralism of perspectives and projects. And it is to see that our hope for the future of this community can be grounded in a reasoned faith in a higher power, fighting alongside us for our ideals.

NOTES

1 What has been elided here is important: "What similarity can there possibly be between human laws imposed *a priori* on all experience as 'legislative,' and human ways of thinking that grow up piecemeal among the details of experience because on the whole they work the best? It is this rationalistic part of Kant that pragmatism is expressly meant to overthrow. Both its theory of knowledge and its metaphysics go with an empiricist mode of thought" (Perry 1935, 2:469). It is the task of this paper to answer James's rhetorical question and show how much of Kant's world-view survives the translation into pragmatic empiricism.

2 James himself once suggested this comparison in an unpublished letter to Henry William Rankin, where he writes: "*Adopt your hypothesis, and see how it agrees with life – That is faith. As Kant says I have swept away knowledge in order to make room for Faith;* and that seems to me the absolutely sound and healthy position" (12 June 1897, James Papers, Houghton Library. An excerpt appears in *WB*, 252).

3 Kuklick's claim has not gone unchallenged. Madden and Hare, in their

review of Kuklick's book, write: "The central contentions are that James was a Kantian and an idealist. Kuklick's arguments for these claims, though weak, are clear enough. While we agree that James studied Kant and was in some degree influenced by the Kantian way of approaching the problems of metaphysics and epistemology, we are unconvinced that James was a Kantian fundamentally. James, like Kant, saw as his metaphysical task mediation between rationalism and empiricism, but his way of achieving this mediation was very different from Kant's. His broadening of empiricism cannot be described fairly as Kantian" (Madden and Hare 1978, 58).

4 The best place to start such a study would be Pochmann's (1957) monumental study. For James's massive debt to Renouvier, see Long 1925; for his debt to Lotze, see Kraushaar 1936.

5 It should be noted that I am drawing only on James's writings in the period prior to the publication of *Pragmatism*. While James certainly enters a new phase as a philosopher at this time, I would contend that the fundamental structure of his world-view remains unaltered. But that discussion lies beyond the scope of this paper.

6 "[T]he reduction of the phenomenal Chaos to rational form must stop at a certain point. It is a limited process, – bounded by the number of elementary attributes which cannot be mutually identified, the specific *qualia* of representation, on the one hand, and, on the other, by the number of entities (atoms or monads or what not) with their complete mathematical determinations, requisite for deducing the fulness of the concrete world. All of these irreducible data form a system, no longer phenomenally rational, *inter se*, but bound together by what are for us empirical laws. We merely find the system existing as a matter of fact, and write it down. In short, a plurality of categories and an immense number of primordial entities, determined according to these categories, is the minimum of philosophical baggage, the only possible compromise between the need of clearness and the need of unity" (*EPh*, 54).

7 This abstracts, of course, from our current knowledge of the genetic characterization of species; the point of view here is a metaphysical one. It is important to recognize that in the first instance the doctrines of spontaneous variation and natural selection are not limited to any particular sort of being. All that is required is some mechanism of propagation of characters from one individual to another, and an external force constraining the propagation in limiting the continued existence of the individual.

BIBLIOGRAPHY

I PRIMARY LITERATURE

Original editions

The Principles of Psychology. 2 vols. New York: Holt, 1890.

Psychology (Briefer Course). New York: Holt, 1892.

The Will to Believe, and Other Essays in Popular Philosophy. New York: Longmans, Green and Company, 1897.

Human Immortality: Two Supposed Objections to the Doctrine. Boston: Houghton Mifflin, 1898.

Talks to Teachers on Psychology: And to Students on Some of Life's Ideals. New York: Holt, 1899.

The Varieties of Religious Experience: A Study in Human Nature. New York: Longmans, Green and Company, 1902.

Pragmatism: A New Name for Some Old Ways of Thinking. New York: Longmans, Green and Company, 1907.

The Meaning of Truth: A Sequel to "Pragmatism." New York: Longmans, Green and Company, 1909.

A Pluralistic Universe: Hibbert Lectures at Manchester College on the Present Situation in Philosophy. New York: Longmans, Green and Company, 1909.

Posthumously published

Some Problems of Philosophy: A Beginning of an Introduction to Philosophy. New York: Longmans, Green and Company, 1911.

Essays in Radical Empiricism. New York: Longmans, Green and Company, 1912.

385

The standard edition

The Works of William James. Edited by Frederick H. Burkhardt, Fredson Bowers, and Ignas K. Skrupskelis. Cambridge: Harvard University Press, 1975–1988.

The individual volumes, with date of publication are as follows.

Volume 1   *Pragmatism* (1975)
Volume 2   *The Meaning of Truth* (1975)
Volume 3   *Essays in Radical Empiricism* (1976)
Volume 4   *A Pluralistic Universe* (1977)
Volume 5   *Essays in Philosophy* (1978)
Volume 6   *The Will to Believe* (1979)
Volume 7   *Some Problems of Philosophy* (1979)
Volume 8   *The Principles of Psychology* (3 vols.) (1981)
Volume 9   *Essays in Religion and Morality* (1982)
Volume 10   *Talks to Teachers on Psychology* (1983)
Volume 11   *Essays in Psychology* (1983)
Volume 12   *Psychology: The Briefer Course* (1984)
Volume 13   *The Varieties of Religious Experience* (1985)
Volume 14   *Essays in Psychical Research* (1986)
Volume 15   *Essays, Comments and Reviews* (1987)
Volume 16   *Manuscript Lectures* (1988)
Volume 17   *Manuscripts, Essays and Notes* (1988)

Correspondence

The Letters of William James. 2 vols. Edited by Henry James. Boston: Atlantic Monthly Press, 1920.
Selected Letters of William James. Edited by Elizabeth Hardwick. Boston: David R. Godine, 1961.
The Correspondence of William James. William and Henry. Edited by Ignas K. Skrupskelis and Elizabeth M. Berkeley. 3 vols. Charlottesville and London: University Press of Virginia, 1992–4. Nine additional volumes are planned.

II SECONDARY LITERATURE

Aiken, Henry D. 1962. "American Pragmatism Reconsidered: II. William James." *Commentary* 34: 238–46.
Allen, Barry. 1993. *Truth in Philosophy.* Cambridge: Harvard University Press.

1994. "Atheism, Relativism, Enlightenment and Truth." *Studies in Religion* 23: 167–78.

Allen, Gay Wilson. 1970. *William James*. Minneapolis: University of Minnesota Press.

Allison, Dorothy. 1994. *Skin: Talking about Sex, Class, and Literature*. Ithaca, N.Y.: Firebrand Books.

Austin, J. L. 1962. *Sense and Sensibilia*. Edited by G. J. Warnock. Oxford: Oxford University Press.

Ayer, A. J. 1968. *The Origins of Pragmatism: Studies in the Philosophy of Charles Sanders Peirce and William James*. San Francisco: Freeman, Cooper.

Barrett, William. 1978. *The Illusion of Technique: A Search for Meaning in a Technological Civilization*. New York: Doubleday and Company.

Barzun, J. 1983. *A Stroll with William James*. New York: Harper and Row.

Baym, Nina. 1978. *Women's Fiction: A Guide to Novels by and about Women in America: 1820–1870*. Ithaca and London: Cornell University Press.

1984. *Readers, Writers and Reviewers: Responses to Fiction in Antebellum America*. Ithaca and London: Cornell University Press.

Beasely, Conger. 1990. "In Animals We Find Ourselves." *Orion: Nature Quarterly* 9, 2 (spring): 16–23.

Bennett, Jonathan. 1971. *Locke, Berkeley, Hume*. Oxford: Oxford University Press.

Bergson, Henri. 1959. *Oeuvres*. Paris: Presses Universitaires de France.

Best, Steven, and Douglas Kellner. 1991. *Postmodern Theory: Critical Interrogations*. New York: Guilford Press.

Bird, Graham. 1986. *William James*. New York: Routledge and Kegan Paul.

Boring, Edwin G. 1953. "A History of Introspection." *Psychological Bulletin* 50: 169–86.

1961. *Psychologist at Large: An Anthology and Selected Essays*. New York: Basic Books.

Bourne, Randolph. 1977. *The Radical Will: Selected Writings, 1911–1918*. New York: Urizen.

Bradley, F. H. 1914. *Essays on Truth and Reality*. Oxford: Oxford University Press.

Brennen, Bernard P. 1961. *The Ethics of William James*. New York: Bookman Associates.

Brent, Joseph. 1993. *Charles Sanders Peirce: A Life*. Bloomington: Indiana University Press.

Brink, D. O. 1989. *Moral Realism and the Foundations of Ethics*. Cambridge University Press.

Brodhead, Richard H. 1993. *Cultures of Letters: Scenes of Reading and*

Writing in Nineteenth-Century America. Chicago and London: University of Chicago Press.

Brown, Gillian. 1990. *Domestic Individualism: Imagining Self in Nineteenth-Century America*. Berkeley and Los Angeles: University of California Press.

Bruce, Dickson. 1992. "W. E. B. Du Bois and the Idea of Double Consciousness." *American Literature* 64: 299–309.

Burge, T. 1979. "Individualism and the Mental." *Midwest Studies in Philosophy* 4: 73–121.

——— 1986. "Individualism and Psychology." *The Philosophical Review* 95: 3–46.

Carlson, Thomas Bruce. 1990. "The Pragmatic Individual: From Kant to James." Ph.D. diss., Harvard University.

Carter, Stephen. 1993. *The Culture of Disbelief: How American Law and Politics Trivialize Religious Devotion*. New York: Basic Books.

Cassirer, Ernst. 1981. *Kant's Life and Thought*. Translated by James Haden. New Haven: Yale University Press.

Churchland, Paul. 1984. *Matter and Consciousness*. Cambridge: MIT Press.

Clifford, W. K. 1877. "The Ethics of Belief." *Contemporary Review* 29: 283–309.

——— 1879. "The Influence upon Morality of a Decline in Religious Belief." In his *Lectures and Essays*, vol. 2. London: Macmillan Publishers Ltd.

Cobb-Stevens, Richard. 1974. *James and Husserl: The Foundations of Meaning*. The Hague: Martinus Nijhoff.

Cooper, W. E. 1990. "William James's Theory of Mind." *Journal of the History of Philosophy* 28, 4(October): 571–93.

Cormier, Harvey Jerome. 1993. "William James's Reconception of Truth." Ph.D. diss., Harvard University.

Cotkin, George. 1990. *William James: Public Philosopher*. Baltimore and London: Johns Hopkins University Press.

Croce, Ann Jerome. 1988. "Phantoms from an Ancient Loom: Elizabeth Barstow Stoddard and the American Novel, 1860–1900." Ph.D. diss., Brown University.

Dancy, Jonathan. 1993. *Moral Reasons*. Oxford: Basil Blackwell.

Dancy, Jonathan, and Ernest Sosa, eds. 1992. *A Companion to Epistemology*. Oxford: Basil Blackwell.

Davies, Martin. 1991/92. "Perceptual Content and Local Supervenience." *Proceedings of the Aristotelian Society* 92: 21–45.

Dearborn, Mary V. 1988. *Love in the Promised Land*. New York: Free Press.

Dewey, John. 1897. "The Psychology of Effort." Reprinted in *The Early Works*, vol. 5, edited by Jo Ann Boydston. Carbondale: Southern Illinois University Press, 1972.

——— 1905/10. "The Postulate of Immediate Empiricism." Reprinted in *The*

Middle Works, vol. 3, edited by Jo Ann Boydston. Carbondale: Southern Illinois University Press, 1977.

1908. "What Pragmatism Means by Practical." Reprinted in *The Middle Works*, vol. 4, edited by Jo Ann Boydston. Carbondale: Southern Illinois University Press, 1977.

1920. "The China Lectures of 1920." Reprinted in *The Middle Works*, vol. 12, edited by Jo Ann Boydston. Carbondale: Southern Illinois University Press, 1982.

1925. "The Development of American Pragmatism." Reprinted in *The Later Works*, vol. 2, edited by Jo Ann Boydston. Carbondale: Southern Illinois University Press, 1984.

[1929] 1958. *Experience and Nature*. La Salle, Ill.: Open Court Publishing Company. Reissued, New York: Dover Publications.

1934. *A Common Faith*. New Haven: Yale University Press.

1940. "The Vanishing Subject in the Psychology of James." Reprinted in *The Later Works*, vol. 14, edited by Jo Ann Boydston. Carbondale: Southern Illinois University Press, 1988.

1942. "William James and the World Today." Reprinted in *The Later Works*, vol. 15, edited by Jo Ann Boydston. Carbondale: Southern Illinois University Press, 1989.

1942a. "William James as Empiricist." Reprinted in *The Later Works*, vol. 15, edited by Jo Ann Boydston. Carbondale: Southern Illinois University Press, 1989.

1980. *Art as Experience*. New York: Putnam.

Douglas, Ann. 1977. *The Feminization of American Culture*. New York: Avon Books.

Du Bois, W. E. B. 1944. "My Evolving Program for Negro Freedom." In *What the Negro Wants*, edited by Rayford Logan. Chapel Hill: University of North Carolina Press.

1968. *Autobiography*. New York: International Publishers Company.

1986. *Writings*. New York: Library of America.

1992. *Black Reconstruction*. New York: Atheneum.

Early, Gerald. 1993. *Lure and Loathing: Essays on Race, Identity, and the Ambivalence of Assimilation*. New York: Penguin.

Edie, James. 1987. *William James and Phenomenology*. Bloomington: Indiana University Press.

Emerson, Ralph Waldo. 1983. *Essays and Lectures*. New York: Library of America.

Esposito, Joseph L. 1977. *Schelling's Idealism and Philosophy of Nature*. Lewisburg, Pa.: Bucknell University Press.

Evans, Elizabeth Glendower. 1929. "William James and his Wife." *The Atlantic Monthly*, September, 374–87.

Evans, Gareth. 1982. *The Varieties of Reference*. Oxford: Clarendon Press.

Feinstein, Howard M. 1894. *Becoming William James*. Ithaca and London: Cornell University Press.

Flanagan, Owen. 1984. *The Science of the Mind*. Cambridge: MIT Press.

Flower, Elizabeth, and Murray Murphey. 1977. *A History of Philosophy in America*. New York: Putnam.

Fodor, Jerry. 1992. *A Theory of Content and Other Essays*. Cambridge: MIT Press.

Ford, Marcus Peter. 1982. *William James's Philosophy*. Amherst: University of Massachusetts Press.

Gale, Richard M. 1980. "William James and the Ethics of Belief." *American Philosophical Quarterly* 17: 1–14.

    1991. *On the Nature and Existence of God*. Cambridge University Press.

    1994. "William James on the Identity of Self over Time." *The Modern Schoolman* 71: 165–89.

Geary, Susan. 1976. "The Domestic Novel as a Commerical Commodity: Making a Bestseller in the 1850's." *Papers of the Biographical Society of America* 70: 365–93.

Goodman, Russell B. 1990. *American Philosophy and the Romantic Tradition*. Cambridge University Press.

Gramsci, Antonio. 1971. *Selections from the Prison Notebooks*. Edited and translated by Quentin Hoare and Geoffrey Nowell Smith. New York: International Publishers Company.

Gurwitsch, Aron. 1964. *The Field of Consciousness*. Pittsburgh: Duquesne University Press.

Haldane, J. 1989. "Reid, Scholasticism, and Contemporary Philosophy of Mind." In *The Philosophy of Thomas Reid*, edited by M. Dalgarno and E. Mathews. Dodrecht: Kluwer.

    1992. "Putnam on Intentionality." *Philosophy and Phenomenological Research* 52: 671–82.

Harris, Susan K. 1990. *19th-Century American Women's Novels: Interpretive Strategies*. Cambridge University Press.

Harvey, Van A. 1979. "The Ethics of Belief Reconsidered." *Journal of Religion* 59: 406–20.

Hebb, D. O. 1949. *The Organization of Behavior*. New York: John Wiley and Sons.

Heller, Agnes. 1990. *A Philosophy of Morals*. Oxford: Basil Blackwell.

Hollinger, David A. 1985. "William James and the Culture of Inquiry." In *In the American Province: Studies in the History and Historiography of Ideas*, edited by David A. Hollinger. Bloomington: Indiana University Press.

    1992. "The 'Tough-Minded' Justice Holmes, Jewish Intellectuals, and the Making of an American Icon." In *The Legacy of Oliver Wendell*

Holmes, Jr., edited by Robert W. Gordon. Stanford: Stanford University Press.

Holt, Thomas. 1990. "The Political Uses of Alienation: W. E. B. Du Bois on Politics, Race, and Culture, 1903–40." *American Quarterly* 42: 301–23.

Hookway, Christopher. 1985. *Peirce.* London: Routledge.

——— 1990. "Vagueness, Logic and Interpretation." In *The Analytic Tradition,* edited by D. Bell and N. Cooper. Oxford: Basil Blackwell.

——— 1993. "Belief, Confidence and the Method of Science." *Transactions of the Charles S. Peirce Society* 29: 1–32.

Hopkins, Pauline. 1988. *Of One Blood.* In *The Magazine Novels.* New York: Oxford University Press.

Howe, Mark De Wolfe, ed. 1941. *Holmes–Pollock Letters.* Cambridge: Harvard University Press.

Hughes, H. Stuart. 1958. *Consciousness and Society: The Reconstruction of European Social Thought, 1890–1930.* New York: Alfred A. Knopf.

Humphrey, George. 1951. *Thinking: An Introduction to Its Experimental Psychology.* New York: John Wiley and Sons.

Husserl, Edmund. 1970. *Logical Investigations.* 2 vols. Translated by J. N. Findley. London: Routledge and Kegan Paul. Originally published 1900/1913.

Hutchison, William R. 1977. *The Modernist Impulse in American Protestantism.* Cambridge: Harvard University Press.

Jacoby, Russell. 1987. *The Last Intellectuals: American Culture in the Age of Academe.* New York: Basic Books.

James, Henry. 1984. "Elizabeth Stoddard." In *Essays on Literature, American Writers, English Writers.* New York: Library of America, 614–17.

——— 1984a. "Preface to the New York Edition of Portrait of a Lady." In *French Writers, Other European Writers, The Prefaces to the New York Edition.* New York: Library of America, 1070–85.

Johnston, Mark. 1989. "Dispositional Theories of Value." *Proceedings of the Aristotelian Society* suppl. vol. 63: 139–74.

Kallen, Horace. 1924. *Culture and Democracy in the United States.* New York: Boni and Liveright.

Kant, I. 1952. *Critique of Judgment.* Translated by J. C. Meredith. Oxford: Clarendon Press (Ak. v).

——— 1963. *Idea for a Universal History from a Cosmopolitan Point of View.* Translated by L. W. Beck in *On History.* Indianapolis: Bobbs-Merrill (Ak. viii).

——— 1964. *Groundwork of the Metaphysics of Morals.* Translated by H. J. Paton. New York: Harper and Row (Ak. iv).

——— 1968. *Critique of Pure Reason.* Translated by Norman Kemp Smith. New York: St. Martin's Press (Ak. iii and iv).

1974. *Logic.* Translated by R. Hartman and W. Schwartz. Indianapolis: Bobbs-Merrill (Ak. IX).

Kauber, Peter, and Peter H. Hare. 1974. "The Right and Duty to Will to Believe." *Canadian Journal of Philosophy* 4: 327–43.

Kelley, Mary. 1984. *Private Woman, Public Stage: Literary Domesticity in Nineteenth-Century America.* New York and Oxford: Oxford University Press.

Kloppenberg, James T. 1986. *Uncertain Victory: Social Democracy and Progressivism in European and American Thought, 1870–1920.* New York: Oxford University Press.

Kraushaar, Otto F. 1936. "Lotze's Influence on the Psychology of William James." *Psychological Review* 43: 235–57.

——— 1938. "What James's Philosophical Orientation Owed to Lotze." *Philosophical Review* 47: 517–26.

——— 1939. "Lotze as a Factor in the Development of James's Radical Empiricism and Pluralism." *Philosophical Review* 48: 455–71.

——— 1940. "Lotze's Influence on the Pragmatism and Practical Philosophy of William James." *Journal of the History of Ideas* 1: 439–58.

Kuklick, Bruce. 1977. *The Rise of American Philosophy: Cambridge, Massachusetts, 1860–1930.* New Haven: Yale University Press.

Lamberth, David C. Forthcoming. *Metaphysics, Experience and Religion in William James's Thought.* In *Cambridge Studies in Religion and Critical Thought*, edited by Wayne Proudfoot, Jeffrey L. Stout, and Nicholas Wolterstorff. Cambridge University Press.

Lears, T. J. Jackson. 1981. *No Place of Grace: Antimodernism and the Transformation of American Culture 1880–1920.* New York: Pantheon Books.

Lentricchia, Frank. 1986. *Ariel and the Police.* Madison: University of Wisconsin Press.

Levinson, Samuel. 1978. *Science, Metaphysics and the Chance of Salvation: An Interpretation of the Thought of William James.* AAR Dissertation Series. Missoula: Scholars Press.

——— 1981. *The Religious Investigations of William James.* Chapel Hill: University of North Carolina Press.

Lewis, R. W. B. 1991. *The Jameses: A Family Narrative.* New York: Anchor Doubleday.

Lewis, David. 1984. "Putnam's Paradox." *Australasian Journal of Philosophy* 62: 221–36.

Lewis, Levering David. 1993. *W. E. B. Du Bois: Biography of a Race, 1868–1919.* New York: Henry Holt.

Lightman, Bernard. 1987. *The Origins of Agnosticism: Victorian Unbelief and the Limits of Knowledge.* Baltimore: Johns Hopkins University Press.

Linschoten, Hans. 1968. *On the Way Toward a Phenomenological Psychol-*

ogy: The Psychology of William James. Pittsburgh: Duquesne University Press.

Lippmann, Walter. 1962. *A Preface to Politics.* Ann Arbor: University of Michigan Press.

1985. *Drift and Mastery.* Madison: University of Wisconsin Press.

Livingston, James. 1994. *Pragmatism and the Political Economy of Cultural Revolution, 1850–1940.* Chapel Hill: University of North Carolina Press.

Locke, Alain. 1989. "Who and What is 'Negro'?" In *The Philosophy of Alain Locke*, edited by Leonard Harris, 207–26. Philadelphia: Temple University Press.

ed. 1993. *The New Negro.* New York: Atheneum.

Long, Wilbur. 1925. "The Philosophy of Charles Renouvier and Its Influence on William James." Ph.D. diss., Harvard University.

Lukes, Steven. 1985. "Taking Morality Seriously." In *Morality and Objectivity: A Tribute to J. L. Mackie*, edited by T. Honderich. London: Routledge and Kegan Paul.

Lutz, Tom. 1991. *American Nervousness 1903: An Anecdotal History.* Ithaca and London: Cornell University Press.

Lyons, William. 1986. *The Disappearance of Introspection.* Cambridge: MIT Press.

Macfarlane, Alexander. 1916. *Lectures on Ten British Mathematicians of the Nineteenth Century.* New York: John Wiley and Sons.

MacIntyre, Alasdair, and Paul Ricoeur. 1969. *The Religious Significance of Atheism.* New York: Columbia University Press.

Madden, Edward H., and Peter H. Hare. 1978. Review of *The Rise of American Philosophy*, by B. Kuklick. *Transactions of the Charles S. Peirce Society* 14: 53–72.

Matlack, James H. 1967. "The Literary Career of Elizabeth Barstow Stoddard." Ph.D. diss., Yale University.

Matthiessen, F. O. 1962. *The James Family.* New York: Alfred A. Knopf.

McDowell, J. 1992. "Putnam on Mind and Meaning." *Philosophical Topics* 20: 35–48.

1994. *Mind and World.* Cambridge: Harvard University Press.

McNaughton, D. 1988. *Moral Vision.* Oxford: Basil Blackwell.

Merleau-Ponty, Maurice. 1968. *The Visible and the Invisible – Followed by Working Notes.* Evanston, Ill.: Northwestern University Press.

Milikan, R. 1984. *Language, Thought, and Other Biological Categories.* Cambridge: MIT Press.

Moore, Edward C. 1961. *American Pragmatism: Peirce, James and Dewey.* New York: Columbia University Press.

1966. *William James.* New York: Washington Square Press.

Moore, G. E. 1907–8. "Professor James' 'Pragmatism.' " *Proceedings of the Aristotelian Society*, n.s., 8: 33–77. Reprinted in Moore (1922).

1922. *Philosophical Studies*. London: Routledge and Kegan Paul.

Mouffe, Chantal. 1979. "Hegemony and Ideology in Gramsci." In *Gramsci and Marxist Theory*, edited by Chantal Mouffe. London and Boston: Routledge and Kegan Paul.

Murphey, Murray. 1968. "Kant's Children: The Cambridge Pragmatists." *Transactions of the Charles S. Peirce Society* 4: 3–33.

Myers, Gerald E. 1986. "Introspection and Self-Knowledge." *American Philosophical Quarterly* 23: 199–207.

1986a. *William James: His Life and Thought*. New Haven: Yale University Press.

Niebuhr, Richard R. 1983. *Streams of Grace: Studies of Jonathan Edwards, Samuel Taylor Coleridge and William James*. Kyoto: Doshisha University Press.

Nisbett, Robert E., and Timothy De Camp Wilson. 1977. "Telling More than We Can Know." *Psychological Review* 84: 231–59.

Olin, Doris, ed. 1992. *William James: Pragmatism, in Focus*. London and New York: Routledge and Kegan Paul.

Otten, Thomas. 1992. "Pauline Hopkins and the Hidden Self of Race." *English Literary History* 59: 227–56.

Peirce, Charles Sanders. 1877. "The Fixation of Belief." *Popular Science Monthly* 12: 1–15.

1931–60. *Collected Papers of Charles Sanders Peirce*. 8 vols. Edited by C. Hartshorne and P. Weiss (vols. 1–6) and A. Burks (vols. 7–8). Cambridge: Harvard University Press.

1992. *Reasoning and the Logic of Things*. Edited by K. Ketner and H. Putnam. Cambridge: Harvard University Press.

Perry, Ralph Barton. 1935. *The Thought and Character of William James*. 2 vols. Boston: Little, Brown and Company.

[1938] 1979. *In the Spirit of William James*. Reprint, Westport, Conn.: Greenwood Press.

Pettit, Philip, and John McDowell, eds. 1986. *Subject, Thought and Context*. Oxford: Clarendon Press.

Pochmann, Henry A. 1957. *German Culture in America 1600–1900: Philosophical and Literary Influences*. Madison: University of Wisconsin Press.

Poirier, Richard. 1987. *The Renewal of Literature*. New York: Random House.

1992. *Poetry and Pragmatism*. Cambridge: Harvard University Press.

1993. "Pragmatism and the Sentence of Death." In *Wild Orchids and Trotsky*, edited by Mark Edmundson. New York: Penguin.

Posnock, Ross. 1989. "Assessing the Oppositional: Contemporary Intellectual Strategies." *American Literary History* 1: 147–71.

1991. *The Trial of Curiosity: Henry James, William James and the Challenge of Modernity*. New York: Oxford University Press.

Pratt, J. B. 1909. *What Is Pragmatism?* New York: Macmillan Publishing Company.

Putnam, Hilary. 1975. "The Meaning of Meaning." In his *Mind, Language and Reality*. Cambridge: Harvard University Press.

1981. *Reason, Truth and History*. Cambridge University Press.

1987. *The Many Faces of Realism*. LaSalle, Ill.: Open Court Publishing Company.

1988. *Representation and Reality*. Cambridge: MIT Press.

1990. "James' Theory of Perception." In his *Realism with a Human Face*. Cambridge: Harvard University Press.

1992. *Renewing Philosophy*. Cambridge: Harvard University Press.

1994. *Pragmatism*. Oxford and Cambridge, Mass.: Basil Blackwell.

1994a. "Pragmatism and Moral Objectivity." In his *Words and Life*. Cambridge: Harvard University Press.

1994b. "THE DEWEY LECTURES 1994: Sense, Nonsense and the Senses: An Inquiry into the Powers of the Human Mind." *The Journal of Philosophy* 91: 445–517.

Putnam, Ruth Anna. 1990. "The Moral Life of a Pragmatist." In *Identity, Character, and Morality*, edited by Owen Flanagan and Amélie Rorty. Cambridge and London: MIT Press.

Ratner, S., and J. Altman, eds. 1964. *John Dewey and Arthur F. Bentley*. New Brunswick: Rutgers University Press.

Raymond, Mary E. 1937. "Memories of William James." *The New England Quarterly* 10: 419–29.

Rey, George. 1992. "Semantic Externalism and Conceptual Competence." *Aristotelian Society Proceedings*, n.s., 192, 3: 315–31.

Rhees, R. 1970. *Discussions with Wittgenstein*. New York: Schocken Books.

Rorty, Richard. 1979. *Philosophy and the Mirror of Nature*. Princeton: Princeton University Press.

1982. *Consequences of Pragmatism: Essays 1972–1980*. Minneapolis: University of Minnesota Press.

1986. "Pragmatism, Davidson, and Truth." In *Truth and Interpretation*, edited by Ernest LePore and Brian McGuinness. Oxford: Basil Blackwell.

1994. "Religion as Conversation Stopper." *Common Knowledge* 3: 1–6.

1994a. "Sind Aussagen universelle Geltungsansprüche?" *Deutsche Zeitschrift für Philosophie* 42, 6: 975–88.

1995. "Is Truth a Goal of Inquiry: Davidson vs. Wright." *The Philosophical Quarterly* 45: 281–300.

Forthcoming. "McDowell, Davidson and Spontaneity." *Philosophy and Phenomenological Research.*

Roth, John K. 1969. *Freedom and the Moral Life: The Ethics of William James.* Philadelphia: Westminster Press.

Royce, Josiah. 1908. *Philosophy of Loyalty.* Norwood, Mass.: Macmillan Publishing Company.

   1915. *Studies in Good and Evil.* New York: Appleton.

   1951. *Royce's Logical Essays.* Edited by Daniel Robinson. Dubuque, Iowa: Wm. C. Brown Company.

   1960. *The Letters of Josiah Royce.* Edited by John Clendenning. Chicago: University of Chicago Press.

   1965. *The Religious Aspect of Philosophy.* Glouster, Mass.: Peter Smith Publisher. Originally published 1885.

   1969. *Basic Writings.* 2 vols. Edited by John J. McDermott. Chicago: University of Chicago Press.

   1971. *The Philosophy of Josiah Royce.* Edited by John Roth. New York: Thomas Crowell Press.

Ruddick, Lisa. 1990. *Reading Gertrude Stein.* Ithaca: Cornell University Press.

Russell, Bertrand. 1945. *A History of Western Philosophy.* New York: Simon and Schuster.

   1966. *Philosophical Essays.* London: Allen and Unwin. Originally published 1910.

   1986. *The Philosophy of Logical Atomism and Other Essays, 1914–1918.* Vol. 8 of *Collected Papers,* edited by J. G. Slater. London: Allen and Unwin.

Ryle, Gilbert. 1949. *The Concept of Mind.* New York: Barnes and Noble.

Santayana, George. 1920. *Character and Opinion in the United States.* New York: Charles Scribner's Sons.

   [1920] 1967. *Character and Opinion in the United States.* London: Constable and Company. Reissued, New York: W. W. Norton and Company.

   1923. *Scepticism and Animal Faith.* London: Constable and Company.

Scheffler, Israel. 1974. *Four Pragmatists: A Critical Introduction to Peirce, James, Mead, and Dewey.* New York: Humanities Press International.

Schelling, F. W. J. 1807. "The Relation of Plastic Art to Nature." In Wilshire (1985).

Schiller, F. C. S. 1907. *Studies in Humanism.* London: Macmillan Publishers Ltd.

   1927. "William James and the Making of Pragmatism." *The Personalist* 8, 2: 81–93. Reprinted in Schiller (1934).

   1934. *Must Philosophers Disagree?* London: Macmillan Publishers Ltd.

Schiller, Friedrich. 1965. *On the Aesthetic Education of Man in a Series of*

Letters. Translated by Reginald Snell. New York: Frederic Ungar Publishing Company.

Seigfried, Charlene H. 1978. *Chaos and Context: A Study in William James*. Athens: Ohio University Press.

1990. *William James's Radical Reconstruction of Philosophy*. Albany: State University of New York Press.

Skinner, B. F. 1976. *About Behaviorism*. New York: Vintage.

Smith, Quentin. 1986. *The Felt Meanings of the World: A Metaphysics of Feeling*. West Lafayette, Ind.: Purdue University Press.

Sollors, Werner. 1986. "A Critique of Pure Pluralism." In *Reconstructing American Literary History*, edited by Sacvan Bercovitch. Cambridge: Harvard University Press.

Spencer, Herbert. 1872. *The Principles of Psychology*. 2nd ed. 2 vols. London: Williams and Norgate.

Sprigge, T. L. S. 1993. *James and Bradley*. Chicago: Open Court Publishing Company.

Starbuck, Edwin D. 1943. "A Student's Impressions of James in the Middle '90's." *Psychological Review* 50: 128–31.

Stephen, James Fitzjames. 1874. *Liberty, Equality, Fraternity*. 2nd ed. London: Smith, Elder.

Stoddard, Elizabeth. 1984. *The Morgesons and Other Writings, Published and Unpublished*. Edited by Lawrence Buell and Sandra Zagarell. Philadelphia: University of Pennsylvania Press.

Stout, G. F. 1907. Review of Schiller (1907). *Mind*, n.s., 16: 579–88.

Strouse, Jean. 1980. *Alice James: A Biography*. Boston: Houghton Mifflin.

Sundquist, Eric. 1993. *To Wake the Nations*. Cambridge: Harvard University Press.

Tillich, Paul. 1974. *Mysticism and Guilt Consciousness in Schelling's Philosophical Development*. Lewisburg, Pa.: Bucknell University Press.

Titchener, E. B. 1909. *Lectures on the Experimental Psychology of the Thought-Processes*. New York: Macmillan Publishing Company.

Todes, Samuel. 1989. *The Body and the Material Subject of the World*. New York: Garland Publishing.

Tomisch, John. 1971. *A Genteel Endeavor: American Culture and Politics in the Gilded Age*. Stanford: Stanford University Press.

Veeder, William. 1975. *Henry James – The Lessons of the Master: Popular Fiction and Personal Style in the Nineteenth Century*. Chicago and London: University of Chicago Press.

Watson, J. B. 1919. *Psychology from the Standpoint of a Behaviorist*. Philadelphia: J. B. Lippincott.

1924/1925. *Behaviorism*. New York: The People's Institute Publishing Company.

Weigand, Paul. 1952. "Psychological Types in Friedrich Schiller and William James." *Journal of the History of Ideas* 13: 376–83.

Welter, Barbara. 1966. "The Cult of True Womanhood: 1820–1860." *American Quarterly* 18: 151–74.

Wernham, James C. S. 1987. *James's Will-to-Believe Doctrine: A Heretical View*. Kingston, Ontario: University of Toronto Press.

West, Cornel. 1989. *The American Evasion of Philosophy*. Madison and London: University of Wisconsin Press.

1991. *The Ethical Dimension of Marxist Thought*. New York: Monthly Review Press.

White, Morton. 1972. *Science and Sentiment in America: Philosophical Thought from Jonathan Edwards to John Dewey*. New York: Oxford University Press.

Whitehead, Alfred North. 1929. *Process and Reality*. New York: Macmillan Publishing Company.

Wiener, Philip. 1949. *Evolution and the Founders of Pragmatism*. Cambridge: Harvard University Press.

Wild, John Daniel. 1989. *The Radical Empiricism of William James*. Garden City, N.Y.: Doubleday.

Williams, Michael. 1993. *Unnatural Doubts*. Oxford: Basil Blackwell.

Wilshire, Bruce. 1979. *William James and Phenomenology: A Study of 'The Principles of Psychology.'* New York: AMS Press.

1984. *William James: The Essential Writings*. Albany: State University of New York Press.

1985. *Romanticism and Evolution: The Nineteenth Century*. Lanham, Md.: University Press of America.

Forthcoming. "Edie's Hard-Nosed James and the Retrieval of the Sacred." In *James Edie: Phenomenology and Scepticism*, edited by B. Wachterhauser. To be published as a Festschrift for Edie.

Forthcoming (a). *Wild Hunger: Nature's Excitements and Their Addictive Distortions*.

Wittgenstein, Ludwig. 1953. *Philosophical Investigations*. Edited by G. E. M. Anscombe. Oxford: Basil Blackwell.

Wood, Ann D. 1971. "The 'Scribbling Women' and Fanny Fern: Why Women Wrote." *American Quarterly* 23: 3–24.

Woodfield, Andrew, ed. 1982. *Thought and Object: Essays in Intentionality*. Oxford: Clarendon Press.

Wright, Chauncey. 1877. *Philosophical Discussions*. Edited by C. E. Norton. New York: Henry Holt.

Yeazell, Ruth Bernard. 1981. *The Death and Letters of Alice James*. Berkeley and Los Angeles: University of California Press.

INDEX

399